THE EMERALD HANDBOOK OF ENTREPRENEURSHIP IN TOURISM, TRAVEL AND HOSPITALITY: SKILLS FOR SUCCESSFUL VENTURES

THE EMERALD HANDBOOK OF ENTREPRENEURSHIP IN TOURISM, TRAVEL AND HOSPITALITY: SKILLS FOR SUCCESSFUL VENTURES

EDITED BY

MARIOS SOTIRIADIS
University of South Africa, Pretoria, South Africa

United Kingdom – North America – Japan
India – Malaysia – China

Emerald Publishing Limited
Howard House, Wagon Lane, Bingley BD16 1WA, UK

First edition 2018

British Library Cataloguing in Publication Data
A catalogue record for this book is available from the British Library

ISBN: 978-1-78743-530-8 (Print)
ISBN: 978-1-78743-529-2 (Online)
ISBN: 978-1-78743-957-3 (Epub)
ISBN: 978-1-78754-484-0 (Paperback)

Printed and bound by CPI Group (UK) Ltd, Croydon, CR0 4YY

ISOQAR certified
Management System,
awarded to Emerald
for adherence to
Environmental
standard
ISO 14001:2004.

Certificate Number 1985
ISO 14001

INVESTOR IN PEOPLE

CONTENTS

v

PART III
PLANNING THE TOURISM BUSINESS VENTURE

PART IV
MANAGING THE TOURISM BUSINESS

LIST OF CONTRIBUTORS

Agusdin Agusdin	University of Mataram, West Nusa Tenggara, Indonesia
María del Mar Alonso-Almeida	Autonomous University of Madrid, Madrid, Spain
Martha Alicia Alonso-Castañón	Polytechnic University of San Luis Potosi, San Luis, Mexico
Marisol Alonso-Vazquez	University of Queensland, St Lucia, Australia
María José Álvarez-Gil	Universidad Carlos III de Madrid, Madrid, Spain
Stavros Arvanitis	Technological Educational Institute (TEI) of Crete, Heraklion, Greece
Vasiliki Avgeli	Technological Educational Institute (TEI) of Crete, Heraklion, Greece
Hongfei Bao	Jeju National University, Cheju, Republic of Korea
Sébastien Bédé	EM Strasbourg Business School, Strasbourg, France
Yosr Ben Tahar	PSB Paris School of Business, Paris, France
Elricke Botha	University of South Africa, Pretoria, South Africa
Evelyn G. Chiloane-Tsoka	University of South Africa, Pretoria, South Africa
Sylvie Christofle	Graduate School of Management, University of Nice Sophia Antipolis, Nice, France
Leticia Estevez	National University of Avellaneda, Avellaneda, Argentina

Anestis Fotiadis	Zayed University, Abu Dhabi, United Arab Emirates
Vincent Grèzes	University of Applied Sciences and Arts Western Switzerland, Valais, Switzerland
Vanessa Guerrier-Buisine	Graduate School of Management, University of Nice Sophia Antipolis, Nice, France
Coralie Haller	EM Strasbourg Business School, Strasbourg, France
Marta Magadán	University of Oviedo, Oviedo, Spain
Charlotte Massa	EM Strasbourg Business School, University of Strasbourg, France
Claudel Mombeuil	Université Quisqueya, Port-au-Prince, Haiti
Eugenia Papaioannou	Alexander Technological Educational Institute (TEI) of Thessaloniki, Thessaloniki, Greece
Catherine Papetti	Graduate School of Management, University of Nice Sophia Antipolis, Nice, France
Antoine Perruchoud	University of Applied Sciences and Arts Western Switzerland, Valais, Switzerland
María del Pilar Pastor-Pérez	Autonomous University of San Luis Potosi, San Luis, Mexico
Msindosi Sarah Radebe	University of South Africa, Pretoria, South Africa
Nkoana Simon Radipere	University of South Africa, Pretoria, South Africa
Jesús Rivas	International University of La Rioja, Logroño, Spain
Roland Schegg	University of Applied Sciences and Arts Western Switzerland, Valais, Switzerland
Shiwei Shen	Ningbo University, Ningbo, P.R. China
Nataša Slak Valek	Zayed University, Abu Dhabi, United Arab Emirates

Marios Sotiriadis   University of South Africa, Pretoria, South Africa

Magdalena Petronella (Nellie) Swart   University of South Africa, Pretoria, South Africa

Anne Taylor   American Hotel Academy, Brasov, Romania

Cina van Zyl   University of South Africa, Pretoria, South Africa

Stelios Varvaressos   Higher Technological Educational Institute (TEI) of Athens, Athens, Greece

ABOUT THE EDITOR

Marios Sotiriadis is Professor at University of South Africa and Visiting Professor at University of Ningbo, China. Formerly he was Professor of Tourism Business Management Department, TEI of Crete, and Tutor of the Hellenic Open University, Greece. He received his PhD in Tourism Management from the University of Nice Sophia-Antipolis, Nice, France. He is the author of 10 books and monographs, three distance-learning manuals and three e-learning materials on aspects of tourism marketing and management. He has undertaken a variety of research and consultancy projects for both public and private organisations of the tourism industry. Professor Sotiriadis's research and writing interests include tourism destination and businesses marketing and management. His articles have been published by international journals and presented at conferences.

PREFACE

Academic contributions have explored the subject of entrepreneurship in general and in the tourism context in particular. Such a development is a logical process appropriate to a challenging and interesting subject area. Before launching into the chapters, there is a need to explain why this book is required in the marketplace. First, the growing recognition of entrepreneurship and its significant contribution to job creation, tourism development and offering of high quality experiences underpin this book's production. Second, this topic is increasingly recognised as an interesting area for academic research and scholarship, and educational/training programmes. Third, although several books are available on entrepreneurship in general, the few edited volumes on the subject of tourism entrepreneurship have mainly an academic focus. Much of the academic literature on entrepreneurship (beyond some books that are now dated) is in journal article format, so this in itself partially justifies the need for a handbook such as this one that is more accessible to a wider audience. The main elements of the handbook are presented below.

THE BOOK'S AIM

This book is designed to fill a void in the academic and industry fields. It is unique because it adopts a comprehensive approach to considering the key issues and aspects of planning and operating business ventures in tourism. The rationale and main aim of the book are to provide potential tourism entrepreneurs with the necessary skills and tools for identifying and implementing an entrepreneurial activity. Given the predominant and ever-increasing role of entrepreneurship in tourism, the theme and purpose of the book are very topical. This book offers three major advantages: (1) it focuses on entrepreneurship in tourism-related industries; therefore, it provides contextualised theory and practice in these industries, (2) it takes an entrepreneurial perspective, a practical approach without neglecting the academic rigour and (3) it encompasses case studies and examples to show to readers how theory is or can be applied in practice.

The editor and contributors of this book are guided by the aim to explain and illustrate the essential knowledge, the main issues and aspects of the topic in a clear style — simplifying as far as possible and relating the principles within a carefully structured narrative and integrated framework supported by short case studies drawn from current practice. We wish this book to be read and appreciated by students and industry practitioners alike.

THE BOOK'S AUDIENCE

This volume is proposed to be a practical handbook for entrepreneurship in tourism-related industries. It would serve as a guide for those studying entrepreneurship and preparing for entrepreneurial careers as well as a reference for the practical use of entrepreneurs at the planning, implementation, operation and evaluation stages of building a tourism business. For prospective academics studying entrepreneurship or for those engaging with the entrepreneurial tourism business, the handbook provides valuable information on the tourism context and business environment. In addition, through practical examples, the importance of developing practical entrepreneurial skills is demonstrated.

As a handbook, the book will be valuable:

- in teaching situations − both academic at the senior undergraduate (specific upper-level courses) and master's levels, and in workshops with current and prospective tourism entrepreneurs. Readers of this textbook will be university students, undergraduate or postgraduate, in tourism businesses-related courses;
- as an actual handbook and reference for those setting up a tourism business. A handbook such as this will be a useful guide as entrepreneurs develop and refine their business concept and operation;
- for students − the book is written to meet the needs of all tourism-related courses and programmes. The material will be relevant to other courses in which service industries are important elements;
- for those working in tourism − the book recognises that entrepreneurship is a very practical subject. It constitutes a valuable contribution to developing the necessary knowledge, competencies and skills of entrepreneurial decision-making and ventures.

Examples from the industry/business world are provided to illustrate real-life practice and give readers a better understanding of entrepreneurship in tourism.

OUR APPROACH TO THE SUBJECT AND THE BOOK'S STRUCTURE

The rationale of the proposed book is based upon the following main concept: to provide students and prospective entrepreneurs with the knowledge, know-how and best practices in order to assist them in planning, implementing and managing business ventures in the field of tourism-related industries. By taking a managerial and marketing perspective, it aims to bridge the strategic and operational functions at business/micro level.

Therefore, the purpose and content of the book focus on analysing the whole process of developing and managing the entrepreneurial process, from the conception of the entrepreneurial idea to the development and implementation of its business plan. The sections and chapters of the book have a rational sequence, reflecting the entrepreneurial and business plan development processes.

The book provides contextualised knowledge of entrepreneurship in the tourism industry and is presented in six parts. The structure is designed to follow a logical development of the subject although, as every entrepreneur or manager knows, the process of planning, managing and marketing a business venture is circular rather than linear. The book is divided into six parts, as outlined below.

"Part I (Tourism: A Consumer-driven Business Field)" clearly explains tourism and its particular characteristics. This part deals with the elements and analytic frameworks of tourism as a set of industries and business activities. It consists of two chapters highlighting the importance of entrepreneurship and entrepreneurs in tourism in order to engage the reader in the central topic of the handbook, and discusses the tourism system and tourism value chain as analytical frameworks for tourism businesses.

"Part II (Tourism Business Environment)" presents and explains the key issues of the business environment in the field of tourism. It discusses tools enhancing the analysis of this environment and highlights the importance of the concepts of creativity and innovation.

"Part III (Planning the Tourism Business Venture)" analyses the issues of planning a business project; that is, moving from the idea or business concept to its implementation. Thus, it focuses on issues that a prospective entrepreneur has to consider and analyse in order to make informed decisions before an investment is made.

"Part IV (Managing the Tourism Business)" examines the main issues of managing the business operation. Once the investment has been completed and the business operation is ready to cater for clientele, the crucial task is to perform the managerial functions in an effective and efficient way. This section consists of six chapters; the latter chapter discusses the implications if the business venture is not successful, and related decisions.

"Part V (Marketing the Tourism Business Offering)" focuses on the tools and processes of marketing the tourism business offering and services.

Finally, "Part VI (Specific Topics of Entrepreneurship in Tourism)" deals with crucial topics and issues that require special attention in terms of entrepreneurship in tourism. The underlying idea is to discuss the specific issues that entrepreneurs should know about the context in which they operate.

In terms of overall content and structure, the book is comprehensive and logically organised. The sequence of chapters is rational and follows the entrepreneurial process.

FEATURES

The book has the following special features:

- A unique structure, which divides activities into analysis of business environment, planning, managing and marketing the business venture, as well as crucial issues requiring special attention in terms of entrepreneurship. This helps to create an understanding of what has to be done to plan and manage a successful venture.
- Twenty-three chapters, one for each of the key elements readers need to understand about entrepreneurship.
- The coverage of topics spans all the stages of the entrepreneurial process.

Each chapter contains the following features to aid understanding:

- *Learning objectives.* Every chapter starts with a comprehensive set of learning objectives addressing the main points covered.
- *Introduction.* It outlines the context and the importance of the issues discussed in the chapter.
- *Case study and examples.* Examples are used to illustrate how the theories work in real-world situations. They describe real-life practices, illustrating the application of approaches and techniques related to the chapter's topic area.
- *Summary.* It condenses the main issues; a synthesis of the key issues presented and some suggestions and recommendations for prospective entrepreneurs.
- *Review questions/questions for discussion.* They appear at the end of each chapter, allowing readers to test their knowledge and understanding.
- *References and Further reading.* It offers some suggestions for additional library resources at the end of each chapter.

Editor's note
I would like to point out the interchangeability of the terms 'enterprise', 'company', 'business', 'venture' and 'organisation'. These terms are used interchangeably throughout the book.

ACKNOWLEDGEMENTS

A handbook like this one is never a one-person effort, but it is the result of a variety of creative minds. Many people have helped or inspired me in my professional and academic career. I would like to thank, in my capacity as editor, all the colleagues who have contributed to the writing of this book, as well as all other people who have provided advice, material and support. Tourism industry practitioners, in particular, with whom I have forged lasting friendships, have helped me to conceive and contextualise this textbook.

PART I
TOURISM: A CONSUMER-DRIVEN
BUSINESS FIELD

CHAPTER 1

ENTREPRENEURSHIP AND ENTREPRENEURS IN TOURISM

Marios Sotiriadis

ABSTRACT

Purpose – *The aim of this chapter is to discuss and highlight the importance of entrepreneurship and entrepreneurs in tourism in order to engage the reader in the central topic of the handbook.*

Methodology/approach – *A literature review was conducted on conceptual issues and practical aspects of entrepreneurs and entrepreneurship. Case studies are included to illustrate the role and contribution of entrepreneurs in the tourism field.*

Findings – *This chapter highlights (1) practical definitions of the terms entrepreneurs and entrepreneurship; (2) main features of tourism entrepreneurs; and (3) the role of entrepreneurs in tourism activities and their contribution to the development of a tourism destination.*

Research limitations/implications – *This chapter is explorative in nature, because the discussion is mostly based on a literature review. Thus, more research-based knowledge and more empirical studies are needed in this field.*

Practical implications – *The chapter presents the main features and characteristics of individuals involved in entrepreneurship, as well as the need for developing the appropriate skills for successful business ventures.*

Originality/value – *This chapter deals with the question of why tourism entrepreneurship is so important in the contemporary context and in the*

The Emerald Handbook of Entrepreneurship in Tourism, Travel and Hospitality:
Skills for Successful Ventures, 3–17
ISBN: 978-1-78743-530-8/doi:10.1108/978-1-78743-529-220181001

business environment of tourism. The practical and entrepreneurial approach of the book is also discussed.

Keywords: Entrepreneurs; entrepreneurship; tourism-related industries; features; contribution; skills

---

Learning Objectives

After studying this chapter, you should be able to:

- present the importance of tourism in the global economy/at the global level;
- provide a definition of entrepreneurship;
- discuss the role of entrepreneurs;
- describe the main features of entrepreneurs;
- briefly present the role and contribution of entrepreneurs in tourism activities and their contribution for the development of a tourism destination.

1.1. INTRODUCTION

The main idea of this volume is to highlight that 'tourism entrepreneurship' is the backbone of tourism-related industries. Therefore, this topic deserves the current and cutting-edge volume that is relevant to practitioners and academics alike. The tourism industry and related businesses are unique in the sense that, from a service perspective, the product is the experience that is co-created by the tourists. Thus, entrepreneurs entering the tourism arena are in need of a dedicated handbook on tourism entrepreneurship that goes beyond the more generic business entrepreneurship literature.

This chapter deals with the question of why tourism entrepreneurship is so important in the contemporary context and in the business environment of tourism. The chapter then discusses the framework of tourism and the business and market environments in which entrepreneurial ventures are designed, managed and developed.

The main aim of this chapter is, therefore, to discuss and highlight the importance of entrepreneurship and entrepreneurs in tourism in order to engage the reader in the central topic of the handbook. First, the importance of tourism-related industries is highlighted. Second, the concepts of entrepreneurship (the business activities) and entrepreneurs (the individuals involved) are discussed and clearly defined. Then, the contribution of entrepreneurship in tourism is outlined.

1.2. THE IMPORTANCE OF TOURISM AND ITS RELATED INDUSTRIES

Tourism and travel are important economic activities in most countries around the world. In 2015, international tourism marked an impressive above-average growth for six consecutive years in terms of international tourist arrivals, with a record total of 1.2 billion tourists travelling the world. Some 50 million more tourists (overnight visitors) travelled to international destinations around the world in 2015 than in 2014 (World Tourist Organization (WTO), 2016). This reflects a 4 per cent growth, or an increase of 50 million tourists who travelled to any international destination during the year.

The latest report by World Travel & Tourism Council (WTTC, 2016) indicated that, for the fifth successive year, the growth of tourism-related industries in 2015 (2.8 per cent) outpaced that of the global economy (2.3 per cent). In total, tourism generated US$7.2 trillion (9.8 per cent of global gross domestic product (GDP)) and supported 284 million jobs, equivalent to one in 11 jobs in the global economy. Tourism-related industries are a key force for good, and it has proven, in the past, that they are strong and adaptable enough to face any challenges. Prospects 2017 remain positive, with international tourist arrivals expected to grow by 4 per cent worldwide (WTO, 2016). Tourism will continue to grow, creating more jobs and bringing in more economic and social benefits.

Further, World Tourism Day 2015 was celebrated around the theme 'One billion tourists, one billion opportunities', which highlighted the transformative potential of one billion tourists. With more than one billion tourists travelling to any international destination every year, tourism has become a leading economic activity (WTO, 2016). Representing more than just economic strength, these achievements reflect tourism's vast potential and increasing capacity to address some of the world's most pressing challenges, including socio-economic growth, jobs creation, inclusive development and environmental preservation. As an economic activity that contributes to as many as one in 11 jobs worldwide, tourism is a valuable source of livelihood for millions of people. Built around the millions of cross-cultural encounters happening every day in different corners of the world, tourism is also a gateway to greater understanding of the world beyond our borders.

Nevertheless, a scanning of the WTO's latest report revealed that the terms 'job creation', 'talent development', 'employment' and 'revenues' appear to be used frequently in tourism, which is not surprising at all. On the contrary, what is surprising is that the concepts 'entrepreneurship' and 'entrepreneurial activity' do not appear a single time and are, in fact, totally absent! There is no doubt that the outcomes and achievements of tourism, at global level, are attributable to micro-, small- and medium-sized enterprises as well as big companies. Further, it is estimated that the above-mentioned aims, set by the WTO, will not be addressed properly without enhancing and promoting entrepreneurship in tourism.

The creation of tourism enterprises — for that provide products and services in facilitation, transportation, attractions, accommodation, catering and travel-related retail businesses — is behind the such impressive achievements and performance. The creation and operation of tourism enterprises offer new employment opportunities, earning of real income, generation of tax revenues and stimulation of other industries and productive activities in the local/regional economic system. However, this business activity 'is not an act of nature, but an act of the tourism entrepreneur' (Koh & Hatten, 2002, p. 22).

The theme of this handbook is not to analyse the economic, social or other contribution of tourism to a region's or country's economic and social developments and well-being; instead, the theme is to provide practical guidance and assistance for the creation and operation of new ventures in tourism.

In this regard, it would be very useful to clarify the concepts of entrepreneurship and entrepreneurs, as there are a multitude of definitions of entrepreneurship and entrepreneur. Let us start by considering the business activity and then the individual.

1.3. ENTREPRENEURSHIP

Many definitions of entrepreneurship are offered by scholars. Some of these are cited below in chronological order. Entrepreneurship is:

- 'the creation of an innovative economic organisation (or network of organisations) for the purpose of gain under conditions of risk and uncertainty' (Dollinger, 1995, p. 7);
- 'the process of creating something new with value by devoting the necessary time and effort, assuming the accompanying financial, psychic and social risks, and receiving the resulting rewards of monetary and personal satisfaction and independence' (Hisrich & Peters, 1998, p. 9);
- 'an activity that involves the discovery, evaluation and exploitation of opportunities to introduce new goods and services, ways of organising, markets, processes and raw materials through organising efforts that previously had not existed' (Shane, 2003, p. 4; Shane & Venkataraman, 2000, p. 218);
- 'a way of thinking, reasoning, and acting that is opportunity obsessed, holistic in approach, and leadership balanced' (Timmons & Spinelli, 2007, p. 79);
- 'the result of a systematic and disciplined process of applying innovation and creativity to opportunities and needs in the market' (Zimmerer & Scarborough with Wilson, 2008, p. 5).

It is evident that two ideas/principles are central to the entrepreneurship concept: (1) the creation and recognition of opportunities, inclusive of the will and initiative to seize those opportunities and (2) the creation of new businesses in conditions of risk and uncertainty in order to make a profit (Timmons & Spinelli, 2007; Zimmerer & Scarborough with Wilson, 2008). According to the latter authors, entrepreneurship involves the application of focused strategies to explore new ideas and new insights to create a product or a service that can either satisfy individuals' needs or solve their problems. Some of these similarities in the definitions include the following terms, used to describe entrepreneurship, and constitute the key features of entrepreneurship: business opportunity recognition, innovation, risk-taking, idea creation, creativity, achievement orientation and resourcefulness.

Shane (2003) suggests that the notion of innovation constitutes a key attribute of entrepreneurship. Zimmerer and Scarborough with Wilson (2008, p. 43) define innovation as 'the ability to apply creative solutions to problems and opportunities to enhance the lives of people'. In this case, creativity is described as the ability to develop new ideas and to discover new ways of looking at opportunities and problems. According to Drucker (1985), innovation is the tool used by entrepreneurs to exploit change as an opportunity. Entrepreneurial ventures thrive on innovation. There are three main types of innovation: process, organisational and marketing (Oberg, 2010). Innovation outputs can be either new ways of doing things, or the development of new products, services or techniques (Porter, 1990). These two concepts and their implications, in terms of tourism entrepreneurship, are discussed in Chapter 5.

It is worth pointing out that (1) successful entrepreneurship is a constant process that relies on creativity, innovation and application in the marketplace and (2) the individual is the main force behind, and at the beginning of, this entrepreneurship process (Zimmerer & Scarborough with Wilson, 2008).

1.4. ENTREPRENEURS

An entrepreneur can be defined as a person who sees an opportunity in the marketplace and establishes a business with the aim of meeting the market's needs. There is a plethora of definitions of the term 'entrepreneur'; some of these are cited below in chronological order. An entrepreneur is:

- 'a person who carries out commercial innovation: modification of existing knowledge and/or practices. If innovation is successful, it leads to a state of creative destruction. Innovation could occur in five forms: offering of new goods/services; new production methods, new sources of supplies; new markets/distribution systems; and/or new management techniques' (Schumpeter (1949), cited in Koh and Hatten (2002, p. 27));
- 'a person who sees an opportunity and assumes the risk (financial, material, and psychological) of starting a business to take advantage of the opportunity or idea' (Hatten, 1997, p. 31).

- 'an individual who is alert to opportunities for trade ... is capable of identifying suppliers and customers and acting as an intermediary where profit arises out of the intermediary function' (Deakins & Freel, 2009, p. 7);
- 'a person who creates a new business in the face of risk and uncertainty for the purpose of achieving growth and profit by identifying significant opportunities and assembling the necessary resources to capitalise on them' (Zimmerer & Scarborough with Wilson, 2008, p. 5).

Ahmad and Seymour (2008, p. 9) proposed the following formal definitions for the purpose of supporting the development of related indicators, mainly statistical data at national level, as recommended by the Organization for Economic Co-operation and Development (OECD):

- Entrepreneurs are those persons (business owners), who seek to generate value, through the creation or expansion of economic activity, by identifying and exploiting new products, processes or markets.
- Entrepreneurial activity is the enterprising human action in pursuit of the generation of value, through the creation or expansion of economic activity, by identifying and exploiting new products, processes or markets.
- Entrepreneurship is the phenomenon associated with entrepreneurial activity.

It should be pointed out that entrepreneurs do not only come up with new ideas, but they also act on them. Based on the above definitions, it looks evident that entrepreneurs identify opportunities and then adopt various means to exploit or develop these opportunities in order to obtain a wide range of outcomes. Literature suggests that entrepreneurs also possess specific characteristics, namely: creativity and innovation, determination and persistence, need for independence, need for achievement and risk-taking, commitment and determination, leadership, opportunity obsession, tolerance of risk, creativity, self-reliance and adaptability and motivation to excel (Longenecker, Moore, Petty, & Palich, 2006, p. 16). The factors that distinguish entrepreneurs most strongly from others in a business/strategic management are innovation, opportunity recognition, process and growth. These characteristics and capabilities are much needed in tourism-related industries.

Case Study 1.1:   A Set of Advice to Starting Entrepreneurs

Two authors (an academic and an industry practitioner) offer advice/tips to budding entrepreneurs based on their vast experience and in-depth case studies analyses in the business field and entrepreneurship. The main tips are outlined as follows:

Qualities: It is important to have a deep understanding of the qualities necessary to succeed in a highly challenging market/industry, and the complexities of decision making along the way.

Catalyst: The most common reason that highly motivated and talented employees leave their job − be it voluntarily or by force − is a disagreement with their boss or with the direction their company is taking. A lifelong job is not the kind of career that most employees are looking for. So, when they get fired, or when they see an opportunity that their boss fails to support, it is not at all uncommon for such an event to be the catalyst that gets them out on to do their own venture.

Full perception and deep understanding of industry environment: The prospective entrepreneurs must appreciate the difficulty of becoming a service provider, in other words, providing tourism and travel services. The service industries involve more complexities, resulting in challenges of becoming an entrepreneur in a service setting.

Learning the hard way: Instead of looking for 'an idea' (so they can become an entrepreneur), the best use of their time is to find a compelling, even painful, problem that their knowledge, capabilities and networks are well suited to resolve. It is quite clear that nobody will pay you to solve a non-problem.

Competencies and skills/abilities: A prospective entrepreneur, who combines expert knowledge with great passion and pride in his/her offering, has higher probabilities of success. However, although pride and passion are necessary, they are just not sufficient. There is a further need for a great deal of persistence and an ability to manage uncertainty. These two, combined with expertise, pride and passion, are vital for an entrepreneur.

Reducing uncertainty: The most important asset for any entrepreneur is his/her network. The network is crucial in their ability to hit the ground running. The team needs to be able to execute on the critical success factors in the industry where the business venture operates. Almost always, despite the entrepreneurial heroes lionised in the popular press, successful entrepreneurship is a team sport, and not just an individual's endeavour.

Tenacious and persistent: Entrepreneurs must be tenacious and persistent in any industry. The 'overnight success' of Starbucks, for example, took more than 20 years of hard work, however, entrepreneurs must also be agile enough to know when to persist and when to pivot. Hence, it is important to indicate how difficult life is as an entrepreneur, without all the sugar-coating that we see in today's media. There are always daunting challenges that a venture will face in entering and trying to become profitable.

Funding: Some business ventures can be started and, sometimes, can rapidly grow, using customer funding, instead of venture capital. The cold hard facts are that the vast majority of fast-growing entrepreneurial companies never raise any venture capital. A prospective businessperson could use customer funding and not raise venture capital. In this regard, Chapter 19 of this handbook provides reliable and updated information on crowdsourcing for tourism ventures.

Some questions to ask yourself before starting a new business: Is there a real market for your idea? Do you really want to compete in the tourism industry? Are you the right person to pursue it? No matter how talented you are or how much capital you have, if you are pursuing a fundamentally flawed opportunity, then you are heading for failure. Therefore, before you launch your lean start-up, take your idea for a test drive and make sure it has a fighting chance of working.

(The authors are: John Mullins, Associate Professor of Management Practice in Marketing and Entrepreneurship at London Business School; and Tiffany Putimahtama, President of United SP Corporation, a family-owned real estate investment company.)

Source: The Case Centre (2017) and Mullins (2013).

Based on the above, where the focus is on what an entrepreneur does, rather than what he or she is, it should be stressed that, an entrepreneur (1) identifies new business opportunities, (2) is creative and innovative, (3) is willing to take calculated risks, (4) obtains financial resources, (5) starts and manages own enterprise(s), (6) is able to market a concept, product or service and (7) organises and controls resources and monitors performance to ensure a sustainable and profitable operation. These ideas and principles are equally valid in the service industries, including tourism.

1.5. ENTREPRENEURSHIP IN TOURISM

According to the WTTC (2016), the total contribution of tourism-related industries to GDP (including wider effects from investment, the supply chain and induced income impacts) was US$7,170.3 billion in 2015 (9.8 per cent of GDP) and is expected to grow by 3.5 per cent to US$7,420.5 billion (9.8 per cent of GDP) in 2016. It is forecasted to rise by 4.0 per cent, per annum, to US $10,986.5 billion by 2026 (10.8 per cent of GDP). Tourism is expected to grow faster than the wider economy and many other industries over the next decade. It is also anticipated that the industry will support over 370 million jobs by 2026.

With regard to the employment, tourism-related industries generated 107,833,000 jobs, directly, in 2015 (3.6 per cent of total employment), and this is forecasted to grow by 1.9 per cent in 2016 to 109,864,000 (3.6 per cent of total employment). By 2026, tourism-related industries will account for 135,884,000 jobs, directly, an increase of 2.1 per cent per annum over the next 10 years.

Obviously, tourism continues to grow, which opens up many avenues for entrepreneurs who are interested in launching a business venture. Tourism and travel include the following industries: accommodation services, food and beverage services, retail trade, transportation services and cultural, sports and entertainment services. It is estimated that more than 90 per cent of the business in tourism-related industries are small- and medium-sized enterprises (SMEs) (European Union (EU), 2015).

The role of SMEs in tourism is very relevant (Getz, Carlsen, & Morrison, 2004; Williams & Shaw, 2011) and especially important when responding to customers' specific demands and providing them with the tourism services requested in a customised way (Novelli, Schmitz, & Spencer, 2006). There is no doubt that SMEs in tourism play a vital role in all types of economies — developed, emerging and developing. SMEs can also be credited for being a key driver in the development and competitiveness of a tourism destination/area. Although large companies have a significant influence on the nature of what is supplied to particular markets, for example, tour operators in relation to mass tourism, the most significant units of offering in most destinations and locations are SMEs and, often, micro enterprises (Getz et al., 2004; Thomas, 2007).

The European Union (EU) recognises that Europe's economic growth and jobs depend on its ability to support the growth of enterprises (EU, 2015). In the EU, the most important sources of employment are SMEs, and the European Commission (EC) stresses that entrepreneurship creates new companies, opens up new markets and nurtures new skills. The EC aims to reignite Europe's entrepreneurial spirit, to encourage people to become entrepreneurs and to motivate more people to set up and grow their own businesses. Its initiatives to promote entrepreneurship are summarised in an Entrepreneurship Action Plan, adopted in January 2013.

Within this framework, the EU has implemented a specific support programme — 'Competitiveness of Enterprises and Small and Medium-sized Enterprises (COSME)' — running from 2014 to 2020 (EU, 2016). The EC aims to promote entrepreneurship and improve the business environment for SMEs, to allow them to realise their full potential in today's global economy. This programme has thematically focused on tourism, in general, and in employment, decent work and capacity building in tourism as well as trade, investment and competitiveness in tourism. The COSME framework programme aims to enhance SME competitiveness, increase tourism demand, diversify offerings and products and enhance quality, sustainability, accessibility, skills and innovation.

Koh and Hatten (2002, p. 23) stress that the perception, decisions and actions of tourism entrepreneurs 'fundamentally determine what, where, and when touristic enterprises will be created in a community, touristic entrepreneurs are the sculptors of a community's touristscape'; in other words, they are the driving force behind a destination's offering/supply. The following case study illustrates this issue.

**Case Study 1.2:   A Partnership to Link with Intermediaries:
Vanuatu Safaris Air Pass**

While tourism has been an important source of foreign exchange for Vanuatu,[1] the benefits have not necessarily extended to communities in the country's outer islands. To generate tourist interest in more remote locations, two strategies were launched: (i) development of a unique experience (island bungalows) and (ii) making travel to the outer islands economical and a clear value-added experience for tourists.

The Vanuatu Island Bungalow Association (VIBA) plays a key role in monitoring the progress of this tourism programme by coordinating bookings and providing continued support to bungalow owners. A bungalow is generally a small bush cabin, built from local materials, without many of the conveniences of a modern hotel. There are also adventure lodges – owned by local chiefs, communities or families – built of local materials in an environmentally friendly way. A maximum of 10 rooms/bungalows are located on each island. The bungalow operators are more likely to protect the marine and coastal resources that serve as tourist attractions.

To develop this new product of island bungalows for Vanuatu's tourism industry, linkages had to be established with Vanuatu's regional airline, island bungalow managers, travel agents and wholesalers, local tour operators and international funding agencies. Without these linkages, the mechanisms to provide bungalow owners with continued support and improvements in product quality, business skills, management and customer service skills training, and marketing would not be possible.

Access to the outer islands was provided by developing a four-coupon air pass – Vanuatu safaris air pass (VSAP) – with the nation's regional air carrier and local inbound operator whereby foreign tourists save 50 per cent on domestic air travel. Each coupon is valid for one domestic flight (regardless of distance), with Vanair, so that tourists can travel to at least 2 of Vanuatu's 18 islands.

The air pass markets the islands as an adventure to experience: adventure tours, indigenous peoples, cultural traditions unchanged for centuries and accommodation in a traditional rural bungalow. The VSAP has benefited the rural areas that have few opportunities to generate cash. Developing small eco-tourism operations diversify their economies, create new jobs and generate tourism revenue. The coordinated marketing programme, with Island Safaris of Vanuatu and Vanair, has led to an increase in the number of bungalows registered with VIBA and has sold 50 passes monthly.

Later, when Island Safaris of Vanuatu and Vanair were reviewing the air pass, several changes were made, which included:

- posting air pass information on Vanair and Vanuatu National Tourism Office websites;
- offering tourists the opportunity to buy an unlimited number of extra coupons; and
- allowing the pass to be bought not just in US dollars but in both Australian and New Zealand dollars.

By offering the air pass for sale in Australian and New Zealand dollars, wholesalers such as Qantas Holiday could promote the air pass to all their 85 agents worldwide. Tourists from Australia and New Zealand are Vanuatu's largest market share. Major supporting partners provided financial aid to support VIBA's partnership programme with Vanair and Island Safaris of Vanuatu.

Through the VIBA and the Tourism Development Council Board meetings, the programme is monitored for issues involving: (1) promotion – to track demand and note changes for future improvements; (2) intermediaries – to make certain that they are providing external assistance and marketing support as agreed upon and (3) rural communities – to ensure tourist revenue is directly benefiting the economy that owns and operates the island bungalows, minimising leakage.

Stakeholders believe results are achieved through working together. Local tourism entrepreneurs are the driving force behind Vanatu's tourism offering; along with public bodies and agencies, they have designed and managed their community's touristscape.

Source: Riddle (2004).

Koh and Hatten (2002), based on a review of the historical thoughts of the entrepreneurs, have identified a number of roles of the entrepreneurs; that is, he/she is an arbitrageur, innovator, market filler, risk bearer, decision maker, creator of an enterprise and coordinator of the production factors. Further, they (Koh & Hatten, 2002, p. 25) suggested the following definition for the tourism entrepreneur:

> [The tourism entrepreneur] is a creator of a touristic enterprise motivated by monetary and/ or non-monetary reasons to pursue a perceived market opportunity .... Of course, the tourism entrepreneur also believes he/she has the ability and skills to entreprendre successfully, and is willing to assume all the risks and uncertainties associated with launching and operating a touristic enterprise.

It is generally believed that the entrepreneurship, in related industries, is one of the main engines and drivers of tourism development.

1.6. THE BOOK'S AIM, OBJECTIVES AND APPROACH

This handbook takes the perspective of the individual, the prospective entrepreneur of a tourism business venture. Thus, its aim is twofold:

1. To contribute to developing skills for entrepreneurship and business initiatives in tourism-related industries (i.e. tourism, travel, hospitality and leisure)
2. To provide practical guidance and assistance to prospective businessperson for his/her entrepreneurial journey in these industries.

The specific objectives are: (1) to provide prospective entrepreneurs with practical guidance to go from the business concept to a profitable and sustainable operation and (2) to present, in a practical way, the analytical frameworks and practical tools/methods needed to minimise the risks involved and maximise the chances for a successful venture.

To address the above aim and objectives, the approach of the proposed book is based on the following concepts as the starting point to present and discuss, in a practical way, the key knowledge and methods/tools:

- *A business idea*: The feasibility and sustainability of any enterprise, as a business activity, depend upon whether it can add any value or provide a service/an offering based on the tourism assets to the current or prospective consumers within a global market − the right offering/service at the right price (value-for-money).
- *The individual*: The focus is on the person wishing to undertake a business initiative and develop and implement a venture/project in the field of tourism. How can he/she proceed? What are the conditions, the prerequisites to make its project a successful business? What are the steps to be taken from the initial concept to the operation of the business? Therefore, the unit of analysis is the person and his/her idea for business venture.
- *Implementation of theoretical knowledge into effective practices/processes*: Most probably, this person (student or businessperson) has a sound understanding of the theoretical backgrounds and needs to move to applications. However, it may transpire that he/she lacks the knowledge and skills of how to apply the theoretical knowledge.

Fig. 1.1 depicts the general approach of the handbook.

Apparently, the focus of the handbook is on the components of 'applying' and 'creating'. It constitutes a contribution to the development of skills of applying the knowledge by presenting in a practical way the adequate/suitable methods and tools.

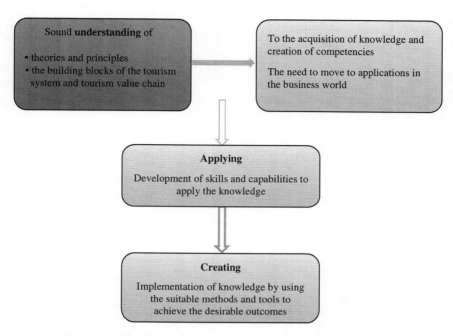

Fig. 1.1. The General Approach of the Book. *Source*: Author

1.7. SUMMARY

The role played by entrepreneurship and entrepreneurs in the field of tourism is undeniable and generally recognised. The main purpose of this chapter was to engage the readers with the central topic of this handbook.

It, firstly, presented and highlighted the importance and the contribution of tourism to the global economy. Then, the two concepts of entrepreneurship and entrepreneurs were clearly defined. The main features and characteristics of individuals involved in business ventures were also outlined. This was followed by an outline of the contribution of entrepreneurship and SMEs in tourism-related industries.

The chapter was completed by presenting and clarifying the main elements of the book, specifically, the aim, objectives, approach and perspective/focus. The following chapters will provide detailed presentations and analytic discussions on key issues and aspects of entrepreneurship in tourism-related industries.

Review Questions

Now you may check your understanding of this chapter by answering the following questions or discussing the topics:

- Discuss the contribution of tourism to the global economy and the economy of your country.
- Outline a definition of entrepreneurship that you believe is the most appropriate.
- Discuss the various definitions of the concept 'entrepreneur' and identify the underlying ideas/principles.
- What are the main features of an entrepreneur?
- Present the main ideas and message from the case study on partnership in Vanuatu.

NOTE

1. Vanuatu, officially the Republic of Vanuatu, is a Pacific island nation located in the South Pacific Ocean. The archipelago, which is of volcanic origin, is some 1,750 kilometres east of northern Australia, 540 kilometres northeast of New Caledonia, east of New Guinea, southeast of the Solomon Islands and west of Fiji. This state/nation is made up of roughly 80 islands that stretch 1,300 kilometres. (Source: https://en.wikipedia.org/wiki/Vanuatu)

REFERENCES AND FURTHER READING

Ahmad, N., & Seymour, R. G. (2008). *Defining entrepreneurial activity: Definitions supporting frameworks for data collection*. OECD Statistics Working Papers, No. 2008/01. Paris: OECD Publishing. doi:10.1787/243164686763

Brookes, M., & Altinay, L. (Eds.). (2015). *Entrepreneurship in hospitality and tourism: A global perspective*. Oxford: Goodfellow Publishers Ltd.

Deakins, D., & Freel, M. (2009). *Entrepreneurship and small firms*. (5th ed.). New York, NY: McGraw-Hill.

Dollinger, M. J. (1995). *Entrepreneurship: Strategies and resources*. Boston, MA: Austen Press.

Drucker, P. (1985). *Innovation and entrepreneurship*. New York, NY: Harper & Row.

European Union. (2015). *Promoting entrepreneurship*. Retrieved from https://ec.europa.eu/growth/smes/promoting-entrepreneurship_en. Accessed on 5 October 2016.

European Union. (2016). *COSME: Europe's programme for small and medium-sized enterprises*. Official website. Retrieved from http://ec.europa.eu/growth/smes/cosme/index_en.htm Accessed on 4 October 2016.

Getz, D., Carlsen, J., & Morrison, A. (2004). *The family business in tourism and hospitality*. Oxfordshire: CABI Publishing.

Hatten, T. S. (1997). *Small business: Entrepreneurship and beyond*. Upper Saddle River, NJ: Prentice Hall.

Hisrich, R. D., & Peters, M. P. (1998). *Entrepreneurship*. (4th ed.). New York, NY: McGraw-Hill.

Koh, K. Y., & Hatten, T. S. (2002). The tourism entrepreneur: The overlooked player in tourism development studies. *International Journal of Hospitality & Tourism Administration, 3*(1), 21–48.

Longenecker, J. D., Moore, C. W., Petty, J. W., & Palich, L. E. (2006). *Small business management. An entrepreneurial emphasis. International edition.* (14th ed.). London: Cengage Learning.

Mullins, J. (2013). *The new business road test: What entrepreneurs and executives should do before launching a lean start-up* (4th ed.). London: FT Press, Financial Times Series.

Novelli, M., Schmitz, B., & Spencer, T. (2006). Networks, clusters and innovation in tourism: A UK experience. *Tourism Management, 27*(6), 1141–1152.

Oberg, C. (2010). Customer roles in innovations. *International Journal of Innovation Management, 14*(6), 989–1012.

Porter, M. (1990). *The competitive advantage of nations.* London: Macmillan.

Riddle, D. I. (2004). Best practice case studies in tourism. In *Small states in transition – From vulnerability to competitiveness.* Port of Spain, Trinidad & Tobago. Vancouver, Canada: CMC Service-Growth Consultants Inc., Ministry of Trade and Industry, Republic of Trinidad and Tobago & Commonwealth Secretariat.

Schumpeter, J. A. (1949). Economic theory and entrepreneurial history. In R. V. Clemence (Ed.), *Change and the entrepreneur* (pp. 253–271). Cambridge, MA: Harvard University Press, Research Center in Entrepreneurial History.

Shane, S. (2003). *A general theory of entrepreneurship: The individual-opportunity nexus.* Cheltenham: Edward Elgar.

Shane, S., & Venkataraman, S. (2000). The promise of entrepreneurship as a field of research. *Academy of Management Review, 25*(1), 217–226.

The Case Centre. (2017). *The case: NakedWines.com.* Retrieved from https://www.thecasecentre.org/ educators/ordering/selecting/featuredcases/NakedWines. Accessed on 5 September 2017.

Thomas, R. (2007). Tourism partnerships and small firms: Power, participation and partition. *International Journal of Entrepreneurship and Innovation, 8*(1), 37–43.

Timmons, J. A., & Spinelli, S. (2007). *New venture creation: Entrepreneurship for the 21st century.* Boston, MA: McGraw-Hill Education.

Williams, A. M., & Shaw, G. (2011). Internationalization and innovation in tourism. *Annals of Tourism Research, 38*(1), 27–51.

World Tourism Organization. (2016). *UNWTO annual report 2015.* Madrid: UNWTO.

World Travel & Tourism Council. (2016). *Travel & tourism: Economic impact 2016.* London: WTTC.

World Travel Market. (2015). *The WTM global trends report 2015.* London: WTM & Euromonitor International.

Zimmerer, T. W., & Scarborough, N. M. with Wilson, D. (2008). *Essentials of entrepreneurship and small business management* (5th ed.). Upper Saddle River, NJ: Pearson/Prentice Hall.

CHAPTER 2

FRAMEWORK FOR TOURISM INDUSTRIES: TOURISM SYSTEM AND TOURISM VALUE CHAIN

Stelios Varvaressos

ABSTRACT

Purpose — *The scope of this chapter is to present in a simple and synoptic way the main components of tourism as a consumer-driven business field. The main purpose of this chapter is to discuss the tourism system and tourism value chain as the analytical frameworks for tourism businesses.*

Methodology/approach — *A literature review was conducted on conceptual issues and managerial aspects of tourism system and value chain.*

Findings — *This chapter highlights the fact that tourism is not a science or a scientific discipline; it is just a body of knowledge. It presents, in a synoptic and clear way, the building blocks of the tourism, that is, the approaches of tourism system and tourism value chain, as well as the concept of tourism experience.*

Research limitations/implications — *This chapter is explorative in nature, because the discussion is mostly based on a literature review.*

Practical implications — *Tourism is a multifaceted activity, which touches upon many different economic activities that are connected as a system. Thus, tourism must be understood as a system that includes interrelated elements working together. The model of a value chain can be applied in*

The Emerald Handbook of Entrepreneurship in Tourism, Travel and Hospitality:
Skills for Successful Ventures, 19–31
ISBN: 978-1-78743-530-8/doi:10.1108/978-1-78743-529-220181002

tourism, both at business and destination levels. Tourists are the focal point
of the global value chain in international tourism.

Originality/value — *This chapter analyses analytical frameworks, models*
and concepts in an integrated way. This analysis is very useful in creating a
better understanding of the tourism industries and the business ventures in
this field.

Keywords: Tourism system; models; analytical frameworks; tourism
experience; value chain; global value chain

Learning Objectives

After studying this chapter, you should be able to:

- define the tourism system and understand its components;
- provide two definitions of the concept 'tourism experience';
- present the model of value chain and explain its significance;
- describe the utility of the value chain analytical framework at destination level;
- explain the main components of the global value chain in tourism.

2.1. INTRODUCTION

Tourism researchers and scholars use the tools, analytical frameworks and
methods provided in various disciplines — such as management, marketing,
geography, sociology, economics and psychology — to consider, examine and
analyse the various issues and aspects of tourism. The reason for this is simple:
tourism is not a science or a scientific discipline; it is just a body of knowledge.

The scope of this chapter is to present in a simple and synoptic way the
main components of tourism as a consumer-driven business field. This synoptic
presentation is necessary because of the different approaches and ways in which
the subject of tourism is conceptualised. Different stakeholders experience and
define tourism in different ways. The issue is further compounded since tourism, as a service industry comprising both tangible and intangible aspects, lends
itself to subjective interpretations (Hall, 2008; Varvaressos, 2013).

Many people consider tourism as an industry. However, tourism is a
multidimensional, multifaceted activity, which touches upon many different
economic activities that are connected as a system. Thus, tourism must be
understood as a system that includes interrelated elements working together to
complete specific purposes. A common means of conceptualising tourism is
that of a system; systems approach promotes the analysis of connectivity

between elements (Mill & Morrison, 2002). Systems theory distinguishes between open and closed systems. An open system interacts with the environment(s) in which it exists, of which tourism is an example.

In this chapter, we are going to present, in a synoptic way, the building blocks of the tourism, or what some authors call 'the visitor economy' (see, for instance, Middleton, Fyall, Morgan, & Ranchhod, 2009). These are the approaches of tourism system and tourism value chain, as well as the concept of tourism experience.

2.2. THE TOURISM SYSTEM

Various models have been developed to describe the tourism system. Two of these are especially relevant: Leiper's model (1990), which is more concise in nature, and Hall's model (2008), which is more elaborate in nature.

2.2.1. Leiper's Tourism System

A tourism system model was suggested by Leiper (1979) and later on updated (Leiper, 1990). Leiper's model conceptualises tourism as an open system consisting of three interrelated basic elements, namely, tourists, geographical elements and tourism industries, as listed below:

- the human component: the tourists departing and returning;
- the geographical elements: tourist-generating region, transit route and tourist destination region, which relates to transport; and
- the industrial/organisational element: tourism industries and business activities that offer facilities and services for tourists.

The tourists are the actors in this system as they are the consumers who initiate the act of travelling, enjoy the experience and recount the happy memories. The three geographical elements are the source market for tourism (origin area), the transit route region (consisting of the activities and attractions to be visited en route) and the destination (hosting area) of the tourists, which is the motive for undertaking the journey. The final element in Leiper's model is the tourism industries that encompass the businesses and organisations responsible for delivering the tourism experience (Fletcher, Fyall, Gilbert, & Wanhill, 2013).

Each of the elements of Leiper's tourism system interacts with the others, not only to deliver the tourism experience, but also to facilitate transactions and the differing contexts within which tourism occurs. In many respects, the tourist destination represents the 'sharp end' of tourism.

Planning and management strategies are implemented at the destination. It is therefore at the destination where the innovations in tourism take place — new products are developed and 'experiences' delivered, making the destination the place 'where the most noticeable and dramatic consequences of the system occur' (Leiper, 1990, p. 23). As for the last element (tourism industry), Leiper suggests that it 'consists of all those firms, organisations and facilities which are intended to serve the specific needs and wants of tourists' (Leiper, 1979, p. 400). Obviously, tourism is an open system; all three elements are subject to influence by external environments (i.e. socio-cultural, economic, political, legal and technological environments).

The value of this model is that the process of tourism is dissected and the tourism industry is shown to contain several activities with functional and spatial connections across the system. Obviously, the tourist is the actor in this system. Tourism may be regarded as a whole range of individuals, businesses, organisations and places, which combine in some way to deliver a tourism experience. While Leiper's basic tourism system provides a snapshot of the tourism industry and illustrates how the different elements relate, it however presents a simplistic picture of rather complex social and economic activities with numerous stakeholders who sometimes have divergent interests (Fletcher et al., 2013).

2.2.2. Hall's Tourism System

Hall (2008) suggested a more detailed tourism system. Unlike Leiper's simplistic model, Hall takes a more detailed analytical approach towards the tourism system. He argues that a tourism system should describe the interrelationships between the various components that make the tourism experience possible, thus the geographical elements and the destination offering or industrial elements.

While acknowledging the importance of the geographical elements in Leiper's model, Hall goes further to refer to the psychological elements and the industry components as well. The psychological elements include the behaviour of tourist consumers, and the industry elements, that is, business and organisations that are providing products and services needed by tourists to fulfil their whole experience (see Table 2.1).

Hall (2008) also provides a more detailed image of the destination production elements (Table 2.2).

The destination production elements of a tourism system provide in-depth analysis of issues relating to the tourist-generating region, the transit route region and the tourist-hosting destination. Hence, the tourism system provides a comprehensive image and perception of the businesses involved in providing services to tourists in the market of origin (demand), the transit route region (transport) and in the tourism destination (supply/offering).

One determining factor and issue of crucial importance that has not sufficiently been taken into account by the models of tourism system is marketing

Table 2.1. The Three Dimensions and Elements of the Tourism System.

Psychological Elements	Geographical Elements	Industrial Elements
Decision to organise a trip Decision to purchase	Generating region	Travel agencies and tour operators Destination and outbound providers Marketing Transport infrastructure
Travel to destination	Transit route	Transport and transit route infrastructure (e.g. motels, highway catering, other services)
Activities at destination Entertainment and social interaction with local communities	Destination region	Local transport, accommodation, catering and entertainment, visitor attractions, retail shops, events and festivals
Travel from destination	Transit route	Transport and transit route infrastructure (e.g. motels, highway catering, other services)
Recollection stage Activities and behaviours on return home	Generating region	On-going marketing activities by tourism destinations and outbound tourism trade (tour operators, travel agencies and online intermediaries)

Source: Adapted from Hall (2008, p. 77).

and its influence on all activities and aspects of tourism. Several authors, mainly Middleton et al. (2009), have highlighted the systematic links between demand and supply, as well as the influence and the role of marketing actions by, for instance, destination and tourism providers seeking to influence demand, tourism behaviour and consumption, as well as respond to consumers' demand for tourist experiences.

The latter concept, 'tourism experience', the concept with a focal interest in services marketing, is briefly presented in the following section.

2.3. TOURISM EXPERIENCE

Much has been written about the concept of experience: definitions, models, aspects, realms/dimensions, characteristics, methods and so on. The concept of 'tourism experience' is both vast and abstract. Let us cite some of the most, in our humble opinion, relevant definitions:

- Experiences are created when 'a company intentionally uses services as the stage and goods as props, to engage individual customers in a way that creates a memorable event' (Pine & Gilmore, 1999, p. 11).

Table 2.2.   Tourism System — Destination Production Elements.

Organisation of Trip	Travel	Arrival and Experience On-site
Tourists' origin area (Source/demand market)	Transport links between home and destination:	Destination transport infrastructure:
Distribution channels for destination in demand market:	• Airlines • Bus and coach services • Railways services • Car hire services • Ferry services	• Airports • Harbours • Railway/Bus stations
• Travel agents/retailers • Tour operators/ wholesalers • Tourism e-mediaries/ online distribution channels	Communication links between generating region and destination that enable the distribution and promotional channels as well as the financial transactions	Commercial transport at destination
		Distribution channels at destination and local providers
Transport infrastructure in generation region		Destination's facilities and attractions:
		• Accommodation • Catering: restaurants and bars • Museum and monuments • Exhibition and conference centres • Natural parks • Retail stores • Events and festivals • Casinos and nightclubs

Source: Adapted from Hall (2008, p. 79).

• Experiences are the 'result of encountering, undergoing, or living through situations. They are triggered stimulations of the senses, the heart, and the mind. Experiences also connect the company and the brand to the customer's lifestyle and place individual customer actions and the purchase occasion in a broader social context. In sum, experiences provide sensory, emotional, cognitive, behavioural, and relational values that replace functional values' (Schmitt, 2003, p. 25).

• 'By "total experience" we mean the feelings customers take away from their interaction with a firm's goods, services, and "atmospheric' stimuli"' (Haeckel, Carbone, & Berry, 2003, p. 18).

Webster's Dictionary defines 'experience' as 'something personally encountered, undergone, or lived through', but experience also means engaging the senses and creating long-lasting memories. A memorable tourism experience must amaze and astonish; therefore, it must (1) create a lasting memory; (2) differentiate one company's product from the competition and (3) involve innovation and (4) be highly unique.

The tourism system approach described in Section 2.2 is an outline of a geographic model of the tourism experience, which begins in the generating region and moves through the transit region into the destination region and then returns to the generating region. This is the spatial approach, the geographic perspective.

When a tourist is motivated to take a leisure or holiday trip, the process begins with deciding, planning and organising the trip, followed by arranging transportation to the destination where the holiday is enjoyed. Obviously, the tourism experiences include more than the on-site experience (Middleton et al., 2009). If we consider the issue of tourism experience in temporal terms, it could be said that it includes the following five phases:

1. Anticipation (pre-trip experience);
2. Travel to (en-route experience);
3. On-site stay (destination/on-site experience);
4. Travel back; and
5. Recollection/reflection.

Depending on their motivation, the pre-trip and en-route phases of a leisure or holiday trip are often seen by tourists as a way of enhancing the perceived quality of the on-site experience. In today's environment of ever more sophisticated consumers, those who deliver memorable customer experiences consistently create superior value and competitive advantage.

2.4. VALUE CHAIN

The concept of value chain is derived from business management and is a model developed by Michael Porter (1985). It is used to describe the process by which businesses receive raw materials, add value to the raw materials through various processes to create a finished product and then sell that end product to customers. In other words, a value chain is a chain of activities that a business operating in a specific industry performs in order to deliver a valuable product or service for the market. According to Porter (1985), the primary activities are inbound logistics, operations, outbound logistics, marketing and sales and service. The support activities are firm infrastructure, human resource management, technology and procurement.

The idea of the value chain is based on the process view of organisations, the idea of seeing a manufacturing or service organisation as a system, made up of subsystems, each with inputs, transformation processes and outputs. Inputs, transformation processes and outputs involve the acquisition and consumption of resources, that is, money, labour, materials, equipment, buildings, land, administration and management. How value chain activities are carried out determines costs and affects profits.

The concept of value chain as decision support tools was added onto the competitive strategies paradigm developed by Porter (1979). It can be applied within two contexts/levels, business/micro and industry, briefly explained in the subsequent sections.

2.4.1. Value Chain at Business Level

The appropriate level for constructing a value chain is the business unit. The value chain categorises the generic value-adding activities of an organisation. Companies conduct value chain analysis by looking at every production step required to create a product/service and identifying ways to increase the efficiency of the chain. The overall aim is to deliver maximum value for the least possible total cost and to create a competitive advantage.

A value chain is therefore a business model that breaks down the flow of production activities into five categories. Each one of these categories is an opportunity for a company to maximise efficiency and create a competitive advantage. The aim of the value chain is, therefore, to increase profits by creating value at each of the five product touchpoints, so the value exceeds the cost associated with the product (Porter, 1985, pp. 11–15).

2.4.1.1. Primary Activities of the Value Chain

The first activity in the value chain is *inbound logistics*, which includes all receiving, warehousing and inventory management of raw materials ready for production. The second activity is *operations* and encompasses all efforts/processes needed to convert raw materials into a finished product or service. *Outbound logistics* is the third activity in the value chain and occurs after all operations are completed and the end product is ready for the consumer. Activities required to deliver a product to the end user are considered part of outbound logistics. *Marketing and sales* are the fourth part of the value chain and include all strategies used to get potential customers to purchase a product, such as distribution channel selection, promotion and pricing. *Service* is the fifth and final step in a company's value chain and describes all activities that create better consumer experiences, such as customer service and repair services. All five primary activities are essential in adding value and creating a competitive advantage.

2.4.1.2. Support Activities

Support activities facilitate the efficiency of the primary activities in a value chain. The four support activities are *procurement*, *technological development*, *human resource management* and *company infrastructure*. Increasing the efficiency of any one of the four support activities increases the benefit to at least one of the five primary activities.

2.4.1.3. Value System

It is believed that the value chain framework is a powerful analysis tool for strategic planning. Capturing the value generated along the chain is the approach taken by many management strategists. The value chain concept has been extended beyond individual businesses; it can apply to whole supply chains and distribution networks. The delivery of a mix of products and services to the end consumer mobilises different economic factors, each managing its own value chain. The industry-wide synchronised interactions of those local value chains create an extended value chain − sometimes global in extent (e.g. tourism). Porter terms this larger interconnected system of value chains the 'value system'. A company's value chain forms part of a larger stream of activities. A value system, or an industry value chain, includes the suppliers that provide the inputs necessary to the company along with their value chains. Once the business has created the products, these products pass through the value chains of distributors (which also have their own value chains), all the way to the consumers. All parts of these chains are included in the value system. To achieve and sustain a competitive advantage, and to support that advantage with information technologies, a company must understand every component of this value system.

2.4.2. Value Chain at Industry/Destination Level

An industry value chain is a physical representation of the various processes involved in producing goods and services, starting with raw materials and ending with the delivered product (also known as the supply chain). It is based on the notion of value added at the link (stage of production) level. This approach has been implemented at destination level, suggesting that the value chain analytic framework provides the chain of activities involved in the production and delivery of a tourism experience. The value chain approach to tourism covers all stakeholders − private and public − involved in delivering a tourism experience (Varvaressos, 2013).

The tourism experience consists of a series of individual experience points provided by multiple entities/service providers, for instance, tour operators, travel agents, airlines, incoming ground operators, hotels, taxis, car hire companies, shops, restaurants, cultural and entertainment services (Braithwaite, 1992). Failure to provide a good experience at any point may undermine the entire experience and accordingly destroy a destination's competitiveness. In other words, the provision of high-quality tourism experiences is a difficult and complex task and requires the harmonisation and coordination of a diverse set of interdependent industries and the public sector.

It is therefore necessary to perform a rigorous assessment of the role of each value chain component in the overall tourism experience, the linkages to other actors and the performance of the service providers, industries and institutions.

The approach emphasises the supply aspects of the tourism experience and aims at providing insights into the factors affecting destination competitiveness. It enables a strategic way of identifying and prioritising critical issues along the chain, and developing targeted actions/interventions to achieve maximum impact. Drawing on the value chain assessment and benchmarking methodologies, specific constraints, challenges and opportunities for action can be identified.

2.4.3. The Global Value Chain in Tourism

As already mentioned, tourism entails a wide range of products and services that interact to provide an opportunity to fulfil a tourism experience comprising both tangible parts (e.g. airlines, hotel and restaurant) and intangible parts (e.g. sunset, scenery, mood) (Judd, 2006, p. 325). A series of assets – historical, natural, cultural, etc. – in destinations is used to promote particular tourism offerings or opportunities aimed at meeting tourists' expectations.

The global organisation of tourism is highly complex due to the numerous offerings and opportunities in destinations all over the world. International airline carriers, cruise liners, outgoing and incoming tour operators and multinational hotel chains are the lead organisations in the tourism global value chain. These organisations cater to all market segments, and they create transnational 'linkages' with tourism destinations in a variety of ownership, alliances and other business strategies. Linkages are the connections between companies along the global value chain. There are three types of linkages:

1. Backward linkages between specific product suppliers (such as artisan crafts, food and drinks) for businesses like hotels;
2. Forward distribution linkages for all tourism companies;
3. Horizontal linkages between companies in the same value chain segment (e.g. excursion providers) who recommend complementary providers (coach or boat for an organised tour).

The tourism global value chain uses the international tourist as a focal point. As stressed by Leiper (2004), without tourists there cannot be tourism. Placing tourists at the centre of the value chain acknowledges that (1) tourists are the fuel and the main driver of tourism; (2) tourism is a demand-driven production system and (3) consumption and production take place simultaneously, as any other services industry.

Following a tourism experience in a value chain details the steps and the providers tourists interact with from the moment they plan for an international journey to the completion of their trip (Christian, 2010). The cumulative activities together represent tourism in its entirety. The main components of the global value chain in tourism are outlined next.

Organising the trip and distribution is the first component, rather than being one of the last stages, as in production-based value chains (i.e. manufacture). This is due to one simple reason: distribution interlinks the supply and demand located in two different countries/markets. The first thing tourists do is to organise and decide how they will purchase their holidays or the components of their trip. Travel agents and tour operators are the main distribution channels. Commonly, travel agents act as the retailers of tourism services (transportation and accommodation), and tour operators are wholesalers. Tour operators purchase blocks of airline seats, hotel rooms and excursion activities and bundle these elements in various package arrangements. The packaged product is then sold via a travel agent or directly. Tourists can also book their trip components directly on providers' websites or through online distribution channels (tourism e-mediaries or online travel agents).

The next stage is international transport. The most common transport mode is international air carriers, but cruise services are a popular option as well. Road and rail transports, although common in Europe and parts of Asia, are typically not a long-haul option. International distribution and transport are based in the outbound countries, but regional distribution and transport operators (incoming) are based in the inbound countries. Inbound countries (destinations) have their own distribution providers and often work directly with international distribution channels.

Destinations have assets and attractions constituting push factors for international tourists. In the destination or hosting area, tourists engage in a number of activities that include local transport, accommodation, catering and excursions (Varvaressos, 2013). Accommodation options include hotels, self-catering units and other forms. Excursions and organised tours are the local activities representative of tourism offering and assets of the destination. Many excursion activities are sold by local operators and carried by local guides. Other local services needed by tourists include catering and retail shopping, which are the needs to be met by local service providers (Varvaressos, 2013).

Except for international airfare, most components of the tourism value chain are characterised by a diverse array of organisational, ownership and operational business structures (Christian, 2010). Large corporations coexist with small and medium enterprises and microbusinesses. International tourism demands a sophisticated level of coordination and marketing that reaches tourists based in numerous countries and regions. Organisations or companies that have management potential, coordination capabilities and marketing prowess carry the most value.

2.5. SUMMARY

Tourism-related industries represent businesses that engage in or influence tourists' experiences and activities. They are the industrial elements, the providers of tourism services that work together in meeting the demands for tourism experiences.

In this chapter, we have presented and explained:

- the tourist system − a very good framework for conceptualising tourism;
- two models providing better understanding and insights in elements and components of tourism activities;
- the whole tourism system − where each and every element of the tourism system is important to offer a valuable experience;
- all components are interrelated and interlinked, so each and every element should operate properly. If one fails to function properly, it will affect the whole tourism system, and consequently the tourism experience;
- the concept of 'tourism experience' and some definitions;
- the model of value chain, an analytical framework that can be applied in tourism, both at business and destination level; and
- a detailed illustration of the global value chain in international tourism with tourists as the focal point.

It is believed that all the above elements, models and concepts would be very useful in studying and creating a better understanding of the tourism industries and the business ventures in this field.

Review Questions

Now you may check your understanding of this chapter by discussing the following issues:

- Describe briefly the tourism system and its components.
- Identify and briefly discuss the two main suggestions about the tourism system.
- Discuss two definitions of 'tourism experience' and choose the one that you believe is the most appropriate. Explain why.
- Explain the utility of the model of value chain in tourism businesses or the tourism industry.
- Discuss the differences and similarities of the analytical framework of value chain at destination and business level.
- Identify the main components of the tourism global value chain and the ways in which they are interrelated.

REFERENCES AND FURTHER READING

Armstrong, J. S. (1986). The value of formal planning for strategic decisions: A reply. *Strategic Management Journal, 7*(1), 183–185.

Braithwaite, R. (1992). Value-chain assessment of the travel experience. *Cornell Hotel and Restaurant Quarterly, 33*(5), 41–49.

Bryson, J. M. (2011). *Strategic planning in public and non-profit organizations* (4th ed.). New York, NY: Jossey-Bass.

Christian, M. (2010). Tourism scoping paper. Paper prepared for the Capturing the Gains research network. London: United Kingdom Department of International Development (DFID) supported research project.

Fletcher, J., Fyall, A., Gilbert, D., & Wanhill, S. (2013). *Tourism: principles and practice* (5th ed.). Harlow: Pearson Education.

Haeckel, S. H., Carbone, L. P., & Berry, L. L. (2003). How to lead the customer experience? *Marketing Magazine, 12*(1), 18–23.

Hall, C. M. (2008). *Tourism planning: Policies, processes and relationships* (2nd ed.). Harlow: Pearson/Prentice Hall.

Judd, D. (2006). Commentary: Tracing the commodity chain of global tourism. *Tourism Geographies, 8*(4), 323–336.

Leiper, N. (1979). The framework of tourism: Towards a definition of tourism, tourist, and the tourist industry. *Annals of Tourism Research, 6*(4), 390–407.

Leiper, N. (1990). *Tourism systems.* Occasional Paper 2. Department of Management Systems, Massey University, Auckland, New Zealand.

Leiper, N. (2000). Are destinations 'the heart of tourism'? The advantages of an alternative description. *Current Issues in Tourism, 3*(4), 364–368.

Leiper, N. (2004). *Tourism management* (3rd ed.). Frenchs Forest: Pearson Education.

Middleton, V. T. C., Fyall, A., Morgan, M., & Ranchhod, A. (2009). *Marketing in travel and tourism* (4th ed.). Oxford: Elsevier.

Mill, R., & Morrison, A. (2002). *The tourism system: An introductory text.* Dubuque, IA: Kendall Hunt Publishing.

Mintzberg, H. (1981). What is planning anyway? *Strategic Management Journal, 2*(1), 322.

Mintzberg, H. (1994). Rethinking strategic planning part II: New roles for planners. *Long Range Planning, 27*(3), 22–30.

Okumus, F., Altinay, L., & Chathoth, P. (2010). *Strategic management for hospitality and tourism.* Oxford: Butterworth-Heinemann.

Pine, B. J., & Gilmore, J. H. (1999). *The experience economy: Work is theatre and every business a stage.* Boston, MA: Harvard Business School Press.

Porter, M. E. (1979). How competitive forces shape strategy. *Harvard Business Review*, (March). Retrieved from https://hbr.org/1979/03/how-competitive-forces-shape-strategy. Accessed on 12 October 2016.

Porter, M. E. (1985). *Competitive advantage: Creating and sustaining superior performance.* New York, NY: The Free Press.

Schmitt, B. (1999). Experiential marketing. *Journal of Marketing Management, 15*(1), 53–67.

Schmitt, B. (2003). *Customer experience management: A revolutionary approach to connecting with your customers.* New York, NY: John Wiley & Sons.

Varvaressos, S. (2013). *Tourism economics* (2nd ed.). Athens: Propobos.

PART II
TOURISM BUSINESS
ENVIRONMENT

CHAPTER 3

FEATURES OF TOURISM-RELATED BUSINESSES AND TRENDS IN TOURISM AND TRAVEL MARKETS

Elricke Botha

ABSTRACT

Purpose — *The aim of this chapter is to provide the readers with a brief background to the characteristics of tourism and a synoptic presentation of the main trends in tourism markets and challenges that tourism businesses should deal with.*

Methodology/approach — *A literature review was conducted on the relevant trends that can affect the management and marketing of tourism businesses. Micro case studies were also presented as practical examples of how tourism businesses have adapted to trends.*

Findings — *This chapter highlights the specific characteristics of the tourism industry, as well as the trends in the market/business environment. Tourism businesses need to remain aware of trends and find solutions to adapt their services and activities to take advantage of them.*

Research limitations/implications — *This chapter is explorative in nature because it has made used of extant literature.*

Practical implications — *Tourism entrepreneurs are encouraged to stay abreast of changes in the business environment. Some of the examples provided may only be applicable in the short run but other examples have long-term impact. Valuable solutions are provided for consideration.*

The Emerald Handbook of Entrepreneurship in Tourism, Travel and Hospitality:
Skills for Successful Ventures, 35–51
ISBN: 978-1-78743-530-8/doi:10.1108/978-1-78743-529-220181003

Originality/value — *This chapter analyses several trends affecting the tourism industry from management and marketing perspectives. This analysis gives a better understanding of how these trends specifically affect tourism. This chapter highlights the importance of monitoring the trends and their evolution in the various markets.*

Keywords: Tourism industry; features; trends; markets; technology; tourist consumer behaviour

---

Learning Objectives

After studying this chapter, you should be able to:

- explain the unique characteristics of tourism;
- describe the business environment of tourism;
- illustrate tourism services and markets;
- clarify features of tourism businesses;
- identify unique trends associated with the tourism industry;
- provide strategies for adapting to trends associated with the tourism industry.

3.1. INTRODUCTION

As with most of the literature pertaining to tourism, one should first have a look at the definition of tourism in order to understand the unique nature of tourism management and marketing. The UNWTO (2010) defines tourism as 'the activity of visitors'. A visitor is therefore 'a traveller taking a trip to a main destination outside his/her usual environment, for less than a year, for any main purpose (business, leisure or other personal purpose) other than to be employed by a resident entity in the country or place visited' (UNWTO, 2010). What is most interesting about the tourism industry is the fact that it can be viewed as a system of entrepreneurial and organisational activities, such as hospitality (i.e. accommodation, food and beverage and other operations) and transport and recreation (i.e. activities and attractions) involved in the production of tourism services and products to tourists.

It is worth clarifying the main terms used in this chapter. Firstly, 'tourist services' are all kinds of services needed during the journey, the stay at the destination and while using tourism products. Examples are transport, accommodation, catering, sport and entertainment facilities. Secondly, the 'tourist products', 'tourism offerings' or 'destination mixes' are the attractions and related activities offered by the destination to the current or potential tourists

(Morrison, 2013). 'Tourism experiences' are the output of tourism goods and services (Andersson, 2007). Destinations offer different opportunities of tourism experiences depending on their assets and resources. Thirdly, the term 'market' traditionally denotes the place where the process of buying and selling occurs. In the tourism industry, market means a specific group of buyers (demand/tourists) who buy/purchase specific tourist experiences at particular destinations (supply/offering).

The characteristics of any industry are important because they are of relevance to how managers make decisions – this is no different in tourism (Evans, 2015). Middleton, Fyall, Morgan, and Ranchhod (2009) indicate that travel and tourism's characteristics are so dominant in their implications that the core principles of business decisions should be adapted to ensure success and sustainable operation. It is against this background that tourism businesses require certain strategies to obtain a competitive advantage (Evans, 2015).

Tourism-related goods and services are produced by many industries and companies, which are obliged to collaborate in order to satisfy the consumers' need for tourism experiences. Several characteristics of tourism distinguish it from other industries. The most important ones are outlined in Section 3.2. This is followed by the synoptic presentation of the main trends in the tourism markets, along with the challenges that tourism destinations and businesses should deal with.

3.2. FEATURES OF TOURISM-RELATED BUSINESSES

3.2.1. General Conditions of Business Environment

An interesting fact is that there is no actual tourism industry as it is not limited to a single industry producing products and services to tourists. The number of stakeholders involved in supplying tourism products and services to tourists is heterogeneous. These stakeholders range from suppliers (e.g. accommodation), distributors (e.g. travel operators or travel agents), competitors, partners, governments (i.e. law enforcement, grants or support) and other firms carrying out complementary activities to fulfil tourist needs (Song, 2012). In this section, we attempt to highlight the main features of tourism supply.

Tourists at the core of the supply chain management: At the core of tourism supply chain management is demand management (Song, 2012), which focuses on satisfying guests' needs and earning profit. As Decrop (2010) explains, consumers deal with a multitude of brands available in many product categories, and hence, final choices are ultimately driven by constraints and opportunities. It is the harmony between different suppliers that affects the satisfaction of consumers regarding the tourism industry.

Providers in the tourism supply chain: Four tiers of providers are evident in the tourism industry. The first tier is known as service providers (e.g. accommodation), the second tier is input providers (e.g. food and beverage suppliers), the third tier is the tourists and an optional tier, the intermediaries (Piboonrungroj & Disney, 2015). Selecting the correct suppliers is perhaps the most important aspect since tourists view the tourism product as a whole and specific aspects of the service delivery are not seen as separate entities. Tourism businesses have to consider several collaborations to provide the most efficient tourism product or service (see also Chapter 8). These collaborations are known as horizontal collaboration (either within the same product — intra-collaboration — to obtain economies of scale or between products in the same sector — inter-collaboration) and vertical collaboration (upstream collaboration, e.g. service provider and retailer) or downstream (e.g. service provider and intermediary) (Piboonrungroj & Disney, 2015).

Information technologies as the backbone of tourism supply chain management: Information technologies, such as the Internet, intranet and software, are essential for integrating operation systems and sharing information for effective collaboration in the tourism industry (Piboonrungroj & Disney, 2015). Tourism businesses that incorporate information technologies enjoy growth regarding both financial and non-financial aspects (performance). Information technologies are an effective means of promoting collaboration with real-time information on usage (demand), availability (supply) and requirements (the gap between the two).

It is believed that one should consider the characteristics of tourism to gain a better understanding of the challenges faced by tourism businesses in managing supply chain (Song, 2012).

3.2.2. Features of Tourism Services and Markets

Tourism has specific characteristics that influence the management and marketing of related businesses.

3.2.2.1. Main General Characteristics of Services and Tourism Services

Evans (2015) explains that the tourism industry, including hospitality and events, has certain key characteristics that are important for any manager to consider. These characteristics direct managers to make important decisions about their businesses and the guidelines they should follow.

The most recognised characteristic is that *tourism services are intangible in nature.* Unlike physical products, tourism services cannot be seen, smelt, touched or heard (Evans, 2015; Kotler, Bowen, & Makens, 2014) and are therefore difficult to be bought because one cannot test or distribute the services as they are done for physical products. Closely associated with intangibility is the fact that services' production is *inseparable* from consumption and hence happens at the same time (Kotler et al., 2014). The implication of this is that the customers are more concerned about the service quality and satisfying customers can therefore be quite difficult to accomplish (Evans, 2015). Service performance is determined by employees' attitudes and behaviour (Middleton et al., 2009). Since consumption and production take place at the same time, this also means that services can be *perishable*. If no production or consumption takes place, the 'product' is not sold and no income is generated (Evans, 2015). Tourism services are similarly *heterogeneous* or *variable*. Service delivery may vary from one employee to the other or even fluctuate from day to day. Kotler et al. (2014) suggest that tourism industries could reduce variable services by (1) investing in good hiring and training programmes, (2) standardising the service-performance process and (3) monitoring customer satisfaction.

Apart from the above characteristics, which are common to all services, there are additional features to tourism.

3.2.2.2. Particular Characteristics of Tourism Services

Three additional features are highly relevant to tourism services. First, *demand fluctuations* or *seasonality* due to factors such as climate, school holidays, public holidays or even religious events or political reasons. These fluctuations have many managerial implications such as cash flow management, labour decisions, product pricing and relevant marketing campaigns at off seasons (Evans, 2015).

Second, tourism products are also *interdependent* on one another. For example, most consumers need to combine several tourism services in order to travel to an overseas destination. Some of these services may be independent from the main destination. The success of a tourism product therefore depends on the supply chain of many other tourism businesses or suppliers on which they depend (Evans, 2015). Tourism entrepreneurs have to make crucial decisions on ensuring quality suppliers, distributors or competitors, or trying to gain a culture of cooperation and foster rigorous quality standards (Evans, 2015). Many tourism businesses opt for partnerships and collaborative projects like marketing or co-branding (Middleton et al., 2009).

Third, tourism has high *fixed costs and relatively low operating costs*. The initial costs to start a business requires large investments. Due to the the intangibility nature of tourism products, the tourism industry is opting for high quality tangible aspects in order to ensure that the customers experience higher quality. For instance, compare a five-star hotel to a three-star hotel. The cost associated with the additional services such as under-floor heating and high-cost bathroom fixtures is much higher than those offered in a three-star hotel. Tourism businesses therefore have to make important marketing decisions (Kotler et al., 2014).

Contrary to the above, some tourism opportunities also offer *ease of entry* to the market. Different from the accommodation industry, other industries like travel agents do not incur high costs (Evans, 2015). These types of tourism opportunities have minimal capital investment, few staff and even low operating expenses, which make it more attractive as small-to-medium enterprises (SMEs). One of the consequences of this attractiveness is, however, that it is also easier for competitors to enter the market, and the tourism business should therefore consider options like diversification (new products and new markets) or new product development (new products and existing markets) (Kotler et al., 2014).

The main objectives of tourism supply management are therefore to improve tourist satisfaction, to reduce seasonality, to gain higher monetary values, to retain tourism sustainability and to reduce demand uncertainty, to name but a few (Song, 2012; Tigu & Călărețu, 2013). In other words, entrepreneurs and managers should make the right managerial decisions to overcome the various hurdles associated with the characteristics of tourism on a strategic, tactical and operational level.

3.2.3. Special Features of Tourism Businesses

Let us look at some special features of tourism businesses having an impact on their management and marketing.

People-oriented: The tourism industry predominantly builds upon people. One the one hand, the tourism industry delivers products to people (i.e. tourists) and on the other hand people (i.e. employees) — employees deliver it and customers are usually part of the 'product' (Kotler et al., 2014). Tourism businesses usually refer to their employees as their most valuable asset. External factors such as seasonality and a lack of formal education and training are issues that affect the service quality and sustainability of employment in the tourism industry (Nickson, 2013).

Long-term market development: Investing in any segment of the tourism-related industries is costly and therefore a long-term venture. Every tourism business must evaluate market segments against size and growth, structural attractiveness and business objectives and resources to determine whether they can obtain sustainable advantages over their competitors (Kotler et al., 2014).

High capital investment and immobility: From a property perspective, there are two fundamental aspects to consider in capital investment. The physical properties of tourism businesses (i.e. buildings, facilities and equipment) require substantial capital investment. The value of the property, however, is primarily derived from the surplus revenue associated with the operational management (Pechlaner & Frehse, 2010). The return on an investment will take several years to show positive results. The emphasis is therefore placed on innovative management practices to overcome seasonality and competition and to make sure that monthly overheads are covered and to make a profit.

Inflexibility: Tourism businesses are highly vulnerable to external shocks and therefore difficult to manage with flexibility. Some of these aspects may include fluctuations in demand or even external factors such as natural disasters. Entrepreneurs typically try to manage their businesses by identifying risks to which the tourism business may be susceptible, assessing the possible impacts of those risks and developing contingency plans in reacting effectively (Evans, 2015). For a more detailed presentation, see Chapter 13.

Imitability: Services and offerings by tourism providers are generally easy to copy. It is not easy to avoid or avert the offering of similar packages and to achieve a competitive, unique selling proposition.

Cooperative nature of competition: Enterprises that would normally see themselves as being in competition, work in a cooperative way to jointly promote their destination and to cater for their customers (Morrison, 2013).

All the above-mentioned characteristics have to be taken into account for management and marketing functions or activities. Based on the above, it could be stressed that tourism is the sum of a range of coordinated efforts and collaborative actions.

The prudent entrepreneur who takes the time to prepare a comprehensive business plan and takes a longer-term view to tourism investment can reap substantial financial gain.

3.3. TRENDS IN THE TOURISM AND TRAVEL MARKETS

Scanning and monitoring the macro-environment for actual or potential changes to the social, technological, economic, environmental and political factors will assist tourism businesses to effectively plan for specific supply chain aspects (Evans, 2015; Morrison, 2013).

Trend is a 'general development or change in a situation or in the way that people are behaving' (Cambridge Dictionary, 2017). Trends therefore have an influence on markets and impact businesses. This section outlines the main emerging trends in the global tourism industry, identified and highlighted by official and business reports. It is important to notice that these trends are classified into two fields or areas: consumer behaviour and technology. However, it should be quite clear that they are interconnected or interlinked in the sense that some of the changes in consumers are enhanced and supported by technological developments. The first is the main driver of tourism activities and the latter is the tool that facilitates actions.

3.3.1. General Situation

With more than one billion tourists travelling to an international destination every year, tourism has become a leading economic activity, contributing just over 10 per cent of the global gross domestic product (GDP) and almost

7 per cent of the world's total exports in 2016 (WTTC, 2017). Representing more than just economic strength, these numbers reflect tourism's vast potential and increasing capacity to address some of the world's most pressing challenges, including socio-economic growth, providing sustainable livelihoods, fostering peace, inclusive development and environmental preservation (UNWTO, 2015).

As an economic activity behind as many as one in 10 jobs worldwide (WTTC, 2017), tourism is a valuable source of livelihood for millions of people. In 2016, the international tourism industry has outperformed the global economy's growth (WTTC, 2017). The first half of 2017 has already produced 369 million international overnight tourists (UNWTO, 2017), resulting in 21 million more than in the same period in 2016 (the total international visitors for 2016 were 1,235 million and it is expected to be more at the end of 2017) (UNWTO, 2017). Demand remained strong overall, though with mixed results across individual destinations due to strong exchange rate fluctuations, increased safety and security concerns and the drop in oil prices and other commodities, which increased disposable income in importing countries but weakened demand in exporting countries (UNWTO, 2016).

The growth in tourism demand from emerging markets continues with a steady pace, as large rising middle classes, especially from Asia and Latin America, are willing, and more able than ever, to travel both within and beyond their borders. Much of this growth is being driven by higher consumer spending as the recovery from the recession gathers pace and is becoming firmly established.

Tourism forecasts over the next 10 years also look extremely favourable, with the predicted growth rates of an average of 3.3 per cent annually (UNWTO, 2016) and continue to be higher than the growth rates in other industries (WTTC, 2017). Capitalising on the opportunities of this tourism growth will require destinations to create favourable business climates for investment and human resource support necessary to facilitate successful and sustainable tourism.

3.3.2. Emerging Trends in Tourism Consumer Behaviour

Consumers' attitude and behaviour are changing faster than ever before. Nowadays, tourist consumers are more experienced, more demanding and online/connected. More specifically, consumption patterns shifted after the economic crisis, leading to a rise in demand for very good value-for-money tourism services (Morrison, 2013). Consumers search for value for money combined with experiences that are more authentic during their travels and holidays. The trend towards choosing value-for-money products has accelerated during the recession as discretionary leisure and business travel budgets have been cut.

Demand for more authentic tourism experiences: Alternatively, this is also called 'slow tourism'. The emphasis is not so much on 'slow' but more on what alternative tourism may accomplish. Meng and Choi (2016) explain that this phenomenon relates to immersing oneself in the landscape and taking in the sights, which usually results in authentic experiences. These activities may include deep engagement with unspoilt nature or places; cultural heritage by means of production, preparation and consumption; slow activities like training, education or community engagement; and alternative transportation like bicycles or walking. Perceptions of authenticity are therefore a critical decision-making factor for tourists since they increase the attractiveness of the destination (Meng & Choi, 2016). It is therefore necessary to find out how visitors experience authenticity at destinations. Jiang, Ramkissoon, Mavondo, and Feng (2017) suggested that authenticity could be increased by managing the destination's image, improving staff friendliness, investing in quality infrastructure and embedding elements of feelings and emotions in positioning and marketing activities.

The *effect of technology and/or information technologies* on people's daily lives has brought about several changes in consumer behaviour. The tourism industry is one of the most affected industries. As mentioned previously, information technologies are the backbone of the tourism supply chain. Operating systems like the global distribution system (GDS) assist travel agents to book the necessary products and services from multiple tourism providers. The most profound change due to information technologies can be viewed from the consumers' perspective. A definitive shift in power from tourism providers to tourism consumers appeared since consumers now have greater access to information and prices via the *Internet* (Standing, Tang-Taye, & Boyer, 2014). Consumers have become increasingly value-conscious, with the Internet providing unlimited scope for prior comparison and greater transparency of the guest experience on a global scale. Easier accessibility to *mobile phones* helps consumers to look for a different perspective than web-based viewing — looking for an experience on their mobile phones. Tourism businesses are increasingly adding GPS functionality, filtering options to retrieve the desired product/service quickly, customisation based on previous search results and even incorporating social media platforms (Rheem, 2010). Tourists also take part in co-creating each other's experiences by editing and reviewing destinations (Gasser & Simun, 2010). This phenomenon is also called the participatory web where tourists increasingly share their travel images, stories and reviews by means of *social media* platforms such as Flickr, Facebook, YouTube, Travelblog and TripAdvisor (Munar, Gyimòthy, & Cai, 2013). These platforms are now integrated into the decision-making process. The fact that information technologies brought about several *new distribution channels* and changes in power structures within the tourism industry further reinforces this argument (Buhalis & Foerste, 2015). Well-informed consumers are now 'unbundling' the whole booking experience by self-booking directly with suppliers or through new channels.

Contrary to the above, the impact of high information and communication technologies use also created a trend of 'digital detox' for some tourists. They typically travel outside the range of telecommunications and Internet to places beyond mass tourism (Matoga & Pawłowska, 2016).

Environmental awareness is usually more closely related to ecotourism, but these days more and more consumers are increasingly environmentally aware (Rao, 2014). The growing consumer interest in *fitness and experiential tourism* is likely to boost active holidays. Consumers see *well-being or health as part of their travel experience*. Some of the motivations for wellness tourism include rejuvenation; socialisation and excitement; hedonism; obsession with health and beauty; relaxation and escape (Dimitrovski & Todorović, 2015).

Looking for adventure: Tourists are looking for opportunities to explore lesser-known (off-the-beaten tracks) destinations, discover untouched, unique places, push the boundaries of their comfort zone and create unforgettable memories (Rao, 2014).

Millennials, also known as Generation Y, are also adding to the complexity of delivering tourism products. Some of the noticeable characteristics of these tourists are: they have precise budgets and opt for inexpensive accommodation; they often travel in groups and love to socialise; they have flexible schedules; they travel to learn more about other people's cultures and heritage – adding to the authentic experience mentioned earlier – and they like to spend time in an active manner like hiking or surfing (Pădurean, Nica, Hornoiu, & Tănase, 2014). Tourism businesses are therefore encouraged to develop new tourism models based on technology, mobile appliances, networks and smartphones to serve this market (Costa, Montenegro, & Gomes, 2016).

An economy of *collaboration or sharing* is popular all over the world; the peer-to-peer online platforms are successful in providing transport, accommodation and dining services. Enabled by technological innovations, the sharing economy presents significant competition to the traditional tourism providers who are usually highly regulated (OECD, 2016). Some of the strategies suggested by Dichter and Seitzman (2017) to address the competition include enabling digitally integrated customer journeys (e.g. tracking order options); receiving instantaneous, single-click peer/customer feedback (e.g. digital real-time conversations); creating a personalised service (e.g. adding services to the package on the spot); and designing authentic, non-commoditised experiences (e.g. different room designs).

Although the traditional forms of vacations will persist, some tourists are more interested in niche tourism. Due to several trends associated with wellness, health or digital detoxification, niche tourism is also on the increase. These tourists have specific needs and motivations to cater for.

3.3.3. Technological Developments: Information and Communication Technologies

Technology in the form of digital information and telecommunications will remain the driving force behind the tourism industry's process of change (Conrady & Buck, 2010). Google's managing director of travel, Rob Torres (2017), suggests that tourism businesses should consider delivering mobile experiences that assist the tourist – leverage mobile technologies like GPS, location attraction suggestions and offline functionalities; and developing fast page loading times.

Tourists are increasingly connected to the Internet. Through their mobile phones, tourists can book a number of tourism-related products and services like online bookings (transport, accommodation and restaurants) and social media to review products and services (OECD, 2016). Specific technological advances include the following:

- Wearable electronics are expected to innovate strategies of businesses in the near future. Some of the advances in these electronics are also evident in tourism where people can do virtual tours of attractions or sightseeing to make informed decisions (UNWTO, 2016).
- Technology is about to transform the tourism experience to make it richer and more enjoyable on the basis of tourists' personal preferences.
- New technology continues to disrupt traditional tourism as tourists connect with tourism companies across multiple devices including mobile phones and wearables. Instant messaging (e.g. WhatsApp and WeChat) is set to overtake social media for customer service, bookings and payments.
- The rise of e-tourism is transforming the industry with personalised tourism services in order to create enjoyable experiences suited to a traveller's individual preferences.

All the above-mentioned trends have a considerable impact on and raise challenges and opportunities for tourism businesses and destinations.

3.4. CHALLENGES FOR TOURISM BUSINESSES AND DESTINATIONS

The high speed of technological change – transforming approaches and tools for business processes – requires a fast response from tourism businesses. The following list discusses the main challenges (Buhalis & Foerste, 2015; Castro, Ferreira, & Ferreira, 2016; Costa et al., 2016; Morrison, 2013; Schuckert, Lui, & Law, 2015; Wang, Li, & Li, 2013):

- New patterns of consumer behaviour mean that the most successful businesses will be those that are able to most efficiently engage with consumers and clearly differentiate their offering from their competitors.

- Tourism providers need to embrace the online world and must ensure that they deliver their offering through multiple and ever-changing channels.
- Tourism companies need to be swift to embrace wearable electronics as part of their strategies targeting always-connected consumers in order to remain competitive.
- The challenge is to be present and easy to reach by consumers throughout the whole tourism experience in terms of notifications, assistance, service and additional bookings. This is expected to be a key area of competition in the tourism industry over the next few years, with companies increasingly focusing on the period after the booking was made as well as during the whole tourism experience.
- This represents a challenge for tourism companies, which need to build a flexible technological architecture to follow their customers from one device to another.
- The most interesting developments are taking place in mobile technology, where companies are embracing social media more than ever as part of their marketing strategies.
- These trends also create a new challenge for companies: customer reviews and spontaneous uploads mean that it can be used as a strategic tool in promotions, online sales and reputation management.
- A gradual shift to personalised marketing in tourism is already evident, with each consumer treated in a different way due to the collection of data from smart devices.
- Technical giants and online travel agents (OTAs) lead the way. In future, all the large tourism companies are expected to provide personalised mobile services with more detail, features and services related to tourism destinations.
- Destinations and businesses have to pay attention to established/developed markets, but also to emerging ones. According to UNWTO (2016), arrivals in emerging economies will exceed those in advanced economies by 2020.
- The combination of cloud services, Internet of things and end-user Internet service systems is allowing tourism destinations to become smart tourism destinations. This functionality creates greater competitiveness and delivers services to tourists according to their searches/preferences.
- Investing in reinforcing data security to protect guests and the organisation's reputation.
- Yield management tools will be developed and extended to improve operational efficiency and cost management.
- Customer choices are driven by quality, uniqueness/authenticity and new experiences. Price, quality and convenience will continue to drive consumer spending, but sustainability will increasingly be part of the decision-making process.
- There is a need to understand different generational needs and values due to multigenerational travels. According to OECD (2016), multigenerational

travel (i.e. three generations of a family taking a holiday together) is becoming more common.

- Develop a multi-channel approach with increasing use of mobile smartphone technology. Developing this capacity will enable providers to ensure their services fit the quick response needs of today's 'on-the-move' consumer.

Tourism providers and companies who are able to understand and meet the needs of new tourist consumers will be the most successful.

3.4.1. Current Performance and Long-term Outlook

Over the past six decades, tourism has experienced continued expansion and diversification to become one of the largest and fastest-growing economic industries in the world (UNWTO, 2016). Many new destinations have emerged in addition to the traditional favourites of Europe and North America. An ever-increasing number of destinations worldwide have opened up to, and invested in tourism, turning it into a key driver of socio-economic progress through the creation of jobs and enterprises, export revenues and infrastructure development (UNWTO, 2016).

Forecasts point to a continuation of growth in international tourist arrivals. What is the long-term outlook? International tourist arrivals worldwide are expected to increase by 3.3 per cent a year between 2010 and 2030 to reach 1.8 billion by 2030, according to UNWTO's long-term forecast report 'Tourism towards 2030'. Between 2010 and 2030, arrivals in emerging destinations (+4.4 per cent a year) are expected to increase at twice the rate of those in advanced economies (+2.2 per cent a year). The market share of emerging economies increased from 30 per cent in 1980 to 45 per cent in 2015, and is expected to reach 57 per cent by 2030; equivalent to over one billion international tourist arrivals (UNWTO, 2016). Tourism is likely having a prosperous future.

Micro Case 3.1: Hotels Adapting to Consumers and Technological Advances

Even though some of the following examples are based on large hotel chains, the emphasis of the examples is rather on how small changes can assist an entrepreneur to adapt to consumer and technological trends.

Several hotels have done some research on consumer and other technological advances and adapted their product offerings accordingly. *The Washington Post* (2017) identified six ways hotels adapted to the Millennials generation (and other technological advances). These strategies are outlined below with additional examples from other hotels in general.

Aspiring to social-media-worthy: Adding a piece of beautiful art not only appeals to the guest staying there but would possibly also appeal to the social group following that guest, focusing on art that is 'shareable'.

Connecting guests with local attractions: Hotels are placing local guides in rooms with local community favourite locations to visit. Many guests are opting for an active lifestyle while travelling and choose some hotels for their health and fitness amenities. Some hotels are capitalising on applications for fitness and offer a complimentary map on MapMyFitness to extended stay guests. Other hotels offer local events to guests staying at the hotel by means of showcasing traditional dances, food trucks with local dishes or wine and beer tasting of local breweries or wine farms.

Revamping room services and menus: Guests would rather explore the city and hotels and customising their normal services to serve numerous needs. These services are delivered by means of vegan options, 'restaurant-to-go', environmentally packaging and ordering on-site and off-site food via applications.

Changing traditional hotel space functionalities: The traditional lobby with a front desk has lost its purpose. Hotels are revamping these spaces since guests can check-in via customised apps. Some hotels have changed the lobby to suit guests who would like to work. These spaces include numerous plugs, free Wi-Fi and easy access food and beverages. Some hotels even went as far as making guest rooms smaller by emphasising detail in or optimising communal spaces to urge guests to explore hotel amenities and the local area (Neirbi Analytics, 2017).

High-tech approaches: Hotels are creating their own apps with numerous services (e.g. check-in, check-out, ordering food or towels). Making use of smartphones, however, goes beyond the use of apps or normal functionalities. Some hotels, these days, have also opted to use guests' smartphones to unlock rooms instead of key cards. In-room technologies could include streaming Netflix, music or surfing the web.

Prioritising social consciousness: Hotels are focusing on social consciousness by operating more environmentally friendly with through paperless operations, solar panels and switching air conditioners and lights automatically off when no one occupies the room. Added to this, social consciousness is also practiced through inspiring dialogs with an on-site expert about art or the interior and infrastructure design of the hotel (*The Washington Post*, 2017).

3.5. SUMMARY

Due to the continual growth of tourism-related markets, tourism businesses should continuously monitor the trends in the business environment and be susceptible to adapt to future changes.

The tourism industry has specific characteristics that need a different approach to managing and marketing services. Added to this, the trends associated with the tourism industry should encourage careful thought as to how tourism businesses should be managing and marketing their offering. Tourism businesses should be aware of these trends, as well as how to adapt their services and activities to take advantage of them.

Tourist consumers have a wide range of needs and tastes that will have to be catered for by a variety of tourism businesses and services. These products and services, however, should offer quality as well as something unique. The power has shifted from the tourism business to the tourism market. Customers are in control of what they see, when they want to see it and how they want to react to information. This was mainly due to technological advancements, which have created a demand for tourism businesses to be more flexible to the information they would like to distribute. Customers demand simplified information spread over numerous platforms. Social media and the sharing economy are now part of the decision-making process and would help customers to customise their trips. Even though mass tourism still has its place in the industry, tourists are opting for travelling as part of their well-being and consider health and fitness as part of their travel arrangements.

Review Questions

Review your understanding of this chapter by answering the following questions or discussing the topics:

- What are the unique characteristics of tourism that require a different approach to managing a business successfully?
- Discuss the business environment of tourism.
- Which trends are affecting the management of tourism businesses?
- How should tourism businesses adapt to trends in consumer behaviour and technological developments?

REFERENCES AND FURTHER READING

Andersson, T. D. (2007). The tourist in the experience economy. *The Scandinavian Journal of Hospitality and Tourism, 7*(1), 46–58. doi:10.1080/15022250701224035

Buhalis, D., & Foerste, M. (2015). SoCoMo marketing for travel and tourism: Empowering co-creation of value. *Journal of Destination Marketing & Management, 4*(3), 151–161. doi:10.1016/j.jdmm.2015.04.001

Cambridge Dictionary. (2017). Trend. *Cambridge Dictionary*. Retrieved from http://dictionary.cambridge.org/dictionary/english/trend

Castro, C., Ferreira, F. A., & Ferreira, F. (2016). Trends in hotel pricing: Identifying guest value hotel attributes using the case of Lisbon and Porto. *Worldwide Hospitality and Tourism Themes, 8*(6), 691–698. doi:10.1108/WHATT-09–2016-0047

Conrady, R., & Buck, M. (2010). Preface and overview. In R. Conrady & M. Buck (Eds.), *Trends and issues in global tourism* (pp. V–IX). Heidelberg: Springer.

Costa, J., Montenegro, M., & Gomes, J. (2016). Global trends challenging tourism organisations and destinations today: What are the likely solutions? *Worldwide Hospitality and Tourism Themes, 8*(6), 716–719. doi:10.1108/WHATT-09–2016-0057

Decrop, A. (2010). Destination choice sets: An inductive longitudinal approach. *Annals of Tourism Research, 37*(1), 93–115. doi:10.1016/j.annals.2009.08.002

Dichter, A., & Seitzman, N. (2017). What's really driving the growth of the sharing economy? In *WTTC: Global economic impact and issues*. Retrieved from https://www.wttc.org/-/media/files/reports/economic-impact-research/2017-documents/global-economic-impact-and-issues-2017.pdf

Dimitrovski, D., & Todorović, A. (2015). Clustering wellness tourists in spa environment. *Tourism Management, 16*(2), 259–265. doi:10.1016/j.tmp.2015.09.004

Evans, N. (2015). *Strategic management for tourism, hospitality and events* (2nd ed.). London: Routledge.

Gasser, U., & Simun, M. (2010). Digital lifestyle and online travel: Looking at the case of digital natives. In R. Conrady & M. Buck (Eds.), *Trends and issues in global tourism* (pp. 83–89). Heidelberg: Springer.

Jiang, Y., Ramkissoon, H., Mavondo, F. T., & Feng, S. (2017). Authenticity: The link between destination image and place attachment. *Journal of Hospitality Marketing & Management, 26*(2), 105–124. doi:10.1080/19368623.2016.1185988

Kotler, P. R., Bowen, J. T., & Makens, J. C. (2014). *Marketing for hospitality and tourism* (6th ed.). Boston, MA: Pearson Education Limited.

Matoga, Ł., & Pawłowska, A. (2016). Off-the-beaten-track tourism: A new trend in the tourism development in historical European cities. A case study of the city of Krakow, Poland. *Current Issues in Tourism*, 1–26. doi:10.1080/13683500.2016.1212822

Meng, B., & Choi, K. (2016). The role of authenticity in forming slow tourists' intentions: Developing an extended model of goal-directed behavior. *Tourism Management, 57*(5), 397–410. doi:10.1016/j.tourman.2016.07.003

Middleton, V. T. C., Fyall, A., Morgan, M., & Ranchhod, A. (2009). *Marketing in travel and tourism* (4th ed.). Oxford: Butterworth-Heinemann.

Morrison, A. M. (2013). *Marketing and managing tourism destinations*. New York, NY: Routledge.

Munar, A. M., Gyimòthy, S., & Cai, L. (2013). Tourism social media: A new research agenda. In A. M. Munar & S. Gyimòthy (Eds.), *Tourism social media: Transformations in identity, community and culture* (Vol. 18, pp. 1–18). Tourism Social Science Series. Bingley: Emerald Group Publishing Limited.

Nearbi Analytics. (2017). *Hotel trends: Marketing to Millennials*. Retrieved from http://www.neirbi.com/blog/hotel-trends-marketing-millennials/

Nickson, D. (2013). *Human resource management for hospitality, tourism and events*. New York, NY: Routledge.

OECD. (2016). *OECD tourism trends and policies*. Retrieved from http://www.keepeek.com/Digital-Asset-Management/oecd/industry-and-services/oecd-tourism-trends-and-policies-2016_tour-2016-en#.WalgobIjF0w#page3

Pădurean, M. A., Nica, A. M., Hornoiu, R. I., & Tănase, M. O. (2014). Trends in tourism consumption behaviour of the young generation. *Quality – Access to Success, 15*(5), 110–116. Retrieved from https://search.proquest.com/docview/1624972978/fulltextPDF/5382B63D52AB4D7CPQ/1?accountid=14648

Pechlaner, H., & Frehse, J. (2010). Financial crises and tourism. In R. Conrady & M. Buck (Eds.), *Trends and issues in global tourism* (pp. 27–38). Heidelberg: Springer.

Piboonrungroj, P., & Disney, S. M. (2015). Supply chain collaboration in tourism: A transaction cost economics analysis. *International Journal of Supply Chain Management, 4*(3), 25–31.

Rao, R. S. (2014). Emerging trends in hospitality and tourism. *International Journal of Research – Granthaalayah, 1*(1), 1–8. Retrieved from http://granthaalayah.com/Vol1Iss1.html

Rheem, C. (2010). What is next for European online travel? In R. Conrady & M. Buck (Eds.), *Trends and issues in global tourism* (pp. 299–309). Heidelberg: Springer.

Schuckert, M., Lui, X., & Law, R. (2015). Hospitality and tourism online reviews: recent trends and future directions. *Journal of Travel & Tourism Marketing*, *32*(5), 608–621. doi:10.1080/10548408.2014.933154

Song, H. (2012). *Tourism supply chain management*. New York, NY: Routledge.

Standing, C., Tang-Taye, J. P., & Boyer, M. (2014). The impact of the internet in travel and tourism: A research review 2001–2010. *Journal of Travel & Tourism Marketing*, *31*(1), 82–114. doi:10.1080/10548408.2014.861724

The Washington Post. (2017). Six ways hotels are targeting the millennial market (and benefiting us all). *The Washington Post*. Retrieved from https://www.washingtonpost.com/lifestyle/travel/six-ways-hotels-are-targeting-the-millennial-market-and-benefiting-us-all/2017/06/29/244c0646-5852-11e7-a204-ad706461fa4f_story.html?utm_term = .98aa09d7b7c2. Accessed on 16 August 2017.

Tigu, G., & Călărețu, B. (2013). Supply chain management performance in tourism continental hotel chain case. *Supply Chain*, *XV*(33), 103–115.

Torres, R. (2017). Technology trends & the future of travel. In *World Travel and Tourism Council (WTTC): Global economic impact and issues*. Retrieved from https://www.wttc.org/-/media/files/reports/economic-impact-research/2017-documents/global-economic-impact-and-issues-2017.pdf

UNWTO. (2010). *International recommendations for tourism statistics 2008*. Retrieved from https://unstats.un.org/unsd/publication/Seriesm/SeriesM_83rev1e.pdf#page=21

UNWTO. (2015). *World tourism day: Celebrating the billion opportunities brought about by the tourism sector*. Retrieved from http://wtd.unwto.org/content/official-messages-world-tourism-day

UNWTO. (2016). *UNWTO tourism highlights: 2016 edition*. Retrieved from http://www.e-unwto.org/doi/pdf/10.18111/9789284418145

UNWTO. (2017). Strong tourism results in the first part of 2017. *UNWTO World Tourism Barometer*, *15*(June). Retrieved from http://cf.cdn.unwto.org/sites/all/files/pdf/unwto_barom17_03_june_excerpt_1.pdf

Wang, D., Li, X., & Li, Y. (2013). China's "smart tourism destination" initiative: A taste of the service-dominant logic. *Journal of Destination Marketing & Management*, *2*(2), 59–61. doi:10.1016/j.jdmm.2013.05.004

World Travel and Tourism Council (WTTC). (2017). *WTTC: Global economic impact and issues*. Retrieved from https://www.wttc.org/-/media/files/reports/economic-impact-research/2017-documents/global-economic-impact-and-issues-2017.pdf

CHAPTER 4

STRATEGIC ANALYSIS AND COMPETITION ANALYSIS

Marios Sotiriadis

ABSTRACT

Purpose – *This chapter's aim is to outline and highlight the components of strategic planning and management framework, as well as the value and utility of strategic analysis and competitor analysis.*

Methodology/approach – *Extensive literature review was conducted on conceptual issues and management aspects of human resources management. A practical approach has been adopted and implemented to illustrate the value of strategic analytical tools.*

Findings – *This chapter provides a description and an understanding of how the analyses and tools of strategic planning and management could be used to plan and implement a business venture better. It discusses the tools enhancing the analysis of the business environment in the field of tourism.*

Research limitations/implications – *This study is explorative in nature because the discussion is mostly based on a literature review. It takes more entrepreneurial/practical than academic approach.*

Practical implications – *The analyses of the business environment and of the competition in an industry are tasks of critical importance. If these analyses are adequately performed, the probability of success may increase. This chapter discusses the purpose, the process and the implementation of tools of strategic analysis and competitor analysis. Practical recommendations and steps are also provided.*

The Emerald Handbook of Entrepreneurship in Tourism, Travel and Hospitality:
Skills for Successful Ventures, 53–70
Copyright © 2018 by Emerald Publishing Limited
All rights of reproduction in any form reserved
ISBN: 978-1-78743-530-8/doi:10.1108/978-1-78743-529-220181004

Originality/value — *The analytical frameworks, tools and techniques discussed in this chapter should enhance prospective entrepreneurs to adequately perform their task of analysing the tourism business environment.*

Keywords: Strategic planning; management; business environment; strategic analysis; competitor analysis; tools

---

Learning Objectives

After studying this chapter, you should be able to:

- explain the meaning and process of strategic planning and management;
- briefly describe what is strategic planning and its objectives;
- define key terms pertaining to strategic management;
- provide a definition of strategic analysis;
- discuss three tools of strategic analysis;
- provide a definition of competition/competitor analysis;
- explain the purpose and the process of competition analysis;
- present two tools for analysing competitors.

4.1. INTRODUCTION: MEANING AND PROCESS OF STRATEGIC PLANNING AND MANAGEMENT

This chapter provides a description and an understanding of how the analyses and tools of strategic planning and management could be used to better plan and implement a business venture.

Strategy entails future and long-term thinking and developing a course of action to meet goals and objectives. The strategic management framework (see Fig. 4.1) depicts the process sequentially and definitively. Strategic planning and management includes four phases: (1) strategic analysis of internal (organisation) and external analysis (business environment); (2) setting goals and objectives; (3) strategy formation and (4) strategy implementation (Okumus, Altinay, & Chathoth, 2010). Apparently, it must be clear that the different elements of the strategic management framework overlap and go hand in hand.

The first phase is the strategic analysis that provides the prospective entrepreneur with a clear picture of venture's situation and that includes internal and external analysis. Internal analysis pertains to the analysis of strengths and weaknesses, whereas external analysis pertains to the analysis of opportunities and threats; the analyses together are popularly referred to as SWOT analysis. SWOT analysis enables an entrepreneur to engage in making his/her strategic, long-term decisions — that is where the business should be in, say, five years

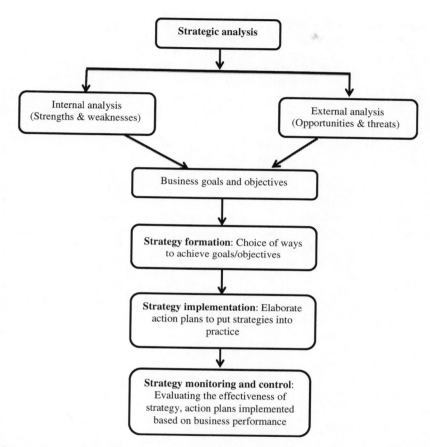

Fig. 4.1. Strategic Planning and Management Framework. *Source*: Author's creation, based on Okumus et al. (2010).

from now. Strategic decisions pertain to choosing an alternative among a set of alternatives that leads to strategy-related success. These decisions have an effect on the enterprise's long-term direction (Olsen, West, & Tse, 2006).

The entrepreneur must then define the venture's goals and objectives. Goals are about what the company aims to achieve in a definite period of time. Goals are planned over the short (a maximum of one year) and long terms (three to five years). This very much depends on the characteristics of the business. Goals (generalised) need to be linked to objectives (specific). Objectives need to be definite and quantifiable (Mintzberg, Lampel, Quinn, & Ghoshal, 2003).

Thirdly, strategic formation is the process of defining the direction of the business's futuristic course of action, which would enable the company to allocate resources in order to achieve the set goals and objectives. An internal and external environment analysis is part of the assessment before strategy is formulated. Strategies clearly identify how the objectives will be met in terms of the plan, and tactics are the actions that operationalise the strategy — those that lead to the attainment of goals and objectives. It must be noted that tactical decisions, which can be immediate or very short term in terms of scope, impact the implementation process in the everyday business operations (Mintzberg et al., 2003; Okumus et al., 2010).

Then, the decisions made must be put into practice. Strategy implementation is the process of putting strategy into action, which includes designing the business structure and related systems. This process leads to effective resource allocation processes, including programmes and activities such as setting budgets, developing support systems, recruiting staff, as well as designing performance evaluation and rewards systems that lead to the attainment of set goals and objectives (Bryson, 2011).

Nowadays, it is not possible or advisable to rely on intuition and luck as the best way to achieve a sustainable and profitable future in the highly competitive tourism marketplace. Strategic planning and management are definitive and formalised approaches that are useful to assist enterprises in achieving their aims, in creating value for customers and owners and in attaining a competitive edge over their competitors (Okumus et al., 2010). Creating a competitive advantage, and subsequently sustaining it over a period of time, requires a formal approach in terms of strategy formation and implementation.

The business/company should engage in constant evaluation of its market position that enables it to develop a strategic perspective on the value creation process. A series of factors in the company's external and internal environments is constantly changing and has an impact on an enterprise's success. A constant and careful scanning of the environment helps to detect any changes in its external environment and enables the enterprise to formulate strategies. Moreover, emphasis must be given to implementing strategies, including the implementation of monitoring and control systems that help to evaluate the strategies chosen, to implement the action plans and to enhance business performance.

The following sections deal with some of the analytical tools enhancing an entrepreneur to conduct this task more effectively.

4.2. STRATEGIC PLANNING

4.2.1. What Is Strategic Planning?

Strategic planning is a business management activity that is used to set priorities and focus on energy and resources. It constitutes a management tool that helps an enterprise to assess and adjust its direction in response to a changing environment. Bryson (2011) argues that strategic planning is a set of concepts, procedures and tools designed to assist entrepreneurs and managers with their tasks. The same author defines strategic planning as 'a disciplined effort to produce fundamental decisions and actions that shape and guide what an organisation is, what it does, and why it does it' (Bryson, 2011, p. 10).

It is an enterprise/company's process of determining the future direction, defining its strategy and making decisions on allocating its resources to pursue this strategy (Bryson, 1988). Generally, strategic planning deals with three key questions (Armstrong, 1986):

1. What do we do?
2. For whom do we do it?
3. How do we excel?

Strategic planning process involves preparing the best way to respond to the circumstances of the company's environment. Authors suggest that being strategic means being clear about the company's objectives, being aware of the organisation's resources and incorporating both so as to be consciously responsive to a dynamic environment (Mintzberg, 1994; Okumus et al., 2010).

With regard to the strategic planning, three crucial aspects must be pointed out.

1. A very efficient approach to strategic planning is to adopt a systems approach that starts with the end in mind (for more details, see Chapter 2).
2. The managerial activity is focused on results, the drivers of results and performance improvement.
3. It focuses on the needs of customers.

All these features of strategic planning render this managerial activity very useful to small enterprises and big corporations alike.

4.2.2. Strategic Planning: Some Practical Tips

Strategic planning is critical to business success as it enables the entrepreneur to better understand the competitive environment. Strategic planning describes where the prospective entrepreneur wants the venture to go, though not necessarily how it is going to get there; it defines the destination that the enterprise is heading towards. Smallbusiness.chron.com (2016) suggests some practical tips, which are summarised below.

- *Function of strategic plans*: Strategic plans are, by definition, focused on the long term: typically, the strategic plan covers a three-year period. The plan sets the goals for the enterprise and outlines how resources will be used in attaining the goals. Strategic plans are expressions of ownership dreams and visions of successful results. Strategic planning functions as the 'design' just as a blueprint functions as the 'how' to build something. The strategic plan displays the completed goal. In smaller businesses strategic planning is usually focused on the overall enterprise.

- *Effective planning*: To effectively plan an enterprise's future, we must know where we are now (current situation), where we want to go (aim/goal) and how we intend to get there (strategy). The continuous process of planning addresses changes in the external/business environment.
- *Improvise*: This process involves out-of-the-box thinking. There is no one right way to create effective strategic planning. It is, by definition, brainstorming at its best. Since it depends on creativity and out-the-box thinking, there is no perfect way to design a successful strategic plan. The more we understand our enterprise/venture and the business environment, the better a winning strategic plan we will create.
- *Use methods and analytical frameworks*, such as SWOT analysis. A SWOT (standing for strengths, weaknesses, opportunities, and threats) analysis is an efficient way to prepare for developing a strategic plan. Identifying these four critical components of the enterprise existence is often the primary building block of strategic plans. This technique can be effectively used as the foundation for strategic goals for a small business. For a more detailed presentation of this analytical tool, see Section 4.3.2.1.
- *Envisioning goals and then defining strategies*: The true essence of strategic planning is how to achieve an enterprise's objectives. Strategic thinking, which is often overlooked in a smaller business, identifies the methods that the entrepreneurs will take to reach their goals. For example, if they believe that developing an e-commerce function would help achieve increased sales volume, they should in turn identify the right method to use and apply the right strategy to achieve the business goals. By selecting the strategy, they have defined the method to employ in the detailed specifications in business plan.
- *Strategy defines action*: As critical as business planning is to the success of an enterprise, all plans are useless unless followed by action. An additional side benefit of strategic planning is the natural action plan that stems from identifying the preferred strategy. Thus, strategic planning defines the rudiments of the action plan to achieve the desirable results.

4.3. STRATEGIC ANALYSIS

4.3.1. Definition and Considerations for Application

Strategic analysis is the process of developing a strategy for a business/enterprise by researching the business and the environment in which it operates (Business Dictionary, 2016). BNET Business Dictionary defines strategic analysis as 'the process of conducting research on the business environment within which an organization operates and on the organization itself, in order to formulate strategy'. Definitions of strategic analysis often differ, but the following three attributes are commonly associated with it:

1. Identification and evaluation of data relevant to strategy formulation;
2. Definition of the external and internal environment to be analysed;
3. A range of analytical methods that can be employed in the analysis.

The strategic analysis for a business is one of the most basic and useful tools for strategic business planning; its main purpose is to understand the business environment. It should be pointed out that market intelligence data are integral information for understanding current market trends in the tourism industry (Varvaressos, 2013). The data can be effectively used for conducting a comprehensive situational analysis for a tourism business and the implications this analysis might have for its future strategic direction. Examples of potential sources are (1) Euromonitor (www.euromonitor.com) and (2) Travel and Tourism Intelligence (www.t-ti.com; www.tourism-intelligence.com) (Dale, 2005).

Analytical methods and tools — the main ones are presented in the following subsection — are the key to ensuring that consistency and rigour are applied to the analysis. There are a number of important considerations to be aware of when using analytical tools, which briefly presented below:

- Gather all information needed to assess the situation.
- The tool must help to answer the question that the enterprise has asked for. Define the business problem or goal that necessitates the analysis, for instance, differentiates offering. A clear definition of what issue the strategic analysis should answer will help guide the effort towards success.
- The expected benefit of using the tool needs to be defined and it must be actionable. The more clearly the tool has been defined, the more likely the analysis will be successful.
- Many tools benefit from input and collaboration with other people, functions or even enterprises. There should be sufficient time for collaboration and advance warning should be given so that people can accommodate the analysis.
- Proper use of analytical tools may be time-consuming. It is important to ensure that the people involved are aware of this. Otherwise, they may not be able to provide the necessary commitment to complete the analysis.

The aim of the analytical tool is to sharpen the focus of the analysis and to ensure a methodical, systematic approach. It is important to exercise caution when interpreting the results of strategic analysis. It should be pointed out that a strategic analysis is subjective by nature; we have to be certain that in developing and analysing information and competitive intelligence we are as honest and accurate as possible. Entrepreneurs should use the information derived from the analysis to define how to best use their strengths, remedy their weaknesses, optimise any predicted opportunities and counter any perceived threats.

4.3.2. Tools of Strategic Analysis

The most common analytical methods used in strategic analysis are the SWOT analysis, PEST (or PESTEL OR SCEPTICAL) analysis and Porter's five forces analysis.

4.3.2.1. SWOT Analysis
SWOT is an acronym for the major components or areas of the analysis: strengths, weaknesses, opportunities, and threats. Within these four areas, we attempt to define the organisation's position relative to the competition and operational environments. It is a simple but widely used tool that helps in analysing and understanding the strengths, weaknesses, opportunities and threats involved in a business project or activity. It is a straightforward model to create the foundation of a strategy (Moutinho, 2000).

This level of analysis enables an organisation to determine whether there are factors present that will aid in the achievement of specific objectives (due to an existing strength or opportunity) or if there are obstacles that must be overcome before the desired outcome can be realised (due to weaknesses or threats). The process starts by defining the objective of the business project or activity and identifies the internal and external factors that are important to achieve the objective. The strengths and weaknesses are usually internal to the enterprise, while the opportunities and threats are usually external. Often these are plotted on a simple 2 × 2 matrix in 4 quadrants, as depicted in Table 4.1.

As mentioned above, the process of SWOT analysis evaluates a company's strengths, weaknesses, market opportunities and potential threats to provide competitive insights into the potential and critical issues that impact the overall success of the business. Further, the primary goal of a SWOT analysis is to identify and assign all significant factors that could positively or negatively impact success to one of the four categories, providing an objective and in-depth look at the business.

It should be pointed out that the various internal and external factors are prioritised so that time is spent concentrating on the most significant factors. This should include a risk assessment to ensure that high risk or high impact threats and opportunities are clearly identified and are dealt with in priority order.

Once we have established the specific values (weightings) related to the business offerings within the four quadrants of the SWOT analysis, we can develop a strategic plan based on the analysis. For example, once we have identified our inherent strengths, we can leverage them to pursue the opportunities best suited

Table 4.1. SWOT Analysis with Examples.

Strengths	Opportunities
Positive attributes internal to the enterprise and within its control Examples: resources, competitive advantages, aspects related to the business that entrepreneur does particularly well, focusing on all the internal components that add value or offer enterprise a competitive advantage	External factors that represent the motivation for the business to exist and prosper within the marketplace. A critical issue is timing. Examples: market potential and growth, lifestyle changes, resolution of current problems, new projects/services and innovations
Weaknesses	**Threats**
Factors that are within enterprise's control yet detract from its ability to obtain or maintain a competitive edge Examples: limited expertise, lack of resources, limited access to skills or technology or poor physical location. Weaknesses encapsulate the negative internal aspects to the business that diminishes the overall value of the products or services provided	External factors beyond the control of enterprise that have the potential to place the entire business at risk Examples: ever-present threat is competition Other threats: unsustainable price increases by suppliers, increased government regulation, economic downturns, shifts in consumer behaviour. Aim: the creation of a contingency plan that will enable enterprise to quickly and effectively address these issues should they arise

to our enterprise, effectively reducing potential vulnerability related to threats. In the same way, by identifying our enterprise's weaknesses with regard to external threats, we can develop a plan that will enable us to eliminate or minimise them.

It is important to remember that SWOT analysis can be influenced (and often quite strongly) by those who perform the analysis. So, it would be a good idea to have an outside business consultant reviewing the results to provide the most objective plan.

4.3.2.2. PEST Analysis

An analysis of the macro-environment is crucial in determining the factors that have a direct impact and/or might influence the strategic direction of an organisation. A number of different concepts can be used to analyse the external macro-environment in an attempt to identify those factors that may have an impact upon the organisation, either in terms of being a threat or an opportunity (Dale, 2005).

PEST (which stands for Political, Economic, Socio-cultural and Technological) analysis is a scan of the external macro-environment in which an enterprise exists. It is a useful tool for understanding the political, economic, socio-cultural and technological environment that an enterprise operates in (Enz, 2010). It can be used for evaluating market growth or decline, and as such the position, potential and direction for a business.

- Political factors include government regulations such as employment laws, environmental regulations, taxation policy and political stability.
- Economic factors include economic growth, interest rates, inflation and currency exchange rates. These affect the cost of capital and operating expenses of an enterprise.
- Social factors include population growth, age demographics, lifestyle and fashion, and attitude towards health (e.g. nutrition). These impacts on the consumer's needs and the potential market size for an enterprise's goods and services.
- Technological factors are those that influence barriers to entry, make or buy decisions and investment in innovation, such as automation, investment incentives and the rate of technological change.

PEST factors can be classified as opportunities or threats in a SWOT analysis. It is often useful to complete a PEST analysis before completing a SWOT analysis (Harrison & Enz, 2004). Other authors (see, for instance, Evans, Campbell, & Stonehouse, 2003) use the STEEP (Socio-Demographic, Technological, Economic, Environmental and Political Influences) approach to analyse the external/broad environment. Whilst recognising the shortcomings of these approaches, Peattie and Moutinho (2000) put forward the SCEPTICAL (Social, Cultural, Economic, Physical, Technical, International, Communications and infrastructure, Administrative and institutional, Legal and political) model as a more relevant concept for analysing those factors within the external tourism environment.

4.3.2.3. Five Forces Model
The analysis of the immediate competitive (micro-strategic) environment is important for understanding the strengths and weaknesses of the competition and the company's relative position in the industry. It is upon this basis that the company can then go on to formulate strategies that enable a strategic advantage to be gained over competitors.

The most popular model for doing this is Porter's 'Five Forces Model' (Porter, 1998), a simple framework for assessing and evaluating the competitive strength and position of an enterprise. According to Porter, there are five forces which determine the competitive intensity and attractiveness of a market. The five forces model helps to identify where power lies in a business situation. This is useful both in understanding the strength of a company's current competitive position, and the strength of a position that a company may look to move into.

Strategic analysts often use Porter's model to understand whether new products or services are potentially profitable. By understanding where power lies, the theory can also be used to identify areas of strength, to improve weaknesses and to avoid mistakes. The five forces are as follows (Businessballs, 2016):

1. *Supplier power*: An assessment of how easy it is for suppliers to drive up prices. This is driven by: the number of suppliers of each essential input, the uniqueness of their product or service, the relative size and strength of the supplier and the cost of switching from one supplier to another. Factors: supplier concentration, importance of volume to supplier, cost relative to selling price.
2. *Buyer power*: An assessment of how easy it is for buyers to drive prices down. This is driven by: the number of buyers in the market, the importance of each individual buyer to the organisation and the cost to the buyer of switching from one supplier to another. Factors: buyer information, buyer volume, buyer price sensitivity, buyer switching costs, bargaining leverage. If a business has just a few powerful buyers, they are often able to dictate terms.
3. *Competitive rivalry*: The key driver is the number and capability of competitors in the market. Many competitors, offering undifferentiated products and services, will reduce market attractiveness. Factors: number of competitors, size of competitors, industry growth rate, differentiation and exit barriers.
4. *Threat of substitution*: For instance, buyer switching cost, buyer propensity to substitute and product differentiation. Where close substitute products exist in a market, it increases the likelihood of customers switching to alternatives in response to price increases. This reduces both the power of suppliers and the attractiveness of the market.
5. *Threat of new entry*: Profitable markets attract new entrants, which in turn erodes profitability. Unless incumbents have strong and durable barriers to entry, for example, patents, economies of scale, capital requirements or government policies, profitability will decline to a competitive rate. Factors: switching costs, economies of scale, learning curve, capital requirements and patents.

Note that this model is not perfect. For example, Evans et al. (2003) apply Porter's competitive forces model to the context of the European airline industry, whilst acknowledging the model's limitations.

4.4. COMPETITION (OR COMPETITOR) ANALYSIS

4.4.1. Definition and Purpose

Competition analysis has been defined as 'identifying our competitors and evaluating their strategies to determine their strengths and weaknesses relative to those of our own product or service' (Entrepreneur, 2016).

Competition analysis in strategic management and marketing is an assessment of the strengths and weaknesses of current and potential competitors. This analysis provides both an offensive and defensive strategic context to identify opportunities and threats.

A competitor analysis is a critical part of a company's marketing plan. A marketing competitor analysis is a critical part of a company's marketing strategy. By doing the analysis, an entrepreneur can formulate how to run the business. This can be seen as a reactive approach; in other words, an entrepreneur's strategy is a reaction to how his competitor will run his company. With this evaluation, an entrepreneur can establish what makes his product or service unique – and therefore what attributes he should emphasise in order to attract his target market.

The following are some of the common questions while doing a marketing competitor analysis.

- Who are our competitors?
- What products or services do they sell?
- What is each competitor's market share?
- What are their past and current strategies?
- How do their strategies affect our business?
- What type of tools and media are used to market/promote their products or services?
- What are each competitor's strengths and weaknesses?
- What potential threats do our competitors pose?
- How big of a threat are they to our enterprise?
- What potential opportunities do they make available for us?

A quick and easy way to compare our product or service to similar ones in the market is to make a competition grid. Down the left side of a piece of paper, write the names of four or five products or services that compete with ours. To help us generate this list, think of what our customers would buy if they didn't buy our product or service. Across the top of the paper, list the main features and characteristics of each product or service. Include such things as target market, price, size, method of distribution and extent of customer service for a product. For a service, list prospective buyers, where the service is available, price, website and other features that are relevant. A glance at the competition grid will help us see where our product fits in the overall market (Entrepreneur, 2016).

Competition analysis is an assessment of the strengths and weaknesses of current and potential competitors. The analysis seeks to identify weaknesses and strengths that an enterprise's competitors may have, and then use that intelligence to improve efforts with the enterprise (Business Dictionary, 2016). The purpose of the competitive analysis is, therefore, to determine the strengths and weaknesses of the competitors within our market, strategies that will provide us with a distinct advantage, the barriers that can be developed in order to prevent competition from entering our market and any weaknesses that can be exploited (Entrepreneur, 2016; Varvaressos, 2013).

4.4.2. The Process: How to Conduct a Competition Analysis

The process of conducting a competition analysis encompasses seven steps, as presented below (Marketing 91, 2016).

4.4.2.1. Step 1: Identify Current and Future Competitors in the Market

The first step of performing a competition analysis is to identify our current and potential competitors. There can be two ways of completing this step: (1) look at them from a consumer's point of view and (2) look at them from the competitors' point of view.

The best way to identify competitors is by looking at them from a consumer's point of view; think like a consumer would and attempt to identify their major strengths and weaknesses. Why would a consumer prefer the competitors' services? Is it because they do things differently or their quality is the best? Either way, these things are like strengths for the competitors. We attempt to respond to a crucial question: why would consumers prefer our competitors to our own enterprise?

On the other hand, looking at them from competitors' point of view will help us understand their business better. We look at their resources and assets and how we would counter them in the marketing field. We try to see what their weaknesses are and how we would take advantage of these.

4.4.2.2. Step 2: Finding Market Share

Once we have identified the competition, the second step is to know their market share; their presence in the marketplace. At the same time, we attempt to identify the reasons for their business or sales performance: good distribution channels (easily available/ accessible), high quality, low price or good value for money.

4.4.2.3. Step 3: Performing SWOT

Once we know the market share and we have completed our analysis, we need to determine the strengths, weaknesses, opportunities and threats for each of our competitors. This will show where our enterprise currently stands, who we need to benchmark against to move forward and what strategies can be most effective to stay on top and be competitive. The SWOT will provide the foundations for the steps we can take to move ahead of our competition.

4.4.2.4. Step 4: Build Competition Portfolio

Once we know the strengths and weaknesses of our competitors, and the opportunities and threats in the business environment, we can build a competition portfolio. A competition portfolio will include each and every product of our competitors, their features, logistics, etc. This portfolio should be treated like a management information system and must be updated from time to time by following up on competitive intelligence.

4.4.2.5. Step 5: Plan Strategies

Now that we have a full image and perception of our competition portfolio that provides a line of action, it presents two scenarios.

1. If the competition is superior, then we have two ways to move forward:
   - try the same strategies as top competitor and slowly move to the top and
   - be innovative and try to directly take a market share.
2. If the competition is average we can reach to the top through some effort, implementing the best strategies to equal and better their performance. Focus and devote energy and resources to achieve this.

4.4.2.6. Step 6: Execute Strategies

Put into practice (implement) the suitable strategies and ensure their effective implementation. At the same time, it is very important to have a contingency plan and to anticipate any reactions by competitors; a contingency plan while executing strategies is very important. At the same time, there must be a degree of flexibility and adaptability to handle unforeseen situations and events.

4.4.2.7. Step 7: Monitor and Follow-up

The main aim of this step is to quantitatively and qualitatively measure the response to the implemented strategy. At the same time, we might put into practice a strategy which gets an excellent response from consumers. It is crucial to obtain feedback from the clientele and market so as to know at all times whether the strategies are working effectively. Thus, following up is essential for long-term competition analysis.

In the end, whatever strategies we implement, our competitors are going to respond. Thus, competition analysis would have to be regularly revised, monitored and updated. Competition analysis helps us to pinpoint our current standing in the market and the future direction we should take.

4.4.3. Tools for Analysing Competitors

The two most commonly used tools in analysing competitors are: (1) four corners analysis and (2) competitor array.

4.4.3.1. Four Corners Analysis

The four corners analysis is a useful tool for analysing competitors (Porter, 1998). It emphasises that the objective of competitive analysis should always be to generate insights into the future. The 'four corners' refer to four diagnostic components that are essential to competitor analysis: future goals, current strategy, assumptions and capabilities.

The model can be used to (1) develop a profile of the likely strategy changes a competitor might make and how successful they may be; (2) determine each competitor's probable response to the range of feasible strategic moves other competitors might make and (3) determine each competitor's probable reaction to the range of industry shifts and environmental changes that may occur.

Understanding the following four components can help predict how a competitor may respond to a given situation.

1. *Motivation − drivers*: Analysing a competitor's goals assists in understanding whether they are satisfied with their current performance and market position. This helps predict how they might react to external forces and how likely it is that they will change strategy.
2. *Motivation − management assumptions*: The perceptions and assumptions that a competitor has about itself, the industry and other companies will influence its strategic decisions. Analysing these assumptions can help identify the competitor's biases and blind spots.
3. *Actions − current strategy*: A company's strategy determines how a competitor competes in the market. However, there can be a difference between 'intended strategy' (the strategy as stated in annual reports and public statements) and the 'realised strategy' (the strategy that the company is following in practice, as evidenced by business actions). Where the current strategy is yielding satisfactory results, it is reasonable to assume that an enterprise will continue to compete in the same way as it currently does.
4. *Actions − capabilities*: The drivers, assumptions and strategy of an enterprise will determine the nature, likelihood and timing of a competitor's actions. However, an enterprise's capabilities will determine its ability to initiate or respond to external forces.

We should not overlook the motivational factors that are generally the key drivers of competitive behaviour.

4.4.3.2. Competitor Array

Another interesting technique or tool to conduct the competitor analysis is by using the competitor array. It is a simple tool where we follow a few steps to determine how our competitors are performing. The steps are as follows:

- *Define the industry*: Describe the nature of the industry we and our competitors are in and the scopes available to produce our goods and services.
- *Find out our competitors*: An industry is likely to have multiple competitors. We need to find out who is our genuine competitor that can match our level.
- *Determine the consumers*: Find out who our customer base is and what their level of expectation is.
- *Key success factors*: Identify what factors are the leading prospects in becoming successful. It does not matter if those factors have been used by us or our competitors.
- *Rank/prioritise* those factors by assigning a weight to each one.
- *Rate competitors*: Give each competitor a rating based on their respective weights on the key factors.

This process will help us realise which competitor is contributing more in the market, which is part of the competitor analysis. We can then develop our management and marketing strategy properly.

4.5. SUMMARY

The analyses of the business environment and of the competition in an industry are tasks of critical importance. If these analyses are adequately performed, the probability of success may increase.

This chapter has outlined and highlighted the components of strategic planning and management framework, as well as the value and utility of strategic analysis and competitor analysis. We have considered:

- the meaning and process of strategic planning and management;
- what strategic planning is and suggested some practical recommendations;
- the definition of strategic analysis and what we should consider for its application;
- three tools of strategic analysis: SWOT analysis, PEST analysis and the Five Forces Model;
- a definition and the purpose of competitive analysis;
- how this competitor analysis is carried out (i.e. the process);
- the most common tools for conducting a competitor analysis.

The analytical frameworks, tools and techniques discussed in this chapter should enhance prospective entrepreneurs to adequately perform their task of analysing the tourism business environment.

Review Questions

Now you may check your understanding of this chapter by answering the following questions or discussing the topics:

- Explain the process of strategic planning and management. Why is it useful?
- Describe what strategic planning entails in practical terms.
- What is strategic analysis and why do we conduct it?
- Present the analytical framework of SWOT and apply it in a business project you are familiar with.
- Differentiate between PEST analysis and the Five Forces Model.
- Explain in practical terms what competition analysis is.
- Briefly present the process of competitor analysis.
- Discuss the two tools for analysing competitors; are there any differences and similarities?

REFERENCES AND FURTHER READING

Armstrong, J. S. (1986). The value of formal planning for strategic decisions: A reply. *Strategic Management Journal, 7*(1), 183–185.

Bryson, J. M. (1988). A strategic planning process for profit and non-profit organizations. *Long Range Planning, 21*(1), 73–81.

Bryson, J. M. (2011). *Strategic planning in profit and non-profit organizations* (4th ed.). New York, NY: Jossey-Bass.

Business Dictionary. (2016). Definitions. *Business Dictionary*. Retrieved from http://www.business-dictionary.com/definitions. Accessed on 10 October 2016.

Business Directory. (2006). Strategic analysis. *Business Directory*. Retrieved from http://dictionary.bnet.com/definition/Strategic+Analysis.html. Accessed on 10 October 2016.

Businessballs. (2016). Porter's five forces. *Businessballs.com*. Retrieved from www.businessballs.com/portersfiveforcesofcompetition.htm. Accessed on 12 November 2016.

Dale, C. (2005). *Strategic management for tourism: Resource guide*. London: The Higher Education Academy, Hospitality, Leisure, Sport and Tourism Network.

Entrepreneur. (2016). Competitive analysis. *Entrepreneur.com*. Retrieved from https://www.entrepreneur.com/encyclopedia/competitive-analysis/article/25756. Accessed on 20 November 2016.

Enz, C. A. (2010). *Hospitality strategic management: Concepts and cases* (2nd ed.). New York, NY: John Wiley & Sons.

Evans, N., Campbell, D., & Stonehouse, G. (2003). *Strategic management for travel and tourism*. Oxford: Butterworth-Heinemann.

Harrison, J. S., & Enz, C. A. (2004). *Hospitality strategic management: Concepts and cases*. New Jersey, NJ: John Wiley & Sons.

Marketing 91. (2016). Competitor analysis. *Marketing91.com*. Retrieved from http://www.marketing91.com/7-steps-competitor-analysis/. Accessed on 4 December 2016.

Mintzberg, H. (1994). Rethinking strategic planning part II: New roles for planners. *Long Range Planning, 27*(3), 22–30.

Mintzberg, H., Lampel, J., Quinn, J. B., & Ghoshal, S. (2003). *The strategy process: Concepts, contexts and cases.* Harlow: Pearson.

Moutinho, L. (2000). Strategic planning. In L. Moutinho (Ed.). *Strategic management in tourism* (pp. 259–281). Wallingford, CT: CABI.

Okumus, F., Altinay, L., & Chathoth, P. (2010). *Strategic management for hospitality and tourism.* Oxford: Butterworth-Heinemann.

Olsen, M. D., West, J., & Tse, E. (2006). *Strategic management in the hospitality industry* (3rd ed.). New York, NY: Prentice Hall.

Peattie, K., & Moutinho, L. (2000). The marketing environment for travel and tourism. In L. Moutinho (Ed.). *Strategic management in tourism* (pp. 17–40). Wallingford: CABI.

Porter, M. (1996). What is strategy? *Harvard Business Review*, (Nov/Dec), 61–78.

Porter, M. E. (1985). *Competitive advantage: Creating and sustaining superior performance.* New York, NY: The Free Press.

Porter, M. E. (1998). *Competitive strategy: Techniques for analyzing industries and competitors.* New York, NY: The Free Press.

Quick, M. B. A. (2007). *An online knowledge resource for business administration.* Topics are presented as frameworks and summaries on the various subjects of business administration, including strategic analysis. Retrieved from www.quickmba.com/strategy. Accessed on 23 November 2016.

Smallbusiness.chron.com. (2016). Strategic planning. *Smallbusiness.chron.com.* Retrieved from http://smallbusiness.chron.com/strategic-planning-important-business-2671.html. Accessed on 5 December 2016.

Varvaressos, S. (2013). *Tourism economics* (2nd ed.). Athens: Propobos.

CHAPTER 5

INNOVATION, CREATIVITY AND TOURISM

Marta Magadán and Jesús Rivas

ABSTRACT

Purpose — *The main aim of this chapter is to show the paramount role that both creativity and innovation have in order to state competitive advantages in tourism.*

Methodology/approach — *The approach is based both on literature review and on various business cases to underline the ideas derived from the literature review.*

Findings — *An entrepreneurial mind must be creative and innovative. This simple idea takes a special value in tourist businesses because of the need to survive in a global market full of competitive actors, dynamism and volatility of preferences in consumers' attitudes.*

Research limitations/implications — *This chapter is an approaching essay based mainly on a general literature review supported with several case studies.*

Practical implications — *Tourism entrepreneurs must take into account the role that creativity and innovation have for their business plans. These two dimensions are the head and tail of the same coin that will help them not only to create value for tourist customers but also to make the difference between them and their competitors.*

The Emerald Handbook of Entrepreneurship in Tourism, Travel and Hospitality:
Skills for Successful Ventures, 71–88
ISBN: 978-1-78743-530-8/doi:10.1108/978-1-78743-529-220181030

Originality/value — *This chapter shows the connections between creativity, innovation and competitive advantages, and their critical value for any entrepreneur who wants to deploy a successful business venture.*

Keywords: Innovation; creativity; entrepreneur; competence; competitive advantage

---

Learning Objectives

After studying this chapter, you should be able to:

- present the necessity for creativity and innovation in tourism;
- explain the key role of both creativity and innovation in entrepreneurship;
- provide a definition of creativity and innovation;
- discuss the various forms and types of innovation;
- analyse the factors driving innovation;
- present the interrelations between innovation and entrepreneurship;
- discuss some cases of innovation in the field of tourism entrepreneurship.

5.1. INTRODUCTION

The tourism industry comprises activities that are scattered in nature, time and space, which need to be combined and assembled dynamically, and involves gathering together actors located far apart in the physical, organisational, as well as cognitive senses. Innovation and creativity can be fundamental tools in strategic management in any tourism business. In fact, the tourism-related industries operate within highly competitive and challenging environments. Changing conditions in the business environment and markets continually force providers of tourism services to offer consumers new and modified products and services to remain competitive, focusing on the respect of value perceptions of markets and stakeholders.

As the world becomes more complex, tourism-related industries continually undergo change and new global challenges force companies to adapt to this new, accelerated and discontinuous environment. Tourism markets are characterised by rapid growth, and as a result, the tourism provider's creativity is a *sine qua non* condition for nurturing and improving the enterprise's market position. Creativity is generally manifested in an extensive way and implies that tourism providers anticipate the needs and desires of customers and identify new offerings. It should be noted that the theme of this chapter is not to study a new form of tourism — that is creative tourism — but to reflect about the impact of innovation and creativity on tourism entrepreneurship and businesses.

The business environment and markets are posing a series of paramount challenges for all entrepreneurs: (1) organizational skills — competitiveness of tourism enterprises is significantly dependent on their capacity to transform service provision into a creative process of satisfying consumers' individual needs. New and innovative ways of doing business are imperative and (2) resilience skills — entrepreneurs must be able to adapt their rationale and businesses to the various and complex changes that can appear, for instance, in markets, productive processes or in customer relationships, in order to handle smartly all the unforeseen situations.

As supposed, innovation and creativity form part of both types of skills and are the raw material and input that determine success in any tourism venture. The importance of innovation as the key driver of sustainable success and business performance has been well documented in various studies. The main ideas and suggestions of these studies are as follows:

- Innovation is a vital element for the survival and growth of companies.
- Rogers (1993) suggested five important attributes of innovation that affect innovation diffusion. Any innovation perceived by receivers that allows having (1) greater relative advantage, (2) more compatibility, (3) better observability, (4) easier trialability and (5) less complexity will be adopted more rapidly than other innovations.
- Innovation is playing a vital role in services and, unquestionably, is particularly important in the tourism industry.
- An ability to innovate is widely regarded as adding to the competitiveness of tourism businesses and destinations.

5.2. THE IMPERATIVE FOR CREATIVITY AND INNOVATION IN TOURISM

Let us put it straightforward: in tourism-related industries, there is an imperative for the entrepreneurs to be creative and innovative because of the continuous shifting of landscape of tourism. In this regard, the following aspects are of significant importance: (1) globalization: no frontier — less barriers — to access to new markets, and a more increasing pressure from new competitors; (2) digitalisation: new ways of operating a tourism business by means of communication and information technologies that impact on almost every organisational subsystem and aspect; (3) new consumers: more informed, more experienced and more concerned about their impact — social, cultural or environmental — on their visited destinations and (4) new trends and fashions: arising from the need of collecting diverse experiences across the whole lifecycle of tourist consumers.

It is important to see innovation as systematic or integral to the tourism system as a whole. Innovation pervades all components of the tourism system, whether it is the individual tourist who creates new ways of travelling seeking for unique experiences, the small accommodation unit that creates its first website, or the restaurant that introduces new dishes to appeal to an emerging market segment. It is believed that the implementation of creative ideas ultimately leads to innovation. Furthermore, innovation in tourism stems from everyday practice and interaction. Even though radical innovations do occur in tourism, they are often developed externally, particularly when they involve new technologies, that is, when introducing technological changes, adaptive innovations are more frequently used by tourism businesses. This is the case of tourism 'e-mediaries', for example Orbitz.com and Booking.com, and online review forums, for example Tripadvisor.com (Sotiriadis, Loedolff, & Sarmaniotis, 2015).

As stressed, tourist consumers are nowadays very different from previous generations (see Table 5.1). As the demand for tourism services become more segmented, specialised and sophisticated, tourism-related enterprises face the challenge to constantly changing their offering, rethinking their daily operations and processes, improving their organisational structure and business model and finding new ways of communicating and interacting with consumers and other stakeholders in the market (Moutinho, 2011). Tourism enterprises need creativity to be competitive as satisfying the ever increasingly demanding consumers has become even more difficult than ever. Nowadays, consumers are tech savvy and want a high quality experience. They are also very experienced, have unlimited 24/7 access to information and do know what are quality standards and good value for money (Misrahi, 2015).

Tourism markets are booming and there is always room for innovation, like most other industries. In this regard, the technology is very useful, providing interesting innovations that are changing the way consumers experience travel:

Table 5.1.   Main Trends in Tourism Consumer Behaviour.

Trends	Elements/Features
Smart consumer	• Wants honest, transparent offerings • Empowered to build personalised travel packages • Offers should be different and creative • Online and offline content should be seamless • Create own unique path in between
Uniqueness search	• Consider themselves 'explorers' vs tourists • Collaboration between traveller and brand • Want customised travel plans • Expect authentic overseas experience
Social interaction	• Travellers want to feel valued • Stay connected 24/7 • Desire to engage with brands • Social media is their playground

Source: Authors' elaboration, adapted from Misrahi (2015).

always connected, customised experiences (do-it-yourself), electronic guides/ websites for seamless experiences. In fact, most of these innovations deal with technology and their potential application on tourism activities from very diverse dimensions and perspectives. While these innovations are now the new norm, 10 years ago, they would have been unheard of. New innovations might continue to transform the way we travel in the next decade.

This is valid at micro/business level. Some authors consider that innovation in tourism may be enhanced through facilities which generate 'indirect infusion of knowledge into the destinations' (Hjalager, 2002, p. 470), such as nature parks, cultural institutions, sports, events and other leisure facilities. This type of operators — which provide services complementary to the core tourism product; that is transportation and accommodation — are generally more likely to adopt and adapt innovations generated in the academic field. The role of complementary services in enhancing creativity and innovation in the tourism industry is, indeed, significant. In the tourism value chain, the prevalence of one complementary service leads to the emergence of new offerings of experiential activities. Thus, these services, due to their diversity and quality, create the premises and foundations for creative thinking and enhanced innovation — linking both — at the heart of tourism value chain. This supports the shift from tangible to intangible competitive advantage.

5.3. DEFINITIONS, FORMS AND TYPES

Creativity and innovation in any organisation are vital to its successful performance. For a better understanding of the links between entrepreneurship, innovation and creativity, there is a need for a clear definition of the latter two concepts.

5.3.1. Definitions

Literature defines creativity as the generation of novel and useful ideas. Stein (1994, p. 1) suggests that creativity 'is a process that results in novelty which is accepted as useful, tenable, or satisfying by a significant group of others at some point in time'.

Creativity is an important attribute and asset in the development of human capital. Only with a creative and innovative workforce can a nation prosper and achieve economic growth (Porter, 1990). Any national economy depends very much on the degree of creativity and innovativeness of their people. 'Creativity' has been the common ingredient and starting point for innovation from the First to the Fourth Industrial Revolution, and it can now be stated that 'creative capital' is the main active for building a society of knowledge.

In short, creativity is the seed of all innovation. The successful creation of new products, new services or new business practices starts with a person or a team thinking up a good idea, and developing that idea beyond its initial state. The conversion of creative ideas into actual new products and processes has long been considered a central challenge in the management of innovation and in the creation of new ventures.

The concept of innovation as an outcome or innovative performance was firstly presented in Schumpeter's (1934) innovation theory, wherein it is stated that the creation of new knowledge or new combinations of existing knowledge are transformed into innovations in the enterprise. Innovation, understood as performance, is a visible result of the ability to generate knowledge, and its utilisation, combination and synthesis for the introduction of products, processes, markets or new types of organisations or more improved ones. This conceptualisation clearly separates innovation from little changes in the production or delivery of products, such as the extension of product lines, service components incorporation or product differentiation. Academic literature gave to us a wide variety of definitions in relation with innovation; Table 5.2 summarises some of the most popular definitions in chronological order.

An underlying idea to almost all definitions is that the acceptance and implementation are key issues; innovation involves the capacity to change and adapt.

5.3.2. Creativity and Innovation in the Context of Knowledge Management

Knowledge management is 'a set of organizational design and operational principles, processes, organizational structures, applications and technologies that helps knowledge workers dramatically leverage their creativity and ability to deliver business value' (DeTienne & Jackson, 2001, p. 2). Creativity and innovation are at the very heart of, the cutting edge of knowledge management. Gurteen (1998) argues that creativity and innovation concern the process of creating and applying new knowledge. If knowledge management (KM) is to have any real impact on the way we do business, then it has got to be about making radical changes in the way that we utilise knowledge. It needs to be about creating new knowledge, applying knowledge. In other words, KM needs to fundamentally focus on creativity and innovation.

In conclusion, a more useful approach is to consider and approach creativity as the process of generating ideas while regarding innovation as the sifting, refining and most critically the implementation of those ideas. Creativity deals with divergent thinking, while innovation deals with convergent thinking. Put shortly, creativity is about the generation of ideas, and innovation is about putting them into action. Creativity — coming up with new ideas — is not enough. We need innovation — the taking of new or existing ideas and

Table 5.2. Innovation – Definitions.

Author	Definition
Thompson (1965, p. 2)	'Innovation is the generation, acceptance and implementation of new ideas, processes products or services.'
Kimberly (1981, p.108)	'There are three stages of innovation: innovation as a process, innovation as a discrete item including, products, programs or services; and innovation as an attribute of organizations.'
Kanter (1983, pp. 20–21)	'The process of bringing any new, problem solving idea into use. Ideas for reorganizing, cutting costs, putting in new budgetary systems, improving communication or assembling products in teams are also innovations. Innovation is the generation, acceptance and implementation of new ideas, processes, products or services.'
West and Farr (1990, p. 9)	'The intentional introduction and application within a role, group or organization of ideas, processes, products or procedures, new to the relevant unit of adoption, designed to significantly benefit the individual, the group, organization or wider society.'
Damanpour (1996, p. 694)	'Innovation is conceived as a means of changing an organization, either as a response to changes in the external environment or as a pre-emptive action to influence the environment. Hence, innovation is here broadly defined to encompass a range of types, including new product or service, new process technology, new organization structure or administrative systems, or new plans or program pertaining to organization members.'
Plessis (2007, p. 21)	'Innovation as the creation of new knowledge and ideas to facilitate new business outcomes, aimed at improving internal business processes and structures and to create market driven products and services. Innovation encompasses both radical and incremental innovation.'
Enz and Harrison (2008, p. 215)	'The invention of a new service, product, process, or idea. Innovation includes existing ideas that are reapplied or deployed in different settings for different customer groups.'
Wong, Tjosvold, and Liu (2008, p. 2)	'Innovation can be defined as the effective application of processes and products new to the organization and designed to benefit it and its stakeholders.'
Barcet (2010, p. 51)	'Introducing something new into the way of life, organization, timing and placement of what can generally be described as the individual and collective processes that relate to consumers.'
Hjalager (2011, p. 127)	'The creation of better or more effective products, processes, services, technologies, or ideas that are accepted by society, markets, and government.'

Source: Authors' elaboration.

turning them into action. This requires the application of existing knowledge and the development of appropriate new knowledge. Also, coming up with new ideas is the food of innovation. Innovation is a far tougher proposition than creativity.

5.3.3. Forms and Types of Innovation

Authors suggest four main types of innovation: product, process, organisational and marketing innovation. The first two can be considered as technical innovation, and the rest as management innovation.

- *Product innovation*: This is considered to be 'realised' only when both wholly new products (radical innovation) and already existing but substantially improved products (incremental innovation) are introduced on the market. This includes significant improvements in technical specifications, components or materials, embedded software, etc. Incremental innovations come mostly from the work of engineers and technicians and from market studies, while radicals rely mainly on science (OECD, 2005).
- *Process innovation*: One of the most widely accepted types of innovation is process innovation (Camisón & Villar-López, 2014). These innovations address how an organisation does its business, for instance electronic sales using online distribution channels. Process innovations can be characterised as new methods of producing and/or delivering products and services. Literature suggests that the most commonly used approach to categorise the benefits associated with process innovation is according to their significance. These benefits might be direct (cost savings), indirect (improved relationships with customers and suppliers) or strategic benefits (forge closer business partnerships).
- *Organisational innovation*: This is defined as the introduction of new organisational methods for business management in the workplace and/or in the relationship between an organisation and external associates (OECD, 2005). With regards to the positive outcomes of organisational innovation, it provides a challenging and satisfying work environment which leads to enhanced job satisfaction and self-fulfilment by employees.
- *Marketing innovation*: The OECD (2005) defines marketing innovation as the effectuation of new marketing methods involving important changes in packaging, product design, promotion, pricing or placement. The benefits associated with marketing innovation include better ways of targeting and addressing customer needs, opening up new markets or differentiating a company's product or service in the market with the intention of increasing sales performance. Moreover, marketing innovation could assist in the development of new marketing tools and methods for targeting consumers more efficiently.

5.3.4. Technological Innovations

Within technological innovation, most common classifications distinguish between two opposite types: one which differentiates between product innovation and process innovation, and another which classifies the degree of novelty as either incremental or radical innovation. The outputs of the process of techno-logical innovation, which is materialised in product-related innovations, can stem from the development or introduction of new materials, intermediate pro-ducts, or new components or product features. In the case of innovation results related to processes, they may be associated with the development or introduc-tion of new equipment, an increase in the degree of automation of processes, a redistribution of the production processes or the use of new energy sources. On the contrary, radical innovation produces fundamental changes in dominant practices and in the knowledge available in a company or an industry, while incremental innovation represents instead marginal changes with respect to usual practices and knowledge.

Tourism-related industries are the most successful business on Internet (because they are information-dominated) bringing fundamental and radical changes.

There is an overemphasis on technological innovations probably because these are tangible. However, it should also be pointed out the need of an integrated approach to innovation considering both technological and non-technological aspects. Implementing such an integrated approach requires the consideration of the emerging business models, novel marketing approaches, customer management, service delivery, distribution channels and discovery tools. Online co-innovation communities are enabling customers to share, discuss and advance their ideas. Such dynamic environments not only provide compa-nies with rich sources of innovation, but also push service providers to continu-ously innovate and redesign their services. Innovative technologies and business models have revolutionised the tourism-related industries. Examples of such innovations are mobile booking, electronic luggage tags, bring your own device, smartphone boarding passes, hotel service optimisation systems, guest device connectivity tools, wearable devices to identify guests and tablet menus.

Innovations in the hospitality and tourism industries follow a trajectory of service innovation modes, differing from a product innovation. Such innova-tions have increased operational efficiency as well as created more value for customers. Service innovations determine ways of creating and delivering more value to customers through technology or processes. It involves continuous improvement and streamlining ideas to empower employees and consumers. New types of customer experiences have emerged as a result of innovation. Innovative collaborations between enterprises that operate in different indus-tries are also shaping the tourism-related industries. For example, the Wine Routes or other thematic clusters provide a series of culinary or creative experi-ence opportunities.

A challenge for providers of tourism services is finding the optimal mix of digital and human interactions to create personalised customer experiences while respecting their privacy. The tourism industry presents structural features that distinguish it from other services, and these characteristics can easily damage the process of knowledge generation and transfer or act as a barrier to investment in technology.

The first characteristic of this type is the heterogeneity, which usually leads to standardised services. The relative lack of quality standards in the industry can diminish market transparency, and deteriorates innovation as well. The second structural characteristic is the case of the fragmented nature of the industry, dominated by small firms (Hjalager, 2006). Of course, smaller firms could be extremely innovative, but the reduced size may also be an obstacle to achieving an optimal rate of innovation, which often leads to diseconomies of scale that affect the profitability of R&D investments, market research and new products.

A third important structural feature of the tourism industry is that few firms create technologies; they prefer to buy technologies from outside the company rather than internal R&D departments. Knowledge transfer is hampered in tourism by a value chain with a low level of cumulative innovation (Weiermair & Peters, 2002) and where technology and innovation diffusion opportunities are penalised by the weak cooperative relationship with customers and other suppliers. These characteristics of the innovation process stimulate companies to make incremental innovations based on the knowledge previously available within the organisation to minimise the high economic efforts involved in their development, associated risks and probability of failure. This general situation is observed with greater emphasis on tourism, allowing imitators and adapters to prevail over genuine innovators (Hjalager, 2002).

5.4. DETERMINING FACTORS

According to numerous studies, there are various factors that foster innovation. These factors are product-related, market-related, process-related and organisation-related including teamwork and collaboration; decentralised approval processes; excellent communications; a learning-focused innovation orientation and an overall innovation orientation that produces capabilities for innovation.

A valuable study was conducted by Ottenbacher (2007) who investigated the success factors of hospitality innovations and how they relate specifically to different performance dimensions (see Table 5.3).

Tourism enterprises create innovations to achieve different performance objectives, and the findings of this study identify the descriptive dimensions determining the accomplishment of each form of innovation success. It is argued that (1) companies should ponder the emphasis between the product, market, process and organisational factors to deliver market performance, financial performance, or employee and customer relationship enhancement and (2) there is still little comprehensive follow-up of user-oriented innovation in tourism and its impact on improvements and quality assurance.

Table 5.3. Factors Positively Influencing Innovation Classified into Performance Dimensions.

Performance Dimensions	Measured in Terms Of	Key Success Factors Driving Performance
Market performance	Opening new markets, attracting new customers and market share	Market responsiveness, effective marketing communication, raising awareness (benefits of the new service and convinced customers to try them) and tangible quality (offer high quality)
Financial performance	Total sales, profitability, cost efficiencies and enhanced profitability and sales of other services	Attractiveness of target markets for new services; strategic human resource management, employee involvement in the process (at the idea generation, planning and design stages of the new service) and prelaunch activities (in the earlier stages of the process, include a market study, a financial analysis and the development of a detailed service concept)
Employee and customer relationship enhancement	Incorporating positive employee feedback, competencies of employees, improved customer satisfaction and loyalty and the image of the enterprise	Employee commitment (employee understanding, motivation and commitment), behaviour-based evaluation (evaluation of front-line employees' performance) and empowerment (power and autonomy to exercise control over job-related situations and decisions)

Source: Authors' elaboration, adapted from Ottenbacher (2007).

5.5. INTERRELATIONS WITH ENTREPRENEURSHIP

Innovation and entrepreneurship (or the creation of new businesses) are connected because the entrepreneurial mind-set is essential to founding new businesses as well as rejuvenating existing ones. According to Drucker (1985), innovation is the tool of entrepreneurs by which they exploit change as an opportunity. It is quite clear that innovation combines invention with commercialisation, making it easy to realise why innovation and entrepreneurship are so closely linked. Developing a new service, product or process is not enough; the innovative enterprise must know how to convert an idea into a service or a product that is appealing and attractive to consumers. In many instances, the new idea requires the creation of a new business to produce and sell the idea to consumers. However, innovation within existing companies is also possible. Innovation outputs can either be new ways of doing things, or the development of new products, services or techniques (Porter, 1990).

In the broadest sense of the term, entrepreneurship is the creation of new business. It involves opportunity recognition or creation, assembling resources to pursue the opportunity and managing activities that bring a new venture into existence. Some ventures are complete start-ups, while other ventures are pursued within an existing organisation. It is believed that:

- Entrepreneurship is often envisioned as a discovery process that entails channelling resources towards the fulfilment of a market need. For a start-up to be successful, this often means meeting a need better than other companies. Entrepreneurial discovery may be viewed as the intersection of a need and a solution. Entrepreneurial activity occurs anytime an entrepreneur is capable to link a need with a solution in such a manner that a new business emerges.
- Entrepreneurial ventures, whether independent or within established corporations, might be viewed as experiments. They try to determine, for example, the size of a market, or whether a technology or way of competing is promising.

Therefore, entrepreneurship is a high-risk activity. The primary tasks/activities associated with a new venture are recognition or creation of an opportunity and the creation of a business plan (see Chapter 9).

Some other points should be also highlighted (Hall & Williams, 2008). First, there is a focus on technological innovations, but organisational ones are significant and valuable. Second, tourism services must be dynamic, fluid, constantly adjusting to customers' demands, and facing increasing competition. Third, the distinctive features of tourism services should be considered: (1) tourism services involve close interaction between the producers and consumers of services: basically, a customer becomes co-creator or co-producer; (2) the importance of the human factor: given the importance of consumer experiences in services, innovation is likely to focus as much on quality as on quantity. The human capital, understood as skills and competencies, is particularly important. Soft skills, such as interpersonal relationships, appropriate bodily behaviour and welcoming attitudes, often described under the rubric of 'emotional labour', are at a premium in the drive for quality-enhancing innovations and (3) the role of organisational factors: organisational innovations are particularly important in services.

The production of new combinations of products is an important source of innovation in tourism services, and this draws on Normann's concept of 'bundling' (Normann, 1984). Tourism providers can increase their sales and reduce unit costs by providing bundles of complementary services. As Van der Aa and Elfring (2002) argue, in many new combinations the components are not all that novel. Rather, the new concept derives its novelty from the way the components are combined. Hence, the key to innovation is finding novel ways of linking service components, thereby creating value for customers.

All these elements and features should constitute the foundations/ground for directions and strategies to achieve innovative approaches and services. It is useful to complete this chapter by highlighting some practical considerations, drawn from suggestions by Duverger (2012) and Hall and Williams (2008):

• Tourism is increasingly characterised by changes in markets and consumer preferences, in drives for competitiveness, in technology and in the organisation of factors of production. As a result, the products and processes of tourism are constantly being modified, seemingly at an increasing rate.
• Tourism has always been subject to changes, reflecting shifts in tastes and preferences, technologies and politico-economic conditions. But globalisation trends have modified the stage on which innovations are played out, and the rhythm of change has intensified in recent years by developments in information and communication technologies.
• The future of the tourism-related industries will be shaped by delivering meaningful, personalised branded experiences for consumers. Knowing what people want, meeting their expectations and creating memorable experiences consistently is the key.
• The experiential dimension defines successful companies as much as the finer points of product design.
• Value-for-money and new business models such as crowdsourcing will become more prevalent in the market supported by the ongoing importance of (mobile) social media.
• Innovation largely depends on key organisational competencies, such as employee competency and market orientation.
• An innovation-oriented enterprise knows how to listen to its employees and customers; however, choosing which customer or employee to listen to might be paramount to finding radical innovative ideas.
• Extract innovative service ideas from the market before they materialise as competing market offerings.
• Not only are innovative service ideas present, in the marketplace, but also that the best ideas most likely exist within the minds of current and past dissatisfied clients, the latter of which is often referred to as 'service defectors'.

5.6. INNOVATION AND CREATIVITY IN TOURISM: SOME SUCCESS CASES/BEST PRACTICES

This section outlines three cases related to the successful adoption and implementation of innovation and creativity in the field of tourism industry.

Case 5.1:   Technological Innovation in Marketing and Business Alliances

Barceló Hotel Group has reached an agreement with Expedia (a tourism e-mediary or online travel agent OTA) to integrate the latter's advanced dynamic packet platform into the brand website. This option is already available on the chain's website both in the US and UK, and soon will be expended to the other markets.

Expedia's technology will allow Barceló to offer a new combined reservation option for its hotels, to customers booking from the US and UK websites, including alternative flights operated by the more than 500 airlines with which the OTA collaborates. According to Expedia data, compared to exclusively accommodation reservations, the packages not only double, on average, the duration of the stay and the advance reservations, but they also reduce by half owing to the cancellations. Raúl González, CEO of Barceló Hotel Group, indicated, 'This new collaboration agreement with Expedia fits in naturally with us because it allows us to offer our customers, from our own website, a pioneering and unique experience for booking dynamic packages. Expedia is a leader in technology and our goal is to continue exploring how the relationship between Barceló and Expedia can evolve beyond distribution to generate business for our partners'.

On the other hand, Cyril Ranque, President of Lodging Partner Services (Expedia Group), pointed out,[1] 'The launch and start-up of this collaboration with Barceló is a clear sign that our large volume of investment in technological innovation has fruitful benefits for our hotel partners, which is strengthened by the fact that Expedia's hotel chains collaborate with us in the development of this type of breakthrough and pioneering initiative that brings value beyond traditional distribution'. This marketing alliance constitutes a win-win business collaboration.

Case 5.2:   The Innovation in Experiences at RH Hotels: The First Glass Pool Suspended in Spain[2]

RH Hotels is one of the leading chains in environmental management and the only one with eight of its establishments certified with ISO 14064-1 Carbon Footprint.

RH Hotels inaugurated in its Hotel RH Don Carlos, a terrace solarium, with the first suspended glass swimming pool of the Peninsula, located in its sixth plant, to 30 metres of height. With this addition, RH Hotels confirms its commitment to offer increasingly attractive and innovative facilities in its hotels, with a clearly differentiated offer providing its customers with new experiences.

The Hotel RH Don Carlos has a second heated swimming pool with retractable cover in its spa, equipped with sauna, Turkish bath, heated jacuzzi and rain shower. From both you can see spectacular views of the city of Peñíscola and its Papa Luna Castle.

Case 5.3:   The Commercial Innovation of 'Concept' Hotels[3]

The segmentation strategies put in place by several chains are leading to the emergence of 'concept' hotels, some of which are beginning to be successful in the marketplace. In this way, what began as a bet — as in many cases with investments of millions of euros — is today a valuable market proposition/offering to certain market segments.

Hotels for 'millennials': For example, to capture and retain the millennial audience (youngsters from 18 to 33 years old), Marriott launched the Moxy brand a couple of years ago. Equally, the trademark of NH is trying to be fitted to the 'millennials'.

More recently, Accor Hotels has also created its new JO & JOE brand, directed to the 'millennials'. This new concept aims to responding to the expectations of 'millennials' who travel for work and leisure, and who adopt the new concepts of sharing, spontaneity and experience. Through this new generation of hotels (with 50 destinations covered in 2020, always in the urban centre and in 'living spaces'), Accor seeks precisely to adapt to a broad international community of clients with a millennial, prescriptive mentality that comes to revolutionise the market.

Premium hotels for the X generation: Parents of millennials are the baby boomers (born in the late 1950s and in the 1960s), while millennials' 'older brothers' are members of the X generation (those born in the 1970s and early 1980s).

For those segments with a disposable income above the average and belonging to the X generation are available new hotel brands, such as NH Collection or The One (group H10). These are establishments that respond to a concept of luxury somewhat more classic, but not too old, so they can also attract the baby boomer generation.

Hotels for hedonists: Nevertheless, hotel chains are not only segmented by age groups and spending power, but also by lifestyles and aspirations. From this perspective, new concepts and brands have emerged focusing on a hedonistic segment for those with enough income and wishing to pamper themselves, such as W (Starwood group recently acquired by Marriott), ME (Meliá Hotels), Hard Rock or Ushuaïa.

The main goal of these new hotel brands is to differentiate themselves from the competition, attract diverse profiles of clients and delight them in such way during their stay that they wish to repeat the experience and become loyal customers to the brand.

Hotels for tourists from other cultures: Another option is creating specific hotel concepts for consumers coming from a specific geographical area of the world, with a different cultural background and idiosyncrasy; for example, the case of the brand PengYou by the Spanish hotel chain Meliá for the Chinese market. Also, Meliá and NH focus their strategy on China with a customised offering. Another example is the so-called Islamic hotels.

5.7. SUMMARY

Creativity and innovation are considered a major source of competitive advantage in the business arena. Innovation must be seen not so much as a series of end products but as a persistent, linked but shifting set of endeavours over time. Enterprises can be perceived as holding an envelope of capabilities, and these will be drawn on and deployed in different ways to address the changing needs of customers. This opinion is supported by the resource-based strategic management approaches that view a company as a bundle of resources and competences. The challenge of tourism-related industries/enterprises is to develop resources and competences that drive innovations.

Tourism services depend on human interaction and interpersonal exchanges that entail perceptions, emotions and feelings, which are impossible to standardise to the experiences offering. In fact, if innovation is understood as a process rather than a result; it may be found in any enterprise or industry. Innovation may proceed from little adjustments in a daily process of continuous improvement, carried out by almost all the organisational actors, at all levels. The message for entrepreneurs and managers in the tourism-related businesses is evident. Most of the success factors are directly controllable. There are no easy answers to innovation success in the tourism industries. Success in tourism innovation is not the result of doing one aspect competent; success is a combination of many factors in place and doing many things well, as highlighted by Ottenbacher (2007).

In short, our main goal and wish are to encourage every tourist businessperson to implement measures to widen the effects of creativity and innovations in their present or future enterprises by pointing out all the potential and actual virtues inside of these two concepts, which ultimately are the head and tail of the 'success' coin.

Review Questions

Now you may check your understanding of this chapter by answering the following questions or discussing the topics below:

- Describe the main difference between creativity and innovation.
- Discuss why creativity and innovation are necessary in tourism.
- Present a definition of creativity and of innovation.
- Consider the four types of innovation (product, process, organisation and marketing). Find examples of tourism businesses having adopted and implemented each one of these types.
- Which one of innovation types do you consider more commonly spread in the tourist industry? Why?
- State the main difference between radical and incremental innovation. From your point of view, which one is more spread in tourist businesses? And what could be the reasons for this?
- Present the main factors driving innovation.
- Discuss the interrelations between innovation and entrepreneurship.

NOTES

1. See hosteltur.com. Accessed on 18 July 2017.
2. Retrieved from hosteltur.com. Accessed on 27 June 2017.
3. Adapted from hosteltur.com. Accessed on 2 January 2017.

REFERENCES AND FURTHER READING

Barcet, A. (2010). Innovation in services: A new paradigm and innovation model. In F. Gallouj & F. Djellal (Eds.), *The handbook of innovation and services: A multidisciplinary perspective* (pp. 49−67). Cheltenham: Edward Elgar.

Camisón, C., & Villar-López, A. (2014). Organizational innovation as an enabler of technological innovation capabilities and firm performance. *Journal of Business Research, 67*(1), 2891−2902.

Damanpour, F. (1996). Organizational complexity and innovation: Developing and testing multiple contingency models. *Management Science, 42*(5), 693−716.

DeTienne, K., & Jackson, L. A. (2001). Knowledge management: Understanding theory and developing strategy. *Competitiveness Review: An International Business Journal, 11*(1), 1−11.

Drucker, P. (1985). *Innovation and entrepreneurship.* New York, NY: Harper & Row.

Duverger, P. (2012). Using dissatisfied customers as a source for innovative service ideas. *Journal of Hospitality & Tourism Research, 36*(5), 537−563.

Enz, C., & Harrison, J. (2008). Innovation and entrepreneurship in the hospitality industry. In B. Brotherton & R. Wood (Eds.), *The Sage handbook of hospitality management* (pp. 213−228). London: Sage Publications.

Gurteen, D. (1998). Knowledge, creativity and innovation. *Journal of Knowledge Management*, *2*(1), 5–13.

Hall, C., & Williams, A. (2008). *Tourism and innovation*. New York, NY: Routledge.

Hjalager, A. M. (2002). Repairing innovation defectiveness in tourism. *Tourism Management*, *23*(5), 465–474.

Hjalager, A. M. (2006). The marriage between welfare services and tourism—A driving force for innovation? *Journal of Quality Assurance in Hospitality & Tourism*, *6*(3–4), 7–29.

Hjalager, A. M. (2011). Strategic innovation in tourism business. In L. Moutinho (Ed.), *Strategic management in tourism* (2nd ed., pp. 127–140). Oxfordshire: CAB International.

Kanter, R. M. (1983). *The change masters: Innovation for productivity in the American corporation*. New York, NY: Simon & Schuster.

Kimberly, J. R. (1981). Managerial innovation. In P. C. Nystrom & W. H. Starvuck (Eds.), *Handbook of organizational design* (Vol. 1, pp. 84–104). New York, NY: Oxford University Press.

Misrahi, T. (2015). Five innovations transforming the travel industry, travel & tourism industries. *World Economic Forum*, 10 September. Retrieved from https://www.weforum.org/agenda/2015/09/5-innovations-transforming-the-travel-industry/

Moutinho, L. (Ed.). (2011). *Strategic management in tourism*. Oxfordshire: CAB International.

Normann, R. (1984). *Service management, strategy and leadership in service businesses*. Chichester: John Wiley & Sons.

OECD. (2005). *The measurement of scientific and technological activities*. (3rd ed.). Oslo Manual. Paris: OECD EUROSTAT.

Ottenbacher, M. (2007). Innovation management in the hospitality industry: Different strategies for achieving success. *Journal of Hospitality & Tourism Research*, *31*(4), 431–454.

Plessis, M. D. (2007). The role of knowledge management in innovation. *Journal of Knowledge Management*, *11*(4), 20–29.

Porter, M. (1990). *The competitive advantage of nations*. London: Macmillan.

Rogers, E. M. (1993). *Diffusion of innovations*. New York, NY: The Free Press.

Schumpeter, J. A. (1934). *The theory of economic development*. Cambridge, MA: Harvard University Press.

Sotiriadis, M., Loedolff, C., & Sarmaniotis, C. (2015). Tourism e-mediaries: Business models and relationships with providers of tourism services. In D. Gursoy, M. Saayman, & M. Sotiriadis (Eds.), *Collaboration in tourism businesses and destinations: A handbook* (pp. 225–240). Bingley: Emerald Group Publishing Limited.

Stein, M. I. (1994). *Stimulating creativity*. New York, NY: The Mews Press Ltd.

Thompson, V. A. (1965). Bureaucracy and innovation. *Administrative Science Quarterly*, 1–20.

Van der Aa, W., & Elfring, T. (2002). Realizing innovation in services. *Scandinavian Journal of Management*, *18*(2), 155–171.

Weiermair, K., & Peters, M. (2002). Innovation and innovation behaviour in hospitality and tourism: Problems and prospects. In *Fifth Biennial Conference, Conference proceedings in Tourism in Asia: Development, Marketing and Sustainability*, Hong Kong, China (pp. 600–612).

West, M. A., & Farr, J. L. (1990). *Innovation and creativity at work*. New York, NY: John Wiley & Sons.

Wong, A., Tjosvold, D., & Liu, C. (2008). Innovation by teams in Shanghai, China: Cooperative goals for group confidence and persistence. *British Journal of Management*, *20*(2), 238–251.

PART III
PLANNING THE TOURISM
BUSINESS VENTURE

CHAPTER 6

THE ENTREPRENEURIAL PROCESS AND LEGAL ISSUES

Cina van Zyl

ABSTRACT

Purpose – *This chapter deals with the process perspective of entrepreneurship, that is, what prospective entrepreneurs should do and how they do it (the processes they use) to launch a new venture in the tourism field. The main purpose of this chapter is to explain what the entrepreneurial process is, the steps/phases to transit from idea to enterprise and the risks involved.*

Methodology/approach – *General review was conducted on conceptual issues and managerial aspects of the entrepreneurial process and legal issues.*

Findings – *This chapter highlights that the entrepreneurial process undergone by entrepreneurs is dual in nature, both in terms of action and thinking process. Given that the failure rate of new ventures is high, there is a need to focus on the importance of understanding the dynamics of entrepreneurship, the action process of the prospective entrepreneur and the potential risk impact.*

Research limitations/implications – *This chapter is explorative in nature because the discussion is based on a general review.*

Practical implications – *Prospective entrepreneurs should follow specific steps, a rational process to establish their business venture and to protect its operations against any event. Thus, any new business should manage risks appropriately, as well as record insurance to cover for unforeseen events.*

The Emerald Handbook of Entrepreneurship in Tourism, Travel and Hospitality:
Skills for Successful Ventures, 91–108
ISBN: 978-1-78743-530-8/doi:10.1108/978-1-78743-529-220181031

Originality/value — *This chapter provides an overview of the entrepreneurial process and legal risk issues that may affect the success of a new venture. The hands-on approach is particularly useful in dealing with the entrepreneurial mind when exploring new business ventures in the tourism field.*

Keywords: Entrepreneurial process; dynamics; influencing factors; integrative model; legal issues

---

Learning Objectives

After studying this chapter, you should be able to:

- define the entrepreneurial process;
- explain the main phases of entrepreneurial process;
- describe the main influencing factors and the dynamics of this process;
- write notes on the integrative model of the cognitive processes that foster entrepreneurial action to show the value thereof;
- discuss the main legal issues and aspects of entrepreneurship;
- present an overview of the legal issues to be addressed by start-ups and early stage companies.

6.1. INTRODUCTION

Entrepreneurship is a highly complicated and uncertain journey in which entrepreneurs embark upon a range of activities over an extended period in order to make an original idea into a materialised business (Van de Ven, Polley, Garud, & Venkataraman, 2008). Also, inevitably, failure is a natural and inseparable part of the entrepreneurial journey. Even if the prospective entrepreneurs have the right characteristics to be successful, their dream might still fail along the journey.

In this chapter, we are going to present what the entrepreneurial process is — the steps/phases to transit from idea to enterprise. This chapter deals with the process perspective of entrepreneurship, that is, what prospective entrepreneurs should do and how they do it (the processes they use) to launch a new venture.

The entrepreneurial process includes the steps/phases to transit from idea to enterprise. This process begins with action, the creation of a new business/enterprise including the antecedents to its creation, scanning the environment for opportunity, the identification of the business opportunity to be pursued and the evaluation of the feasibility of the new venture. It should be pointed out that the feasibility evaluation is the topic of the following chapter (Chapter 7).

Various definitions were suggested about the entrepreneurial process. According to Burns (2007), the full model of entrepreneurial process consists of 10 stages ranging from the first one 'motivated to make the difference', passing through 'creativity and innovation', 'spotting, creating and exploiting opportunities', 'ways of managing obstacles', 'find the required resources' to the most important stage of creating capital. Bygrave and Zacharakis (2010) suggested that 'an entrepreneur is someone who perceives an opportunity and creates an organization to pursue it' and 'the entrepreneurial process involves all the functions, activities, and actions associated with perceiving opportunities'.

This chapter focuses on the initial stages of this entrepreneurial process. As it has already been mentioned, entrepreneurs are looking to capitalise on an opportunity in the market. In simple terms, the entrepreneurial process presents the stages of transition from idea conceptualisation to opportunity exploitation (Hoyte, 2015).

The entrepreneurial process is opportunity driven. It is about the 'doing with ideas' and turning these ideas into reality. Ideas and opportunities are the beginning of the entire entrepreneurial process. In order to come up with ideas and turn them into opportunities, a prospective entrepreneur should scan the environment and see the bigger picture: the opportunity, the market, clients/customers, competition and the whole business environment that influence the current situation and future prospects. The aim of this chapter is to explain the phases of decision-making and the factors that are interrelated and may affect the success of a new venture. The legal issues that every new entrepreneur must handle are outlined in the last section of the chapter.

6.2. THE ENTREPRENEURIAL PROCESS

The entrepreneurial process describes the entrepreneurial actors (prospective entrepreneurs) as they go through from idea conceptualisation to entrepreneurial opportunity exploitation. The process follows various phases from the initial idea stage to the ultimate decision to initiate the venture (Hoyte, 2015). It is believed that the entrepreneurial process begins with the birth of opportunity ideas and encompasses four phases as depicted in Fig. 6.1.

This simplified model of the four phases of the entrepreneurial process helps us in understanding the entrepreneurial experience or journey.

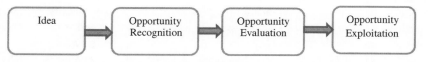

Fig. 6.1. Four Phases of the Entrepreneurial Process. *Source*: Author's creation, adapted from Shane and Venkataraman (2000).

The main terms and four phases of the entrepreneurial process are presented below.

6.2.1. Ideas and Opportunities

The notion of ideas is an important initial phase of the entrepreneurial process. Ideas interact with real-world conditions and entrepreneurial creativity at a point in time to produce an opportunity around which a new venture can be created (Timmons, 1999). The lack of an agreed upon definition for what an idea is makes it difficult to differentiate it from an opportunity. Recent research acknowledges the overlap between an idea and an opportunity, but more importantly, it emphasises that although opportunities begin as ideas it is the action that is needed to transform them into something substantive. Entrepreneurship is about action in the face of uncertainty. It is believed that ideas are a necessary, but not sufficient condition for opportunities to emerge because they merely represent opportunity beliefs — beliefs about the amount of uncertainty the entrepreneurial actor perceives and his/her willingness to bear this uncertainty (McMullen & Shepherd, 2006).

Firstly, an opportunity may mean different things to different people and secondly, an opportunity may always exist for some people and never exist for others. If three people were asked to describe what an opportunity is, there would undoubtedly be three different responses. An opportunity is an appropriate or favourable time or occasion (e.g. their meeting afforded an opportunity to exchange views). An opportunity can also be described as a situation or condition favourable for the attainment of a goal (e.g. starting a business). An opportunity can be a good position, chance or prospect, as for advancement or success (e.g. job advancement).

Eckhardt and Shane (2003, p. 336) stated that entrepreneurial opportunities were 'situations in which new goods, services, raw materials, markets and organizing methods can be introduced from the formation of new means, ends or means-ends relationships'. This definition implies that entrepreneurial opportunities exist as objective artefacts waiting to be discovered by alert entrepreneurs (Shane, 2003; Wood, Williams, & Gregoire, 2012). Seen from a process perspective centred on entrepreneurial action, it becomes more important to understand the unfolding experience of the entrepreneur's thoughts and actions vis-á-vis emergent opportunities (Wood et al., 2012).

Perhaps the biggest misconception about an idea for a new business is that it must be unique. Too many would-be entrepreneurs are obsessed with finding a unique idea.

The idea per se is not what is important. Developing the idea, implementing it and building a successful business are the important aspects of entrepreneurship. The prospective entrepreneurs who are unable to identify their market and customers are not ready to start a business. They have only found an idea and have not yet identified the market and gathered the resources they will need. Rushing to open a business without adequate planning can lead to costly mistakes (Bygrave & Zacharakis, 2010).

6.2.2. *Opportunity Recognition*

The creation and/or recognition of opportunities is at the heart of the entrepreneurial process (Timmons, 1999). The opportunity has, at this stage, already been isolated and defined as entrepreneurial. Opportunities are discoverable; some persons can identify and others cannot recognise these opportunities. The source of opportunities is assumed to arise exogenously from changes in technology, consumer preferences or other contextual factors within an industry or market. The prospective entrepreneurs search and scan the environment for business opportunities. They might learn cognitive processes that improve one's ability to identify opportunities. To the extent that entrepreneurs can learn creative, imaginative and speculative thinking they can become more proficient finders and creators of opportunities (Dimov, 2004).

A cognitive lens places alertness as an outcome of the entrepreneur's unique knowledge or higher-level learning. Prior knowledge gained from social networks, among other sources, were antecedents of entrepreneurial alertness. With specific reference to the discovery and exploitation of entrepreneurial opportunities, Shane (2000) proposed three dimensions of prior knowledge that are important: prior knowledge of markets, prior knowledge of how to serve markets and prior knowledge of consumer problems. Whether entrepreneurs search or are alert to entrepreneurial opportunities, prior knowledge and learning are important facets of opportunity recognition.

6.2.3. *Opportunity Evaluation*

This was seen as resulting from entrepreneurial intentions derived from feasibility and desirability perceptions plus a propensity to act on opportunities (Shapero & Sokol, 1982). More recently, Haynie, Shepherd, and McMullen (2009) arguing from a resource-based perspective (RBV) showed that existing knowledge resources are fundamental to entrepreneurs' judgement of recognised opportunities. Moreover, Dimov's (2010) study of venture emergence by nascent entrepreneurs revealed that entrepreneurs' evolving judgement may be described as opportunity confidence and linked to early planning.

While these contributions focused more on the individual entrepreneur's judgement in terms of beliefs, skills and/or traits, work by McMullen and Shepherd (2006) shed light on entrepreneurs' ability to evaluate different types of opportunities. The same authors suggest that entrepreneurs' judgement extends beyond beliefs to actions specific to evaluating the feasibility and desirability of entrepreneurial opportunities. The field of judgement and decision-making is about 'how people ... combine desires and beliefs (and this includes personal values, goals, knowledge and means) to choose a course of action' (cited in McMullen & Shepherd, 2006, p. 141). Dimov (2007) also emphasised the importance of 'doing' or 'acting' when he stated that creativity and insight play an essential role in the birth of opportunity ideas. Therefore, the transition from ideas to opportunities is dependent both on cognitive and action processes.

6.2.4. Opportunity Exploitation

This is where the link between idea conceptualisation and opportunity exploitation is a 'black box'. This 'black box' exists because the focus has been on expounding/clarifying the mechanisms behind opportunity recognition and opportunity evaluation discretely rather than exploring the mechanisms required to transition through these phases of the entrepreneurial process. Research by Wood et al. (2012) on the cognitive processes that foster entrepreneurial action represents recent attempts to understand how entrepreneurs transition from having an idea to deciding to exploit it. Wood et al. defines entrepreneurial action as 'efforts by individuals to identify, develop and/or pursue ideas for introducing new products, services and/or business models in particular markets' (2012, p. 208) and highlight that for entrepreneurial action to ensue, entrepreneurs must shift from one type of cognitive processing to another as they move through the phases of opportunity recognition and evaluation.

This work offers an integrative model of the cognitive processes that foster entrepreneurial action. It shows how an entrepreneur's thinking evolves from the emergence of an opportunity idea to the initiation of concrete entrepreneurial acts by drawing attention to several cognitive inflection points that indicate changes in mental processing as entrepreneurs move through the process of entrepreneurial action. The proposed model comprises four classes of cognitive processing required at different stages of the entrepreneurial action process. Specifically, attention cognitive processes prior to the identification of entrepreneurial opportunities, association cognitive processes at the stage of opportunity recognition, rule-based cognitive processes for opportunity evaluations and cognitive processes of intentions to transition from opportunity evaluation to entrepreneurial action. Such an entrepreneurial process is depicted in Fig. 6.2.

This model depicts the cognitive processes associated with the transition from idea to opportunity exploitation. Its aim was to identify and explain the different cognitive processes at work as an entrepreneur's mind move through the phases of the entrepreneurial process.

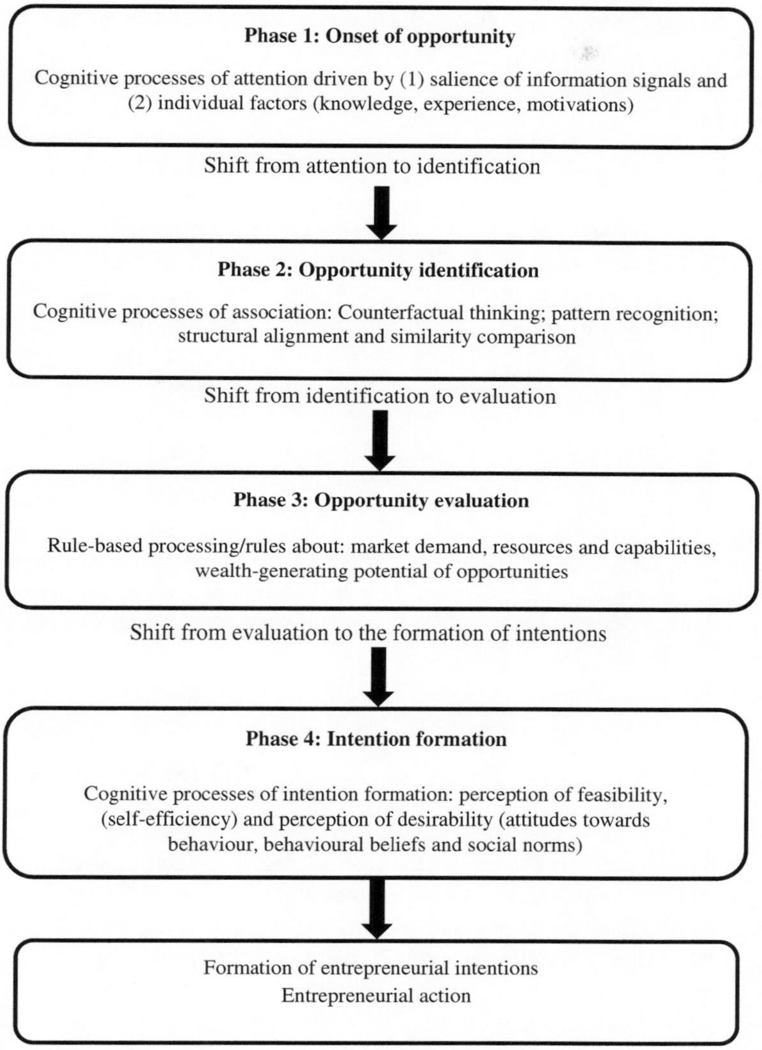

> **Phase 1: Onset of opportunity**
>
> Cognitive processes of attention driven by (1) salience of information signals and (2) individual factors (knowledge, experience, motivations)

Shift from attention to identification

> **Phase 2: Opportunity identification**
>
> Cognitive processes of association: Counterfactual thinking; pattern recognition; structural alignment and similarity comparison

Shift from identification to evaluation

> **Phase 3: Opportunity evaluation**
>
> Rule-based processing/rules about: market demand, resources and capabilities, wealth-generating potential of opportunities

Shift from evaluation to the formation of intentions

> **Phase 4: Intention formation**
>
> Cognitive processes of intention formation: perception of feasibility, (self-efficiency) and perception of desirability (attitudes towards behaviour, behavioural beliefs and social norms)

> Formation of entrepreneurial intentions
> Entrepreneurial action

Fig. 6.2. Four Phases of the Entrepreneurial Process. *Source*: Author's creation, adapted from Wood et al. (2012).

6.2.5. *Entrepreneurial Intent*

Entrepreneurial intent refers to the intention of an individual to start a new business. The existence of an entrepreneurial opportunity; its identification by the prospective entrepreneur and the conscious decision of the entrepreneur to exploit that opportunity are among the requisite steps necessary in the entrepreneurial process (Shane, 2003). Shapero and Sokol (1982) suggest that the process of forming intentions may prove complex. They have developed a model on what influences entrepreneurial intentions (the expected entrepreneurial behaviour). Shane (2003) claims that desirability, feasibility and a propensity to act are the most crucial factors influencing an individual's intention to start a venture, his/her actual personal attitude. Moreover, specific desirability and perceived self-efficacy are described as important foundations for the perceptions of feasibility.

It is believed that there are some key antecedents to opportunity/entrepreneurial thinking (Van Auken, Fry, & Stephens, 2006): (1) salient information signals from environment; (2) idiosyncratic individual factors (e.g. 'pull' motivators, issues one cares about) and (3) 'push' motivators (e.g. career/life situations).

Based on this discussion we may suggest that prospective entrepreneurs act swiftly on an initial idea to make it feasible and launch their new idea.

The ideas and opportunities are the beginning of the entire entrepreneurial process. A prospective entrepreneur should scan and see the whole picture: the opportunity, the market, customers, competition and the whole business environment that influence the current situation and future prospects. Furthermore, the behaviour and attitude of prospective entrepreneurs are affected by a range of factors and different dynamics depending on the phase of the entrepreneurial process. This is the topic of the next section.

6.3. INFLUENCING FACTORS AND DYNAMICS

There is a series of personal, sociological and environmental factors that give birth to a new enterprise: alternative career prospects, economic situation, family and friends, role models and availability of resources. Bygrave and Zacharakis (2010) indicated that the prospective entrepreneurs will get their ideas through their present line of employment or experience.

Bygrave (2004) proposes a model that highlights the personal attributes and environmental factors that influence the venture at each stage. In his model of the entrepreneurial process, the author presents the entrepreneurial process as a set of stages and events that follow one another. These stages are: the idea or conception of the business, the event that triggers the operations, implementation and growth. Bygrave's model raises issues that suggest the need for research that would incorporate the dynamic perspective in the understanding of the entrepreneur and entrepreneurship. He highlights the critical factors that drive the development of the business at each stage. Table 6.1 lists the various categories of factors – personal, environment, sociological and organisational – and the various phases of entrepreneurship on which these factors have an impact.

Table 6.1. Influencing Factors Depending on the Phase of Entrepreneurial Process.

Factors	Influencing the Phases
Personal: achievement, locus of control, ambiguity tolerance, risk taking, personal values, education, experience	Innovation and triggering event
Environment: opportunities, role models, creativity	Innovation and triggering event
Personal: risk taking, job dissatisfaction, job loss, education, age, commitment	Triggering event
Environment: competition, resources, incubator, government policy	Triggering event
Sociological: networks, teams, parents, family, role models	Implementation and growth
Personal	Implementation and growth
Entrepreneur	Implementation and growth
Leader	Implementation and growth
Manager	Implementation and growth
Commitment	Implementation and growth
Vision	Implementation and growth
Environment: competitors, customers, suppliers, investors, bankers, lawyers, resources, government policy	Implementation and growth
Organisational: team, strategy, structure, culture, products	Growth

Source: Author's elaboration, adapted from Bygrave and Zacharakis (2010).

Entrepreneurial traits are mainly shaped by personal attributes and the environment. Let us briefly present each one of the factors that influences a person to embark on an entrepreneurial journey.

6.3.1. Personal Attributes

Personal attributes are the characteristics of entrepreneurs that make them different from non-entrepreneurs. Various authors (e.g. Bygrave & Zacharakis, 2010; Thompson, 2004) suggest that a successful entrepreneur has amongst other some of the following characteristics:

- Ability to identify opportunities;
- Be agent for change (they do new and different things);
- Develop tenacity and creativity;
- Need for realisation;
- Willingness to be independent, locus of control (an intense desire to be in control of one's own destiny);

- Take initiatives and calculated risks;
- Able to react to stressing situations;
- Commitment, establish and actively strive to achieve goals;
- Leadership skills, persuasion and a network of contacts;
- Understand the business field (has good business sense);
- Planning and systematic monitoring;
- Requirement for quality and efficiency;
- Dedication, seeking wealth and a forward-looking vision.

They are also achievers, have ambitions to be successful and are risk-takers. Instead of using psychological terms to describe the entrepreneurs' characteristics, Bygrave (2004) uses a set of everyday words, which he named 'The 10 Ds', of which the most significant are listed below:

- *Dream/Vision*: Entrepreneurs have a vision of what the future could be like for them and their businesses, and have the ability to implement their dreams.
- *Decisiveness*: They make decisions swiftly. Their swiftness is a key factor in their success.
- *Determination*: They implement their ventures with total commitment, without being averted by any obstacle.
- *Dedication*: They are totally dedicated to their business; they work tirelessly.
- *Devotion*: They love what they do, with full devotion to their venture.
- *Details*: Entrepreneurs must be on top of the critical details.
- *Destiny*: They want to be in charge of their own destiny, not relying on other persons.

6.3.2. Environmental and Sociological Factors

Prospective entrepreneurs are also influenced by certain environmental and sociological factors, such as:

- *Role models*: prospective entrepreneurs come into contact with role models primarily in their home (parents), social environment or at work;
- The local business environment (i.e. favourable conditions);
- *Family culture*: family responsibilities play an important role in the decision whether to start a venture;
- *Age*: the trade-off between the experience that comes with age and the optimism and energy of youth and
- *Contacts*: a network of personal relationships is helpful and supportive of new venture.

It is believed that the environmental factors interact with personal characteristics to increase the tendency towards launching a venture (Bygrave, 2004).

However, it should be pointed out that, in the succeeding stages of the enterprise, from implementation to full organisational development in the growth stage, other personal attributes become important. These are vision, leadership, entrepreneurial spirit, management ability and commitment. Therefore, there is an evolving dynamic in the entrepreneurs' attributes, meaning that the behavioural profiles change and additional abilities develop as the organisation grows in size and complexity.

6.3.3. Understanding the Dynamics of Entrepreneurial Process

A significant number of ventures do not ever achieve success. One of the main reasons for the high failure rate is the entrepreneurs' lack of ability to develop and manage their businesses. This underpins the importance of understanding the dynamics of entrepreneurship and the role of the entrepreneur as the main actor in this process.

The dynamic approach shows the shifting importance given to personal, environmental and sociological attributes throughout the evolution of the enterprise/business. The dynamic approach focuses on the personal attributes and contributes to understanding the values, characteristics and actions of the entrepreneur over time. It is believed that there is a strong emphasis on *knowing how to do* and not on *knowing how to act*. However, the importance of the person and his/her trajectory, intentions, world vision, values, belief, that is, on *knowing how to be*, is a critical factor. As such, the integration and harmonisation of the affective and cognitive dimensions become necessary. Nassif, Ghobril, and da Silva (2010) suggest an approach combining the affective and cognitive dimensions. Entrepreneurs give more importance to affective attributes at the beginning of the venture, and progressively emphasise the cognitive aspects. Affective aspects, such as perseverance, courage, personal motivation, acceptance of risks, optimism etc., are predominant at the beginning of the venture, especially in the business conception or initial phase.

It should be pointed out that there are two different types of activities in the start-up process: (1) planning activities to establish the new venture and to signal cognitive legitimacy to outside stakeholders and (2) operational activities for the purpose of managing, marketing and establishing the new venture in the market. It is believed that (1) there is a variation in the importance of the affective and cognitive aspects for the entrepreneur over time, (2) the importance of affective and cognitive aspects changes at each phase of the venture development and (3) the environmental factors and entrepreneur values influence the speed of this evolution/change.

The legal issues that an entrepreneur may be confronted with, liability aspects and the role of contracts are discussed next.

6.4. LEGAL ISSUES AND ASPECTS OF ENTREPRENEURSHIP

This section outlines the legal issues that constitute an integral part of decision-making during the entrepreneurial process. The section considers the key issues of law, legal protections and contractual arrangements to protect business assets.

It should be pointed out that compliance with governmental and other regulatory constraints is a critical issue. Regulatory compliance affects enterprises in all types of industries. A start-up must make sure to comply with all regulatory requirements (registration, taxation regime, licences, etc.). It is important to find out what type of records and other documents should be generated and maintained by the business. The laws, which apply to a business, will vary depending on a range of different factors, such as the country and the type of business entity.

6.4.1. Choice of the Appropriate Business Entity/Structure

There are multiple business structures available, and using the best structure can be critical to ensuring that a company is successful. One of the first decisions that will need to be made by a start-up enterprise is to choose a form of business organisation. In order to make such a determination, an entrepreneur will need to focus on the likely capital structure of the organisation (i.e. who are the likely or targeted equity owners of the business) and the exit strategy (sale, dissolution, etc.).

Legal entities vary depending on the country (partnership, corporation, limited liability company, etc.); however, all forms of business entities have advantages and disadvantages. The factors to consider in selecting an appropriate business entity are liability, tax implications, complexity of formation and management, capital (initial and ability to raise capital) and credibility in the business world, amongst others. The choice on an appropriate business entity should be based on key criteria such as capital structure, taxation regime, flexibility, managerial issues and regulatory requirements.

6.4.2. Protection of Intellectual Property Rights

Any commercial or artistic innovation or any unique name, symbol, logo or design is an asset for the entrepreneur. Therefore, it must be protected from unauthorised use by others. The following is a brief description of the types of intellectual property that enterprises should be concerned with protecting.

- *Patents on inventions*: A patent is an exclusive right granted by a country to an inventor, allowing the inventor to exclude others from making, using, selling, or offering for sale his or her invention in that country during the life of the patent, although this right is subject to any prior rights that others may have to related inventions.

- *Trademarks*: A trademark may consist of a name, phrase, symbol or device that identifies and distinguishes the source of goods/services of one party from those of others. Trademark law is designed to prevent confusion among the consumers regarding the source of goods or services. A person or business who has trademark rights may prohibit others from using the same or a similar trademark in connection with the sale of goods or services under circumstances that could result in confusion of consumers. Having a URL does not automatically give the entrepreneur trademark rights to the name.
- *Copyrights*: Copyright protection is available for original works of authorship, such as written works (books and manuals), computer programs (software), databases, dramatic works, and audio and video works. Copyright protects only the way in which the idea is expressed, not the actual idea. Copyright owners have the exclusive right to copy, publicly perform and distribute the copyrighted material and to prepare derivative works. Copyrights can be transferred and/or licensed.
- *Licensing*: This is an arrangement between two parties, that is proprietary right owner/patentee and the licensee. Licensing is done to either expand a business or to start a new venture. The patent owner may give permission to, or license, other parties to use the invention on mutually agreed terms. Licensee pays royalty/fees against the right to use (Skaist, 2015).

6.4.3. Liability Issues and Insurance

A company must comply with legal specifications of a product under the regulations. Product liability claims include the following types:

- *Negligence*: anywhere in production and marketing process, entrepreneurs or employees give bad advice or malpractice;
- *Warranty*: overstating the product's benefits;
- *Strict liability*: defective products for sale (food and beverages);
- *Misrepresentation*: material facts on advertisements and other promotional materials (hidden costs);
- *Premises liability*: someone falls/gets hurt on company's property;
- *Contractual liability*: violation of contract provisions; and
- *Employees*: generally, every company should limit their liability as much as possible before taking in any new employees (Reynolds, 2015).

Any new business or start-up should manage risks appropriately as well as insurance, which is a cover against any risk or unforeseen events. Companies should have insurance coverage to cover any form of liability. The main types of insurance coverage include: property (fire, burglary, robbery and business interruption); life (protects the business continuity); casualty (physical injury or property damage) and employees' compensation (for on-job injury).

6.4.4. Contracts

A contract is a legally binding agreement between two parties. Entrepreneurs usually contract with either of landlords, providers or suppliers, vendors, contractors and clients. Contractual agreements are needed for leases (office space in buildings, equipment, vehicles, systems), as well as with independent contractors, clients, services and other transactions.

It should be pointed out that written contracts must be preferred over verbal ones, because the former are termed as valid and legally enforceable. The various types of contracts must take cognisance of aspects in Section 6.4.3 to cover all possible liability issues. Generic contracts are freely available on the Internet, and each country hosts its own legal system; however, contracts between two parties should be custom-made for the entrepreneur's specific venture, or needs. In the case of SME's contracts with clients or any other parties, must be reasonable and fair at all times as this holds an element of legal risk. Legal risk is the possibility that lawsuits, adverse judgements or contracts that turn out to be unenforceable can disrupt or adversely affect the operations or condition of a business.

The involvement of legal advice upfront about the day-to-day running of the business will make sense once the business starts to grow. This will in assist the prospective entrepreneur to mitigate any form of legal risks, especially in the fields where an elevated risk has to be expected. Examples are business processes in which complex legal issues have to be addressed so that the expert knowledge available should be supplemented by a separate legal assessment, as well as the development of new products, activities in new business lines or markets (above all, international business). When new processes are established, it is generally necessary to address the question of whether legal aspects could be relevant and, if yes, to consult lawyers depending on the concrete requirements. This is to ensure that the relevant legal requirements are met and that the enforcement of rights does not fail due to unclear or inadequate wordings or due to lacking evidence resulting from insufficient documentation or the set-up of the contract. Refer to Table 6.2 where it indicates examples of internal and external causes per category and legal risk implications.

In general, matters covered by special laws result in special legal risks for the entrepreneur within their scope and, therefore, need to be given special attention in the fields concerned, such as:

- the consumer protection regulations applicable to contracts with clients/consumers, notably a country's Consumer Protection Legislation;
- the provisions of Labour Law, including health and safety at work;

Table 6.2. Examples of Internal and External Causes per Category and Legal Risk Implications.

Category	Internal Causes			External Causes External Events
	People	Processes	Systems	
Examples of legal risk causes	Excessive additional work, executive demands on employees	Consumers are advised according to wrong specifications	System failure prevents the processing of consumer/client orders	Changes in tax jurisdiction
Legal risk	Claims resulting from the violation of labour law	Claims resulting from the violation of consumer protection law	Claims resulting from the non-performance of contractual duties	Payment of additional income tax

Source: Author's creation, adapted from Oesterreichische Nationalbank (2006), Reynolds (2015) and Skaist (2015).

- the provisions of a jurisdiction's Data Protection Regulations (e.g. client privacy and loss of client data) are particularly important in the information technology field. For entrepreneurs in tourism cyber security, this is of utmost importance.

Overall, the following important types of legal risk can be identified:

- *Risks from incorrect or imprecise contractual provisions* that lead to adverse effects due to mistakes made in the wording of contracts. Such mistakes may have direct consequences (for example, an unlawful clause invalidates the entire contract or an essential part of it) or may entail indirect effects (for example, an imprecise wording allows diverse interpretations resulting in a long and risky legal dispute for the entrepreneur).
- *The risk that claims are unenforceable due to lacking evidence*, which is typically caused by a process failure or a staff/employee mistake. In most cases, the mistakes relate to the documentation of business transactions (absence of a client's signature or authority to proceed with a transaction, lost documents, etc.).
- *Shortcomings in business processes or mistakes made by employees*, claims may also be unenforceable as they are barred by time or due to a failure to observe time limits. For example, if the entrepreneur is to be the provider of the service, factors to consider are: on what terms and conditions is it taking place, the pricing and payment terms thereof and timely delivery upfront within the next 30 days.

It is clear that the entrepreneur should be knowledgeable on the roles and responsibilities of contracts for all parties involved from people, processes and systems to cover any unforeseen risk to culminate from the endeavour. It is advisable to draw up an entrepreneurial checklist to cover all the legal issues and aspects of entrepreneurship of their business.

6.5. SUMMARY

The entrepreneurial process undergone by entrepreneurs is as much an action process as it is a thinking process. The model depicted in Fig. 6.2 highlights the mental/cognitive processes associated with the process. We have seen an integrative model of entrepreneurial action with phases of pre-opportunity identification, identification, evaluation and intention formation. It shows how an entrepreneur's thinking evolves from the emergence of an opportunity idea to the initiation of concrete entrepreneurial acts by drawing attention to several cognitive inflection points that indicate changes in mental processing as entrepreneurs move through the process of entrepreneurial action. The ideas and opportunities are only the beginning of the entire entrepreneurial process. It is recommended that the prospective entrepreneur should scan and see the bigger picture: the opportunity, the market, customers, competition and the entire business environment that influence the current situation and future prospects. Furthermore, the behaviour and attitude of prospective entrepreneurs are affected by a range of factors and different dynamics depending on the phase of the entrepreneurial process.

We know that a significant number of ventures do not ever achieve success which just once again illustrate the importance of understanding the dynamics of entrepreneurship and the action process of the prospective entrepreneur. However, a shifting importance is given to personal, environmental and sociological attributes throughout the evolution of the new enterprise/business. The unique characteristics and actions of the entrepreneur should be acknowledged. As a prospective entrepreneur, there is a strong emphasis on *knowing how to do* and not on *knowing how to act*. A critical factor is the importance of the person and his/her trajectory, intentions, world vision, values, belief; that is, on the *knowing how to* and *when to* in order to shape tomorrow.

Nevertheless, a number of key legal issues need to be considered, which forms an integral part of decision-making during the entrepreneurial process. Prospective entrepreneurs should also bear the following in mind: issues of law, legal protections and contractual arrangements of their start-ups to protect the business's assets. The decision on the choice of the appropriate business entity/structure (partnership, corporation, limited liability company, etc.) should be based on certain criteria such as capital structure, taxation regime, flexibility, managerial issues and regulatory requirements.

Any commercial or artistic innovation or any unique name, symbol, logo or design is an asset for the entrepreneur and must be protected from the onset of the business in order to prevent unauthorised use by others. In other words, the intellectual property rights of the new venture are of paramount importance and should be protected early on. Furthermore, any new business or start-up should manage risks appropriately as well as insurance which is a cover against any risk or unforeseen events. Companies should have insurance coverage as soon as it is feasible to cover any form of liability. The involvement of legal advice or lawyers upfront about the day-to-day running of the business is recommended once the business starts to grow in order to assist the prospective entrepreneur to mitigate any form of legal risks, especially when dealing with people, processes and systems. In general, matters covered by special laws (Consumer Protection Legislation, Labour Law, Data Protection Regulations) result in special legal risks for the prospective entrepreneur within their scope and, therefore, need to be given special attention in the fields concerned.

Review Questions

Now you may reflect and test your understanding of the entrepreneurial process and all legal issues as covered in the chapter by answering the following questions or discussing the topics:

- Define the entrepreneurial process and explain the four phases of the entrepreneurial process.
- Present the influencing factors the prospective entrepreneur may be confronted with depending the phase of entrepreneurial process they might found themselves to be in.
- Discuss the importance of personal attributes of an entrepreneur as well as the unique characteristics they may possess which leads to success.
- Illustrate your understanding of the topic by describing the dynamics of the entrepreneurial process.
- Identify the various legal issues for prospective entrepreneurs to be addressed by start-ups at an early stage of the company's existence. Why is a contract such an important legal document?

REFERENCES AND FURTHER READING

Baron, R. A., & Shane, S. A. (2007). *Entrepreneurship: A process perspective* (2nd ed.). Mason, OH: South-Western College Publishing.

Brookes, M. (2015). Entrepreneurship as a process. In M. Brookes & L. Altinay (Eds.), *Entrepreneurship in hospitality and tourism: A global perspective* (pp. 25–40). Oxford: Goodfellow Publishers Ltd.

Burns, P. (2007). *Entrepreneurship and small business* (2nd ed.). Hampshire: Palgrave/Macmillan.

Bygrave, W. D. (2004). The entrepreneurial process. In W. D. Bygrave & A. Zacharakis (Eds.), *The portable MBA in entrepreneurship*. Hoboken, NJ: John Wiley & Sons.

Bygrave, W. D., & Zacharakis, A. (2010). The entrepreneurial process. The portable MBA in entrepreneurship (Chapter 1), (4th ed.). Published online: 8 November 2011. doi:10.1002/9781118256121.ch. Retrieved from http://onlinelibrary.wiley.com/doi/10.1002/9781118825 6121.ch1/summary. Accessed on 15 September 2017.

Dana, L.-P. (Ed.). (2011). *World encyclopaedia of entrepreneurship*. Cheltenham: Edward Elgar Publishing.

Dimov, D. P. (2007). From opportunity insight to opportunity intention: The importance of person-situation learning match. *Entrepreneurship Theory and Practice, 31*(4), 561–583.

Dimov, D. P. (2010). Nascent entrepreneurs and venture emergence: Opportunity confidence, human capital, and early planning. *Journal of Management Studies, 47*(6), 1123–1153.

Dimov, D. P. (2004). The individuality of opportunity recognition: A critical review and extension. In J. Butler (Ed.), *Research in entrepreneurship and management, Vol. 4: Opportunity identification and entrepreneurial behaviour* (pp. 135–161). Charlotte, NC: Information Age Publishing.

Eckhardt, J. T., & Shane, S. A. (2003). Opportunities and entrepreneurship. *Journal of Management, 29*(3), 333–349.

Haynie, J. M., Shepherd, D. A., & McMullen, J. S. (2009). An opportunity for me? The role of resources in opportunity evaluation decisions. *Journal of Management Studies, 46*(3), 337–361.

Hoyte, C. A. S. (2015). *Making sense of entrepreneurial opportunities*. PhD thesis, University of Nottingham. Retrieved from http://eprints.nottingham.ac.uk/28826/1/PhD%20Thesis_Cherisse%20Hoyte.pdf. Accessed on 10 August 2017.

McMullen, J. S., & Shepherd, D. A. (2006). Entrepreneurial action and the role of uncertainty in the theory of the entrepreneur. *Academy of Management Review, 31*(1), 132–152.

Nassif, V. M. J., Ghobril, A. N., & da Silva, N. S. (2010). Understanding the entrepreneurial process: A dynamic approach. *BAR - Brazilian Administration Review, 7*(2), 213–226.

Oesterreichische Nationalbank. (2006). *Guidelines on operational risk management*. Vienna: Otto-Wagner-Platz.

Reynolds, H. (2015). *Legal issues for entrepreneurs*. Retrieved from https://www.meetup.com/Legal-Issues-for-Startups-and-Entrepreneurs/. Accessed on August 20, 2017.

Shane, S. (2000). Prior knowledge and the discovery of entrepreneurial opportunities. *Organization Science, 11*(4), 448–469.

Shane, S. (2003). *A general theory of entrepreneurship: The individual opportunity nexus*. Northampton, MA: Edward Elgar Publishing Inc.

Shane, S., & Venkataraman, S. (2000). The promise of entrepreneurship as a field of research. *Academy of Management Review, 25*(1), 217–226.

Shapero, A., & Sokol, L. (1982). The social dimensions of entrepreneurship. In *The Encyclopedia of entrepreneurship* (pp. 72–90). Englewood Cliffs, NJ: Prentice Hall.

Skaist, M. (2015). *Legal issues for the entrepreneur*. Stradling Yocca Carlson & Rauth Attorneys at Law, California.

Thompson, J. L. (2004). The facets of the entrepreneur: Identifying entrepreneurial potential. *Management Decision, 42*(1/2), 243–258.

Timmons, J. A. (1999). *New venture creation: Entrepreneurship for the 21st century*. (4th ed.). Burr Ridge, IL: Irwin.

Van Auken, H., Fry, F., & Stephens, P. (2006). The influence of role models on entrepreneurial intentions. *Journal of Developmental Entrepreneurship, 11*(2), 157–167.

Van de Ven, A., Polley, D., Garud, R., & Venkataraman, S. (2008). *The innovation journey*. Oxford: Oxford University Press.

Wood, M. S., Williams, D. W., & Gregoire, D. A. (2012). The road to riches? A model of the cognitive processes and inflection points underpinning entrepreneurial action. In A. C. Corbett & J. A. Katz (Eds.), *Entrepreneurial action* (Vol. 14, pp. 207–252). Advances in Entrepreneurship, Firm Emergence and Growth. Bingley, UK: Emerald Group Publishing Limited.

CHAPTER 7

FEASIBILITY ANALYSIS AND STUDY

Stavros Arvanitis and Leticia Estevez

ABSTRACT

Purpose — *The main purpose of this chapter is to define the concept, scope and importance of a feasibility study when developing a new business venture. It also presents the main components of a feasibility study by describing a feasibility study template.*

Methodology/approach — *A literature review was conducted on conceptual issues and practical aspects of the feasibility analysis and study by presenting a hypothetical case of study of a boutique hotel.*

Findings — *This chapter highlights the importance of both feasibility analysis and study, and the main reasons why all entrepreneurs should carry them out. It presents a simple template that shows the key components of a feasibility study and also a hypothetical case of study of a boutique hotel that helps in relating the concepts and ideas previously developed.*

Practical implications — *This chapter introduces both theoretical and practical approaches by presenting a model or template on how to develop the feasibility analysis and study. This template can be applied at any stage of assessment process of a business project.*

Originality/value — *The concept of a feasibility study is accompanied by a practical template and a case study. This approach contributes to a better*

The Emerald Handbook of Entrepreneurship in Tourism, Travel and Hospitality:
Skills for Successful Ventures, 109–129
ISBN: 978-1-78743-530-8/doi:10.1108/978-1-78743-529-220181019

understanding of the value and utility of feasibility analysis and study in assessing tourism business ventures.

Keywords: Feasibility study; analysis; template; business ventures; case study; tourism

---

Learning Objectives

After studying this chapter, you should be able to:

- present the concept, importance and scope of a feasibility analysis and study;
- identify the key components of a feasibility study;
- understand how to approach and carry out a feasibility study through the analysis of a template;
- relate the concepts and ideas developed in this chapter by analysing a hypothetical case study of a boutique hotel.

7.1. INTRODUCTION

A feasibility study is an analysis of how successfully a business venture or project can be completed, accounting for factors that affect the project. A feasibility study tests the viability of an idea, a project or a new business. The goal of a feasibility study is to emphasise problems that could occur if a project is pursued and could determine whether, after all significant factors have been considered, the project should be pursued. In the business field, feasibility studies also allow a business to address where and how it will operate, potential obstacles, competition and the funding needed to get the business up and running.

A feasibility study aims to objectively and rationally uncover the strengths and weaknesses of a proposed venture, opportunities and threats present in the environment, the resources needed to carry through and ultimately the prospects for success. It is clear that a feasibility study evaluates the project's potential for success; therefore, perceived objectivity is an important factor in the credibility of the study for potential investors and lending institutions. It must therefore be conducted with an objective, unbiased approach to provide information upon which decisions can be based.

A well-designed feasibility study should provide a historical background of the business project or venture, a description of the product or service, details of the management and marketing policies and strategies, financial data and statements and legal and other regulatory requirements. A feasibility study can also lead to the development of marketing strategies that convince investors or a bank that investing in the business venture is a wise decision. Before we move forward, it would be very useful to clarify the definition of the term.

A feasibility study (or analysis) is an analysis and evaluation of a proposed business idea or project to determine whether it is technically feasible, is feasible within the estimated cost and will be profitable. Feasibility studies are almost always conducted where large sums are at stake (*Business Dictionary*, 2012). According to the *McGraw-Hill Dictionary of Scientific and Technical Terms* (2003), a feasibility study is:

- a study to determine whether a plan is capable of being accomplished successfully;
- an analysis of the possibilities for a project, which typically includes factors regarding zoning, alternativeness, building codes, financial, environmental and design;
- a detailed investigation and analysis conducted to determine the financial, economic and technical advisability of a proposed business project.

In this chapter, we are going to present and analyse the key issues and aspects of a feasibility study from the perspective of a new business venture. Section 7.2 focuses on an overview and the components of a feasibility study. Section 7.3 deals with the format or template of a feasibility study. Then, Section 7.4 moves on to present a detailed example of a feasibility study related to a new business project for a boutique hotel.

7.2. FEASIBILITY STUDY: OVERVIEW AND COMPONENTS

What is a feasibility study? As the name implies, a feasibility study is an analysis of the viability of an idea. The feasibility study focuses on helping to answer the essential question of 'should we proceed with the proposed business/project idea?' All activities of the study are directed towards helping answer this question. Feasibility studies can be used in many ways, but primarily focus on proposed business ventures. Prospective entrepreneurs with a business idea should conduct a feasibility study to determine the viability of their idea before proceeding with the development of a business. Determining early that a business idea will not work saves money and time.

A feasible business venture is one where the business will generate adequate cash flow and profits, withstand the risks it will encounter, remain viable in the long term and meet the goals of the entrepreneurs. The venture can be either a start-up business, the purchase of an existing business, an expansion of current business operations or a new enterprise for an existing business.

It should be pointed out that a feasibility study is only one step in the business idea assessment and business development process. A feasibility study is usually conducted after producers have discussed a series of business ideas or scenarios. The feasibility study helps to 'frame' specific business scenarios so they can be studied in depth. During this process, the number of business alternatives under consideration is usually quickly reduced. Prospective entrepreneurs may investigate a variety of ways of organising the business and positioning their offering in the marketplace.

In the field of project management, feasibility studies are used to determine potential positive and negative outcomes of a project before investing a considerable amount of time and money into it. From this perspective − that is project management − the most popular model of feasibility study in the field of systems and technology is 'TELOS' (technical, economic, legal, operational and schedule).

- *Technical feasibility*: Is the business idea/project a practical proposition? A technical feasibility study can identify the potential challenges and problems that the system may encounter technically based on the requirements and goals of the business.
- *Economic feasibility*: An economic feasibility study reports on the cost factors of a proposed plan to an organisation. The two main questions are: Is the system cost-effective? Do benefits outweigh costs?
- *Legal feasibility*: Is there any conflict between the proposed system and legal requirements, for instance, legal interdictions? Environmental and social aspects should also be considered in this section.
- *Operational feasibility*: Are the current work practices and requirements adequate to support the new system? An operational feasibility report focuses on the effectiveness of the function of the operations of an organisation, in other words, achieving greater efficiency and cost savings.
- *Schedule feasibility*: Schedule feasibility is a measure of how reasonable the project timetable is. Can the system be developed in time? Are the project deadlines reasonable? It is necessary to determine whether the deadlines are mandatory or desirable.

When a feasibility study on tourism is carried out, there are some sensitive aspects and issues that are specific to the tourist activity and will affect the business venture, such as seasonality, local or hosting community and the political, social and economic situation of the target markets. All these factors should be taken into consideration.

A feasibility study has five *main components*:

- *Description*: provides a layout of the business, the site and location, the products and/or services to be offered and how they will be delivered.
- *Market feasibility* (market analysis and assessment): describes the business environment, that is, the industry, the current and future market potential, competition, prospective clientele, target market segment and sales estimations.

- *Organisational feasibility*: a definition of the corporate and legal structure of the business. This may include information about the founders, their professional background and the skills they possess necessary to get the company off the ground and keep it operational.
- *Technical feasibility*: lays out details on how a good or service will be delivered, which includes transportation, business location, technology needed, materials and staff.
- *Financial feasibility*: provides all financial-related information; a projection of the amount of funding or start-up capital needed, what sources of capital are available and what kind of return can be expected on the investment.

Let us consider the above-mentioned components in more detail.

7.3. TEMPLATE OF FEASIBILITY STUDY

As already pointed out, the main purpose of a feasibility study is to fully examine and to critically look at the business idea in order to determine whether it is worth investing time and money. A feasibility study covering the main issues of a business project can help to reveal whether your idea has a high probability of success. It should be pointed out that all of the required elements of a feasibility study are adequately covered, in order to perform it properly. The outcome of this study is a confirmed solution for implementation or a negative decision to not proceed.

This section outlines the format or contents of reporting on a feasibility study. Hereafter, a feasibility study template is suggested and can be used to:

- assess the feasibility of any type of business project;
- research the business problem or opportunity;
- identify all of the alternative solutions available;
- review each solution to determine its feasibility;
- list any risks and issues with each solution;
- choose a preferred solution for implementation; and
- document the results in a feasibility report.

An effective and high-quality feasibility study consists of 10 stages, as presented next.

7.3.1. Executive Summary and Introduction

Prior to the introduction, a summary (usually two pages) highlights the main issues, conclusions and suggestions of the study. The executive summary provides an overview of the content of the feasibility study. This section is important in that it provides a higher level summary of the detail contained within the rest of the document.

The introduction deals with the provision of background information about the proposed business, data collection method, the proposed name and purpose of the business.

7.3.2. Description of the Business

The second part deals with a statement about the prospective investors or entrepreneurs, the business, the product to be offered, the nature of the industry and the opportunities available to exploit. Issues to be addressed include:

- Do the prospective entrepreneurs have the experience and skills to successfully launch the business?
- What are the products or services on offer?
- Who will be the potential consumers, the clientele and the targeted market segment?
- What are the factors that will affect the proposed business positively and negatively?
- What are the business potential and the opportunities for future expansion?

7.3.3. Market Feasibility: Market Analysis and Assessment

This section is one of the most difficult to prepare and yet one of the most important. Almost all aspects of the feasibility report depend on the market assessment. It is therefore advisable that prospective entrepreneurs should prepare this section first. In addition, enough time and skill should be devoted to this issue.

A market research should be carried out in order to examine the marketability of the product or services and investigate whether there is a potential market for the product or services. If a significant market for the product or services cannot be established, then there is no project. In other words, a market assessment will help to determine the viability of a proposed product in the marketplace. The market assessment will help to identify opportunities in a market or market segment. If no opportunities are found, there may be no reason to proceed with a feasibility study. If opportunities are found, the market assessment can give focus and direction to the construction of business scenarios to investigate in the feasibility study. A market assessment will provide much of the information for the marketing feasibility section of the feasibility study.

This involves determining the current and potential demand for the product or services in the target market, the customers' profile or characteristics and sales forecast over the first three to five years.

The prospective entrepreneurs should have a clear idea of the market in which they will be operating their business. Market feasibility should cover the following (indicating the sources of data and methods used to arrive at providing answers or information):

- *Demand or market*: What is the demand? Who are the customers (their profile) for the proposed product or service?
- *The market size*: The number of potential customers, who they are and their location. What are the factors affecting market growth?
- *Competitor analysis*: Addressing questions such as: Who are the competitors? What are their weaknesses (and ways to take advantage)? What is their strength (and ways of offsetting this strength)?
- *Offering*: What characteristics or aspects of the product appeals to the potential customers? What is the business's unique selling proposition?
- *Marketing policies and strategies*: How will the company market its product or services? Some topics which should be included are: How does it differentiate itself from its competitors? Who is the target market? What are the sales policies and strategies? What are the distribution channels? What types of marketing will it utilise? Marketing efforts must be focused on the right target groups in order to yield the greatest return on investment.

7.3.4. Description of Products or Services

This section of the feasibility study provides a high-level description of the products and/or services that are being considered as part of the feasibility study. The purpose of this section is to provide detailed descriptions of exactly what the company is considering, so this information can be applied to the following sections of the analysis. It is important that this description captures the most important aspects of the products and/or services that the organisation is considering, as well as how it may benefit customers and the organisation.

It also describes the existing marketplace for the products and/or services the company is considering. It may describe who the target market consists of for these products or services, who the competitors are, how products will be distributed, and why customers might choose to buy our products/services.

7.3.5. Management Team and Staff Members

The management team is the key to the successful launching of a new business venture. Prospective entrepreneurs must look for a committed management team with balanced technical, managerial and business skills and experience in launching the proposed business. The questions answered by this section include:

- What are the key management roles or positions in the company? Who are the key management members?
- What are the exact duties and responsibilities of the key members of the management team (Job descriptions)?
- Will the business be independently managed by owners or are they employing specialists?
- How many skilled, semi-skilled and unskilled employees would they require? Is it possible to find skilled employees on site or location?
- Do they require supportive professional services (accountant, etc.)?
- What is the monthly and annual cost of labour?

These are important considerations as they may result in increased operating expenses.

7.3.6. Technical Specification

This section describes the location, facilities, buildings, machinery and equipment, raw materials and components utilities. Issues or questions to be addressed include:

- Location: Where will the company be located and why?
- The facilities needed to conduct the proposed business, for instance, building, space.
- The processes involved in the production of the products or service delivery.
- The raw materials and the equipment needed. Technical specifications and price?
- Management and administrative needs or requirements and expenses (power, water, etc.).

7.3.7. Examination of Critical Risks and Problems

The aim in this part is to identify and describe the implicit assumption about the major risks and problems of the proposed venture project. This should include a description of the risks relating to the business environment, the company, the market appeal of the products or services and the timing and financing of the venture.

The identification and description of risks of a business project demonstrate the skills of the prospective entrepreneur and increase the credibility of the business venture. Among the issues to address are:

- What are the threats posed by potential changes in the industry or business environment?

- Are sales projections reasonable (not overly optimistic)?
- What are the difficulties likely to be encountered in collaborating with providers and other partners (e.g. intermediaries)?
- Will the company face difficulties in obtaining the needed funding?
- What impact will government policies, such as taxation, regulations and monetary policy, have on the business?
- What are the potential challenges that direct and indirect competition are likely to pose?
- What are the difficulties or challenges that the tourist destination may face in the short and medium term?

All these issues are of crucial importance to a sustainable and profitable business venture.

7.3.8. Marketing Plans

The marketing plans describe the overall planning to achieve the marketing aim and objectives, such as marketing policies and strategies in the fields of product or services, pricing, sales, distribution and promotion or communication tools, media and techniques. The questions addressed by the marketing plan include:

- What are the targeted market segments?
- How will the potential customers be identified and attracted?
- What are the offering's characteristics and features?
- What types of pricing strategy will be adopted and why? Which prices will be charged?
- Which are the distribution strategies and channels?
- Which are the best sales policies and strategies for my business?
- Which promotional and communications tools will be to attract the prospective customers?

This part of the feasibility study only outlines the main points; their detailed analysis should be presented in a business plan.

7.3.9. Financial Feasibility: Projections and Plan

The prospective entrepreneur needs to consider the financial requirements to make it viable.

The financial plan provides the basic foundation for evaluation of a business venture or project. The purpose is to indicate and assess the financial viability of the venture.

This part of the feasibility study provides a description of the financial projections the new initiative is expected to yield versus additional costs. Financial projections are one key aspect of new project selection criteria. There are many ways to present these projections. Net present value (NPV), cost-benefit calculations and balance sheets are just some examples of how financial projections may be illustrated. This part should also provide the assumptions on which the illustrated financial projections are based.

In case of a new project, financial viability can be judged on the following parameters:

- *Investment and financing funding*:

  — Total estimated cost of the venture: How much money do we need to start up? How much capital for the business, now and in the future?
  — Funding sources: How will the capital requirement be raised? Own capital or loans? How do we intend to fund the business during the start-up phase?
  — Capital structure: How will the funds be used? What are the major areas of expenditure?

- *Turnover and cost structure* (operating expenses):

  — What price would the customers pay for our products or services?
  — What is the sales forecast?
  — Estimate the fixed and variable costs.
  — Break-even point analysis: What is our break-even point? How long will it take to reach break-even sales volume?

- *Cash flow analysis and profitability*:

  — How much working capital will be needed to sustain operations?
  — Cash flow analysis: monitor and control cash in order to meet the project income and cash flows. Projected cash flow statement.
  — Estimate profitability and calculate the return on investment.

Hence, the financial plan should cover the following areas and prepare the following financial statements:

- forecasted profit and loss account;
- forecasted cash flow statement;
- projected balance sheet.

7.3.10. Results, Evaluation, Conclusion/Recommendations and Decision

This part deals with the use of various methods to evaluate the worth of the business project or investment. These include the average rate of return on investment, payable period and discounted cash flow methods. In evaluating project proposals, a prospective entrepreneur intends to answer the following questions:

- What are the profitability and feasibility of the proposed project?
- Will the business venture meet the expectations?
- What is the number of years required to receive the initial cash investment (payback period)?
- Will the present value of future net cash flow be positive or negative?

The feasibility study's conclusions should outline in depth the various scenarios examined and the implications, strengths and weaknesses of each. The potential entrepreneurs need to study the feasibility study and challenge its underlying assumptions. This is the time to be sceptical. Feasibility studies do not suddenly become positive or negative. The analysis rarely renders overwhelmingly positive results. The study will help assess the trade-off between the risks and rewards of moving forward with the business project.

It should be pointed out that it is not the purpose of the feasibility study to decide whether or not to proceed with a business idea. It is the role of the potential entrepreneurs to make this decision, using information from the feasibility study and input from consultants. The final decision is one of the most critical in business development. It is the point of no return. Once they have definitely decided to pursue a business scenario, there is usually no turning back. The feasibility study will be a major information source in making this decision. This indicates the importance of a properly developed feasibility study.

7.4. REPORT ON BUSINESS FEASIBILITY STUDY: EXAMPLE OF BOUTIQUE HOTEL

A feasibility study should consider all issues and aspects we have seen in the previous section. From the above presentation, it is clear that a good feasibility study helps to objectively decide whether or not to proceed with a business project. In this section, we will look at an example of a feasibility study in order to better illustrate the related issues and aspects.

Let us suppose that we have a business idea for a boutique hotel. As a prospective entrepreneur, we have to investigate and analyse all issues. Our findings and suggestions should be reported in the following subsections.

7.4.1. Executive Summary

This is the summarised version of the feasibility study. It must adequately cover the major points of the feasibility study on one or two pages.

The ABC Company – 'ABC Boutique Hotel' – is determined to become a hotel operation for business and leisure tourists, a comfortable and convenient place to have an enjoyable stay experience. With the growing demand for high-quality modern design hotels (family-operated units), ABC Boutique Hotel will capitalise on its proximity to the Business District of the city X to build a core group of repeat customers.

ABC Boutique Hotel will offer its guests a comfortable and enjoyable stay. The company will operate a three-storey hotel unit within walking distance from the business district. The operators are the owners of this building that will be converted and decorated appropriately. The owners and new operators have also provided $1 million of the required $1.3 million start-up funds. The remaining capital will be obtained through Z Bank commercial loans.

The company is expected to grow sales revenue from $320,000 in the first year of operation (2017) to $400,000 in year three. As ABC Company will strive to maintain a 65 per cent gross profit margin and reasonable operating expenses, it will see net profits grow from $120,000 to $200,000 during the same period.

7.4.2. The Company

ABC Company is a limited liability company. It provides hotel services (accommodation, food and beverages) in its 1,200 square meter building located near the business district of the city X. The company's investors are John and Mary S. who own 100% of the company, equally shared. The start-up loss of the company is assumed at $30,000.

Mission: ABC Boutique Hotel will strive to create a unique hotel unit where guests can enjoy a comfortable and relaxing stay in town. It will provide guests with a convenient location, great ambience, friendly customer service and an experience of high quality. The company will operate as a smart hotel to achieve a profitable and sustainable operation to the satisfaction of clientele, shareholders and staff.

Objectives: The ABC Company's objectives for the first operating year are: (1) become selected as the 'Best Boutique Hotel' in the business district, (2) achieve profits by the end of the first year and (3) achieve and maintain a 65 per cent gross margin.

7.4.3. Service/Product Description

This section should provide a description of service. The service experience consists of hotel services (room, healthy breakfast and beverages). ABC Boutique Hotel will offer its guests the best hotel experience in the city. This will be achieved by providing good value for money, high-quality hotel services and food and beverages at the right price.

The rooms will be double and single with private en-suite bathrooms. Décor will be modern and minimalist. The public spaces − reception, lounge bar and breakfast area − will be decorated and equipped in the same way, servicing the boutique hotel concept. Free books and magazines will be available to the guests in the lounge. In the same area − reception lounge − a cosy wine bar will be operating. The buffet breakfast will offer healthy options.

7.4.4. Market Analysis and Assessment

In this section, we have to provide an assessment of the market demand for our services. This is a crucial step, because it should determine whether or not a market exists for the business idea.

Assessing the market size for a new business is a tricky but critical part of a feasibility analysis. For a business idea to work, we must attract enough customers willing to spend enough money on our hotel services to provide sales revenue that covers our operating expenses and renders a profit. Potential customers will prefer a new business only if they perceive the value provided by that new business to be greater than the value provided by existing competitors. To attract customers, we must convince them that we are providing something better, more convenient or of a higher quality at the same price. In short, we must create a perception that we have a competitive advantage. This advantage can be based on many different characteristics (e.g. location, service experience, skilled and friendly staff). Our offering must be distinctive, different and competitively superior to the existing competing businesses.

7.4.4.1. Market Assessment

It consists of identifying our markets, determining market factors that create demand for our services and forecasting the potential demand for them. It should identify opportunities or threats facing the proposed business. Describe the market research technique (telephone surveys, personal interviews, sales figures on existing products, statistical and published information in your target area) that we used to find answers to the questions below. Main issues and aspects to be examined include:

Market and clientele:

- What is the size of the market? Who is buying the hotel services (i.e. target market)?
- How many customers are there? Who are they? How are they segmented?

- What are the major trends affecting the hotel market? What is the growth rate of the market?
- What are the market trends and other factors (demographics, lifestyle) affecting the hotel service?

Price and sales:

- How has the price changed in the last five years?
- What determines price on hotel service, quality, demand or tourist trade (intermediaries)?
- What is the projected sales volume?

Competition (for more detailed analysis see 'competition analysis' below)

- How many hotel operations are there already?
- How does each compete? What do they say about each other?
- What are their strengths and weaknesses?
- How successful are they? What does it take to succeed in the hotel business?

7.4.4.2. Market Analysis

The hotel company should use a market analysis to project sales volume for its new hotel venture. The analysis can provide essential information required in a business plan or feasibility study. Using the market analysis findings, we can estimate the financial potential of the venture by creating financial projections (see Section 7.4.7). Market analysis encompasses the following elements:

- *Industry trends*: Studying industry trends is one of the first steps in conducting a market analysis. It is very helpful to identify opportunities and threats in the industry that may affect the operation's profitability. A question that needs an answer is: What was the evolution of demand for hotel services in the last five years?
- *Location and facility*: Location is a critical consideration because it affects the ability to draw customers. It is important that the hotel's site be accessible, convenient and attractive to our market. Typically, we will have already selected either a location or a concept for our hotel based on market factors. It is important that the location and concept complement each other.
- *Competition analysis*: We have to assess the competitive strengths and weaknesses of existing hotel units and learn from their successes and failures. First, we must identify how many operations are in our market area. We must then identify those units that appeal to the types of customers (market

segments) that we plan to serve (boutique hotels or medium price range). We consider providing answers to the following questions:

— Who are our major competitors? Do we know the sales and market share of each competitor? What is their business performance, are they doing well?
— What are the major strengths of each? What are the major weaknesses of each?
— Do we know of any competitor's plans for expansion? How can we compete with our competition?

- *Concept evaluation and refinement*: Concept involves the entire hotel experience, not just the type of room or breakfast offered. Elements that define a boutique hotel's concept include décor, lighting, menu, type of breakfast, service, price, location and size. Even the name of the operation conveys a sense of the concept. An effective concept establishes a hotel's identity. It distinguishes the operation from others in the market area and allows the hotel to attract particular market segments/groups. Understanding customer preferences is essential in developing an appropriate concept. Using data already gathered, the task is to refine the concept and evaluate its suitability for our target market.

7.4.5. Marketing Strategy

For the feasibility study, a brief outline of the marketing strategy will suffice, whilst the business plan should provide a more detailed description. Main issues are the following:

- Ways to access the market; what distribution methods will we use? Online travel agents (e.g. booking.com), specialist travel agents, tour operator?
- The competitive advantage or benefits of our service experience in relation to the competition.
- The elements of our offering that attract customers. How is our offering differentiated from the competition?
- Price: Which pricing methods will be used?
- Communications and/or promotion: promotional methods, tools and media
- Partnerships: any alliances and collaborations already concluded.

7.4.6. Management Capability

Another issue to be examined and clarified is the management capability and skills to manage and run the operation effectively. Hence, we have to describe:

- the requirements for the management positions and responsibilities of those personnel;

- the skills/expertise we will need to bring to the business;
- existing capabilities within the business (related to qualifications and experience of owner).

7.4.7. Financial Feasibility: Financial Analysis and Projections

The next step is to examine whether the business project is financially feasible. Besides, the financial feasibility is a requirement for loan approval by banks. First, we have to estimate the sales or revenue that the business will generate. We usually use two general principles:

1. *Be conservative*: We underestimate the potential sales, as it is always easier to adjust the costs (operating expenses) for a higher-than-expected level of sales than it is to control our costs when the sales estimate is too high.
2. *Make a range of sales estimates (scenarios)*: We estimate the potential sales in a number of ways and compare figures. We try to see how different the results are. Be conservative and pick the smallest or more pessimistic estimate of the group, or be aggressive and take an average.

Market analysis findings provide a sound basis for realistic financial projections. These projections will help us determine the financial feasibility of the business venture. The accuracy of our revenue projections and costs will be dependent on the reliability of the marketing predictions. Important considerations to determine profitability include the following information:

- Take into account all operating expenses, variable and fixed, that should be allocated to the new enterprise.
- All information needed to prepare projected statements for the next three to five years, such as profit and loss account, cash flow forecast and balance sheet.
- Estimate the sales volume required to reach the break-even point.
- Time needed for the business to become profitable.

It should be pointed out that the first issue to be estimated is the required financing, the required funding to enter the market and feasibility of raising capital (if necessary). Beginners often underestimate the amount of money needed to start, and they do not allow for working capital (i.e. the money needed to finance inventory and first months of operation).

7.4.7.1. Financial Projections
At this point in our market analysis, you have completed all data collection related to the market. We should be in position to estimate the sales potential

based on market factors. Sales in a hotel operation are a function of the number of guests served (overnights) and spending per customer/person or overnight (average spending). While there are no formulas for calculating the sales potential, prior research is always helpful to make more informed and reasonable estimates. The steps that follow are outlined below:

Projecting customer volume: We should be able to make projections of the hotel's customer volume potential based on understanding of our competitive position in the market and on estimates of volume of other hotel operations. The customer volume projection worksheet helps us estimate how many customers or overnights we will serve. The worksheet can be easily completed based on the following instructions:

- Divide the operating year into seasons that describe the variability of business (peak season, middle season and off-season). Enter the number of weeks in each season in the appropriate box.
- For each season, estimate the number of daily guests/overnights. Sum the daily overnights to determine the weekly totals.
- Calculate the number of overnights per season by multiplying the projected number of weekly overnights by the number of weeks in that season.
- Sum the totals from each season to determine forecasted annual overnights.

Projecting average spending: Average spending includes room, food (breakfast) and beverage sales. It should be projected on a daily and weekly basis. We have to make sure that average overnight spending represents an affordable and acceptable price value that is consistent with our hotel concept and the target markets we hope to attract. Pricing should be competitive with other similar hotel operations in our target market.

Projecting sales volume: Sales are calculated for each day or week by multiplying the projected number of overnights by the average spending.
We use the following formula to calculate projected annual sales:

$$\text{Total overnights} \times \text{average spending} = \text{annual sales volume}$$

Other sales estimation methods:

- *Industry or association data*: Use hotel industry-specific statistics on the performance of individual operations to estimate the sales of the new business.
- *Market potential or market share*: Determine the potential of the market (i.e. the total of all sales in the service category in which we will compete). Multiply the per capita figure by the number of

people in our target market for an estimate of market potential. Next, calculate our share of the market. To begin, estimate our share as equal to that of our smallest competitor, or estimate our share as equalling the average competitor in the market. In any case, be sure not to assume we will take over the market, particularly in the short run.

• *Similar business in similar location*: One of the most reliable ways to estimate sales performance of a new business is to look for similar enterprises in similar areas. This may be the most reliable of all the methods, because it allows us to accurately gauge how we might perform based on similar performances by competitors.

• *Sales of existing competitors*: Look at our competitors in the marketplace and estimate their sales.

In any case, we must begin our own estimate of economic feasibility for the hotel business with a good, conservative estimate of our anticipated sales. Once we have completed our projections, we have to compare the annual overnights, average spending and sales projections with industry averages of similar operations. If reasonable, we may use these sales projections as performance goals for the future.

7.4.7.2. Break-even Analysis

The next step is to estimate operating expenses or costs, which is often much easier than estimating sales. The costs must be divided into two basic categories: fixed and variable.

1. Fixed costs are expenses that do not vary with the level of sales, such as rent, manager's salary, utilities, insurance and other operating expenses.
2. Variable expenses are directly related to sales, and include items such as raw materials (food and beverages) and energy.

Next, we calculate our break-even, the sales level at which the unit has neither a profit nor a loss. When we compare our break-even to our estimated sales, we will have a rough idea whether or not our hotel business is financially feasible.

As we estimate break-even, we use quantities that describe the relationship between our prices and our variable costs. Hence, in the hotel industry we work with the contribution percentage.

Let us consider the following hypothetical example:

Fixed monthly expenses: Total $10,000

If the gross margin is 65 per cent (or variable costs are 35 per cent), then our break-even is calculated as follows:

$$\text{Break-even sales in dollars} = \text{total fixed costs} \times \text{gross margin \%}$$
$$= \$10,000/0.65 = \$15,385 \text{ per month.}$$

If the average spending per overnight is \$80, then we need 192 overnights to achieve break-even sales. Estimating break-even allows us to determine the necessary sales per day, per month and per year. Then we can compare that with realistic estimates of the expected sales. Knowing what it takes to break even can give us an idea of whether or not we have a potentially feasible business idea.

7.4.7.3. Financial Performance — Statements
Based on the previous financial projections and information, we are now in a position to have the following projected financial statements: profit and loss account, cash flow statement and balance sheet.

7.4.8. Findings, Conclusions and Recommendations

This part of the feasibility study summarises the findings of the feasibility study and explains why this course of action is or is not recommended. It is therefore a suggestion as to the feasibility of the new hotel business. This section should be brief, since most of the detail is included elsewhere in the document. Additionally, it should capture the likelihood of success for the business idea being studied.

7.5. SUMMARY

If we would like to start a new business, we must thoroughly and objectively analyse the feasibility of our business idea. Failure to do so can have a tremendous personal cost as far as finances, personal relationships and family ties are concerned. A huge volume of information is available on how to start a small business and assist prospective entrepreneurs with these decisions.

A feasibility analysis constitutes a preliminary evaluation of a business idea to examine whether it is worth pursuing. In performing a feasibility analysis, we will:

- Evaluate whether we and our management team possess the characteristics most common to entrepreneurial success.
- Assess the market for our new business idea.

- Estimate the basic financial feasibility of our business, including potential sales revenues, fixed and variable operating expenses and break-even analysis.
- Finally, make an informed decision about whether or not our idea is still attractive and practical.

The feasibility study is, therefore, a critical step in the business assessment process. If properly conducted, it may be the best investment we ever made. Once decisions have been made about proceeding with a proposed business, they are often very difficult to change. We may need to live with these decisions for a long time.

It should be pointed out that *a feasibility study is not a business plan*. The separate roles of the feasibility study and the business plan are frequently misunderstood. What are the main differences? The feasibility study provides an investigating function. It addresses the question: 'Is this a viable business venture?' The business plan provides a planning function and outlines the actions needed to take the proposal from 'idea' to 'reality'. The feasibility study outlines and analyses several alternatives or methods of achieving business success. The business plan deals with only one alternative or scenario. The feasibility study is conducted before the business plan; the latter is prepared only after the business venture has been deemed feasible. If a proposed business venture is considered feasible, a business plan is usually constructed next, which provides a 'roadmap' of how the business will be created and developed. The business plan provides the 'blueprint' for project implementation. If the venture is not deemed feasible, efforts may be made to correct its deficiencies, other alternatives may be explored or the idea is dropped.

The topic of the business plan will be considered separately in a distinct chapter (see Chapter 9).

It is clear that the feasibility study represents a common-sense approach to planning. There are numerous reasons why we should conduct a feasibility study. Conducting a feasibility study is a good business practice. If we examine successful businesses, we will find that they did not go into a new business venture without first thoroughly examining all of the issues and assessing the probability of business success. Other reasons to conduct a feasibility study are: (1) it gives focus to the project and outlines alternatives, (2) it narrows business alternatives, (3) it identifies new opportunities through the investigative process, (4) it identifies reasons not to proceed, (5) it enhances the probability of success by addressing and mitigating factors early on that could affect the business project, (6) it provides quality information for decision-making, (7) it provides documentation that the business venture was thoroughly investigated and (8) it helps in securing funding from banks and other monetary sources.

Review Questions

Check your understanding of this chapter by answering the following questions or discussing the topics below:

- What is a feasibility analysis and study?
- What are its scope and objectives?
- Which are the main components of a feasibility study?
- How does one conduct a feasibility study? How should it be organised?
- What are the differences between a feasibility study and a business plan?
- Does the example of the feasibility study described above refer to the considerations previously developed in the chapter?

REFERENCES AND FURTHER READING

Berrie, M. (2008). *Initiating phase – Feasibility study request and report*. Retrieved from http://www. entrepreneurshipsecret.com/. Accessed on 15 July 2017.

Business Dictionary. (2012). *Feasibility study*. Retrieved from http://www.businessdictionary.com/ definition/feasibility-study.html. Accessed on 10 July 2017.

Investopedia. (2017). What is a 'feasibility study'? *Investopedia.com*. Retrieved from http://www. investopedia.com/terms/f/feasibility-study.asp. Accessed on 12 August 2017.

Justis, R. T., & Kreigsmann, B. (1979). The feasibility study as a tool for venture analysis. *Business Journal of Small Business Management, 17*(1), 35–42.

McGraw-Hill Education. (2003). *McGraw-Hill dictionary of scientific and technical terms* (6th ed.). New York, NY: The McGraw-Hill Companies, Inc.

Reilly, M. D., & Millikin, N. L. (1996). *Starting a small business: The feasibility analysis*. MontGuide, MT 9510, College of Business, Montana State University, Bozeman, Montana.

Small Business Development Corporation. (2017). *Will my business idea work?* Retrieved from https://www.smallbusiness.wa.gov.au/business-topics/starting-a-business/feasibility-of-the-business-idea/. Accessed on 13 July 2017.

The Free Dictionary. (2017). *Feasibility study*. Retrieved from http://encyclopedia2.thefreediction-ary.com/Feasibility+analysis. Accessed on 13 July 2017.

The Secrets of Entrepreneurship. (2017). *The characteristics of an entrepreneurial spirit*. Retrieved from http://www.entrepreneurshipsecret.com/category/entrepreneurship/. Accessed on 12 August 2017.

CHAPTER 8

COLLABORATIVE FORMS AND STRATEGIES FOR BUSINESS VENTURING IN TOURISM INDUSTRIES

Marios Sotiriadis

ABSTRACT

Purpose — *In this chapter, we aim to analyse the role and benefits of a strategic approach to business partnerships and suggest suitable forms and strategies. Thus, the chapter's purpose is to present the methods and models for business venturing applied in the tourism-related industries.*

Methodology/approach — *This chapter takes a perspective of the small business/prospective entrepreneur and analyses how the collaborative methods can contribute towards the business venture's development and success. Literature review was conducted on issues and aspects of collaboration. Examples of best practices are used to illustrate the collaborative forms.*

Findings — *This chapter builds on extant bibliography to discuss the relevance of collaboration as well as its contribution within the tourism business environment. The study provides practical guidance and recommendations for the critical importance of adopting and implementing collaborative forms and strategies. Cooperation and collaborating could make a significant contribution in designing, managing and marketing services and experiences.*

The Emerald Handbook of Entrepreneurship in Tourism, Travel and Hospitality:
Skills for Successful Ventures, 131—150
ISBN: 978-1-78743-530-8/doi:10.1108/978-1-78743-529-220181005

Research limitations/implications — *This study is explorative in nature because the discussion is based on a literature review. It takes more entrepreneurial/practical than academic approach.*

Practical implications — *Entrepreneurs should carefully consider the various collaborative options at the initial stage of their business venture in order to increase the probabilities of success. By entering into a business venture, tourism providers can also provide appealing experience opportunities and extra customer value. However, some key issues need to be considered and resolved in order to realise the potential benefits.*

Originality/value — *This chapter offers prospective entrepreneurs practical guidance of and insights in collaborative forms and strategies.*

Keywords: Collaboration; forms; strategies; management and marketing benefits; destination level; business venturing

---

Learning Objectives

After working through this chapter, you should be able to:

- explain why various forms and strategies of collaboration are necessary in tourism industries;
- present the nature of tourism experiences and describe the potential benefits of collaboration;
- identify the three most common forms of collaboration at destination level;
- describe the various methods/strategies for business partnership and alliances between tourism providers and entrepreneurs;
- discuss the main characteristics of collaborative strategies, as well as their potential challenges and opportunities for prospective entrepreneurs;
- present and discuss examples of best practices illustrating the collaborative approaches and forms in tourism-related industries.

8.1. INTRODUCTION

Within the context of a globalised market and volatile business environment, all tourism enterprises and companies, regardless of their size, have to make strategic decisions (Brotherton, 2003; Okumus, Altinay, & Chathoth, 2010). Tourism enterprises are exposed to strategic risks related to increased uncertainty in their business and market environments, mainly as a result of globalisation and digital revolution. They are attempting to address the related issues and challenges by cooperating with other enterprises within the same industry or in related businesses. Many enterprises have realised that entering into partnerships and alliances with competitors, suppliers and customers is an opportunity to build strengths (Dixit & Sotiriadis, 2015; Okumus et al., 2010).

Some strategic decisions about a new business venture are of crucial importance in achieving a successful and sustainable operation. A prospective entrepreneur might decide to move forward with his/her business project independently, without partnering with other business or organisations. This is the first of two strategic options; the other one being to collaborate with other existing businesses due to the potential managerial and marketing benefits.

Collaboration and partnership in business ventures are the topic of this chapter; it deals with the collaborative strategies and methods applied in tourism-related industries. The chapter thus provides a presentation of methods and models for business venturing. It takes a perspective of the small business/ prospective entrepreneur and analyses the various collaborative strategies and how these methods can contribute towards the business venture's development and success.

The business environment and the drivers for collaboration between tourism enterprises, as well as the resulting benefits, are outlined in Section 8.2. This is followed by the presentation of the various collaborative forms at destination level (Section 8.3). The next section (Section 8.4) deals with the collaborative strategies between enterprises – at micro level – for business venturing.

8.2. BUSINESS CONTEXT AND DRIVERS FOR COLLABORATION

This section outlines the main features of tourism industries and trends in the business environment; it also deals with the main factors influencing collaboration in the tourism industry. Academic research and business reports have documented and highlighted the main challenges that tourism enterprises have to address (see, for instance, Middleton, Fyall, Morgan, & Ranchhod, 2009; Morrison, 2013). The key issues and challenges are in the fields of tourist consumer behaviour and business environment. Consumers are changing faster than ever before in both attitude and behaviours, and the tourism industries – traditionally more focused on the physical product – are waking up to a consumer who is demanding consistent delivery of the service promise. Tourism providers that are able to understand and meet the needs of these new consumers will be the most competitive; the main challenge is to be capable of responding creatively to new consumers' behaviours and trends (Sotiriadis & Sarmaniotis, 2016).

Furthermore, within this increasingly challenging business environment, a particular characteristic of the tourism industries emerges, namely interdependence. Tourism can be viewed as comprising five component segments/industries: accommodation/hotels, attractions, transport, travel trade/organisers and destination organisations (Middleton et al., 2009; Varvaressos, 2013). The five segments are inextricably interlinked and there are strong relationships between them, which make up the wider tourism experience. The providers of tourism services are all linked and depend upon one another, that is, there is interdependence between them. Within this context collaboration is a necessity rather than a luxury (Gursoy, Saayman, & Sotiriadis, 2015).

This section aims at (1) outlining the characteristics of tourism industries, (2) highlighting the concept of experience and its crucial significance in the tourism field due to the interdependence in tourism offering and (3) presenting the managerial and marketing benefits resulting from collaboration.

8.2.1. Characteristics of Business Environment and Tourism Industries

The two main features of tourism business environment are the industry's structure and the importance of the independent small-sized businesses. We focus on three major characteristics of tourism-related industries at global level: (1) fragmentation: the supply is highly fragmented, with a large number of small-sized and family-run enterprises. Particularly, the hospitality industry is very fragmented, as it consists of many small- and medium-sized enterprises producing and selling undifferentiated products or services in a highly competitive marketplace; (2) high seasonality: a high demand during five to six months, followed by low demand and (3) labour intensity: a high number of employees, especially in the hotel industry (Dixit & Sotiriadis, 2015; Page & Connell, 2006; Varvaressos, 2013).

Three main factors affect the business environment and market conditions: (1) globalisation (together with the concentration of power in a few corporations and branding); (2) technological developments, for instance information and communication technologies (ICTs) and (3) changes in consumer behaviour (preferences and requirements/expectations). It is worth stressing that these factors are interconnected and influence one another.

In today's increasingly competitive global business environment, competition takes place not only among individual enterprises, but also among providers of the whole tourism experience. Many of those companies involved in the delivery of the tourism experience are small- and medium-sized tourism enterprises (SMTEs) with limited resources and organisational capabilities, which make their survival a challenge. Studies indicate that the global tourism market no longer involves single businesses, but rather consists of spatial or thematic destinations composed of a cluster or network of tourism-related operations

(Gursoy et al., 2015; Lazzeretti & Petrillo, 2006). Considering the fact that most tourism-related industries are in a highly competitive business environment and have to deal with rapidly changing market conditions, working closely with all actors involved in the production and delivery of a tourism experience is vital for survival and success.

It has been stressed that, given the inevitable structural diversity of tourism-related industries and their domination by small businesses, there is no logical alternative to the development of destination collaboration involving local tourism businesses and other local stakeholders. It is exactly because of this fragmentation that all actors taking part in the value chain should deal with issues such as integration, collaboration and networking of their activities. The fact that a group of SMTEs can compete globally by cooperating locally highlights the importance of collaborative forms in tourism-related industries and destinations.

8.2.2. Tourism Offering and Experiences

As already mentioned, the nature of tourism industries is an important reason for rendering collaboration. Tourism is a set of industries that offers a 'series of experiences' achieved through a combination of products and services. According to Middleton et al. (2009), destinations are providers of experiences and can increasingly be seen as aggregations of businesses, consisting of mainly SMTEs. Moreover, from a supply perspective, a tourism destination is a spatial unit encompassing a complex system of initiatives, plans and actions; and a number of diverse actors, roles and environmental factors that interact to determine its performance (Lazzeretti & Petrillo, 2006; Weidenfeld, Butler, & Williams, 2011). The main challenge in the tourism industries is to offer special and memorable experiences.

From a demand perspective, tourists desire a series of services that allows multiple options and packages offering a multitude of experience opportunities. For visitors, the 'product' is the total experience, covering the entire amalgam of all aspects and components of the experience, including attitudes and expectations (Varvaressos, 2013). In other words, tourist's experience consists of a series of services and products offered by businesses that operate separately. Ideally, each of those services a tourist receives from different companies is a value-adding service or a value-adding experience.

As already seen in a previous chapter (see Chapter 2), the value chain of a destination includes a number of actors involved in offering and delivering all tourism-related services; and a series of businesses, interactions, resources and knowledge streams are involved in the creation and delivery of value to the end-consumer. This creates a need for integration of the whole range of supply chain activities, because service delivery failures of any businesses involved in the delivery of a tourism experience are likely to have significant negative consequences for the whole system. Any dissatisfactory experience with any service aspect decreases tourists' satisfaction with tourism services (Gursoy et al., 2015). One way of minimising the possibility of customer/visitor dissatisfaction during the whole tourism experience is to work closely with providers of a variety of products and services that produce and deliver the tourism experience (Weidenfeld et al., 2011).

It is believed that enterprises must be in open and constant communication with other providers of tourism services. Through close collaboration with the other parties involved, a tourism provider is able to offer a high degree of personalisation. Thus, collaborative strategies are becoming an important form of business activity in almost all tourism-related industries, particularly in view of the realisation that tourism companies are competing globally, as tourism-related industries are global by definition and nature (Dixit & Sotiriadis, 2015).

8.2.3. Potential Benefits of Collaboration

Collaborative strategies can provide SMTEs a range of opportunities to operate and strive in a competitive global business environment. Forming and becoming part of a collaborative entity is becoming increasingly important as markets become more and more competitive. As markets reach maturity, cooperation among businesses becomes more important for survival (Gursoy et al., 2015).

The various collaborative forms and strategies can generate a series of management and marketing benefits, including these (Novelli, Schmitz, & Spencer, 2006; Sotiriadis & Sarmaniotis, 2016): resource development and knowledge transfer between participants; exchange of valuable marketing information and technology; improved quality of service; improved business performance; encouraging different ways of coordination; improved organisational flexibility in addressing and meeting customers' requirements; innovation capacity; value chain establishment and enrichment; enhanced visibility; business referral and cross-marketing activities with other partners/members; the opportunity to enter other partnerships on a national and international level; building up local businesses' critical mass and enhancing improvement of local resources.

Collaboration with a selected few companies as opposed to collaboration with a large number of different companies has been shown to positively impact company performance and innovation outcomes. A plethora of studies have shown that collaboration can be a powerful tool towards higher achievement and increased productivity since collective efficacy can significantly boost groups' aspirations, motivational investment, morale and resilience to challenges (Eisingerich & Bell, 2008).

All the above benefits influence businesses' willingness to cooperate, create alliances and actively work towards the long-term benefits derived from a collaborative use of resources. Services are combined in order to deliver the specific experience that tourists seek. Several studies examined formation and contributions of collaborative approaches in tourism, for instance spa and health tourism (Novelli et al., 2006), rural tourism (Sotiriadis, Tyrogala, & Varvaressos, 2009), tourism innovation (Fabry, 2015) and creative tourism (Couret, 2015). They all reported that in an environment which is saturated and highly competitive, alliances and partnerships are vital strategies for an enterprise's survival and growth, as well as to meet tourists' requirements.

8.3. FORMS OF COLLABORATION AT DESTINATION LEVEL

According to the *Collins English Dictionary*, collaboration is 'working with each other to do a task'. It is a recursive process where two or more people or organisations work together to realise shared goals. This is more than the inter-section of common goals seen in cooperative ventures; it is a deep, collective determination to reach a common objective. Collaboration in business can be found both at inter- and intra-organisational level and ranges from a simple partnership to a complex multinational corporation (Eisingerich & Bell, 2008).

Collaborative approaches can be utilised not only between organisations operating in the same industry, but also between synergistically related organi-sations. Companies can choose to cooperate with companies that are involved in the production and delivery of tourism experiences by implementing various forms of cooperation structures. Cooperation among companies can vary from a simple collaboration on a marketing activity to formation of an official partnership to deliver a specific service.

The most common collaborative forms at destination level are partnership, cluster and product club, outlined below.

8.3.1. Partnerships

It is an arrangement in which parties agree to cooperate to advance their mutual interests (UberStudent, 2011). The most common definition of partner-ship refers to a partnership formed between one or more businesses in which partners (owners) cooperate to achieve common business aims. Partnerships exist within, and across, industries; all types of organisations may partner to increase the likelihood of each achieving their goals and to amplify their reach. A typical example of a partnership is a strategic alliance, that is, an agreement between two or more parties to pursue a set of agreed upon objectives while remaining independent entities. In a strategic alliance partnership, partners may provide resources such as products, distribution channels, production capabilities, project funding, capital equipment, knowledge, expertise or intellectual property. The alliance is a form of cooperation that aims for synergy, where each partner hopes that the benefits from the alliance will be greater than those from individual efforts (Rigsbee, 2000).

8.3.2. Clusters and Clustering

A cluster is simply a collection of businesses or industries within a particular region (or other spatial zone) that are interconnected by their products, markets and other businesses or organisations, such as suppliers, with which they interact. Porter defines clusters as 'geographic concentrations of interconnected companies, specialised suppliers, service providers, firms in related industries, and associated institutions (for example, universities and trade associations) in particular fields that compete but also co-operate' (Porter, 1998, p. 197). Clustering is a process that enables participants to exploit their synergies and complementarities between their outputs. Clustering can generate several benefits, including economies of scale, a focus on cooperation and innovation, increased synergies and productivity, knowledge transfer, joint marketing, increased competitiveness and sustainable competitive advantage (Gursoy et al., 2015).

A cluster is, therefore, a progressive form of business network, which has strong business objectives focusing on improving sales and profits. It enables the exchange of information and technology, encouraging coordination and collaboration within the cluster. In essence, clusters are characterised by a variety of participants that transcend organisational boundaries and structures. Clustering requires strong commitment from cluster members in order to achieve a set of common goals. Clusters can increase the performance, innovative capacity and local businesses' critical mass (Porter, 2000). An example is 'Tourism Cluster Paris Val d'Europe', France (http://www.clustertourisme. com/60/) (Fabry, 2015).

8.3.3. Product Clubs

Gomis et al. (2010) provided the following definition of a product club (related to the wine routes of Spain): A tourism product club is a group of companies that have agreed to work together to develop new tourism products or increase the value of existing products and collectively review the existing problems that hinder profitable development of tourism. Tourism product clubs share an interest in a segment of the tourism industry and aim to increase variety and quality of products available (packages, events, activities and experiences) or develop new products for a specific market segment. The group is committed to conducting a programme of development of tourism products for a period of at least three to five years.

Product clubs may be formed with or without the intervention of a destination management/marketing organisation (DMO), but in several cases DMOs have been involved in creating these partnerships of tourism stakeholders (Morrison, 2013).

Themed routes, circuits and trails or itineraries constitute a similar form of collaboration or type of destination partnership. The role of trails and routes as part of the tourism offering has been explored and their centrality to the tourist experience is well documented. A route is often based on modern-day conceptualisation and designation of a circuit or course that links partnering tourism providers as well as similar natural or cultural features into a thematic linear corridor. It is believed they have an important role in managing tourism resources/attractions and as facilitators of tourism experiences. This concept of route is used for management and marketing purposes, providing opportunities for experience, enjoyment and satisfaction to a destination's visitors. UNWTO's Silk Road is great example of touring routes linked by a common theme that can be used for marketing and branding purposes as well (Morrison, 2013).

8.4. COLLABORATIVE STRATEGIES FOR BUSINESS VENTURING

Collaborative strategies in the business, such as alliances and networks, are seen as a framework providing SMTEs with managerial and marketing opportunities to operate locally and in a globalised and competitive business environment (Fyall & Garrod, 2005; Gursoy et al., 2015; Sotiriadis et al., 2009). The issue of networks and alliances creation and how they can be used as an innovative process to support SMTEs' ventures has been examined by scholars (see, for instance, Novelli et al., 2006). The most common collaborative strategies/methods for business venturing (at business/micro level) are business alliance, network, management contract, franchising and consortium, as outlined next.

8.4.1. Business Alliances

A business alliance is an agreement between two or more businesses to advance common goals and to secure common interests. It is usually motivated by cost reduction and improved service efficiencies for customers. Alliances are often bounded by a single agreement with equitable risk and opportunity share for all parties involved and are typically managed by an integrated project team. An example of this is the code sharing in airline alliances (e.g. STAR Alliance). There are five basic categories or types of alliance (Kuglin & Hook, 2002):

1. *Sales alliance*: an agreement between two or more companies to jointly market their complementary products and services.
2. *Solution-specific alliance*: an agreement between two or more companies to jointly develop and sell a specific marketplace solution.
3. *Geographic-specific alliance*: that which is developed when two or more companies agree to jointly market or co-brand their products and services in a specific geographic region.
4. *Investment alliance*: an agreement between two or more companies to join their funds for mutual investment.
5. *Joint venture*: an alliance that occurs when two or more companies agree to jointly undertake economic activity.

It is worth pointing out that, in many cases, alliances between companies can involve two or more categories or types of alliance.

8.4.2. Business Network/Networking

A business network is a form of social network for businesses (Kokkonen & Tuohino, 2007). Networking is a socio-economic activity performed by groups of like-minded businesspeople to identify, create or act upon business opportunities. There are several prominent business networking organisations that create models of networking activity that, when followed, can allow a businessperson to build new business relationships and generate business opportunities at the same time (Österle, Fleisch, & Alt, 2001). Many managers contend that business networking is a more cost-effective method of generating a new business than marketing efforts (e.g. promotional activities). This is because business networking is a low-cost activity that involves more personal commitment than company resources.

Networking must be seen as a process that enables the partnering members to exploit their synergies and the complementarities between their outputs. This collaborative framework has been extensively used in tourism industries, with niche markets gaining from network building when their businesses are competing and collaborating at the same time, as they provide a series of business benefits for the providers involved (Novelli et al., 2006; Sotiriadis et al., 2009). Business networking can be conducted in a local business community or on a larger scale via the Internet. A successful example is the Creative Tourism Network (Couret, 2015).

Micro Case – Example 8.1: A Business Network in the Hotel Industry: Voluntary Hotel Chain

A voluntary chain is a very good example of a business network in the hotel industry. It constitutes a business partnership that involves independent hotels having common quality criteria. The main role of a voluntary hotel chain is to contribute to better management activities and to enhance the marketing communications and sales campaigns of hotel members. There are 37 voluntary hotel chains in France, for example, Hotels & Preference (H&P), Châteaux & Hôtels of Collection and PML Hotels. Let us briefly look at the example of H&P.

H&P is a French international hotel group composed of 150 mainly 4- and 5-star hotels. A hotel chain established in 2000, H&P today has more than 140 remarkable locations in 22 destinations worldwide, offering many activities such as golf, spas and gastronomy. The chain offers high-quality service. It meets the expectations of customers enjoying luxury hotels as relaxing places with an intimate and friendly atmosphere. Each hotel meets high-quality standards regardless of its category.

H&P also has a hotel selection boasting spas and golf courses. The chain offers a 'preference warranty' that includes: the lowest price/best rate guaranteed, customer service care, customers' verified reviews and handpicked hotels.

To the potential members/partners, the chain is a world of elegance and tradition. H&P offers a contemporary level of standing and impeccable service, accompanied in its development of upscale independent authentic hotels to continually improve their image and positioning through marketing tools, sales and online communications. In less than 14 years with nearly 10,000 rooms, H&P has become one of the top five independent luxury hotel chains. Its ambition is to significantly grow members' revenue across the leisure, corporate and business fields by offering increased visibility, thanks to eight international sales offices, a strong Internet presence and promotion through travel agencies. By linking hotel property to H&P, a hotelier secures a significant place within the network of boutique and luxury hotels.

Source: Hotels and Preference (2015), cited in Sotiriadis and Sarmaniotis (2016).

Micro Case – Example 8.2:   Otium in Italy: Network to Provide Attractive Guest Experiences

This collaboration is in the form of a 'grand tour' network. Independent boutique hotels join forces to offer an eighteenth-century experience. This new 'grand tour' is being offered by OTIUM, a nascent collaboration between independent owner-managed boutique hotels. The initial idea found its roots in the passion of three independent Italian hotel operators who realised the importance of discovering the true meaning of hospitality and uniqueness of the Italian culture.

The aim of this venture, 'Otium in Italy' – in the form of a business network – is to provide experience opportunities for a journey that 'speaks to the senses and the soul, a place to be accepted for what we are, and discover who we want to be' (Otium in Italy, 2015). It offers a new way to travel Italy through the discovery of places and people. The idea is to connect through a unique journey, with stays at an exclusive collection of Italian homes, whose owners have been able to create unique places that ensure guests feel not only at home, but also part of the community and local culture. The network's aim is to create a group of linked properties that (1) tourists can conveniently book and travel between and (2) offer history, character, tradition and the chance to meet and be personally looked after by the owners. The objective was to have between eight and 12 in the network by the end of 2016.

The network's main marketing concept is to provide experience opportunities while exploring Italy, a lifestyle grand tour. The network offers an immersive itinerary that challenges and inspires the savvy traveller on a deeply personal level, creating emotion through the powerful medium of storytelling. The objective is to discover Italy through a sequence of landscapes, manners, cities and monuments. The network offers travelling experiences around knowledge, culture, creativity and enjoyment.

8.4.3. Management Contracts

In the case of hospitality management contracts, the property owner provides the infrastructure requirements, while the hotel operator provides management expertise. These contracts do not create parity in the agreement between the two parties, similar to franchising agreements. The contractual relationship between the owner and the operator is such that the operator is given exclusive rights to manage the property, while the owner assumes the venture's financial risks (Brotherton, 2003). Table 8.1 illustrates the opportunities and challenges for both parties involved (Brotherton, 2003; Dixit & Sotiriadis, 2015).

Table 8.1. Opportunities and Challenges in Management Contract.

	For Property Owner	For Hotel Operator (Hotel Chain)
Opportunities	• Expertise of hotel operator • An established brand/loyal customers • Operating standards and systems • Centralised reservation system • Less responsibility and accountability	• Brand growth • Little capital investment required (no financial risk) • A vehicle to expand into new markets • Economies of scale
Challenges	• No direct involvement in management of hotel • Little personal recognition • Management fees to operator	• Does not own assets • Lack of homogeneity; the daily management and quality control are weak • Possible involvement from owner • Owner feels neglected

Source: Dixit and Sotiriadis (2015).

Although both companies combine specialised assets, the value of the operating company's expertise has more perceived value than the value of the infrastructural requirements provided by the owner. The crucial issue in management contracts is negotiation and clear agreement on the kind of provisions (general, financial, operational and marketing).

8.4.4. *Franchising*

Franchising is popular in the hotel and restaurant industry, with the greatest number of franchises found in the fast-food industry. Franchising is when two independent companies form a contractual agreement giving one (the franchisee) the right to operate a business in a given location for a specified period of time under the other firm's (franchisor) brand. Franchisees agree to give the franchisor a combination of fees and royalties, usually in the form of a percentage of unit sales in restaurants or a percentage of room sales in hotels. Also included in these agreements is an advertising contribution paid to the franchisor as a percentage of unit revenues. Franchising constitutes an alliance between at least two companies, where each side benefits from the skills and resources held by the other. Hotels are operated by individual franchisees (owners) paying royalties to the parent company for the privilege of operating under a brand name (Lashley, 2000). Independent hotels benefit from the global brand name of the international hotel chain and its reservations system. The foreign franchising firm gains a quick, often smooth, access to a new market without the risk involved in ownership (Lashley, 2000).

Hospitality companies engage in what is called business-format franchising, which is when the franchisor sells a way of doing business to its franchisees (Enz & Harrison, 2008). According to Athiyaman and Go (2003, p. 143, cited in Brotherton, 2003), 'Franchising … is linked to the proliferation of branding that is evident in the international hospitality industry. The franchise method can be either applied to licensing a single franchisee or a master license.' Accord, Holiday Inn, Sofitel, Hyatt and Cendant are examples of hotel companies that have used such agreements to rapidly expand both their domestic and international markets. The restaurant industry offers numerous examples, such as McDonald's, Kentucky Fried Chicken (KFC) and Ocean Basket, to name a few (Tassiopoulos, 2011).

Likewise, as far as management contracts are concerned, this alliance offers the franchisee a number of opportunities, but at the same time he/she has to address some challenges (see Table 8.2).

In a hospitality franchise agreement, although the two companies involved typically share assets, the risk exposure is not equally shared. The franchisor is exposed to lower risks than the franchisee, who meets the infrastructural requirements of the agreement. The franchisor meets the product, technology, marketing and training aspects of the agreement for a fixed and/or variable fee. A crucial issue in the preliminary stage is the selection of franchisee partner. Altinay, Brookes, and Aktas (2013) suggest that franchisees use two distinct approaches, processes and criteria to select their franchisor partners.

Is franchising less risky than going into business on one's own? While conventional wisdom might say yes, current research suggests that joining a new and small franchise may be more risky than starting one's own business because success depends on the capacity of the franchisor and the other few franchisees to make the entire chain work. The likelihood of failure is lower when one joins

Table 8.2.   Opportunities and Challenges in Franchise Agreements.

	For the Hotel Business (Franchisee)	For the Hotel Operator (Franchisor)
Opportunities	A well-known brand name, established customer base, assistance with set-up (instructions and technical knowhow), established standards and procedures, financial advice and mass marketing — therefore, a low failure rate	Expansion of the chain, financial growth, brand expansion, guaranteed income (monthly fees), less capital investment in infrastructure, less responsibility for expenditure and less accountability
Challenges	High start-up costs, strict terms and conditions, limited negotiation power, management regulation and control, cost of monthly fees, limited flexibility and high standardisation	Potential loss of control, franchisee unable to maintain standards and closer monitoring

Source: Author's creation, retrieved from Enz and Harrison (2008) and Dixit and Sotiriadis (2015).

an established chain with many units, such as Pizza Hut. It is important to understand that franchising is not without risks (Enz & Harrison, 2008).

An entrepreneur considering franchising as their method of doing business needs to keep in mind that multi-unit franchisee ownership is common in the hospitality industry. The multi-unit franchisee will have far more bargaining power in their transactions with the franchisor, and hence the new entrepreneur needs to consider their own long-term ownership strategy (Enz & Harrison, 2008). Success as a franchisee is not automatic. The success of franchise alliances is dependent on leveraging franchisors' knowledge and thus on the franchisors' transfer capacity and the franchisees' ability to apply the knowledge transferred. An entrepreneur has to put as much effort into a franchise business as any other independent business. Research, ongoing training and implementing effective sales and marketing strategies are also an ongoing requirement to improve success for the franchise business (Tassiopoulos, 2011).

8.4.5. Consortium

Hotel consortium is defined as 'an organisation of hotels, usually, but not necessarily owned autonomously, which combine resources to establish joint purchasing/trading arrangements and operate marketing services. These aims will often be achieved through the setting up of a centralised office whose activities will be financed through a levy/subscription on member hotels' (Litteljohn, 1982, cited in Slattery, Roper, & Boer, 1985). The same authors have identified five examples of collective endeavours among hotels, each of which has a claim to be classified as a type of consortium: (1) marketing consortia (e.g. Leading Hotels of the World and Preferred Hotels), (2) marketing and purchasing consortia (e.g. Best Western), (3) referral consortia (e.g. Nikko Hotels), (4) personnel and training consortia (e.g. Concord Hotels) and (5) reservations systems (e.g. Utell and Expotel).

The independent hotel operators have been attracted to the consortia mainly for security, access to markets, better visibility and increased sales. That is why it is easier and quicker for consortia to persuade hotels into membership than it is for hotel companies to build a new hotel, to conclude a management contract or to sell a franchise.

Micro Case – Example 8.3: Best Western Hotels and Resorts

Best Western International, Inc., operator of the Best Western Hotels & Resorts brand, operates about 4,100 hotels and motels located in over 100 countries and offers accommodations for all types of tourist. The consortium, with its corporate headquarters in Phoenix, Arizona, was founded by MK Geurtin in 1946.

Business model: Best Western provides reservation and brand identity services for all of its worldwide hotels. It has multilingual reservation centres in Phoenix, USA and Italy. Best Western charges its members a rate that is based on an initial cost plus a fee for each additional room. It also publishes a list of standards that each hotel needs to maintain.

Independently owned and operated, each brand has its own personality and style, but all share the same commitment to delivering superior customer service, exceptional value and modern amenities. The hotels are allowed to keep their independent identity. Though they must use Best Western signage and identify themselves as a Best Western hotel, the hotels are allowed the option of using their own independent name as part of their identity (for example, *Best Western Gateway Inn*, in Aurora, Colorado, USA).

In 2011, Best Western changed its branding system (after starting a similar idea in 2002 in some areas of Europe and Asia), with three levels of progressively more amenities and features: *Best Western*, *Best Western Plus* and *Best Western Premier*. Since it no longer operates under a single brand, Best Western concurrently modified its slogan in 2011 from '*the world's largest hotel chain*' to '*the world's largest hotel family*'.

Source: https://www.bestwestern.com/en_US/about.html, 2017.

In travel trade, a consortium refers to an organisation made up of independent travel agents and agencies. They work together to increase buying power, commissions and amenities they are able to provide clients. Agents and agencies must meet a threshold sales volume requirement in order to be invited to join a consortium. Member benefits include marketing programmes, commission overrides, agent training and education, familiarisation trips, technical tools, client referrals and networking opportunities (Varvaressos, 2013). Consortia negotiate with hotels, resorts, cruise lines and other suppliers on behalf of their agent members. The resulting 'preferred supplier' relationship benefits agency clients in the form of upgrades, room amenities and special promotions not available to the general public. Some of the most well-known consortia include Virtuoso, Signature Travel Network, Ensemble Travel Group and Vacation.com.

Micro Case – Example 8.4:   Small Luxury Hotels of the World

Small Luxury Hotels (SLH) is a hotel consortium in the upscale/luxury market segment. A means of consortium differentiation is SLH's development of special customer experiences via the development of an extensive range of personalised packages that guarantee that 'little something extra'. SLH has set out to deliver ultimate active, gastronomic, spa or cultural experiences to targeted customers. In addition, SLH now recognises that its pursuit of excellence does not need to be at the expense of the environment or the community in which a hotel operates. Through its 'Caring Luxury' initiative, SLH encourages its hotel members to adopt responsible environmental, economic and social practices, which at the same time provide enriching and rewarding experiences for hotel guests. By practising Caring Luxury, SLH properties help to maximise the positive effects of tourism, such as creating jobs and benefiting small businesses, enhancing guests' awareness of local culture and traditions and identifying ways to conserve and protect local surroundings.

Source: Small Luxury Hotels (www.slh.com) and Fyall and Garrod (2005) (in Sotiriadis & Sarmaniotis, 2016).

8.5. SUMMARY

The relevance of collaboration within tourism and travel, as well as its contribution within the tourism business environment, has been acknowledged and well documented. This chapter has built on extant bibliography and has provided to prospective entrepreneurs practical guidance of and insights in collaborative forms and strategies by illustrating theoretical issues and aspects with practical examples and best practices.

It has been pointed out that tourism experiences are multidimensional and quite complex, and tourism providers must address the resulting challenges by adopting adequate approaches. It is believed that (1) collaboration is a necessity rather than a luxury in a highly competitive tourism business environment and (2) cooperation and partnering could make a significant contribution in designing, managing and marketing services and experiences.

We have seen the most common forms of collaboration at destination level — that is partnership, cluster and product club — as well as the strategies that retain most currency, most preferred between tourism enterprises, namely business network, alliance, management contract, franchising and consortium. Overall, this chapter provided practical guidance and recommendations for the critical importance of adopting and implementing collaborative forms and strategies both at tourism destination and business level.

The various models of business cooperation and partnering serve as a very useful and efficient framework for management and marketing purposes, especially in the field of niche tourism markets, such as meetings, incentives, conventions and exhibitions (MICE), experiential tourism, health and wellness, gastronomic/culinary, ecotourism and creative tourism, because of the nature of tourists' experience and the variety of involved actors/businesses. Some micro cases were used to illustrate best practices and business world examples.

Prospective entrepreneurs should seriously and carefully consider the various collaborative options at the initial stage of their business venture in order to increase the probabilities of success. Investment in business collaborative ventures and alliances is a good investment because it constitutes a potential source of sustainable competitive advantage. By entering into a business venture, tourism providers can also provide appealing experience opportunities and extra customer value.

Nevertheless, a number of key issues need to be considered and resolved in order to realise the above-mentioned potential benefits. Prospective entrepreneurs should bear in mind and take into account the following factors: (1) The collaboration and combination of forces and resources is not a magic recipe for business success. It must be well planned; only a collaborative platform wisely designed creates a series of business benefits. Such a platform can offer a way of extending, enriching and deepening tourists' experiences; (2) The main aims of a collaborative strategy are threefold: creating an appealing and attractive offering, achieving a competitive advantage and generating business and market diversification; (3) Members/partners should share consistent values and should be focused on the same targeted market segments; it is therefore imperative to select the appropriate partners; (4) The arrangement also needs to be financially attractive to all participants, striking an equitable balance and (5) The choice of the appropriate collaboration structure (contractual form) is equally important.

The strategic decision whether a prospective entrepreneur goes for independent venture or a collaborative strategy is of critical importance.

Review Questions

Now you may check your understanding of this chapter by answering the following questions or discussing the topics below:

- Why is collaboration necessary in tourism industries?
- Discuss the potential benefits of collaboration.
- Present the forms of collaboration at destination level.
- Discuss the various methods/strategies for business alliances between tourism entrepreneurs.
- What are the potential challenges and opportunities for prospective entrepreneurs in the field of collaboration and partnerships?

REFERENCES AND FURTHER READING

Altinay, L., Brookes, M., & Aktas, G. (2013). Selecting franchise partners: Tourism franchisee approaches, processes and criteria. *Tourism Management*, *37*(1), 176–185.

Brotherton, B. (2003). *International hospitality industry*. London: Taylor & Francis.

Collins English Dictionary – Complete & Unabridged 11th edition. Retrieved from www.collinsdictionary.com. Accessed on 10 October 2016.

Couret, C. (2015). Collaboration and partnerships in practice: The creative tourism network. In D. Gursoy, M. Saayman, & M. Sotiriadis (Eds.), *Collaboration in tourism businesses and destinations: A handbook* (pp. 191–203). Bingley: Emerald Group Publishing Limited.

Dixit, S. C., & Sotiriadis, M. (2015). Strategic alliances in the hospitality industry as an expansion strategy: An Indian perspective. In D. Gursoy, M. Saayman, & M. Sotiriadis (Eds.), *Collaboration in tourism businesses and destinations: A handbook* (pp. 77–94). Bingley: Emerald Group Publishing Limited.

Eisingerich, A., & Bell, S. (2008). Managing networks of inter-organizational linkages and sustainable firm performance in business-to-business service contexts. *Journal of Services Marketing, 22*(3), 494–504.

Entrepreneur.com – Franchise Zone. Retrieved from www.entrepreneur.com/franchises/index.html. Accessed on 10 December 2016.

Enz, C., & Harrison, J. (2008). Innovation and entrepreneurship in the hospitality industry. In B. Brotherton & R. Wood (Eds.), *The Sage handbook of hospitality management* (pp. 213–228). London: Sage Publications.

Fabry, N. (2015). Potential contribution of collaborative forms in tourism innovation: a focus on tourism cluster. In D. Gursoy, M. Saayman, & M. Sotiriadis (Eds.), *Collaboration in tourism businesses and destinations: A handbook* (pp. 285–298). Bingley: Emerald Group Publishing Limited.

Fyall, A., & Garrod, B. (2005). *Tourism marketing: A collaborative approach.* Clevedon: Channel View Publications.

Gomis, F. J. D. C., Lluch, D. L., Civera, J. M. S., Torres, A. M. A., Molla-Bauza, M. B., Poveda, A. M., ... Pedregal, A. M. N. (2010). Wine tourism product clubs as a way to increase wine added value: The case of Spain. *International Journal of Wine Research, 2*(2), 27–34.

Gursoy, D., Saayman, M., & Sotiriadis, M. (2015). Introduction. In D. Gursoy, M. Saayman, & M. Sotiriadis (Eds.), *Collaboration in tourism businesses and destinations: A handbook* (pp. xv–xxvi). Bingley: Emerald Group Publishing Limited.

Hotels & Preference. (2015). Official website. Retrieved from http://www.hotelspreference.com/fr/. Accessed on 23 October 2015.

Kokkonen, P., & Tuohino, A. (2007). The challenge of networking: Analysis of innovation potential in small and medium-sized tourism enterprises. *The International Journal of Entrepreneurship and Innovation, 8*(1), 44–52.

Kuglin, F. A., & Hook, J. (2002). *Building, leading, and managing strategic alliances: How to work effectively and profitably with partner companies.* New York, NY: American Management Association.

Lashley, C. (2000). *Franchising hospitality services.* Oxford: Butterworth-Heinemann.

Lazzeretti, L., & Petrillo, C. (Eds.). (2006). *Tourism local systems and networking.* Oxford: Elsevier.

Middleton, V. T. C., Fyall, A., Morgan, M., & Ranchhod, A. (2009). *Marketing in travel and tourism* (4th ed.). Oxford: Elsevier.

Morrison, A. M. (2013). *Marketing and managing tourism destinations.* New York, NY: Routledge.

Novelli, M., Schmitz, B., & Spencer, T. (2006). Networks, clusters and innovation in tourism: A UK experience. *Tourism Management, 27*(6), 1141–1152.

Okumus, F., Altinay, L., & Chathoth, P. (2010). *Strategic management for hospitality and tourism.* Oxford: Elsevier.

Österle, H., Fleisch, E., & Alt, R. (2001). *Business networking: Shaping collaboration between enterprises.* New York, NY: Springer.

Page, S. J., & Connell, J. (2006). *Tourism: A modern synthesis* (2nd ed.). London: Thomson Learning.

Porter, M. (1998). *On competition: A Harvard Business Review book.* Boston, MA: Harvard Business School Publishing.

Porter, M. (2000). Cluster and new competitive economics. *Journal of the Economic and Social Comparison, 2*(1), 21–31.

Rigsbee, E. R. (2000). *Developing strategic alliances.* Mississauga: Crisp Learning.

Slattery, P., Roper, A., & Boer, A. (1985). Hotel consortia: Their activities, structure and growth. *The Service Industries Journal*, 5(2), 192–199.

Sotiriadis, M., & Sarmaniotis, C. (2016). Collaborating to provide attractive hotel guests' experiences. In M. Sotiriadis & D. Gursoy (Eds.), *The handbook of managing and marketing tourism experiences* (pp. 175–194). Bingley: Emerald Group Publishing Limited.

Sotiriadis, M., Tyrogala, E., & Varvaressos, S. (2009). Contribution of networking and clustering in rural tourism business. *Tourismos: An International Multidisciplinary Journal of Tourism*, 4(4), 35–56.

Tassiopoulos, D. (2011). Franchising. In D. Tassiopoulos (Ed.), *New tourism ventures: An entrepreneurial and managerial approach* (pp. 147–179). Claremont, SA: JUTA.

UberStudent. (2011). *Become a partner or sponsor*, 30 April. Retrieved from http://www.uberstudent.org/mod/resource/view.php?id=27. Accessed on 30 June 2015.

UNWTO. (2013). UNWTO Silk Road Programme. Retrieved from http://silkroad.unwto.org/en/content/. Accessed on 8 November 2016.

Varvaressos, S. (2013). *Tourism economics* (2nd ed.). Athens: Propobos.

Weidenfeld, A., Butler, R., & Williams, A. W. (2011). The role of clustering, cooperation and complementarities in the visitor attraction sector. *Current Issues in Tourism*, 14(7), 595–629.

PART IV
MANAGING THE TOURISM BUSINESS

CHAPTER 9

MANAGEMENT AND BUSINESS PLAN

Marisol Alonso-Vazquez, María del Pilar Pastor-Pérez and Martha Alicia Alonso-Castañón

ABSTRACT

Purpose − *The aim of this chapter is to present an overview of how entrepreneurs' management activity can be assisted by utilising business plans. The main purpose of this chapter is to guide prospective tourism entrepreneurs to make a reflection on management decision-making when starting up a micro-, small- or medium-sized tourism venture.*

Methodology/approach − *This chapter was built on a review of management literature and authors' industry experiences.*

Findings − *This chapter suggests that a well-designed business plan can help prospective entrepreneurs to (1) facilitate their decision-making, (2) minimise their risk perception and (3) increase their venture's success probability.*

Research limitations/implications − *This chapter is descriptive in nature to illustrate how business plans are useful instruments for decision-making in management and marketing areas.*

Practical implications − *The practical/entrepreneurial approach practical of this chapter contributes to highlight the utility and value of a business plan for any micro, small or medium tourism, travel, leisure or event venture.*

The Emerald Handbook of Entrepreneurship in Tourism, Travel and Hospitality:
Skills for Successful Ventures, 153−168
Copyright © 2018 by Emerald Publishing Limited
All rights of reproduction in any form reserved
ISBN: 978-1-78743-530-8/doi:10.1108/978-1-78743-529-220181020

Originality/value − *This chapter is useful for prospective entrepreneurs who are planning to launch a venture but have not decided yet how to shape and start a tourism business venture.*

Keywords: Entrepreneurs; management; decision-making; business plan; components; tourism business venture

---

Learning Objectives

After working through this chapter, you should be able to:

- relate the management functions to tourism ventures;
- discuss the importance of managing strategic, tactical and operational decision-making;
- explain a range of decision-making biases;
- identify types of data collection, such as primary and secondary information, to support effective decision-making;
- produce a business plan for your venture.

9.1. INTRODUCTION

Tourism ventures, like any other businesses, are systems that require human, material, financial and technological resources to achieve entrepreneurs' goals. Coordinating these resources effectively and efficiently is the main objective of management, as this will contribute to the sustainability of the venture. This introduction revisits the definition of management and its main functions, with the aim of contextualising the use of business plans.

One of the most common definitions of management is the following:

> Management is the process of planning, organising, leading and controlling the use of resources to accomplish performance goals. (Schermerhorn, 2008, p. 17)

The management process includes four main management functions: planning, organising, leading and controlling.

The *planning* function relates to the entrepreneurs' evaluation of the situation of their venture within their specific context (Linstead, 2009). This context includes the venture relationship with its political, economic, social, technological, legal and environmental settings. This evaluation can be conducted at all stages of the venture. Its purpose is to identify internal or external situations that can contribute to or prevent the entrepreneur from reaching their venture's goals.

The *organising* function is executed when the entrepreneurs specify the activities and responsibilities that will be carried out in the venture (Robbins, 2003). However, as time passes and the business grows, entrepreneurs have to delegate operational processes to other staff or external contractors. Sometimes it is convenient to subcontract services to other businesses via outsourcing or freelance services, to alleviate the entrepreneurs' workload or to overcome their lack of know-how or expertise in specific areas. Small ventures commonly subcontract cleaning, finance and marketing.

The *direction* function is executed when entrepreneurs actually manage and guide the desired path of the venture. Two elements that enable this management are communication and motivation via leadership (Schermerhorn, 2008). Effective communication will contribute to identifying potential issues and finding alternatives to improve the performance of the venture. Gaining a better understanding of employees' drivers of motivation to work is another way to improve the venture's performance. Entrepreneurs have to bear in mind that employees' motivations vary and can be situational. Therefore, entrepreneurs have to be open to listening to their employees' drivers of motivation and be ready to negotiate (Mikkelsen, Jacobsen, & Andersen, 2017).

The *control* function is executed when the entrepreneurs are supervising and verifying that the planned actions have been conducted as requested and the expected results achieved (Robbins, 2003; Shermerhorn, 2008). This principle is a continual process that implies a constant revision of the venture processes and results to achieve the best outcomes (Linstead, 2009).

The aim of this chapter is to present the basic elements that assist prospective entrepreneurs to execute their management functions. Firstly, the concept of decision-making as a fundamental activity of management is presented. This is followed by a description of the different types of decision-making, their biases and their impact on entrepreneurs' decision-making (Section 9.2). The next section deals with sources of data collection and the design of a business plan to support entrepreneurs' management (Section 9.3). Finally, the chapter ends with a micro case that illustrates the process of starting up a tourism venture (Section 9.4).

9.2. MANAGEMENT DECISION-MAKING

Decision-making is an essential part of managing a venture (Bazerman & Moore, 2008). One of the most relevant choices entrepreneurs make is to start-up their own business. This decision is considered transcendent because its consequences may change the entrepreneurs' lifestyle forever. There are three types of decisions: operational, tactical and strategic, which differ in terms of scope.

9.2.1. Managing Strategic, Tactical and Operational Decision-making

Strategic decisions are those that imply a long-term goal, and they are related to all components of the venture. For instance, decisions related to starting up the venture, its legal structure or giving up on this idea are examples of strategic decision-making. To identify strategic decision-making, it is important to reflect on (1) the nature of the problem, (2) the information that is available to the decision-maker and (3) the hierarchical position of the decision-maker in the organisation.

Depending on the nature of the problem, the decision could be programmed or non-programmed (Weihrich, Cannice, & Koontz, 2008). If the decision is repetitive and is associated with structural situations that are somehow predictable, then the decision is considered a programmed decision. Ideally, organisations should define procedures, policies and norms that rule the process of programmed decision-making (Robbins & Coulter, 2009). For this reason, these types of decisions are conducted by staff in lower levels of the hierarchy. Entrepreneurs commonly make programmed decisions during the start-up of a venture. Non-programmed decisions are those for which there are no particular rules that set a possible choice. These decisions are more frequent, more difficult and more complex because there is a lack of information about possible actions and a need for creative solutions.

There are three types of contexts where entrepreneurs deal with decision-making. These are certain, uncertain and risk (Courtney, Lovallo, & Clarke, 2013; Weihrich et al., 2008). These contexts are classified depending on how much control the entrepreneurs have over the problem variables, the information available and the predictability of the results. There is risk when entrepreneurs have no clues about the result of making a specific decision, but there is information that partially controls the variables that facilitate their decision-making. Finally, there is uncertainty when there is no available information, no control over the variables and no idea of the results of the decision-making. In cases of uncertainty, entrepreneurs assign subjective probabilities based on intuition, judgement or experience (Weihrich et al., 2008). However, entrepreneurs should bear in mind that there is more risk if their decision-making is based on subjective rather than objective assumptions.

Tactical decisions are often programmed decisions undertaken in situations of risk based on a venture's strategic decisions (Robbins & Coulter, 2009). For example, setting the prices of a tourism venture's services is a strategic decision, while planning a sales promotion activity within a specific timeframe is a tactical decision. Entrepreneurs have to decide how tactical decisions will be implemented and who will be in charge of implementation, because their workload will increase as the venture expands (White & White, 2017).

Operational decisions are programmed decisions because they provide a solution to daily situations related to the main activity of the venture (Robbins & Coulter, 2009). Decisions of this type are normally taken under predictable conditions and are part of daily operations, for example, what to do if clients complain about their service, miss their booked tour because they overslept or get sick in the middle of a trip. Other examples are related to running the venture, such as paying suppliers or assigning tasks. These decisions are sometimes taken by the entrepreneurs when the ventures are small in size. However, it is expected that with growth these types of decisions will be delegated to employees.

9.2.2. Identifying Decision-making Bias

Entrepreneurs can be influenced by their own cognitive or emotional prejudices, which may lead them to make inadequate choices. Bias is 'a departure from the normative model in a particular direction' (Drucker, 2010, p. 57). Identifying the existence of this bias is relevant for entrepreneurs because its presence can lead them to formulate wrong questions.

These cognitive or emotional prejudices are the so-called decision-making biases (Baron, 2007; Harel, 2015; MacMaster, Archer, & Hirth, 2015; Robbins & Coulter, 2014; Zhang & Cueto, 2015). Usually, these biases are combined. For example:

Overconfidence bias: A strong sense of confidence is an inherent characteristic of entrepreneurs. However, a sense of overconfidence may overestimate the entrepreneurs' performance. For instance, some entrepreneurs make the decision to start-up a business even though the risk and the uncertainty of success are high (Salamouris, 2013). In other words, entrepreneurs' overconfidence in their capabilities and knowledge makes them start a business when other individuals are more reluctant.

Overoptimism bias: This sense of overconfidence overlaps with overoptimism, which refers to overestimating the likelihood of positive events and underestimating the likelihood of negative events (Sharot, 2011; Zhang & Cueto, 2015). This attitude enforces the motivation to start-up a business.

Confirmation bias: The combination of the previous two biases leads entrepreneurs to confirm their own predictions about their decision-making and minimise its negative aspects. In fact, entrepreneurs under these biases tend to eliminate information that contradicts their choices. Simultaneously, they look only for sources that confirm their beliefs rather than those that challenge their way of thinking. For example, entrepreneurs under this confirmation bias misunderstand their clients' needs and expectations or their competitors' threats (Harel, 2015).

Action-oriented bias: This bias for action implies that entrepreneurs take action even though resources are scarce. Entrepreneurs under the effect of this bias do not devote time to analyse the feasibility of their ideas; instead, they take action with their limited resources and information (MacMaster et al., 2015).

Self-interest bias: Another common bias is self-interest. An entrepreneur does what is best for himself/herself (Baron, 2007), and therefore makes choices that provide immediate results rather than long-term benefits.

Loss aversion bias/Self-fulfilling prophecy: The bias of self-fulfilling prophecy refers to potential entrepreneurs who are reluctant to take a risk (also known as loss aversion bias) and focus on risk rather than on potential profits to make their decisions. This perception of high risk, along with a lack of confidence in their entrepreneurial capacities, does not allow entrepreneurs to materialise their venture.

To minimise the consequences of these biases, entrepreneurs have to be aware of their existence and reflect on how these biases can influence their decision-making (Robbins & Coulter, 2014). Creating an open-minded attitude and behaviour that receives feedback from and provides feedback to staff members, external experts and customers, can also mitigate the effect of these biases.

9.2.3. Sources of Information Supporting Management Decision-making

Entrepreneurial decision-making always involves taking risks, which are mitigated when the entrepreneur has access to relevant information. This information is paramount, particularly when the entrepreneur has to make decisions in uncertain circumstances. The following are the basic elements for reducing risk while making decisions (Courtney et al., 2013):

- Previous knowledge about the operation and management of businesses, either empirical or academic;
- Previous industry experience related to the new venture;
- Analytical thinking, logical reasoning and entrepreneurial intuition;
- Access to reliable and qualitative sources of information.

Arguably, one of the most relevant elements mentioned above is access to information. Adequate sources of information are helpful in identifying alternatives courses of action to address an issue or solve a problem. These sources must be relevant, up to date, accurate, trustworthy and cost-effective (Chartered Management Institute, 2013). Information can be collected by means of two methods: primary and secondary.

Primary information is collected directly by observing, questioning or counting a specific phenomenon that is being studied. Common examples of collecting primary information are surveys, interviews or observations of current or potential clients. These activities could be organised by the entrepreneurs themselves or by marketing agencies or independent consultants. Another example is conducting an expert panel. The information needed is collected from industry experts who share their knowledge and expertise by discussing specialised topics (Courtney et al., 2013).

Secondary information is collected by gathering information by third parties for their own purposes. An example of this type of information is desk research. This research consists of collecting news, scientific articles, specialised books, governmental databases and statistics (Chartered Management Institute, 2013). An application of this type of research is the use of statistical information to create a target market profile. Another example is case study analysis, which benchmarks the decisions other small business entrepreneurs make regarding possible problem-solving or identification of a solution (Courtney et al., 2013).

The advantages of using primary data are: they are relevant to the venture and more up to date than secondary information. However, these are costly and therefore are not feasible. Two advantages: easily available and accessible (Chartered Management Institute, 2013). However, secondary data can be wide-ranging, so it may not be relevant for the small business. As a result, entrepreneurs are encouraged to use primary data as much as possible. This type of data is particularly relevant to identifying the main components of the venture structure and to facilitating the entrepreneurs' decision-making. In this regard, an extremely useful instrument is the business plan.

9.3. MANAGEMENT PLANNING: BUSINESS PLAN DESIGN

The business plan is a practical tool for entrepreneurs to use in designing their venture. This tool helps entrepreneurs to plan a business idea before taking action (Corbett & Katz, 2016). The feasibility of the entrepreneurial idea has been assessed by a feasibility analysis and study (presented in Chapter 7).

The purpose of a business plan is to map the future of the venture, to get to the entrepreneurs' desired destination (Sahlman, 1997). It is likely that the business plan will change during the journey. However, the business plan can keep entrepreneurs on track. Another purpose of conducting a business plan is to present the business idea to potential investors or when requesting a bank loan (Mason & Stark, 2004). The business plan is a tool where the essential components of the venture are described in a clear and consistent manner. These components mainly include aspects related to the venture's structure, its finances and the market.

9.3.1. The Venture Component

This component describes the aspects of a venture's identity and legal composition. It includes the business details in terms of its legal and management structure, that is, the registration details, business premises, organisation chart, ownership and management, description of products or services, description of the key job positions, legal considerations, operations and other related plans. It also includes the vision, mission and goals.

The *vision* statement briefly outlines the future of the business. The *mission* statement concisely describes what the business does, including its services and value proposition as well as its growth potential. The *goals* are the venture's aims, while the *objectives* state the activities needed or the steps to be taken towards achieving the goals. These goals and objectives can be linked with the concept of sustainability. Ventures can be sustainable in the sense of their commitment to (1) minimising their negative environmental impacts, (2) being socially responsible and (3) creating shareholder value (Frederick, O'Connor, & Kuratko, 2013). In the past, there was a belief that sustainability was a separate section of the business plan. Today, sustainability can be a philosophy that is embedded in the processes and systems of the venture to increase its chances of survival in the long term (Werbach, 2011). Therefore, entrepreneurs have to think about their own definition of sustainability and identify potential environmental, social and economic harms while doing their activity, as well as practices that should be implemented to mitigate the impact of potential harms.

The *legal structure* of the venture, *registration*, *licences* and *permissions* are other important aspects of the venture component (Timmons, Spinelli, & Tan, 1994). Entrepreneurs have to register their business in their state or territory. If it is only an idea, entrepreneurs have to research the process of registering a business in their location. They have to decide if they will use a trading name, and the business's legal structure (this issue is presented in more detail in Chapter 6). The local taxation authorities will provide a unique business registration or unique company number, which will be the identity of that particular business. Entrepreneurs also have to make decisions about registering domain names or websites, if applicable. Regulations around the world stipulate guidelines and requirements in this field.

In this component, the *management owner/s'* details and background are described. This section is particularly important to delimit the liability and responsibility of the venture. This section has to define who will be responsible for running the business (e.g. the owner or someone on his/her behalf). In the case of a partnership, it is important to state the percentage share and role in the business. If the business will have employees, their job descriptions must be provided in the business plan.

Entrepreneurs have to identify all the regulations affecting their business (Corbett & Katz, 2016), for example, consumer law, business law or law related to the tourism/hospitality industry. Based on the regulatory framework, entrepreneurs can consider potential risk ranked by likelihood of happening and then determine the possible impact they might need to prevent or design action plans to minimise these risks. Once these risks and action plans have been identified, decisions about types of insurance can be made. More detail regarding legal issues is presented in Chapter 6.

The venture component of a business plan must include the provided products or services. In the tourism industry, services rather than physical products are provided. For example, tours, accommodation, bookings are considered services, while T-shirts, souvenirs and postcards are considered physical products. These services are described in this component from the following perspectives: (1) market position, (2) unique selling proposition, (3) anticipated demand for each service or product, (4) pricing strategy, (5) value to the customer and (6) growth potential. These perspectives are considered in the corresponding components on finance and marketing. However, an executive summary is presented in the introduction to the business plan.

It is particularly important to identify and describe the operational processes for delivering services. For example, if there are third parties such as suppliers, then the processes must be precisely described. Operating hours, communication channels used, payment types accepted and credit policy are other types of information related to business processes that should also be provided.

9.3.2. The Finance Component

The finance component starts setting the venture's financial objectives, which can be stated in the form of sales or profit targets (Brooks, 2015). In this section, entrepreneurs also identify how much capital they need to start the venture and where they will obtain the funds. The proportion of loans, investors, personal savings or government funding should be stated in this component as well. It is common for start-ups to provide assumptions of seasonal adjustments, drought or interest rates. This component must also include all related funds and financial resources needed to start the venture.

This section encompasses the main financial statements in terms of forecasts. These are: (1) balance sheet, (2) profit and loss statement and (3) cash flow forecast. These financial statements are further explained in Chapter 10. However, some general considerations are presented below.

The *balance sheet* includes financial resources owned by the venture (assets) and the claims against these resources (liabilities). These claims come from creditors and owners. Assets can be tangible, such as land and equipment, or intangible, such as patents and copyrights. Another classification may be the one referred to as current assets, such as cash, inventory, prepaid expenses for the following three years, and fixed assets, such as leasehold, property and land, furniture, vehicles and equipment. Concerning liabilities, the balance sheet includes the current or short-term liabilities, such as credit cards payable, accounts payable, interest payable, accrued wages, income tax and long-term liabilities, such as loans that are not due and payable within the next 12 months. Finally, an important liability is the owner's equity, that is, what remains after the firm's liabilities are subtracted from its assets (Kuratko, 2017).

The *profit and loss statement* includes sales revenue less cost of goods sold expected for the following three to five years. Information from sales forecasts and expenses projections is used to calculate the net income projections. The entrepreneur should know how profit varies if sales differ from those forecasts. The *break-even analysis* calculates the total sales needed to break even. In the *annual cash flow forecast* the expected cash flow, which includes cash incoming and cash outgoing to determine cash balance, is analysed.

Sometimes an entrepreneur should present their personal financial statement, where personal assets, liabilities, income and expenses are listed. This is intended to inform potential external investors about the entrepreneur's capability and skills (McKeever, 2017). Once the venture is on track, the financial forecasts and statements can be used to manage the venture on a daily basis and monitor the actual performance or results.

9.3.3. The Market Component

In this component, entrepreneurs define the unique selling proposition and conduct research to evaluate the market — potential clients and competitors. This evaluation approach is called market-driven because the unique selling proposition offered will be influenced by market trends and the customers' needs instead of the entrepreneur's production or service convenience (Schindehutte, Morris, & Kocak, 2008).

Market positioning refers to the effort to lead consumers' perceptions of a product or service compared to the competition (Brooksbank, 1994). To create a market positioning statement it is important to identify the target customers, identify this market's needs and fears, tailor a statement that spreads the message to meet their needs and overcome their fears and, finally, support this statement by providing evidence (Osterwalder, Pigneur, Bernarda, & Smith, 2014). Chapter 15 of this book presents more detailed information about marketing tourism services.

A SWOT analysis has been carried out in the feasibility study. This analysis enables prospective entrepreneurs to evaluate the strengths and weaknesses of their venture as well as the opportunities and threats in the business environment (Helms & Nixon, 2010). This issue is presented in Chapters 4 and 7. *Market research* aims at gaining a better understanding of the market groups and segments to be targeted. This analysis includes a description of potential customers as well as the services or products and the quantity that would meet their needs. This type of information helps entrepreneurs to know the best way to target their products or services to them.

An analysis of a venture's direct competition is also part of this section. The assessment of competitors should contain their estimated percentage of market share, unique value to customers, strengths and weaknesses. After analysing the market research, entrepreneurs can identify the most appropriate marketing strategy to enter into a particular market, to target and attract the selected market segment. This includes sales promotion and advertising to communicate the product or service's unique value proposition to attract customers' awareness and generate sales.

The *marketing strategy* to start-up the venture needs to be planned by the entrepreneur and stated in this section. The design of this strategy will depend on whether the product or service is entering into a new or existing market (Jain & Haley, 2009). According to McDonald (1996), if the venture is entering into an existing market with an existing product or service, then a marketing strategy of market penetration would be appropriate. If the venture is entering into a new market with an existing product or service, then the market development strategy would be appropriate. Either of these two strategies will have its own (1) sales promotion and advertising objectives, (2) expectations of achievements and (3) action plans. The sales promotion and advertising efforts need to express the product or service's value proposition. This proposition briefly highlights how the product or service benefits customers over the competitors (Osterwalder et al., 2014). To make an efficient sales promotion, entrepreneurs should select the appropriate communication channels, the expected percentage of overall sales via these channels, their integration with other channels (if any) and the advantages and disadvantages of using them. Finally, the entrepreneurs have to set a specific timeframe for the marketing strategy and the action plan to achieve the objectives.

For further information on how to develop a business plan, entrepreneurs can refer to the business model template by Osterwalder and Pigneur (2010). This template is a tool or framework that helps new entrepreneurs to design their own business plan in a practical way. It contains the main elements of the venture and their relationships, expressing the logic underlying the nature of the business (Osterwalder & Pigneur, 2010). This will help entrepreneurs to assess the business's performance with respect to added value, customer relationships, the creation process and financial aspects. This business plan template has recently been used to integrate the three pillars of sustainability (economic, environmental and social) into the business philosophy. For further information, refer to the sustainability triple-layered business model template by Joyce and Paquin (2016).

9.4. MICRO CASE STUDY: MANAGING A TOURISM-RELATED START-UP BUSINESS

This case study is based on hypothetical elements to illustrate the way a business plan could be useful in efficiently managing a business venture by making appropriate decisions.

Three entrepreneurs decided to start a tourism venture. One of their main reasons for launching their own business was their passion for nature and travel within their own area, San Luis Potosí, Mexico.

9.4.1. Making Decisions Based on Suitable Sources of Information

These entrepreneurs conducted market research with a focus on identifying a unique value proposition for their nature-based tourism product or service, to make the right decisions. In order to achieve this, they identified relevant information. Their market research contained the following steps and outcomes:

1. *Collection and analysis of secondary data*: This information was gathered from a review of local and national news as well as governmental information provided by the Minister of Tourism and/or tourism professionals and other associations. These entrepreneurs focused their review on the facts that provided them with evidence to support their decision-making for establishing a tourism venture. The key points found in the secondary information were:

   - México was one of the top five countries with significant biodiversity. In the world rankings, it was in second place in ecosystems diversity and fourth due to its species diversity (*La Jornada*, 2015). This information was identified in the local news, searching with the key words 'Mexico' and 'tourism'.
   - The approximate average expenditure by tourists in the nature-based tourism segment was US$2,700 versus US$900 in the conventional/leisure tourism segment (*La Jornada*, 2015). This information was identified in local news.

- San Luis Potosí was one of the top five nature-based tourism destinations, along with Chiapas, Chihuahua, Oaxaca and Veracruz (Visit Mexico, 2017). This information was identified in Visit Mexico that is the official website of the Ministry of Tourism.

2. *Collection and analysis of primary information*: This information was gathered from networking and personal interviews with experts in the field of nature-based tourism destinations. The entrepreneurs attended the most important event for nature-based tourism in Latin America, Adventure Travel Mexico Expo (ATMEX), which is organised by the Adventure Travel Trade Association. The purpose of the interviews and networking was to gather information, which was input to making the following decisions: (1) whether to start the venture or not, (2) selecting the targeted market segment, (3) selecting the targeted segment between adventure activities and nature or wildlife experiences and (4) selecting their unique value proposition to differentiate them from their competitors or other tour operators.

After evaluating the key points of the primary and secondary information, the entrepreneurs analysed the strengths, weaknesses, opportunities and threats (SWOT) of the potential venture. They then identified a unique opportunity that contributed to shaping their initial entrepreneurial idea as local tourism operators. They identified a potential niche market. This market consisted of public high schools that needed to provide learning experiences involving recreation and tourism. These schools were subsidised by the government. Therefore, these entrepreneurs shaped their value proposition under the premises of providing nature-based tours for teenagers within a safe and educational setting. These tours included camping, low-risk adventure activities, lessons on how to survive in a natural environment and nature-based learning activities, such as identification of flora and fauna and migration patterns of animals.

Although the financial situation seemed feasible, there was still uncertainty about the social acceptance of this tourism offering. One of the main potential obstacles was the negative perception of the presence of crime in natural isolated areas. This perception would stop parents from allowing their children to participate in such tours. Another potential obstacle was the risk involved in having teenagers do adventure activities without a previous assessment of the required level of skills and physical condition. These entrepreneurs wondered if their decision was not biased. They knew that perhaps their overconfidence in doing adventure activities and their love of nature might have interfered with identifying other potential risks in offering this type of adventure service to the specific targeted market segment.

9.4.2. Using the Business Plan to Help Entrepreneurs to Make Better Decisions

As a consequence, the entrepreneurs made the decision to invest more time in planning and developing a business plan. This plan helped them to clarify the concept of the scheduled tourism offering, identify the main components of the venture and the specific actions they had to take in determining their vision, and implement suitable actions.

The components of this plan included:

- The philosophy of the venture, encompassing the mission, vision, general goal and specific, measurable, attainable, realistic and timely (SMART) objectives;
- The legal structure of the venture, including the registration, premises, management, organisational chart, insurance, legal considerations, licences and permissions;
- The market analysis, consisting of market research, target markets, industry and competition analysis, environmental and safety analysis, as this is key to the value proposition of their tourism offering, as well as a communications plan (promotion and advertising);
- The finance component, encompassing assumptions, objectives, initial investment capital and forecasts for balance sheet, profit and loss statement, cash flow and a break-even analysis.

After a thorough assessment or evaluation of the business plan, they made the decision to target a different market segment: the 18–45 age-group instead of teenagers aged 12–18.

9.5. SUMMARY

This chapter focused on management decision-making for prospective entrepreneurs in tourism ventures. We have seen how a well-designed business plan can significantly assist entrepreneurs in their decision-making. Making analytical decisions can minimise entrepreneurs' perception of risk and uncertainty (Bazerman & Moore, 2008). Management planning can be assisted by instruments such as a business plan, which is a detailed action plan that describes and analyses the main elements of the venture's structure, finance and market (Corbett & Katz, 2016), including mission, goal and objectives, management, organisational chart, licences, targeted market segments, competition and communications plan (promotional actions), as well as forecasted investment capital, balance sheet, profit and loss statement and cash flow statement. A suitable and realistic business plan can help prospective entrepreneurs to make the right management decisions for the short and long term.

Review Questions

Check your understanding of this chapter by answering the following questions or discussing the topics below:

- What is your own definition of management?
- Why would you consider it important to manage strategic, tactical and operational decision-making?
- What is your evaluation of your possible decision-making bias?
- How would you prevent your personal decision-making bias?
- What are the different purposes of a business plan?
- Discuss the content and components of a business plan.

REFERENCES AND FURTHER READING

Baron, J. (2007). *Thinking and deciding* (4th ed.). New York, NY: Cambridge University Press.

Bazerman, M. H., & Moore, D. A. (2008). *Judgment in managerial decision making* (7th ed.). New York, NY: Wiley.

Brooks, R. (2015). *Financial management: Core concepts* (3rd ed.). London: Pearson.

Brooksbank, R. (1994). The anatomy of marketing positioning strategy. *Marketing Intelligence & Planning, 12*(4), 10–14.

Burmeister, K., & Schade, C. (2007). Are entrepreneurs' decisions more biased? An experimental investigation of the susceptibility to status quo bias. *Journal of Business Venturing, 22*, 340–362.

Chartered Management Institute. (2013). *Pathways to management and leadership. Unit 5002V1: Information-based decision making*. London: Chartered Management Institute.

Corbett, A. C., & Katz, J. A. (2016). *Models of start-up thinking and action: Theoretical, empirical, and pedagogical approaches*. Bingley: Emerald Group Publishing Limited.

Courtney, H., Lovallo, D., & Clarke, C. (2013). Deciding how to decide. *Harvard Business Review, 91*(11), 62.

Drucker, P. F. (2010). *Men, ideas and politics*. Boston, MA: Harvard Business Review Press.

Dunn, B. (2015). Adventure Travel Mexico (ATMEX) highlights outdoor opportunities. *Huffingtonpost*, 16 September. Retrieved from http://www.huffingtonpost.com/bryen-dunn/adventure-travel-mexico-a_b_8131318.html

Frederick, H., O'Connor, A., & Kuratko, D. F. (2013). *Entrepreneurship: Theory, process, practice* (3rd ed.). Melbourne: Cengage Learning.

Harel, Y. (2015). Entrepreneurs should watch out for cognitive biases and the curse of knowledge. *Entrepreneur*, November. Retrieved from https://www.entrepreneur.com/article/252499

Harvard Business Review Staff. (2013). You can't be a wimp, make the tough calls. *Harvard Business Review*, (November). Retrieved from https://hbr.org/2013/11/you-cant-be-a-wimp-make-the-tough-calls

Helms, M. M., & Nixon, J. (2010). Exploring SWOT analysis – Where are we now? A review of academic research from the last decade. *Journal of Strategy and Management, 3*(3), 215–251.

Jain, S. C., & Haley, G. T. (2009). *Marketing planning and strategy*. Melbourne: Cengage Learning.

Joyce, A., & Paquin, R. L. (2016). The triple layered business model canvas: A tool to design more sustainable business models. *Journal of Cleaner Production, 135*, 1474–1486.

Kavoura, A., & Andersson, T. (2016). Applying Delphi method for strategic design of social entrepreneurship. *Library Review*, *65*(3), 185−205, doi:10.1108/LR-06-2015-0062

Kuratko, D. F. (2017). *Entrepreneurship: Theory, process, practice* (10th ed.). Melbourne: Cengage Learning.

La Jornada. (2015, August). Busca SLP seguir creciendo dentro del top cinco de los destinos de turismo de naturaleza [SLP looking forward to be part of the top five natured-based tourism destinations]. *La Jornada*. Retrieved from http://lajornadasanluis.com.mx/ultimas-publicaciones/busca-slp-seguir-creciendo-dentro-del-top-cinco-de-los-destinos-de-turismo-de-naturaleza/

Linstead, S. (2009). *Management and organization: A critical text*. New York, NY: Palgrave Macmillan.

MacMaster, B., Archer, G., & Hirth, R. (2015). Bricolage: Making do with what is at hand. In T. Baker & F. Welter (Eds.), *The Routledge companion to entrepreneurship*. London: Routledge.

Mason, C., & Stark, M. (2004). What do investors look for in a business plan? A comparison of the investment criteria of bankers, venture capitalists and business angels. *International Small Business Journal*, *22*(3), 227−248.

McDonald, M. (1996). *Marketing planning*. London: Kogan Page Publishers.

McKeever, M. P. (2017). *How to write a business plan* (13th ed.). Berkeley, CA: Nolo.

Mikkelsen, M. F., Jacobsen, C. B., & Andersen, L. B. (2017). Managing employee motivation: Exploring the connections between managers' enforcement actions, employee perceptions, and employee intrinsic motivation. *International Public Management Journal*, *20*(2), 183−205.

Osterwalder, A., & Pigneur, Y. (2010). *Business model canvas*. Self-published.

Osterwalder, A., Pigneur, Y., Bernarda, G., & Smith, A. (2014). *Value proposition design: How to create products and services customers want*. Hoboken, NJ: Wiley.

Pentland, A. (2013). Beyond the echo chamber. *Harvard Business Review*, (November). Retrieved from https://hbr.org/2013/11/beyond-the-echo-chamber

Robbins, S. P. (2003). *Management*. Upper Saddle River, NJ: Prentice-Hall.

Robbins, S. P., & Coulter, M. A. (2014). *Management* (12th ed.). London: Pearson.

Robbins, S. P., & Coulter, M. K. (2009). *Organisations and behaviour*. London: Pearson Custom.

Sahlman, W. A. (1997). How to write a great business plan. *Harvard Business Review*, *75*(4), 98−109.

Salamouris, I. (2013). How overconfidence influences entrepreneurship. *Journal of Innovation and Entrepreneurship*, *2*(8). Retrieved from doi:10.1186/2192-5372-2-8

Schermerhorn, J. R. (2008). *Management* (9th ed.). New Jersey, NJ: John Wiley & Sons.

Schindehutte, M., Morris, M. H., & Kocak, A. (2008). Understanding market-driving behavior: The role of entrepreneurship. *Journal of Small Business Management*, *46*(1), 4−26.

Sharot, T. (2011). The optimism bias. *Current Biology*, *21*(23), 941−945.

Timmons, J. A., Spinelli, S., & Tan, Y. (1994). *New venture creation: Entrepreneurship for the 21st century* (Vol. 4). Burr Ridge, IL: Irwin.

Trimi, S., & Berbegal-Mirabent, J. (2012). Business model innovation in entrepreneurship. *International Entrepreneurship and Management Journal*, *8*(4), 449−465.

Visit Mexico. (2017). Visit San Luis Potosi. Retrieved from https://www.visitmexico.com/en/main-destinations/san-luis-potosi. Accessed on 10 September 2017.

Wasserman, E. (n.d.). How to write the financial section of a business plan. *Inc.com*. Retrieved from https://www.inc.com/guides/business-plan-financial-section.html

Weihrich, H., Cannice, M., & Koontz, H. (2008). *Management: Globalization and entrepreneurship perspectives*. Beijing: Economic Science Press.

Weihrich, H., Cannice, M. V., & Koontz, H. (2013). *Management: A global, innovative, and entrepreneurial perspective* (14th ed.). New York, NY: McGraw-Hill Education.

Werbach, A. (2011). Strategy for sustainability. *Strategic Direction*, *27*(10). doi:10.1108/sd.2011.05627jaa.013

White, D., & White, P. (2017). Building your management team as your start-up scales is a "make or buy" decision. *Entrepreneurship Theory and Practice*. Retrieved from https://www.entrepreneur.com/article/294699

Zhang, S. X., & Cueto, J. (2015). The study of bias in entrepreneurship. *Entrepreneurship Theory and Practice*, (November). doi:10.1111/etap.12212. Retrieved from https://ssrn.com/abstract=2688310

CHAPTER 10

MANAGING FINANCIAL MATTERS

Marios Sotiriadis

ABSTRACT

Purpose — *The purpose of this chapter is to present the key issues and main aspects of financial management, which also constitute the main concerns of a prospective entrepreneur.*

Methodology/approach — *This chapter takes a perspective of the small business/prospective entrepreneur and analyses how the methods, tools and techniques of financial management can be helpful in operating the business venture. Literature review was conducted on main issues and aspects of financial management.*

Findings — *This chapter builds on extant bibliography to discuss the key issues and main methods of financial management. For any business, irrespective of size, to carry on its operations and achieve its objectives, financial resources are required, and such resources must be managed efficiently and effectively.*

Research limitations/implications — *This study is explorative in nature because the discussion is mostly based on a literature review. It takes more entrepreneurial/practical than academic approach.*

Practical implications — *To contribute to the successful and sustainable operation of a tourism venture, this chapter outlines the key financial issues and presents in a practical way the main methods and techniques used when making operational and investment decisions.*

The Emerald Handbook of Entrepreneurship in Tourism, Travel and Hospitality:
Skills for Successful Ventures, 169–189
Copyright © 2018 by Emerald Publishing Limited
All rights of reproduction in any form reserved
ISBN: 978-1-78743-530-8/doi:10.1108/978-1-78743-529-220181006

Originality/value — *This chapter attempts to equip a prospective entrepreneur with the background knowledge (main competencies), as well as the principal methods and techniques (skills) for managing the financial resources of a venture.*

Keywords: Financial management; budgets; monitoring; analytical techniques; operational and investment decisions; methods

---

Learning Objectives

After studying this chapter, you should be able to:

- explain the critical role of financial management;
- explain the functions of financial management;
- describe the main financial statements/reports;
- discuss the financial planning and budgeting functions;
- explain monitoring financial performance and related ratios;
- apply some analytical techniques for operational decisions;
- describe and apply the main pricing methods;
- explain revenue management and implement the technique of yield management;
- discuss the issue of capital expenditure and investment decisions;
- explain the main methods of evaluating investment projects.

10.1. INTRODUCTION: MEANING, OBJECTIVES AND FUNCTIONS OF FINANCIAL MANAGEMENT

Financial management refers to 'the efficient and effective management of financial resources in such a manner as to accomplish the enterprise's objectives' (Netlibrary, 2017) and is defined as follows:

- 'the management activity that is concerned with the planning, procuring and controlling of the firm's financial resources' (Deepika & Rani, 2014, p. 28).
- 'the planning, directing, monitoring, organizing, and controlling of the monetary resources of an organization' (*Business Dictionary*, 2017).

In any new business venture, there comes a time to consider business finance. For any business/enterprise irrespective of size to carry on its operations and achieve its objectives, financial resources are required, and such resources must be managed efficiently and effectively.

Financial management means applying general management principles — planning, organising, directing and controlling — to the financial resources of the enterprise (Brooks, 2015; Management Study Guide, 2017). Financial management plays a continuous role in both day-to-day management and broader strategic planning of the business (ACCA, 2016). Financial capabilities and skills are critical for efficiently managing financial resources and for monitoring performance, identifying problem areas and new opportunities, and ultimately, helping the business look to the future.

The main objectives of financial management are: (1) to ensure regular and adequate supply of funds to the business, (2) to plan a sound capital structure (a balance between debt and equity capital), (3) to maximise the operational profit without undermining the long-term operation, (4) to ensure to the owner's/ shareholders' adequate returns and (5) to ensure optimum funds utilisation. These objectives can be attained by properly fulfilling the functions of financial management that include planning, procurement and utilisation of funds (Haitham & Jaya, 2015; Management Study Guide, 2017), and more specifically: (1) estimation of capital requirements, (2) determination of capital composition, (3) investment/allocation of funds, (4) management of cash and (5) financial controls.

The aim of this chapter is to present the main issues and aspects of this specialised managerial function, which also constitute the main concerns of a prospective entrepreneur. The remainder of the chapter is structured as follows: first, the main financial statements are briefly presented (Section 10.2); next follows a description of the functions of planning and budgeting (Section 10.3); the third section deals with the operational decisions, i.e. the main methods for pricing tourism services as well as analytical techniques (Section 10.5); and the fourth and last section deals with investment decisions (Section 10.6).

10.2. FINANCIAL STATEMENTS/REPORTS

The three main financial statements produced by an accounting department are the profit and loss statement, the balance sheet and the cash flow statement. These statements are fundamental to the planning and control of business operations and form the basis for monitoring the business's financial performance.

10.2.1. Profit and Loss Statement

This statement summarises the revenue generated and expenses incurred during a period (month, quarter, semester or year) in order to show the result, profit or loss that has accrued. The basic form is shown in Table 10.1.

The direct operating expenses are deducted from sales (revenues) to give the Gross Operating Profit (GOP).

Table 10.1. Profit and Loss Statement.

	In Euros
Sales (revenue)	100,000
Less: Cost of sales (direct expenses)	30,000
Gross operating profit	70,000
Less: Operating expenses	50,000
Nett profit	20,000

10.2.2. Balance Sheets

Whereas the profit and loss report summarises the revenues generated and expenses incurred throughout a period, a balance sheet represents the values of the assets, liabilities and capital of a business at a single point in time, which is normally the last day of the financial period. It provides a snapshot of the business at a particular date; after the stated date these values will be different.

10.2.3. Cash Flow Statement

The cash flow statement provides a summary of how cash has been generated and used during a period. Therefore, it tracks the inflow and outflow of cash resulting from operating, investing and financing activities during a given time period. The term 'cash' refers to both cash and cash equivalents, which are assets readily convertible to cash. The cash flow statement is usually drawn up annually, but may be drawn up more often.

10.3. PLANNING AND BUDGETING

Planning is essential, whether an entrepreneur is starting a new venture, looking at new opportunities for an existing business or updating his/her strategy. Business planning has a critical role to play at every stage in the life of business.

10.3.1. Planning

As discussed in Chapter 9, preparing a business plan assists a prospective entrepreneur in identifying and assessing the opportunities and threats facing his/her venture. It helps to ensure an in-depth understanding of the target market, the competition and the broader business environment. Creating the plan forces us to make choices. We plan how we shall deal with any challenges or how we shall overcome any weaknesses our business may have and make the most of our strengths. We can identify potential pitfalls and work out how to avoid them.

The whole planning process acts as a checklist, helping to ensure that we think about all the important issues. We choose what the best options are. Most importantly, the business plan provides a blueprint, helping to guide the day-to-day management of the business (ACCA, 2016).

Our plan needs to cover the full range of business functions: sales and marketing, purchasing, production, human resources, administration and finance. We also need to be able to turn those plans into numbers, with forecasts of the implications for cash flow and profitability. Financial calculations and forecasts are at the heart of business planning. Drawing our expected revenues and costs together in a cash flow forecast allows us to identify any anticipated cash shortfalls and arrange the financing needs.

Micro Case 10.1:   Start-up Advice

In a start-up business, it is unlikely that it will be possible to recruit an expert to deal with financial issues. Most start-ups find that their first finance recruit is a bookkeeper/accountant. Financial management is typically the responsibility of the owner. The best solution is to seek and follow the right advice:

- Involve the accountant (the key financial adviser) at the planning stage to take full advantage of their expertise in areas such as raising business finance and tax planning.
- Check that their expertise is applicable and that they are helping in the right areas. Make sure that they know how to prepare a cash flow forecast.
- Once the business is up and running, business owners may be under constant pressure to deal with urgent tasks rather than broader business strategy. Meetings with the accountant and other advisers can help to focus on the bigger picture.

The aim should always be to look ahead. The business plan should indicate what the business owner is trying to achieve.

Source: ACCA (2016).

10.3.2. Budgeting

Financial planning encompasses a wide range of topics, from credit control to investment decisions, all which requires accurate financial predictions of the level of business to be achieved in the future. This process of predicting levels of business is called forecasting. Budgets are a formal forecast of the level of business to be achieved over a specific time period (semester/year). A budget is a strategic plan which guides the business owner's steps for the year. It consists not only of financial information, but also of the actions required in order to achieve these financial targets (Harris, 1999). The agreed budget is used as a measure of assessing business performance (see Section 10.4).

There are different parts of a *master budget* which, when combined, will form a full financial plan for the forthcoming year. The main types of budget are as follows:

- *Operating budget*: This is a plan for the revenue and expenditure to be achieved; its format closely resembles a profit and loss statement.
- *Cash budget*: This is a plan for the movement of cash in and out of the business; it is derived from the information in the operating budget.
- *Capital budget*: This is a plan for expenditure required in terms of large equipment and projects needed to achieve the levels of business presented in the operating budget (together, the cash and capital budgets would form a budgeted balance sheet).

A business owner has to forecast sales, services sold and average rate, number of customers and expenditure/spending, cost of sales, operating expenses (wages, energy, etc.). The forecasts for all these elements lead to a budgeted profit and loss statement. The main aim of these forecasts is to enable entrepreneurs to plan all operational issues (operating hours, staffing requirements, purchasing and stocks) more effectively. Forecasts also enhance control of revenue (growth, cash flow, debtors) and expenditure (cash flow, creditors, purchasing).

10.3.3. The Uses of Budgets

Budgets can assist entrepreneurs in profit planning and controlling business operations.

Profit planning: What happens if the business fails to achieve its target? For instance, the forecast occupancy rate for a given year may have been 70 per cent with only 60 per cent achieved. Owners/managers have to analyse the causes and plan remedial actions.

An effective way to determine the likely position when forecast results are under- or over-achieved is to prepare a 'flexible' budget prior to the beginning of period. A flexible budget is simply a budget that can be adjusted to take account of different levels of sales. It does, however, involve analysing the annual budgeted revenues and costs into their fixed and variable components. Once this is done, revenues and costs can be adjusted in line with different levels of sales and thereby determine the impact on profit.

Control: The entrepreneur should be in a position to compare actual results with budget in order to monitor progress. At the end of the budget period, the results are assessed and the actual results typically differ from the budgeted amounts. The causes of these variances need to be determined and appropriate action should be taken.

The results should be evaluated with care. It is possible that the variances are interrelated rather than unrelated, for instance, the increase in sales may have been stimulated by the reduction in prices. With the intimate knowledge of the particular business, the owner/manager will be able to use the variances as a sound basis for understanding and improving future profitability.

10.4. MONITORING BUSINESS PERFORMANCE AND IMPROVEMENT

Good financial control offers far more advantages than merely the ability to keep track of sales and expenses; it can assist in improving the business. Financial controls are very useful because accounting data may be used to generate useful reports, to effectively cash, to properly manage customer and supplier payments and to comply with tax and other regulatory requirements.

10.4.1. Benchmarking/Comparison

The value of financial information is decidedly limited if there is no means of comparison to assess its significance. Current results should therefore be compared against some measure/criterion. The three main sources of information available for comparison are (1) past results, (2) budgeted performance and (3) industry studies.

These measures/benchmarks can help to monitor the business performance. The comparisons may indicate a number of areas that are worth investigating. However, the variances should be interpreted carefully in the context of the level of service provided by the business and should not elicit an impulsive (and possibly inappropriate) cost-cutting exercise. The industry averages give an indication of operating efficiency rather than an enterprise-specific analysis. Therefore, along with budget and previous period comparisons, industry comparisons provide an additional base for monitoring business performance.

10.4.2. Monitoring Improvement

Timely and accurate information enables the entrepreneur to make well-informed decisions that will build business success. Identifying the key performance indicators that have a major impact on the business helps the owner/manager to focus on the issues that really matter. Monthly performance monitoring is essential for long-term success.

Benchmarking the business against competitors and other businesses — for example, comparing key financial ratios and other indicators — can help the owner/manager to identify areas requiring improvement. More detailed analysis can provide deeper insights into opportunities for improvement. For example, analysing competitors' prices and own sales data and margins can help the owner/manager identify areas where a change in pricing might boost overall profitability (ACCA, 2016).

10.4.3. Some Useful Ratios for Financial Performance

10.4.3.1. Profitability Ratios
In order to determine the meaning and significance of a profit figure it needs to be expressed in relation to some other figure such as sales revenue, total assets or owner's equity.

Nett profit ratio. This ratio gives the nett return on sales.

Nett profit ratio = Nett profit before tax/Total sales revenue

= €64,000/€400,000 = 16.0 per cent

Profit before fixed charges ratio. This is an indication of the overall operational efficiency of the business:

Profit before fixed charges ratio = Profit before fixed charges/Total sales revenue

= €133,000/€400,000 = 33.25 per cent

Note: Profit before fixed charges is also referred to as 'gross operating profit' (GOP).

Nett return on total assets ratio. This gives an indication of how the enterprise manages total assets in generating profit. It is also useful for assessing the likelihood of obtaining more equity financing.

Nett return on total assets ratio = Nett profit after tax/Average total assets

= €96,000 = (€560,000 + €640,000)/2

= €96,000/€600,000 = 16.0 per cent

The average total assets are determined by adding the start of year and end of year figures and dividing the total by two.

This is a useful rough indicator when deciding on the purchase and funding of new assets. The resulting ratio of 16 per cent provides a basis on which the earning ability of business assets can be compared to the interest rate for bank loans.

Return on owners' equity ratio. This ratio shows how effectively a business generates profits from operations in terms of the owner's total investment.

Return on equity ratio $=$ Net profit after tax$/$Average owner's equity

€96,000 $=$ (€620,000 $+$ €680,000)$/2$

$=$ €96,000$/$€650,000 $=$ 14.8 per cent

The result shows that the business is generating an annual return of almost €15 for each €100 of owners' equity.

10.4.3.2. Operational Ratios

Revenue per available room (RevPAR). RevPAR is a combination of the average achieved room rate (AARR) and the room occupancy percentage. This ratio overcomes the limitations of using the AARR and occupancy percentage individually where, for instance, high occupancy may be achieved at the expense of a low AARR or, conversely, a high AARR at the expense of a low occupancy.

RevPAR is determined by dividing the rooms' revenue by the number of rooms available:

Revenue per available room $=$ Rooms revenue$/$Number of rooms available

$=$ €832,200$/80$ rooms $=$ €10,402.50 (annually)

This ratio is particularly useful for comparison with similar establishments and with industry averages.

Yield percentage. As an overall indication of the level of business achieved, actual revenue is related to total potential revenue calculated on the basis of 100 per cent room occupancy, and will normally use rack rate (tariff) nett of distributable service charge, value added tax and breakfast (if included) to give maximum attainable revenue.

Yield percentage   = Rooms revenue/Maximum potential rooms revenue

= €1,120,000/1,898,000

= 59 per cent

Maximum potential rooms revenue is calculated as follows:

20 single rooms	€50 × 365 days	= €365,000
60 double rooms	€70 × 365 days	= €1,533,000
Maximum potential rooms revenue		= €1,898,000

The yield percentage is a more global and sensitive ratio than other room statistics.

10.5. OPERATIONAL DECISIONS: PRICING METHODS AND ANALYTICAL TECHNIQUES

In the course of daily operations, entrepreneurs and managers in the tourism-related businesses have to make decisions that affect the financial performance of their business. In this section, the focus is on a practical application of the main pricing methods, two analytical techniques – i.e. break-even analysis or cost-volume-profit analysis (CVP) and profit sensitivity analysis (PSA) – and a technique of revenue management (i.e. yield management).

10.5.1. Pricing Methods

Pricing tourism services requires a sound knowledge of the factors that surround tourism businesses and of the market. For instance, an awareness of customer perception and expectation of product prices in the market segment is required, as well as staying informed about, what competitors are charging for similar items. This section considers (1) how enterprises set prices, (2) the factors that influence pricing decisions and (3) the main methods of pricing. Note that setting an appropriate price is one of the most critical factors in generating revenue.

10.5.1.1. Stages in Setting Prices
Owners/managers of small tourism enterprises adopt a simple approach to setting prices, based upon a combination of statistical data and the current

economic situation. A simple, easy-to-adopt process that may be followed would consist of these steps:

- Analyse the demand/target market.
- Analyse operational features: the cost structure, i.e. fixed costs (do not vary with sales volume) and variable costs (vary in proportion to sales), price and profit relationships.
- Check competitors' offering and current prices.
- Select appropriate pricing methods.
- Review current and potential cost increases.
- Take into account current and forecast inflation.
- Take into account the general economic situation.
- Set prices.

10.5.1.2. Factors Influencing Pricing Decisions

Factors that influence price decisions can be classified into two major categories, as follows (Kotler, 2000):

1. *External environmental factors*: Companies have little (or no) control over these five factors: demand, type and structure of industry, competition, legal/regulatory (taxation policy).
2. *Internal factors*: Companies have considerable control over these seven factors: pricing objectives, costs, resources, positioning (prices must reflect the desired position), distribution channel (commissions), customers (perceptions), product (influence pricing policy).

10.5.1.3. Pricing Methods

Essentially, there are four basic ways of pricing products and services, with numerous variations of each (Harris, 1999). These are briefly presented below.

Cost-plus pricing. Cost-plus pricing sets the selling price of a product based on the cost of production, plus a share of the company's overheads, plus a set percentage profit margin. A form of cost-based pricing is called cost percentage pricing, factor pricing or markup pricing.

The following equation explains cost-based pricing:

$$P = C + f(C)$$

where P = price, C = cost, f = percentage markup.

For example, €10 + 50% markup = €15 price.

The advantages of using cost-plus pricing are that (1) the price is based on factual costings, (2) management judgement is not required, (3) it is the simplest pricing method to implement, (4) it helps management to forecast costs and (5) it can be used as a control mechanism to monitor performance. The disadvantages include that (1) it ignores the price elasticity of demand,

(2) it ignores consumer perceptions of quality and (3) it fails to consider competitors' prices.

Contribution margin pricing. Contribution margin pricing is also known as marginal cost pricing. This pricing approach focuses on maximising contribution margins to recover fixed costs and generate a profit. The method requires an analysis of costs into their fixed and variable categories. Fixed costs are treated as period costs and are not absorbed into the products or services. Prices are set using marginal cost.

Contribution margin pricing facilitates a flexible pricing policy and is used for short-term (tactical) pricing decisions. The method does take account of both the market and the costs.

Going rate pricing. This pricing method is also known as market pricing. In this case, prices are set in relation to the perceived market need, and costs are tailored accordingly. If going rate pricing is to be used, the entrepreneur must be prepared to manage costs in order to ensure that a profit is achieved. This is easier in manufacturing enterprises because they usually contain a high proportion of variable costs, which offers considerable opportunity for cost manipulation. On the contrary, tourism businesses normally contain a low proportion of variable costs, which provides fewer opportunities for cost adjustment.

Where going rate is used rigidly, there is a danger of undermining the quality and consistency of the services which in turn would lead to a drop in demand.

Rate of return pricing (ROR). In the past, some tourism enterprises (e.g. hotels) adhered to a €-per-thousand pricing method to ensure target return on investment (ROI). The target average achieved room rate is calculated on the basis of the total capital invested in the venture.

ROR pricing techniques remain important to help determine the feasibility of a project. The goal of ROR pricing is to find a price structure that provides the required ROI.

Micro Case 10.2:   ROR Pricing Method

The ROR method involves three steps: (1) capital required for the project must be estimated, (2) a target rate of return must be set and (3) the volume of sales required to generate the profit target must be calculated.

A company invests €10 million in a hotel unit. Given a target ROR of 20%, the profit required from the venture is €2 million each year. What volume of sales is needed to produce a nett profit of €2 million?

If the company operates in a market where a net profit on sales of 10% is the norm, then sales revenues of €20 million are required (€2,000,000 × 0.10). The task of the owner/manager is to select a sales mix (total sales from rooms, **F&B** and functions) and pricing policies that can generate the €20 million sales revenue and €2 million profit.

Note: There is no single, universal approach to the formulation of a business pricing policy, nor a single, universal pricing method.

10.5.1.4. Price Promotions
The impact of price promotions needs to be carefully evaluated in the planning stage to protect core revenue business and the business image. In low season, price promotions make a realistic contribution towards fixed costs and justify the cost and effort of their development and promotion. However, caution is called for price-led promotions help to boost sales in low-business periods, but they do have limitations and drawbacks.

Another interesting (and challenging) issue is that of product price bundles, where the enterprise bundles a package of benefits at an all-inclusive price, for example: package holidays, activity leisure breaks, 24-hour conference delegate packages, wedding receptions and set menus (food and drink combinations). Despite the challenges, these bundles have two advantages: the perception of added value and the ease of booking all the features of the bundle at one price in one transaction.

10.5.2. Analytical Techniques

10.5.2.1. Break-even Analysis
The purpose of break-even analysis is to enable management to calculate various cost, volume and profit scenarios in order to make appropriate pricing decisions. A business achieves its break-even point (BEP) when total revenues are equal to total costs and no profit or loss is made. BEP is an important intermediate point that must be reached prior to making a profit (Harris, 1999).

To work out the BEP, the following information is required: fixed costs (FC) and variable costs (VC). Total costs (TC) are the sum of FC + VC.

If the variable costs are 38 per cent and the fixed costs are €85,000.00, what is the sales volume required to achieve the BEP?

$$\text{Sales for break-even} = \text{Fixed costs} + 38 \text{ per cent of sales}$$

$$X = \text{€}85,000 + 0.38X$$

$$0.62X = \text{€}85,000$$

$$X = \text{€}85,000/0.62 = \text{€}137,097.$$

If the customers are spending on average €25.00, the business has to service at least 5,484 clients to achieve the BEP. The break-even figure informs us about the sales needed to cover the fixed and variable costs.

Normally we have to achieve a sales volume for a target profit. The same principle is applied here as for break-even sales volume. How much sales revenue is required to cover fixed costs of €85,000, variable costs of 38 per cent and generate a profit of, let us say, €25,000? The rule is simply to treat profit as a fixed cost, as follows:

$$\text{Sales for target profit} = \text{Fixed costs} + \text{Target profit} + 38 \text{ per cent of sales}$$
$$X = €85,000 + €25,000 + 0.38X$$
$$0.68\,X = €110,000$$
$$= €161,765.00$$

If we divide the above amount by the average spending of clients (€25), the business has to achieve a volume of 6,471 customers to reach target profit.

10.5.2.2. Profit Sensitivity Analysis

Let us presume that we are producing next year's budget and that we would like to improve on the current year's net profit by 8 per cent. In order to achieve this, we could consider a number of options, such as raising prices, increasing the volume of business, cutting costs or a combination of these options.

However, if we increase prices by 8 per cent, will profit rise by 8 per cent? If we reduce costs by 8 per cent, will profit increase by 8 per cent? We are not able to give a precise answer.

In order to objectively determine the influence of different key factors on net profit, we first need to identify the factors and then determine the extent to which each one affects profit. Key factors influencing net profit are: number of clients, average spending/rate, occupancy rate, cost of sales, other variable costs and fixed costs.

It is important to determine the extent to which each factor affects net profit. This can be achieved by applying the PSA. In order to perform a PSA, we need to calculate the 'profit multipliers' of the business we are considering, as follows:

- Identify the key financial and operating factors of the business.
- Assume a change in each key factor of 8 per cent.
- Determine the resulting change in net profit caused by each key factor, holding other factors constant.
- Compute the profit multipliers (PMs) as follows:

$$\text{PMs} = \frac{\% \text{ change in net profit}}{\% \text{ change in key factors}}$$

- Rank the profit multipliers in the order of magnitude and interpret the results.

PSA can assist a business owner in the following ways: (1) it enables the measurement of the relative impact of key factors on net profit, (2) it identifies business orientation (is it cost or market oriented?) and (3) it identifies the most fruitful areas for profit improvement (will the business benefit more by reducing costs, increasing sales volume or raising prices?).

10.5.3. A Revenue Management Technique: Yield Management

Revenue management is about maximising revenues, revenue growth. Entrepreneurs and managers should consider revenue management as an integrated function of business operations. As for the metrics in hotel businesses (ADR, RevPAR or rate of occupancy), the most important in terms of revenue measurement is RevPAR. Revenue management should be viewed as a constant search to optimise the bottom line, even in adverse market conditions where revenue growth may not be possible.

Tourism businesses seek to maximise their potential revenue by using price as a demand management tool. Known as yield management (YM), this is a complex form of price discrimination used to help maximise RevPAR. Because of the focus on sales, YM is also known as revenue management. Room yield is the ratio, given as a percentage, between the actual room sales revenues and the total potential room sales revenue during a given period (see Section 10.4.3).

YM is a technique that assists in the maximisation of revenue from the sale of a product or service bearing two characteristics: (1) perishability over the passage of time and (2) fixed capacity. Clearly, hotel rooms, flight seats and organised tours fit this profile. An unsold room/flight seat is a sale lost forever. Conversely, but similarly, it is impossible to add additional rooms or seats simply because of higher demand.

Essentially, YM works as follows:

- When demand exceeds supply, the objective is to maximise room rate.
- When supply exceeds demand, the objective changes to the maximisation of room occupancy, to some extent even at the expense of average rate.

The formula to calculate yield is: Revenue raised/Revenue potential × 100.

To calculate the yield ratio of a business, the following information is required:

- period of time (day, week, month, quarter, year);
- rooms: number, types and rates;
- potential room revenue;

- rooms sold and
- achieved room rate.

The revenue realised is the number of rooms sold, multiplied by the achieved room rate. The potential room revenue is:

All room types × Number of rooms in each room type × Each room type's rack rate.

Micro Case 10.3: Yield Management

The example in Table 10.2 of a 200-bedroom hotel operating at 80 per cent occupancy with an achieved room rate of €90, for one day, helps to illustrate the method.

Period: One day. Rooms sold: 200 rooms × 80 per cent occupancy = 160 rooms sold

Revenue achieved: Rooms sold × Achieved room rate = 160 × €90 = €14,400.

Total potential revenue: €22,800

$$\text{Yield}(\text{Revenue achieved}/\text{revenue potential}) \times 100$$
$$= (14{,}400/22{,}800) \times 100$$
$$= 63.16 \text{ per cent}$$

If the hotel decided to improve its yield, sacrificing 5 per cent of its occupancy in order to increase the achieved room rate to €110, the yield calculations would be:

Period: One day. Rooms sold: 200 rooms × 75 per cent occupancy = 150 rooms sold

$$\text{Revenue achieved: Rooms sold} \times \text{Achieved room rate}$$
$$= 150 \times €110 = €16{,}500$$

Table 10.2. YM Calculation.

Room Type	Number of Rooms	Rate (€)	Potential Room Revenue (€)
Executive suites	20	180	3,600
Double rooms	60	120	7,200
Single rooms	120	100	12,000

$$\text{Yield}(\text{Revenue achieved/revenue potential}) \times 100$$
$$= (16,500/22,800) \times 100$$
$$= 72.37 \text{ per cent}$$

Software programs have been developed to calculate the complex data and compute the recommended prices quoted to customers. The advantage of YM is that it is a marketing tool designed to tackle the problems caused by the characteristics that typify the service industry. It is always better to sell a room at a low price on a given night rather than have an empty room, because of the low marginal cost to service another room. The disadvantage of YM is the customers' awareness and perception of the variation in prices quoted to them (Harris, 2013).

10.6. INVESTMENT DECISIONS: CAPITAL EXPENDITURE

Financial management drives improvements in the business, as well expansion and growth. This section focuses on the methods that are used to assess capital expenditure. Examples of investment decisions (also known as capital expenditure) include purchasing new equipment, and extending and refurbishing existing facilities. These are often critical decisions for a business because they normally entail large sums of money, long time frames and irreversible commitments.

10.6.1. Investment Decisions

Major investments need careful evaluation to ensure full understanding of the potential financial and business impact. Some crucial questions that need to be asked include the following:

- What increase in profits is expected from making the investment, and how does this compare to the cost of financing?
- How quickly would the investment pay for itself? (The longer it takes, the higher the risks are likely to be.)
- What would be the impact on the cash flow and overall financing position? How can the new investment be best financed without undermining the ability to finance the rest of the business?
- More broadly, how does an opportunity fit in with the existing business and overall strategy?

In order to answer these questions, entrepreneurs may require assistance with financial evaluation which includes preparing a cash flow forecast for the investment, identifying key risk factors and assessing the impact of each (ACCA, 2016).

10.6.2. Investment Evaluation Methods

Common investment evaluation methods include the following:

- *Discounted cash flow (DCF) analysis*: This makes it easy to compare the expected returns from an investment to its initial cost.
- *Internal rate of return (IRR)*: This compares expected returns with the costs of funding.
- *Payback period*: This is a more straightforward measurement which indicates how long it would take to recover the investment.

10.6.2.1. Discounted Cash Flow
This method is the most widely accepted for evaluating investment decisions because it recognises that money has a time value. The fact that the value of money is directly affected by time is expressed in the concept 'interest'. For example: if we discount €1,000 receivable in one year's time back to today's value, we find it is worth €909. Again, if we discount €1,000 receivable in two years' time back to today's value, it will be worth €826 and so on.

10.6.2.2. DCF: Net Present Value Method
This method is based on an assumed minimum rate of return (discount rate) and is usually used to discount (multiply) the future cash flows to their present value. The investment outlay is subtracted from the present value of cash flows, leaving a residual sum which is the Net Present Value (NPV). A decision will be made in favour of a project if the NPV is a positive figure. This method is extremely useful for comparing one capital expenditure project to another. The project with the higher NPV would be selected.

10.6.2.3. DCF: Internal Rate of Return Method
This method requires the calculation of the rate of interest that will reduce the NPV of a project to zero. This enables a direct comparison between the internal rate of return and the required rate. However, care should be taken to not over-emphasise the precise figure of return as the cash flows are only estimates which may vary substantially over the lifespan of the project.

Comparison of two methods: NPV versus IRR. Despite the different approaches contained in the NPV and IRR methods, both always indicate the same 'accept' or 'reject' position for a given project. However, if two projects were being considered and only one could be selected (i.e. mutually exclusive) the NPV and IRR rankings may differ.

Hence, in the process of maximising profitability from our investments, situations will arise where alternative projects need to be ranked in order of potential profitability. In some instances, the NPV and IRR for alternative projects may produce conflicting rankings of potential profitability. The crucial and determining test for the final acceptance of a project is whether or not the IRR compares favourably with the rate of return required by the business. The NPV method is often considered a better method since it uses the same discount rate for alternative proposals, and that rate will normally represent the minimum of acceptable rate.

DCF methods provide an appropriate basis for the evaluation of an investment project because they take into account the time value of money, cash flow and profitability over the entire life of a project (Harris, 1999).

10.7. SUMMARY

Financial management is at the heart of running a successful business, especially a new venture. It directs every activity, from managing cash flow, to tracking business performance, to developing plans that would ensure making the most of opportunities. A prospective or new entrepreneur should fulfil the functions of a financial manager.

To contribute to the successful and sustainable operation of a tourism venture, this chapter outlined the key financial issues and presented in a practical way the main methods and techniques used when making operational and investment decisions. The chapter dealt with the following:

- meaning, objectives and functions of financial management;
- the main financial statements;
- planning and budgeting;
- monitoring performance;
- the pricing process and the leading factors that influence pricing decisions;
- pricing methods;
- analytical techniques and methods for making operational decisions; and
- principal methods of evaluating capital expenditure projects.

This chapter attempted to equip a prospective entrepreneur with the background knowledge (main competencies). It discussed the principal methods and techniques (skills) for managing the financial resources of a venture.

Review Questions

Check your understanding of this chapter by answering the following questions or discussing the topics below:

- Present the objectives and functions of financial management.
- Briefly discuss the three main financial statements.
- Discuss the types and uses of budgets.
- Present the main measures for monitoring financial performance.
- Discuss all factors that influence pricing decisions.
- Evaluate the four main pricing methods.
- Try to apply the break-even analysis in a simple business context.
- Discuss why the profit sensitivity analysis is useful for operational decisions.
- Discuss the method of yield management.
- Present and evaluate the main methods of assessing investment projects.

REFERENCES AND FURTHER READING

Association of Chartered Certified Accountants. (2016). *Financial management and business success – A guide for entrepreneurs*. London: ACCA. Retrieved from www.accaglobal.com. Accessed on 20 August 2017.

Bowie, D., & Buttle, F. (2004). *Hospitality marketing: An introduction*. Oxford: Elsevier, Butterworth-Heinemann.

Brooks, R. (2015). *Financial management: Core concepts* (3rd ed.). London: Pearson.

Business Dictionary. (2017). Financial management. Retrieved from http://www.businessdictionary.com/definition/financial-management.html. Accessed on 4 April 2017.

Deepika, M., & Rani, M. (2014). Managing business finance. *International Research Journal of Management Science and Technology*, 5(4), 28.

Forgacs, G. (2010). *Revenue management: Maximizing revenue in hospitality operations* (12th ed.). East Lansing, MI: American Hotel & Motel Association.

Haitham, N., & Jaya, A. (2015). Current assets management of small enterprises. *Journal of Economic Studies*, 42(4), 549–560.

Harris, P. (2013). *Profit planning* (3rd ed.). London: Goodfellow Publishers.

Harris, P. J. (1999). *Profit planning*. (2nd ed.). Oxford: Butterworth-Heinemann.

Hayes, D. K., & Miller, A. (2010). *Revenue management for the hospitality industry*. New York, NY: John Wiley & Sons.

Kotler, P. (2000). *Marketing management*. New Jersey, NY: Prentice-Hall Inc.

Kotler, P., Bowen, J., & Makens, J. (2003). *Marketing for hospitality and tourism* (3rd ed.). New Jersey, NY: Prentice-Hall Inc.

Legohérel, P., Fyall, A., & Poutier, E. (Eds.). (2013). *Revenue management for hospitality and tourism*. London: Goodfellow Publishers.

Management Study Guide. (2017). Financial management. Retrieved from http://www.management-studyguide.com/financial-management.htm. Accessed on 8 April 2017.

Netlibrary. (2017). Financial management. Retrieved from http://www.netlibrary.cc/articles/eng/ Financial_management. Accessed on 10 April 2017.

Tranter, K. A., Stuart-Hill, T., & Parker, J. (2008). *An introduction to revenue management for the hospitality industry: Principles and practices for the real world*. London: Pearson.

Yeoman, I., & McMahon-Beattie, U. (2004). *Revenue management and pricing: Case studies and applications*. Andover: Cengage Learning EMEA.

Yeoman, I., McMahon, U., & Ingold, A. (2001). *Yield management for the service industries* (2nd ed.). Andover: Cengage Learning EMEA.

CHAPTER 11

PROVIDING SERVICE QUALITY AND CUSTOMER CARE IN TOURISM BUSINESSES

Magdalena Petronella (Nellie) Swart

ABSTRACT

Purpose — *Tourism is a service-intensive industry where tourists' experiences are framed by the quality of service provided. The main aim of this chapter is to offer conceptual guidelines on the service quality expectations and experiences of tourists and how this can be maintained through customer care.*

Methodological approach — *A literature review was conducted where theories relevant to service quality and customer care were explored to design conceptual frameworks and guidelines for small business entrepreneurs/ managers.*

Findings — *Psychological aspects related to the delivery of quality service are influenced by an array of characteristics, variables and managerial perspectives. Furthermore, tourists value the same service quality variables in the service quality assessment of their expectations and experiences.*

Research limitations — *Due to the exploratory nature of this chapter, interpretation of the findings must be done in the context of the discussed literature review with practical examples.*

Practical implications — *Service quality and customer care are essential elements in meeting tourists' expectations. The five-step approach to address the service quality gaps in a tourism business provides valuable guidelines in*

The Emerald Handbook of Entrepreneurship in Tourism, Travel and Hospitality:
Skills for Successful Ventures, 191–206
Copyright © 2018 by Emerald Publishing Limited
ISBN: 978-1-78743-530-8/doi:10.1108/978-1-78743-529-220181007

the inter-relationships between the various aspects related to service delivery. The delivery of quality service is maintained by the creation of good relationships through customer care.

Originality/value — *The illustration of the inter-relationships between analytical frameworks and models provides a unique opportunity for small business entrepreneurs to create an awareness of the delivery of quality service and customer care.*

Keywords: Service quality; customer care; satisfaction; tourist experience; tourist expectations; small business management

---

Learning Objectives

After working through this chapter, you should be able to:

- outline the characteristics of service products in tourism;
- explain why service quality is important in the management of a tourism business;
- discuss the service quality variables that are relevant to a tourism business;
- propose a case study with practical guidelines on service excellence for micro tourism businesses;
- describe the relevance of customer care to a micro business manager.

11.1. INTRODUCTION

Literature is rich with investigations related to service excellence, service quality and customer care and yet this remains a popular research area in tourism (Arabatzis & Grigoroudis, 2010). One of the main reasons stems from the fact that tourism is a people's industry (Cheng, Chen, & Chang, 2008), influenced by different customer behaviours, resulting in many unanswered questions on how to satisfy their needs. Another reason is that the tourism industry is a labour-intensive industry, where tourism experiences are measured in the quality of services they receive during their stay at a tourism establishment. In a global business environment, where tourists from an array of nationalities travel to different destinations, their own cultural background and perspectives often frame their perception of experience. This, together with the fact that tourism employees play an important role in the delivery of quality service creates challenges in the delivery of service quality (Yee, Yeung, & Edwin Cheng, 2010).

Tourists are people, who are the creators of their own experiences (Björk, 2014). These experiences are based on their cognitive (how do they think), conative (how do they feel) and affective (how do they behave) responses (Fishbein & Ajzen, 1975). When experience is interpreted from a 'conative' perspective, reference is made to the physical activity of the tourists; for example, are they clapping hands after the performance of an artist. When tourists are making sense of their experience, for example why did they enjoy the show, it is done from a 'cognitive' experience. Preferences and emotions of tourists are part of their affective experience when, for example, they are engaging with staff at a tourism establishment, and they have a feeling of belonging (Getz, 2012). In many micro tourism businesses, one of the challenges related to service delivery is the delivery of services by inexperienced front-line service providers (employees), who deliver the service from their own understanding of what service quality is, which might not be aligned with international norms and standards. Furthermore, every tourist has a specific perception of what quality is (Swarbrooke & Horner, 1999). This requires more tolerance from tourists to allow employees to deliver services, from their own cultural and behavioural perspectives, that can contribute to an enriching experience at a tourism business. If tourists have an enjoyable experience, they are more likely to return to experience the same service quality, which enhances the economic sustainability of the business (Alegre & Garau, 2010).

Service quality, customer care and service excellence are all ingredients of an 'experience economy', where tourists are willing to pay more for an experience that is considered as exclusive or memorable. This enables tourism businesses and offerings, such as a world heritage site or an accommodation establishment, to develop a sustainable competitive advantage (Middleton, Fyall, & Morgan, 2009). Therefore, we need to know how 'service', 'quality', 'service excellence', 'service quality' and 'customer care' are defined in a tourism context, as this creates a mutual understanding amongst all involved actors (providers and consumers of services).

George (2011, p. 562) defines a *service* as 'any activity or benefit that one party can offer to another that is essentially intangible and does not result in the ownership of anything'. Gronroos (1990, p. 27) is one of the most prominent researchers in service marketing. He defines *service* as:

> ... *an activity or service of activities of a more or less intangible nature that normally, but not necessarily, take place in interactions between customers and service employees and/or physical resources or goods and/or systems of the service provider, which are provided as solutions to customer problems.*

Quality refers to when an 'accommodation establishments should ensure that the products it provides are of an acceptable quality and match or exceed expectations' (adapted from SABS, 2012, p. 16). *Service quality* is defined as '... the delivery of excellent or superior services relative to consumer expectations' (Zeithaml & Bitner, 2003, p. 85), and as '... a customer's perception of service excellence' (Ismail, Haron, & Ibrahim, 2006, p. 740). Furthermore, Page (2015) indicates that a tourism experience instils an emotional response such as excitement, pleasure or satisfaction. This is further enriched through the notion of superior service *(excellence)* that leads to a *tourist service experience* where '... a tourists' experience at all the touch points when visiting the country' (NDT, 2011). However, it is important to recognise that *customer care* has different meanings to different tourists, as it is perceived of whatever the tourists believe it should be (Borton & Borton, 1994). Against this background, it is evident that tourism services are delivered against a broad spectrum of service requirements and understandings.

This chapter aims at providing practical guidelines to prospective tourism entrepreneurs on how to provide service excellence through the adoption and implementation of different service quality strategies. This will ultimately indicate how much the tourism entrepreneurs or managers care about their customers. The discussion starts with an outline of the characteristics of service products in tourism, followed by an explanation on why service quality is important in the management of a tourism business. Service quality variables, relevant to a tourism business, form a foundation for a case study with practical guidelines on service excellence, for micro tourism businesses. The chapter concludes with a description on the relevance of customer care to a micro business manager.

11.2. CHARACTERISTICS OF SERVICE PRODUCTS

Before discussing the concepts of service quality, service excellence and customer care, it is important to understand the context in which tourism services are delivered. As mentioned in the introduction, tourism services are regarded as the 'product' offered by tourism businesses and is described through different characteristics (Evans, 2015). These characteristics are outlined below.

Intangibility: A tourism product cannot be tested or sampled before the consumer uses or experiences it. Tourists buy an experience/offering based on the brand loyalty, price, location and recommendations. Therefore, tourism entrepreneurs need to allocate sufficient resources in communicating and promoting its offering. For example, a guest house must have an operational marketing budget, which includes actions such as advertisement and digital marketing, e.g. online purchase and social media presence.

Inseparability: The delivering of the tourism service and experience (or consumption) take place during the 'moment of truth' or service encounter. Moment of truth is defined as 'the time and place where the customer interacts with the organisation' (Evans, 2015, p. 686). To meet the desired level of service quality, the guest house owner/manager will carefully select one employee to handle all the housekeeping duties. This employee needs to undergo training to develop the appropriate skills for guest services.

Perishability: This means a tourism product cannot be stored for later consumption, for example if a room was not sold for the evening, the potential revenue generated will be lost forever. Tourism entrepreneurs/managers need to understand their market and market needs to have the right quantities of the tourism product available, to have the 'ideal capacity'. This implies that the guest house owner/manager needs to monitor the occupancy rate of the guest house to avoid waste of any resources and to achieve the most cost-effective operation of the business.

Heterogeneity: Not all tourism products are identical. Tourism staff must be motivated to deliver tourism service consistently and within the service quality guidelines of the business. Employees have to be aware of specific tourist needs that must be met by maintaining the same high level of standards throughout the appropriate delivering of the services. This is often easier said than done, as services require an understanding of complex human behaviour during specific circumstances and contexts. For example, usually there are two or more receptionists on duty at a hotel, who have their own personality and might come from different cultural backgrounds. They have received the same training, are using the same phrases to greet guest and follow the same check-in and out procedures. However, their body language might be different and their accent/pronunciation might be different. A tourist having a hearing disability might experience the delivered service as inconsistent and non-identical.

Ownership: Tourists use services and do not 'own' them; therefore, tourism business owners/managers strive to gain loyalty amongst their tourists, satisfy their needs and hope they will visit their establishment again. Loyalty programmes are popular amongst most hotel, airlines and restaurant groups in an attempt to retain the tourists. Relationship marketing, through public relations and promotional activities, aims at giving customers a sense of belonging and a feeling of value for money for the service experience. It is known that some domestic tourists visit the same destination and stay at the same accommodation business every summer holiday. Their repeated visit is motivated by discounts received as a loyal member of the accommodation business, the relationships they have built with the owners and staff, as well as their perception about value-for-money.

11.3. THE IMPORTANCE OF SERVICE QUALITY IN TOURISM

Service quality is one of the important tourism business strategies for gaining a competitive advantage, but this is influenced by the human factor, i.e. the attitude of the owner, manager and employees working in the business. Approximately 90 per cent of a customer's quality learning takes place within the first five service engagements (Iyengar, Ansari, & Gupta, 2007) and are considered to be performed by people. Therefore, the delivery of service quality requires a range of personal and professional skills. A special training is needed to deal with the large degree of personal involvement in the tourism service delivery. One of the biggest challenges with service delivery in the tourism industry is the entry requirements, as the skills requirements are considered easy and do not require extensive knowledge. This notion leads to the dissatisfaction of many tourists and the poor performance of tourism businesses. The development of knowledge, competencies and skills on how to offer quality service can assist in overcoming some of these operational challenges.

Service quality is associated with the flawless or 'zero defect' performance of the business. However, in a service industry such as tourism, service quality is only assessed during the 'moment of truth' when the interaction between the customer and the tourism provider takes place (Evans, 2015). One of the challenges is the delivery of quality services stems from the fragmented experience of many tourists. For example, if a tourist decides to buy a holiday package to the Maldives, the tourism experience involves a range of tourism providers, such as a travel agent, the airlines company, the local transfer company and the resort itself. However, tourists will assess their service experience on the total holiday package and not the individual components/service elements offered by different service providers.

11.4. SERVICE QUALITY VARIABLES IN TOURISM

The owner/manager of tourism business has a selection of service quality models to choose from such as SERVQUAL (Parasuraman, Zeithaml, & Berry, 1988), SERVPERF (Cronin & Taylor, 1992), DINESERV (Stevens, Knutson, & Patton, 1995) and RENTQUAL (Ekiz, Bavik, & Arasli, 2009) to name a few. More recently, Swart (2013) developed a Service Quality Scorecard (SQSC), an assessment tool determining which variables influence service excellence in the business tourism industry. One of the most widely used models in service quality is the SERVQUAL. This model was developed by Parasuraman, Zeithaml, and Berry in the mid-1980s and is defined as 'a framework developed to consider service quality' (Evans, 2015, p. 868). Mill (2011) is of the opinion that the SERVQUAL model remains the most appropriate mechanism to explain guest satisfaction in the tourism-related industries. The five dimensions of the SERVQUAL model are reliability, responsiveness, assurance, tangibility and empathy (Parasuraman et al., 1988). These dimensions/variables are the most popular and most widely used in assessing service quality (Chou, Liu, Huang,

Yih, & Han, 2011; Kuo, Chou, & Sun, 2011). These variables are outlined below.

Reliability is the 'ability to perform the promised service dependably and accurately' (Parasuraman et al., 1988, p. 23). George (2011, p. 464) supports this definition by stating '... the organisation's employees should perform the desired service correctly the first time ...' to meet its promise. In a hospitality business, such as a guest house, this means that the bed must be made correctly the first time, and the waiter must deliver the food order according to the guest's requirements without any mistakes.

Responsiveness is the 'willingness to help customers and provide prompt service' (Parasuraman et al., 1988, p. 23) and the assurance '... that the service is delivered promptly, and the staff are willing and ready to serve and help consumers' (George, 2011, p. 464). When a guest checks in at a guest house, staff must assist him/her immediately and not have to wait for any reason.

Assurance relates to the 'knowledge and courtesy of employees and their ability to inspire trust and confidence' (Parasuraman et al., 1988, p. 23) and 'the ability [of employees] to convey trustworthiness and evoke a feeling of confidence in consumers' (George, 2011, p. 465). During the delivery of the service, a waiter needs to know the menu and be able to make recommendations to the guest on what to order. This will create confidence in the guests that they have ordered the right meal and results in benefit to all actors involved: customers' satisfaction, higher tip service for waiter and better performance for the business.

Tangibility is defined as '... the physical facilities, equipment, and appearance of personnel' (Parasuraman et al., 1988, p. 23) and '... the appearances of physical facilities, equipment, personnel and written materials' (Ismail, Haron, Ibrahim, & Isa, 2006, p. 740). Tourists are exposed to different personalities, behaviours, attitudes and appearances of employees from different cultural backgrounds and expectations. Tourism services become tangible when the employees become part of the tourism experience and frame the image of the business in the mind of the tourists. It is therefore the responsibility of tourism business owner and manager to equip the employees with necessary competencies, capabilities and skills to deliver services to tourists in a flexible and customised way (Evans, 2015).

Empathy portray the 'caring, individualised attention the firm provides its customers' (Parasuraman et al., 1988, p. 23). However, George (2011, p. 465) elaborates on this definition by stating that 'employees need to treat consumers as individuals'. For many tourists, travelling is a stressful experience as travel agents can make incorrect reservations, or they might have misread some instructions about transfers or other services. When incidents like this happen, tourism suppliers need to have empathy towards their clients and try to assist them by providing personal attention and care to resolve the matter immediately.

Against the background of these service quality variables, it is necessary to know that the differences in service quality are measured through gaps, where the difference between tourist expectation and tourist experience are determined. Tourism experience relates to a higher order psychological need, such as prestige and socialising, which contribute to the overall well-being of a tourist (Prebensen, Chen, & Uysal, 2014). To address this psychological need Zeithaml, Parasuraman, and Berry (1990) have identified four gaps in the SERVQUAL model, while Mill (2011) suggests a five-step approach to address these gaps, as indicated in Fig. 11.1.

From Fig. 11.1, it is evident that the four SERVQUAL gaps (Parasuraman et al., 1988) do not follow a chronological order when it is matched with the five-step approach (Evans, 2015; Mill, 2011). This is not critical for the purpose of this discussion; however, it is more important to identify the problems and to note which step addresses which gap in this figure.

- Step 1 focuses on the identification of the problem, which means that the tourism business owner needs to understand WHAT is the problem related to service delivery, before any further action can be taken.
- In Step 2, the tourism business owner needs to manage realistic service offerings by ensuring that the level of promised services meet the expected levels (Gap 4). This means a tourism business, such as guest house, cannot promise porter service and not deliver this to the guests.

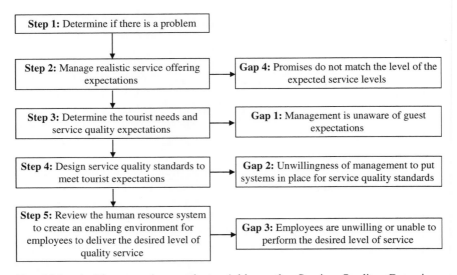

Fig. 11.1. A Five-step Approach to Address the Service Quality Gaps in a Tourism Business. *Source*: Author's creation.

- A determination of the tourist needs and service quality expectations is the next step (Step 3), as the tourism business owner if often unaware of the guest's expectations (Gap 1). For example, guest might expect to have access to coffee and tea services on a 24-hour basis, but the guest house owner might not be aware of this expectation and only offer tea and coffee services from 06:00 until 20:00 daily.
- Tourism business managers and owners are required to design service quality standards to meet tourists' expectations (Step 4); however, they are often unwilling to put systems in place for the required service quality standards (Gap 2). Guest house owners are sometimes reluctant to put policies and procedures in place for the management of service quality, as this requires additional financial resources and often requires the appointment of additional staff to oversee the service quality standards.
- The last step requires a review of the human resources system to create a supportive environment for the employees to deliver the desired level of quality service (Step 5), but this can also lead to unwillingness of employees to render performance of the desired level (Gap 3). Unwillingness of employees to adapt new service quality standards are a challenge in most tourism businesses. It is therefore important to put performance assessment in place for the employees and to motivate them through different staff incentive programmes.

The above-mentioned steps and gaps provide valuable guidelines to owners and managers of tourism business on how to manage the service quality standards in their business.

11.5. SERVICE EXCELLENCE: PRACTICAL GUIDELINES FOR A MICRO TOURISM BUSINESS

One of the biggest challenges in the implementation of the entrepreneurial toolkit amongst micro tourism businesses owners and managers is the lack of experience of being tourists themselves. Some of the tourism entrepreneurs have never travelled outside the geographical boarders of a village or municipality. This situation results in providing tourism services from their own cultural perspective and background. In many cases, in-house skills training is passed on from one employee to another, resulting in a perceived 'correct' service delivery that continues to exist in a tourism business. The intention of the service delivery is genuine, but it becomes evident that the employees 'don't know, what they don't know'. It is against this background that we present practical guidelines on service quality in tourism, as an attempt to enable new tourism business owners/managers to deliver the level of service required by tourists.

Table 11.1.   Measurement of Expectation and Experience of a Service Quality Statement.

With regard to ...	My EXPECTATION of service excellence ...					My EXPERIENCE of service excellence ...				
... how satisfied you are with the level of service quality you have received	1	2	3	4	5	1	2	3	4	5

Source: Author's creation

In a national survey amongst South African domestic tourists in 2012, we asked individuals/tourists to score a number of variables related to their service expectation and experience at accommodation establishments. Respondents had to answer a number of questions about their service quality experience at an accommodation establishment. Two five-point Likert scales were used to measure the guest's expectation and experience of the statement, as indicated in Table 11.1.

If a respondent felt that 'they were always satisfied with the level of service quality received', they had to mark option 5 with a cross (X). If they feel that 'they were always dissatisfied with the level of service quality received', they had to mark option 1. However, if they felt 'that they were satisfied with the level of service quality received, but not always', a mark on option 3 was required to the side that reflected their experience and/or expectations the best. Respondents had to select an option in both scales (the 'my expectation of service excellence' scale as well as the 'my experience of service excellence' scale). The responses from the questions enabled the researcher to determine the scores of each item in the questionnaire (known as the measurement instrument). Scores were related to 'before the visit', 'during their stay' at the accommodation establishment and when they 'left' the establishment, post-experience. We regrouped questions with similar themes, which resulted in the model indicated in Fig. 11.2.

In the following subsections, the questions with the highest scores are reported, as this is an indication of which criteria are the most important in the measurement of service quality at an accommodation establishment, as indicated in Fig. 11.2.

11.5.1. Before Guests Visit the Accommodation Establishment

First, we discuss the expectation results 'before the guests arrive' at the accommodation establishment. These results highlighted that 'easiness to obtain information' about the accommodation establishment was the most important

Fig. 11.2. Experiences and Expectations of Service Quality. *Source*: Author's creation

factor for guest before arrival at the accommodation establishment, for example a guest house. 'Real-time feedback during the making of a reservation', the 'accurate message during the first encounter' and 'updated directions to the establishment' are also important.

Experience results, before the guest arrive at the accommodation establishment, emphasised that guest wants to know what products or services are included in the advertised price. Guests want to obtain information easily about the product and service offerings at the establishment and want updated information delivered to them correctly the first time.

Based on these results, tourists regard the *message and information* shared by the accommodation business as the most important factor to consider before they visit the establishment.

11.5.2. During the Stay at the Accommodation Establishment

Respondents awarded high scores on various *expectation* questions during their stay at the accommodation establishments. The cleanliness of the property's facilities, together with the courteousness of staff were regarded as the most important factors, followed by the ability to resolve the guest's complaints, a value for money experience and the safety of the location and establishment.

Guests were sensitive towards the equal treatment, respectful behaviour and prompt response to their requests. On the other hand, tourists rated the cleanliness of the accommodation establishments the highest in terms of their experience. Guests indicated that they felt safe at the accommodation establishments and locations and experienced that the sleeping conditions were quiet. They experienced the staff to be courteous and willing to assist them.

Service excellence, together with accommodation product offering and quality assurance are the important factors based on the guest's experience and expectations during their stay at the accommodation establishment.

11.5.3. After Guests Having an Experience at the Establishment

Loyalty programmes were regarded as important expectation and experience criteria for guests, followed by their ability to conduct an assessment on their service experience through an online platform (provide an online review). The monitoring and evaluation process are important factors for guests after they have left the accommodation establishment. Guests also regarded to use of up-to-date technology as an important instrument to assess/measure their satisfaction and felt that employees' service delivery has to be measured through a performance appraisal system.

All the criteria mentioned under the three stages of service delivery are important guidelines for tourism business owners and managers on the skills employees require in the delivery of quality service. Training programmes can be delivered based on this information and ensure the correct transfer of skills and knowledge takes place.

11.6. MICRO CASE STUDY: CELEBRATING SERVICE EXCELLENCE IN SOUTH AFRICA

Service excellence is acknowledged as a key driver of a sustainable business and will enable South Africans to deliver an unforgettable customer service experience to tourists (DEAT, 2008). A culture of service excellence means to have the right people in the right jobs, empowerment of front-line employees and a very good understanding of tourists' needs and requirements. One of the great challenges in customer service is the impossibility to quantify customer care, together with the expectation to meet or exceed the tourists' expectations. Customer service relate to the moment-of-truth between the tourist and the employee of the tourism business (George, 2011). Therefore, tourism businesses should consistently monitor, evaluate and continually improve their offering and service provision against criteria such as (1) consistent collection and evaluation of information, (2) accuracy of information, (3) revision and evaluation of monitoring tools, (4) feedback systems, (5) reporting medium of stakeholders and (6) rewards and awards system (Adapted from SABS, 2012, p. 18). Against this background, the Lilizela Awards was created to celebrate service excellence in the South African tourism industry.

The Lilizela Awards acknowledge and reward tourism businesses for the delivery of quality tourism services and products in order to improve the competitiveness of South Africa as a tourism destination. Under this scheme of service excellence, there are five categories, namely (1) accommodation, (2) meetings, exhibitions and special events (MESE), (3) tourist guides, (4) tour operator and (5) visitor experience of the year. The public is invited to nominate and vote for tourism businesses excelling in innovation, excellence and creativity. For more information, one could visit http://www.lilizela.co.za/

11.7. THE RELEVANCE OF CUSTOMER CARE

Customer care is about the ability to look after and create good relationships with tourists. It is expected from business owners, managers and staff to be familiar with the following qualities in providing customer care to tourists (Borton & Borton, 1994):

Act in a professional manner: In the modern information age, tourists value the handling of their personal details with discretion and confidentiality.

Have a positive attitude: Tourism is a people's business, where tourists regard personal interaction as important. Positive tourist responses are elicited through enthusiasm of the employee rendering the services.

Be polite: Politeness is essential at all times and establish good relationships between the tourists and employees providing the services. Polite employees' are also regarded as staff with good manners and are respected for the manner in how they behave towards the tourists.

Be efficient: Attitude, knowledge and skills are the three key characteristics to the efficient delivery of services to tourists. Knowledge support the competence of the staff to provide the services to tourists, while skills are acquired through repetition and practice on the job. However, the staff's attitude and behaviour compliment to the knowledge and skills during the service delivery process.

Be accurate: Tourists consider the accurate, reliable and timely information as one of the most important characteristic for customer. Inaccurate information can result in the loss of valuable time and have financial implications.

11.8. SUMMARY

The aim of this chapter was to provide practical guidelines to tourism entrepreneurs on how to provide service excellence through the adoption and implementation of various service quality strategies. The different concepts were defined in order to provide context for the interpretation of terms such as 'service', 'quality', 'service quality', 'service excellence' and 'customer care'.

The five characteristics − intangibility, inseparability, perishability, heterogeneity and ownership − of service products in tourism context were also presented. Practical examples indicated how these characteristics could be interpreted in tourism context. We have seen the importance of service quality focus in the delivery of flawless performance of service during the decisive encounters (moments-of-truth) and its related challenges from a tourism business perspective. The chapter also highlighted how SERVQUAL is still seen as one of the more appropriate models to assess and measure service quality. Thus, the five dimensions − reliability, responsiveness, assurance, tangibility and empathy − were outlined. This was followed by a useful tool; a five-step approach to address the four gaps in the SERVQUAL model, which provided valuable guidance to tourism business owners, managers and employees on how to address challenges related to service quality. Practical guidelines on service excellence were briefly discussed, based on the results from a national study on service excellence amongst domestic tourists in South Africa, followed by another case study on the celebration of service excellence. The chapter concluded with a discussion on the relevance of customer care in providing high quality service to tourists.

Review Questions

Now you may check your understanding of this chapter by discussing the topics below:

- Define the concept 'service' from a tourism business perspective.
- Explain the concept 'service excellence' from a tourism business perspective.
- Discuss the five characteristics of service products in the tourism context.
- Present why service quality is one of the important tourism business strategies.
- Motivate how the five SERVQUAL variables can be applied in providing services in a tourism business.
- Discuss why customer care is important in the tourism industry.

REFERENCES AND FURTHER READING

Alegre, J., & Garau, J. (2010). Tourist satisfaction and dissatisfaction. *Annals of Tourism Research*, *37*(1), 52–73.

Arabatzis, G., & Grigoroudis, E. (2010). Visitors' satisfaction, perceptions and gap analysis: The case of Dadia-Lefkimi-Souflion National Park. *Forest Policy and Economics*, *12*(3), 163–172.

Björk, P. (2014). Tourist experience value: Tourist experience and life satisfaction. In N. K. Prebensen, J. S. Chen, & M. Uysal (Eds.), *Creating experience value in tourism*. Boston, MA: CABI.

Borton, J., & Borton, L. (1994). *Interpersonal skills for travel and tourism*. London: Longman.

Cheng, J. H., Chen, F. Y., & Chang, Y. H. (2008). Airline relationship quality: An examination of Taiwanese passengers. *Tourism Management*, *29*(3), 487–499.

Chou, C. C., Liu, L. J., Huang, S.-F., Yih, J. M., & Han, T.-C. (2011). An evaluation of airline service quality using the fuzzy weighted SERVQUAL method. *Applied Soft Computing*, *11*(2), 2117–2128.

Cronin, J. J., & Taylor, S. A. (1992). Measuring service quality: A re-examination and extension. *Journal of Marketing*, *56*, 55–68.

DEAT. (2008). *Building a service excellence culture and partnerships in tourism for 2010 & beyond*. Department of Environmental Affairs and Tourism, Ekurhuleni, Gauteng.

Ekiz, E. H., Bavik, A., & Arasli, H. (2009). RENTQUAL: A new measurement scale for car rental services. *Tourism*, *57*(1), 135–153.

Evans, N. (2015). *Strategic management for tourism, hospitality and events* (2nd ed.). Abingdon, UK: Routledge.

Fishbein, M., & Ajzen, I. (1975). *Belief, attitude, intention and behaviour: An Introduction to theory and research*. Reading, MA: Addison-Wesley Publishing Company.

George, R. (2011). *Managing tourism in South Africa* (4th ed.). Cape Town: Oxford University Press.

Getz, D. (2012). *Event studies: theory, research and policy for planned events* (2nd ed.). London, UK: Routledge.

Gronroos, C. (1990). *Service management and marketing: Managing the moments of trust in service competition*. Lexington, MA: Lexington Books.

Ismail, I., Haron, H., Ibrahim, D. N., & Isa, S. M. (2006). Service quality, client satisfaction and loyalty towards audit firms. *Managerial Auditing Journal*, *21*(7), 738–756.

Iyengar, R., Ansari, A., & Gupta, S. (2007). A model of consumer learning for service quality and usage. *Journal of Marketing Research*, *44*(4), 529–544.

Kuo, Y.-C., Chou, J.-S., & Sun, K.-S. (2011). Elucidating how service quality constructs influence resident satisfaction with condominium management. *Expert Systems with Applications*, *38*(5), 5755–5763.

Middleton, V. T. C., Fyall, A., & Morgan, M. (2009). *Marketing in travel and tourism* (4th ed.). Oxford: Butterworth- Heinemann.

Mill, R. C. (2011). A comprehensive model of customer satisfaction in hospitality and tourism: Strategic implications for management. *International Business and Economics Research Journal*, *1*(6), 7–18.

NDT. (2011). *National tourism service excellence strategy*. National Department of Tourism, Pretoria.

NDT. (2013). *Customer service satisfaction levels of domestic tourists at accommodation establishments in South Africa*. Pretoria: National Department of Tourism.

Page, S. (2015). *Tourism management* (5th ed.). London: Routledge.

Parasuraman, A., Zeithaml, V. A., & Berry, L. B. (1988). SERVQUAL: A multiple-item scale for measuring consumer perceptions of service quality. *Journal of Retailing*, *64*(1), 12–40.

Prebensen, N. K., Chen, J. S., & Uysal, M. (2014). Co-creation of tourism experiences: Scope, definition and structure. In N. K. Prebensen, J. S. Chen, & M. Uysal (Eds.), *Creating experience value in tourism*. Boston, MA: CABI.

SABS. (2012). *South African national standard: Tourism service excellence.* SABS, Pretoria.

Stevens, P., Knutson, B., & Patton, M. (1995). Dineserv: A tool for measuring service quality in restaurants. *Cornell Hospitality Quarterly, 36*(2), 56–60. doi:10.1016/0010–8804(95)93844-K

Swarbrooke, J., & Horner, S. (1999). *Consumer behaviour in tourism.* Oxford: Butterworth-Heinemann.

Swart, M. P. (2013). *A business tourist service quality scorecard for predicting business tourist retention.* DCom thesis, University of Johannesburg, Johannesburg.

Yee, R. W. Y., Yeung, A. C. L., & Edwin Cheng, T. C. (2010). An empirical study of employee loyalty, service quality and firm performance in the service industry. *International Journal of Production Economics, 124*(1), 109–120.

Zeithaml, V. A., & Bitner, M. J. (2003). *Service marketing* (3rd ed.). New York, NY: McGraw-Hill.

Zeithaml, V., Parasuraman, A., & Berry, L. L. (1990). *Delivering quality service: Balancing customer perceptions and expectations.* New York, NY: The Free Press.

CHAPTER 12

MONITORING AND ASSESSING BUSINESS PERFORMANCE IN TOURISM: THE CASE OF HOSPITALITY BUSINESS

Magdalena Petronella (Nellie) Swart and Anne Taylor

ABSTRACT

Purpose — *Monitoring and assessment are essential in the measurement of tourism business performance. Therefore, the purpose of this chapter is to illustrate how monitoring and assessment procedures can be applied in the hospitality business.*

Methodological/approach — *A case study and micro examples provide a framework for the monitoring and assessment of business performance in the hospitality business.*

Findings — *This chapter provides reasons why the tourism business uses control measures to monitor business performance. This is complemented with practical steps in the assessment procedures and guidelines for assessments. Different types of assessment procedures together with the characteristics of performance management provide a well-rounded overview to tourism business owners on how to conduct monitoring and assessment.*

Research limitations — *Due to the explorative nature of the monitoring and assessment case study, more empirical studies are needed to investigate and test performance measurement from a developing country perspective.*

The Emerald Handbook of Entrepreneurship in Tourism, Travel and Hospitality:
Skills for Successful Ventures, 207−222
ISBN: 978-1-78743-530-8/doi:10.1108/978-1-78743-529-220181008

Practical implications — *Discussions from the case study support the steps and practical guidelines in the monitoring and assessment of the tourism business.*

Originality/value — *The case study offers new practices into prospective entrepreneurs' measurement and understanding in the monitoring and assessment of business performance.*

Keywords: Monitoring; assessment; control; entrepreneur; hospitality; customer satisfaction

---

Learning Objectives

After working through or studying this chapter, you should be able to:

- state the purpose for the monitoring and assessment of the tourism business performance;
- describe the assessment processes for the monitoring of the tourism business performance;
- discuss the different types of assessment procedures for the monitoring of the performance of a tourism business;
- suggest different characteristics for the monitoring and assessments of tourism business performance to meet differing business needs;
- present a case study of monitoring and assessing the business performance of a small- to medium-sized hospitality enterprise.

12.1. INTRODUCTION

In tourism entrepreneurship, a sound knowledge of different management processes, namely planning, organising, leading and control, are required. Monitoring and assessment of the business's performance are regarded as parts of the 'control' or 'checking' measures for the management of the tourism business and the final components of the management process. The measurement of the tourism business's success is key in the initial strategy formulation process when the initial planning is conducted, as a guideline to ensure the tourism business goals are met. A guiding question tourism entrepreneurs can ask is, 'How do we know if we have been successful?' (Evans, 2015, p. 576). This question aims to measure if the actual business performance was met against the initial stated objectives.

As monitoring and evaluation are related to the control or checking of the management process, it is necessary to have an overall understanding of these concepts. According to Enz (2010, p. 327), a strategic control system is 'a system to support managers in assessing the relevance of the organisation's strategy to its progress in the accomplishment of its goals, and when discrepancies exist, to support areas needing attention'. Van der Wagen (2011) elaborates on this definition by stating the importance in the following of procedures, such as the handling of cash at a guest house, to achieve the performance measures in place. Once sufficient control processes are in place, information is filtered through all the levels in the tourism business which allows timely decision-making when crises occur.

In addition to control, tourism entrepreneurs/managers apply monitoring or evaluation process for the measurement of the success of a business's objectives. As objectives guide the evaluation process, it is important to consider this process during the planning phase. When planning the evaluation task, it is essential to work out what information the tourism entrepreneur/manager requires to be able to make a fair judgement of the business's performance. For example, when a guest checks in at a hotel, a copy of their identity document or passport and residential address are required, which would allow for an analysis of their general demographics. What a pity if they were not asked where they heard about the guest house or who referred them to the place. This information would greatly assist the guest house manager when making a decision on which marketing platforms to use in the promotion of his property. Based on this discussion, it is evident that evaluation supports the quality control process in the tourism business, but it is frequently neglected. It is evident that the monitoring and assessment procedures are an integral part of the overall tourism business strategy and is as important as the planning process.

The theories of monitoring and assessment procedures are mostly universal in tourism businesses, however, the interpretation and application in developing countries offer unique opportunities (Evans, 2015). Before we discuss monitoring and assessment in more detail, it is important to understand *when* we need to apply this process. Monitoring and assessment are done after the planning and implementation process. In Chapter 9, you have learnt about the business plan, where reference is made to the importance of monitoring and evaluating in all the plans you have made for your tourism business. Furthermore, you have learned about the planning checklist and importance of financial controls in Chapter 10, while in Chapter 11 you received guidelines on the importance of monitoring the quality of service we deliver to our tourists and how to take care of them. It is against this background that the monitoring and assessment of a tourism business performance will be investigated.

Therefore, in this chapter, the purpose of monitoring and assessing the tourism business performance is outlined. Assessment processes are proposed for the monitoring of the tourism business's performance, supported by a discussion on differing characteristics to consider during this process. The chapter concludes with a case study of monitoring and assessing the business performance of a small- to medium-sized hospitality enterprise.

12.2. THE PURPOSE FOR THE MONITORING AND ASSESSMENT OF THE TOURISM BUSINESS PERFORMANCE

The purpose answers the question, *why* is it necessary to monitor and assess the performance of a tourism business?

If entrepreneurs and managers do not monitor and control the activities happening in the organisation, they stand a chance of losing the overall control over the tourism business, which can result in financial losses or even liquidation. Therefore, the reasons why tourism businesses use control measures, as proposed by Enz (2010) as well as Erasmus, Strydom, and Rudansky-Kloppers (2014), include the following:

- *Create a link with planning, organising and leading.* As mentioned earlier, control is the last phase in the management process, which is important to measure if the strategic objectives have been achieved. If one of the strategic objectives was to increase the occupancy rate from an average of 50−60 per cent, this needs to be evaluated after a period of time, to determine if the plan was successfully implemented, supported by operational procedures and under the correct leadership.
- *A counter strategy to overcome resistance to change.* At times, tourism entrepreneurs have to change or adapt business strategies in order to stay abreast with changes in market conditions. For example, in the marketing of a guest house, the business owners have traditionally only approached travel agents and developed a website; however, with the emergence of social media, they need to adopt alternate marketing strategies such as having a presence on social media or creating a Facebook profile and Twitter account.
- *Communication on new business strategies.* In the tourism business environment, we are dealing with different people, with differing perceptions and interpretations of messages. It is therefore essential to communicate new business strategies in a format that will be understood by tourists, employees and other relevant stakeholders. By applying a control measure, the action of sending the right messages about the changes in an enterprise's marketing strategy increases understanding.
- *Regular attention to strategic initiatives.* Tourism entrepreneurs easily get distracted away from considering business strategies, once they get caught up in the day-to-day operations of the business. A deliberate focus on control strategies and processes assist any tourism entrepreneur to remain disciplined and focused on the business strategy. With reference to the changes in the enterprise's marketing strategy, the owner/manager is obliged to evaluate Facebook and Twitter as alternative marketing platforms, therefore he/she needs to do regular checks on the impact of these social media platforms on the business's performance (increase of online bookings) and reputation (online reviews).

- *Debating strategic uncertainties.* During the planning phase, tourism entrepreneurs draft strategies with the hope that they will succeed. However, in business not all these strategies are 100 per cent accurate, which requires entrepreneurs to revisit and debate the original strategies. Through constructive debate with stakeholders and after considering industry trends, strategies are updated to address uncertainties that might have arisen.
- *Assist in the management of cost.* Cost saving on daily operational expenses is one of the biggest challenges in a tourism business. Regular monitoring of the operational budget can assist an entrepreneur/manager to design strategies on how to minimise expenses. Profit is always calculated as income minus expenses. So to make more profit in any business, the entrepreneur needs to find ways to increase income and minimise expenses.
- *When tourism businesses expand in size and complexity, organisational control methods can help companies to cope with the expansion.* It is the ideal for most tourism business owners to run a successful business which can be expanded. Business expansion is associated with financial risk, which can be prepared for through regular monitoring and assessment. If a guest house owner decides to open another guest house in a neighbouring town, he/she will use the experiences from the first guest house and not make the same mistakes.

These control measures are just a few examples of reasons why it is important for tourism entrepreneurs to consider the monitoring and assessment of the business' performance.

12.3. ASSESSMENT PROCESSES

Assessment procedures address the question of *how* we can monitor and assess the business's performance. The five steps in the assessment procedures of a tourism business's performance are depicted in Fig. 12.1.

Each of these steps are discussed in more detail below.

Step 1: Plan what you want to achieve.

Planning is the first step in the management process, and therefore tourism entrepreneurs need to plan which objectives they want to achieve after a specific time of operation in order to monitor and assess the success of the business. Performance standards include, for example, the financial profit a guest house has generated over a period of one year; how big the market share is in a specific geographical area; how productive the staff was in the generation of the guest house's profit; and if there was resource capacity for staff development.

Step 2: Check the financial and business environment to see whether the strategic plan is still valid.

In the collection of information on the business environment, both macro and micro environmental factors and financial management are activities the

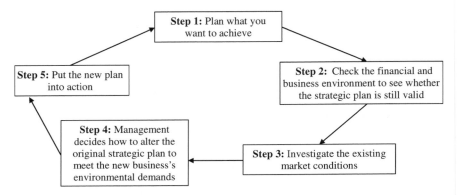

Fig. 12.1.   Steps in the Assessment Procedures. *Source*: Authors' creation.

tourism entrepreneur needs to engage with on a regular basis. All the data and reports must be valid and quantifiable before any comparisons can be made on the expected and actual performance of the tourism business. Reliability is another important factor in the measurement of the actual achievements of the tourism business. Therefore, it is important to determine how much information is required for the comparison on the validity of the business's strategic plan.

Step 3: Investigate the existing market conditions.
Market conditions have a great influence on the supply and demand of tourism services and products. For example, if the currency of a country is strong, the market conditions are more favourable for domestic tourists than for international tourists, as international tourists have to pay more for tourism services. However, if a country's currency is weak, the market conditions is more favourable for international tourists, as it will be more affordable for them to visit the destination. Tourism entrepreneurs need to be sensitive to these market conditions and adapt their tourism product offering to cater to both domestic and international tourists, regardless of currency fluctuations.

Step 4: Management decides how to alter the original strategic plan to meet new business environmental demands.
During the monitoring and assessment process, tourism entrepreneurs need to identify the performance gaps between the planned objective and the achievement of this objective. This is a valuable yardstick to determine the gaps in the performance of the tourism business, and if there is an underperformance, tourism entrepreneurs need to investigate *why* this has happened. If a tourism business is underperforming, entrepreneurs need to decide if the variances are large enough to justify further investigation. Based on the information gathered on the business performance, tourism entrepreneurs need to decide how to adapt

the original business plan to meet the new business demands and achieve the identified targets. More importantly, these corrective actions need to ensure that the same variances do not happen again. Entrepreneurs can apply some strategies to meet the performance targets, such as:

- improve the overall performance of the tourism business;
- revise the previous targets and adapt them to be more reasonable given the current market conditions; or
- lower the performance targets to be more realistic and achievable.

Step 5: Put the new plan into action.

Once the revised plan has been finalised, it must be implemented and put into action. Obviously, the revised plan will also be monitored and assessed after a period of time, as the assessment process will be repeated. The new plan forms the basis for a new cycle of management activities, which requires feedback and review processes to influence planning processes in the tourism business.

Tourism entrepreneurs need to be fair and consistent in the application of the monitoring and assessment procedures of their business. Evans (2015) suggests the following guidelines to ensure an equal and fair assessment of evaluation criteria with guiding questions:

> *Suitability*: *Is the tourism business capable of achieving its strategic objectives?* Entrepreneurs/managers assess the suitability in terms of the opportunities and threats posed by the external business environment. Furthermore, an assessment on how the strengths can address the weaknesses in the internal business environment provides valuable guidance on how to manage the venture.
>
> *Feasibility*: *Is the assessment of the tourism strategy possible?* There are a number of 'internal issues' (culture, competencies of staff and resources) and 'external issues' (customers, competitors, suppliers and government) to consider. A few internal issues include: Do the staff have the right skills to do their work? Is there enough working capital to cover the daily expenses? Does the organisational culture motivate employees to take pride in their work? External issues are difficult to control, such as: How will my competitors respond if I launch a new product? How will tourists react if we launch a new offering? Will the distribution channels support us in this launch/ venture? Does the new product adhere to all institutional regulations?
>
> *Acceptability*: *What is the likelihood for markets to accept the strategy?* Acceptability can be measured through financial tools such as return on investment (ROI) and break-even analyses. Risk and uncertainty is another measurement technique of acceptability, as tourism entrepreneurs need to identify the major risk in the launch of a new product and how to manage the risk in the long term.

12.4. DIFFERENT TYPES OF ASSESSMENT PROCEDURES

In the monitoring and assessment of a tourism business, tourism entrepreneurs and managers can use different types (or kinds) of procedures to measure business performance. Although there are a variety of procedures to choose from, there is no wrong or right procedure to use; it is rather about selecting the correct control procedure that will assist in monitoring the business success, given the circumstances (Evans, 2015, p. 437).

A tourism business, such as an accommodation unit, is subject to the implementation of different types of assessment procedures to achieve its overall objectives. Feedback control and feedforward control, along with physical, human and financial resources are amongst the most popular assessment procedures to use. The strategic direction and the implication of business plans are influenced by feedback control and feedforward control.

Feedback control 'provides entrepreneurs/managers with information concerning outcomes of organisational activities' (Enz, 2010, p. 327). Tourism entrepreneurs/managers design objectives to use later in the measurement of performance of their business. This includes the setting of specific targets as a means to inform the staff members. Business targets make all employees accountable for achieving business objectives. Feedback control is used as a yardstick to alert entrepreneurs/managers when to intervene in the organisational processes. For example, feedback would be required to decide on the date by which a client needs to confirm the final numbers for a function at a restaurant to allow the chef sufficient time to order the necessary supplies for catering requirements. The financial control processes and measures presented in Chapter 10 are a useful control guidance.

Feedforward control enables entrepreneurs/managers to anticipate changes in the tourism business environment, both internal and external, after conducting an environmental analysis and business assessment (Enz, 2010). Environmental discontinuities and new industry regulations are two important aspects tourism entrepreneurs must consider if they want to move their business forward and achieve their organisational goals. Environmental discontinuity is a result of unforeseen and unexpected PEST (political, economic, social and technological) changes. For example, a change in labour regulations can have a serious impact on the working hours of employees and can result in high employee turnover.

In addition to feedback and feedforward control, physical, human and financial resources are used as internal control measures to encourage organisational behaviour that is consistent with the strategic objectives of the tourism business.

12.4.1. Financial Resources

Financial resources must be strictly controlled in the tourism business, and this is vital to successful business operations. Different financial control measures are required to track the resources flow into the tourism business, the financial resources held on the premises of the tourism business, and when the financial resources flow out of the tourism business. Most entrepreneurs/managers have implemented policies and procedures on how the financial resources must be administered.

> **Micro Example 12.1: Financial Resource Control at a Guest House**

Financial resources ensure the sustainable running of a small business, such as a guest house. At the guest house, the owner/general manager is equally responsible for the management of the financial resources. Through the application of regular monitoring and assessment procedures, the general manager can monitor the cash flow in the business and ensure on-time payment of bills. The general manager is accountable for any financial losses and are bounded by the policies and procedures put in place. Another financial control method is the issuing of an invoice and recording the form of payment every time a guest checks out. Payment can be made by means of bank transfers, cash or credit/debit cards, or bill backs.

12.4.2. Physical Control

As most tourism products are intangible, their physical control is a challenge. In this section, we propose application of inventory control, quality control and its measurement, and sharing information as methods to conduct physical control in the tourism business.

Inventory control entails the control of stock in the tourism business. For example, in a guest house, the 'stock' will include amongst other guest amenities, linen and food supplies. This requires regular control to ensure that guests do not take the linen home or for kitchen staff to help themselves to groceries. This is known as shrinkage. If these items are not controlled, the business can suffer from great and regular financial losses, and the quality of the service may deteriorate.

Quality control measures the quality of product or service delivery. In the offering of tourism services, it will mean that the receptionist answers the phone in a specific manner as this is a reflection on the quality of services delivered at the guest house. If a customer service does not meet the guest expectations, it results in dissatisfied guests who will never return to the business, as you have seen in Chapter 11. It is, therefore, important that entrepreneurs/managers develop quality standards and assess the delivery of quality services on a regular basis so they can take appropriate actions if any issues occur.

Sharing information: Sharing of timely and relevant information for management purposes (decision-making) is a vital process in monitoring whether the tourism business goals are met. Control systems function more sufficiently and effectively if adequate information is shared with the entrepreneur/manager, once it has occurred. Information is a critical input in making the right decisions and achieving business objectives.

12.4.3. Human Resources

Tourism is a labour-intensive industry and therefore the control of human resources is a priority in every tourism business. Today, almost all tourism businesses control the productivity of the labour force through an instrument known as 'performance management'. Each employer needs to design an annual performance contract, consisting of key performance indicators (KPIs), which are used to outline if an employee is permanently employed, or the percentage performance bonus he/she will receive at the end of financial year. Turnover intention, employee retention and absenteeism are some of the control measures used to monitor the employees' attitudes and behaviour.

12.5. CHARACTERISTICS TO CONSIDER FOR MONITORING AND ASSESSMENT

Different characteristics are associated with the monitoring and assessment of tourism business performance, such as integration, flexibility, accuracy and assuring guest satisfaction. These are all characteristics synonymous with the business practices followed by entrepreneurs/managers (Erasmus et al., 2014; Van der Wagen, 2011).

Integration indicates the effect of one tourism process on another if they are brought together after a process of monitoring and assessment. In tourism, we are more familiar with the concepts of horizontal and vertical integrations (Evans, 2015). From a monitoring perspective, *horizontal integration* takes place if a tourism business is selling its brand name in different markets around the world. This means that the same hotel brand will be in South Africa, Romania and China. *Vertical integration* occurs if a well-known airline, with an established brand, decides to open a car rental business and a cruise liner using the same brand name.

Flexibility is mostly required in the daily operations of a tourism business. This requires a mutual understanding of all the tourism business's outcomes and the role every stakeholder needs to play to achieve the goal. Through the implementation of sufficient monitoring procedures, employees are empowered to think on their feet and to make quick decisions about changing non-critical procedures when circumstances demand. This results in a more effective way in the running of a tourism business and a desirable attribute of staff members.

Micro Example 12.2: Empowering Waiters through Monitoring Systems

The waiters in a restaurant are the sales agents who are responsible for selling the food and generating the most income out of every guest they serve. It sometimes happens that a regular guest orders from the menu and feels disappointed with the food served, as it is either not what they expected or is not according to their taste. As the waiter knows that the guest is not unreasonable, he must have the authority to allow the guest to order another food item free of charge. In most cases, this will result in an enhanced guest retention and higher guest spending. By giving the waiter this authority, the management not only empowers the waiter but also ensures a more effective running of the restaurant. The incident must be reported so that management is aware of what the case was and the costs incurred.

Accuracy deals with the correctness of information. Monitoring and assessment in the tourism business is based on how accurate/adequate is the information to make informed decisions. Misrepresentation of information can result in the making of decisions with catastrophic results for the business. For example, if a sales person in a travel agency indicates that he/she has sold 10 international holiday packages, the travel agent manager will increase the sales target for the sales agent, which can result in more commission. However, if it was found that the sales agent only sold five packages, the overall sales target for the travel agency as a whole will not be met and can result in financial losses.

Ensuring guest satisfaction: Control systems most often frustrate guests/customers, but sometimes they will endeavour to circumvent the system by trying, for instance:

- to buy alcohol for underage children
- to enter unauthorised areas on the premises or
- to park on the disabled parking bay of the facility, to name a few

In each of these cases, the management must provide staff members with clear guidelines regarding their handling. If a parent insists on buying an alcoholic drink for his/her underage child, the waiter needs to know that the liquor law has preference over guest satisfaction. On the other hand, if a guest has parked on the disabled parking due to his/her back injury and inability to walk long distance, the security guard at the guest house may allow the person to park there, on condition that the vehicle must be moved once a person living with disabilities requires the parking.

The following case study provides an overall summary on how monitoring and assessment (using control) in a hospitality business can be used, after consideration of the business plan (presented in Chapter 9), the financial management (discussed in Chapter 10) and the provision of customer care (see Chapter 11).

12.6. CASE STUDY: USING THE CONTROL PROCESS IN A ROMANIAN ACCOMMODATION BUSINESS (GUEST HOUSE) TO ENSURE GUEST SATISFACTION

Diana and her brother Ionut have inherited a 'pensione' from their parents. The pensione is a small accommodation establishment of eight guest rooms that provided a place for families to spend their holidays during the years of communist rule in Romania. The family also used other rooms on the property for their own accommodation needs. During communism, Romanians would receive holiday vouchers from their employers which could be exchanged for accommodation and food, within a time schedule supported by the government.

The pensione provided a clean and comfortable room, with no frills or extras. The guests made few demands and, as they exchanged coupons for accommodation, they tended to accept the service standards provided to them without any complaints.

When democracy was introduced to Romania in 1989, changes were inevitable. Initially, this enabled the family running the business to purchase their home/business space from the authorities, and they almost expected business to continue as normal. This did not happen. They identified the business opportunity and decided to take the risk to create a family business. With the borders open to international guests, and Romanians able to make free choices regarding their holidays, demands and expectations had changed.

The brother and sister team were naturally resourceful and innovative, having been brought up under a strict and restrictive political past. After a meeting with the other family members, they arrive at a decision to move forward and to embrace the opportunity to run the local small accommodation business, having a homely atmosphere, located in a beautiful natural setting in a small village, near the castle in Bran associated with Dracula.

With some knowledge of management processes, the brother and sister started implementing the management steps — *planning, organising, directing, monitoring and controlling*. The first three steps could be implemented in the business. They are able to implement a *planning process* by doing marketing research, planning a budget and training their employees in the art of providing hospitality services. The market survey provided the information they needed about the changes in the market segment that used to visit the pensione. The survey identified that their guests were a younger generation of Romanian families who were looking for low-cost traditional accommodation. The international guests were students and young budget-conscious tourists looking for a local experience, opportunity to enjoy local cuisine and to appreciate the history and the beauty of an unspoilt environment in the countryside.

With this information, they *organised* their accommodation offering and food selection accordingly. Cost-conscious guests meant that they needed to keep tight control on all spending. Part of their *organising* was to hire the services of a part-time bookkeeper to assist with keeping accurate records of business income and expenses. This proved to be a challenge, as family members saw the income as money available to meet their personal needs. This required good management principles which are enforced by all family members. Accurate financial records enabled the family to approach a bank for a short-term loan to make renovations, mainly improvements to bathroom and kitchen facilities in order to meet health standards and hygiene regulations.

Directing meant that they had to adopt a style which suited them and yet ensured business processes could be implemented effectively and efficiently, as to ensure smooth running of business operations and managing financial resources efficiently. The financial loan proved to be insufficient for the planned changes and improvements, leaving the family take careful decisions about the priorities. Directing also implied setting the standards for customer care required, staff training in guests handling, and building environmental standards to ensure the attractiveness of the business to potential customers.

The most important stage of this management action at this point is *monitoring and controlling*. How do young entrepreneurs *check* that the management plan is implemented properly and that their guests are provided with the best value for money? This required a reverse action thinking process. They needed to *check* their *planning processes* again, *check* their *organising* and *check* their directing style and actions.

They discovered that their guests' profile had changed yet again — the customers wanted to enjoy the accommodation but not the restaurant/meals. The guests choose to enjoy the opportunity to eat at different restaurants in the evenings while on holidays. Only the breakfast option was preferred — with the expectation of a wide international breakfast items to choose from. Requests included fruit juices, cereals and meat items, a tea option, along with the more familiar continental breakfast choices. Guests also requested a buffet service rather than a set breakfast with no choice. Romanian households used to consume few of these items — such as marmalades or breakfast cereals — so the business owners needed to become familiar with the differing eating habits of international guests and to adapt their offering accordingly.

The *planning process* of how guests could obtain information about the guest house and how to make booking also needed to be changed. *Controlling* the process included making online booking options available for potential guests. This meant upgrading their business computer capacity, Wi-Fi access and linking to a booking platform. A user-friendly webpage was created and kept updated. A feedback page is open to potential customers and the management. Online reviews/guest comments are a good tool to keep the management informed about guests' service expectations and level of satisfaction.

Controlling the *organising process* also required their management skills. As their guest bookings had increased by 40 per cent after the initial changes, they needed to *organise* more cleaning staff by re-skilling the kitchen staff in order to assist them in keeping their positions after the breakfast service. Financial *control* measures were also upgraded to include a night audit programme to track daily income more accurately.

Controlling the *leadership* process was more challenging. An autocratic leadership style so common in the Romanian history had to be re-evaluated. Both employer and employees found a participatory management style difficult to adapt to, resulting in slow or delayed decision-making. Following a democratic system was also challenging, as the consequences of some of the decisions would be left to the management to resolve. This process is ongoing.

Being able to take a step backward and *evaluate* their business plans and decisions has been challenging for Diana and Ionut. As most entrepreneurs, they feel very close to their business and find it difficult to be critical of their decisions, and even more difficult to accept changes and challenges in better catering for the market segments. Maturing in their business has helped them to adjust and realign their business to ensure that their guests are getting what they want, to ensure returning guests — the dream of every accommodation entrepreneur!

12.7. SUMMARY

Owning a tourism business, or striving to develop one as an entrepreneur, is the 'stuff' that dreams are made of. We dream of being successful as a person, of being an entrepreneur or a service provider, and of financial success. None of these dreams can be guaranteed in reality. So how do we plan, organise, lead and control to make our dreams come true?

As you become familiar with tourism consumer expectations, you need to define financial and business plans before you can start your tourism venture, and it is equally important to develop a sense and strategy to monitor and assess the business' performance. There are theories that provide ways and strategies to assist an entrepreneur in performing this task and in asking the strategic questions he/she needs to respond to. These theories are known and need to be implemented during the monitoring and assessing of a tourism enterprise. These actions are based on appropriate decision-making and related to business performance, marketing and financial performance, staff training and development to provide the offering and service expected by targeted market segments. Implementing regular assessment procedures to select the persons that work for your business is as important as the process itself. In essence, monitoring and assessing business performance is part of the role of being an entrepreneur/manager. Developing these skills will enhance entrepreneurs in designing and implementing strategies, procedures and techniques to ensure financial sustainability of their business.

Review Questions

Now you may check your understanding of this chapter by answering the following questions or discussing the topics below:

- Define the concept 'strategic control system'.
- Do you have any experience in the monitoring and evaluation of a tourism business? Discuss the main lessons from this experience.
- Can you propose alternative reasons; why it is important for tourism entrepreneurs to conduct regular controls on their business?
- Discuss the five steps in the assessment procedures of a business's performance.
- Suggest guidelines to ensure an adequate assessment of evaluation criteria in the application of monitoring and assessment procedures.
- Discuss the differences between feedback control and feedforward control.
- Debate the relevance of the three physical control measures for a tourism business.
- Outline the measurement and assessment characteristics a tourism entrepreneur/manager can consider in running the business.

REFERENCES AND FURTHER READING

Enz, C. A. (2010). *Hospitality strategic management: Concepts and cases* (2nd ed.). Hoboken, NJ: John Wiley & Sons.

Erasmus, B. J., Strydom, J. W., & Rudansky-Kloppers, S. (2014). *An introduction to business management* (9th ed.). Cape Town: Oxford University Press.

Evans, N. (2015). *Strategic management for tourism, hospitality and events* (2nd ed.). New York, NY: Routledge.

George, R. (2011). *Managing tourism in South Africa* (4th ed.). Cape Town: Oxford University Press.

Legoherel, P., Poutier, E., & Fyall, A. (2013). *Revenue management for hospitality and tourism*. Oxford: Goodfellow Publishers Ltd.

Mullins, L. (2013). *Management and organisational behaviour* (10th ed.). London: Pearson.

Nieman, G., & Nieuwenhuizen, C. (2014). *Entrepreneurship: A South African perspective* (3rd ed.). Pretoria: Van Schaik Publishers.

Page, S. (2015). *Tourism management* (5th ed.). London: Routledge.

Parker, E. (2006). *Eric Parker's road map to business success*. Singapore: Tien Wah Press.

Tassiopoulos, D. (Ed.). (2011). *New tourism ventures: An entrepreneurial and managerial approach* (2nd ed.). Cape Town: Juta.

Van der Wagen, L. (2011). *Event management for tourism, cultural, business and sporting events* (4th ed.). New South Wales: Pearson.

CHAPTER 13

RISK MANAGEMENT IN TOURISM VENTURES

Eugenia Papaioannou and Shiwei Shen

ABSTRACT

Purpose – *This chapter aims to present the key issues and main aspects of risk management (RM), as they relate to tourism entrepreneurship, with a focus on the RM plan and the various strategies used in controlling risks.*

Methodology/approach – *Literature review was conducted and managerial issues and aspects regarding RM in tourism entrepreneurship were highlighted. These issues were illustrated by one example and two case studies from the business world.*

Findings – *This chapter suggests that every probable risk must have a pre-formulated plan to deal with its possible consequences. In the field of tourism entrepreneurship, the elimination of risk by putting safety measures in place is not simply achieved by taking precautions in a haphazard manner. Rather, these tasks require a proactive approach, an intricate and logical plan.*

Research limitations – *This chapter is explorative in nature, based on a literature review and case study analysis. It takes more entrepreneurial/ practical than academic approach.*

Managerial/practical implications – *This chapter provides RM process as a generic framework for entrepreneurs/managers in the identification, analysis, assessment, treatment and monitoring of risk related to their business ventures. It also suggests the appropriate steps to follow to efficiently managing*

The Emerald Handbook of Entrepreneurship in Tourism, Travel and Hospitality:
Skills for Successful Ventures, 223–240
ISBN: 978-1-78743-530-8/doi:10.1108/978-1-78743-529-220181017

risks. Every tourism enterprise should have a strategy and an emergency/contingency plan to address risks.

Originality/value — *This chapter outlines, in a comprehensive and practical way, a strategic approach to risk management for the tourism enterprises. It also highlights the importance and utility of planning and implementing of a suitable strategy to effectively address business-related risks.*

Keywords: Risks; risk management; tourism venture; process; strategy; plan

---

Learning Objectives

After working through this chapter, you should be able to:

- provide a definition of risk management (RM) in general and as it relates to the field of business;
- describe the different steps in the RM process;
- describe the main elements of a standard for RM;
- present and discuss the various strategies of RM;
- discuss a RM plan;
- provide examples of RM.

13.1. INTRODUCTION

Risk management (RM) is about the identification, analysis, assessment, control and avoidance, minimization or elimination of unacceptable risks (Business dictionary, 2016). More formally, RM is defined as:

> ... the identification, assessment, and prioritization of risks followed by coordinated and economical application of resources to minimize, monitor, and control the probability and/or impact of unfortunate events or to maximize the realization of opportunities. (Hubbard, 2009, p. 46)

RM's objective is to assure that uncertainty does not deflect an endeavour from its business goals (ISO, 2009a).

In enterprise RM, a risk is defined as a possible event or circumstance that can negatively influence the organisation in question. It may refer to numerous types of threats caused by the environment, technology, humans, other organisations and politics (Piekarz, Jenkins, & Mills, 2015). The literature suggests that RM is an activity that integrates a recognition of risk, risk assessment, strategies developed to manage it and mitigation using managerial resources (Berg, 2010). The main aim of RM is to reduce different risks occurring within a pre-selected domain to an acceptable level. Note that several RM standards have been developed, including the ISO standards (ISO, 2009a, 2009b) to provide a framework and a more structured approach to managing risks.

This chapter aims to present the main issues and aspects of RM, as they relate to tourism entrepreneurship. The first section deals with the definition of risk and RM, as well as the principles involved. This is followed by a presentation of the standard ISO 31000:2009 and the process of RM, in addition to the steps to implement when addressing risks. The next section is devoted to managerial activities for enterprise RM. Thereafter, the chapter focuses on the main strategies used in controlling risks.

13.2. RISK, RISK MANAGEMENT AND PRINCIPLES OF RISK MANAGEMENT

13.2.1. Definition of Risk

Risk is unavoidable and present in every human situation. It is present in people's daily lives and in all organisations (Berg, 2010). Risk is a term that has been defined many times and in numerous ways, yet the common denominator in all definitions is uncertainty about outcomes. Where definitions differ, is in terms of how they characterise outcomes. In ISO 31000:2009, 'risk' has a very specific meaning: it is defined as the 'effect of uncertainty on objectives' (ISO, 2009a), thus it links risks to objectives. This definition of risk can most easily be applied when the objectives of the organisation are comprehensively and fully stated.

Another description is the following: Risk refers to the uncertainty that surrounds future events and outcomes. It is an expression of the likelihood and impact of an event with the potential to influence the achievement of an organisation's objectives (Berg, 2010). This definition implies that, as a minimum, some form of quantitative or qualitative analysis is required for making decisions about major risks or threats presenting obstacles to the achievement of organisational objectives. For each risk, two calculations are required: its likelihood/probability and the extent of the impact/consequences.

Risks are part of all our lives; they may be internal or external, direct or indirect. According to the definition, a risk involves the possibility that an event will occur and prevent an objective being achieved. RM can help owners/managers exert good control over potential risks in their organisations.

13.2.2. Risk Management

All activities within an organisation involve risks. RM involves anticipating, understanding, analysing and addressing those risks, to make sure the organisation achieves its objectives. Nowadays, the risks we have to manage evolve quickly. Organisations of all kinds face challenging natural, political, socio-economic and cultural influences that make their operating environments uncertain. These influences may impact on the extent to which objectives can be met. We need to make sure we manage risks so that we minimise their threats and maximise their potential.

RM thus refers to the coordinated activities that an organisation takes to direct and control risk. All departments in an organisation continuously manage risk, whether they realise it or not — sometimes more rigorously and systematically, sometimes less so. One well-accepted description of RM is the following: 'RM is a systematic approach to setting the best course of action under uncertainty by identifying, assessing, understanding, acting on and communicating risk issues' (Berg, 2010, p. 81).

Example — Micro Case 13.1:   Implementing an IT System

Let us consider the implementation of an information technology system by a tourism business. The choices of hardware and software are investments/capital expenditure decisions. If the entrepreneur takes the wrong decisions, the consequences will be obvious over the medium term, one to three years. As pointed out 'the associated risks are strategic, and will be taken with the intention of obtaining specific benefits' (IRM, 2010, p. 5).

An IT project is a part of the implementation of strategic plan. This project involves some risks that should be managed efficiently in terms of technical standards, money and time.

Once the project has been carried out and the IT system is in place, there are some operational risks (e.g. hardware breakdown, virus attacks and hackers) to be managed properly. Professional experts indicate that 'these operational risks may be highly significant, and correct procedures will need to be designed and implemented to minimise potential disruptions' (IRM, 2010, p. 5).

RM is about making decisions that contribute towards achieving an organisation's objectives, by managing risk at both the individual activity level and in functional areas. Note that sometimes RM and safety management viewed as being similar, but in practice, safety management is a main and important part of RM which also covers, for instance, financial risks.

13.2.3. Principles of RM

RM as a process is underpinned by a set of principles. The International Organisation for Standardisation (ISO) recommends that the following target areas or principles form part of the overall RM process (ISO, 2009b). The process should:

- create value for the organisation (resources expended to mitigate risk should be less costly than the consequences of inaction);
- be an integral part of overall organisational processes;
- factor into the company's overall decision-making process;
- explicitly address any uncertainty;
- be systematic and structured;
- be based on the best available information;
- be tailorable (flexible/adaptable);
- take into account human factors, including potential errors;
- be transparent and inclusive;
- be dynamic, iterative and responsive to change;
- be capable of continual improvement and enhancement and
- be continually or periodically re-assessed.

RM is the process whereby organisations methodically address the risks attached to their activities. A successful RM initiative should be proportionate to the level of risk in the organisation, as related to the firm's size, nature and complexity. This approach will enable an RM initiative to deliver outputs. The impact or benefits associated with these outputs include more efficient operations, effective tactics and efficacious strategy. Any benefits need to be both measurable and sustainable. The focus of RM is on the assessment of significant risks and the implementation of suitable risk responses (IRM, 2016).

13.3. A STANDARD OF RISK MANAGEMENT: ISO 31000:2009

There are many opinions regarding what RM involves, how it should be implemented and what it can achieve. A number of standards have been developed worldwide to help organisations implement RM systematically and effectively. These standards are designed to help organisations identify specific threats, assess unique vulnerabilities to determine their risk, identify ways to reduce these risks and then implement risk-reduction efforts.

Such standards seek to establish a common view on frameworks, processes and practice and are generally set by recognised international standards bodies or industry groups (IRM, 2016). Conforming to standards is normally a voluntary endeavour, although adherence to a standard may be required by regulators or in terms of a contract. Commonly used standards include:

- ISO 31000:2009 – Risk management: Principles and guidelines;
- Risk management standard – IRM/ALARM/AIRMIC 2002 – developed by the UK's three main risk organisations;

- ISO/IEC 31010:2009 – Risk management: Risk assessment techniques;
- COSO 2004 – Enterprise risk management: Integrated framework.

ISO Standard 31000:2009 – *Risk Management: Principles and Guidelines*, published in 2009, provides a set of principles and guidelines for RM, a framework and a process for managing risk. Here, RM is defined as 'coordinated activities to direct and control an organization with regard to risk' (ISO, 2009a, p. 21). Despite the underlying element of uncertainty, it is often possible to predict risks and to set in place systems and actions designed to minimise their negative consequences and maximise the positive ones.

Large organisations are better equipped and relatively well structured to deal with risks, while maximising benefits. By contrast, due to various limitations, small- and medium-sized enterprises (SMEs) are more exposed to the negative aspects of risk. Due to their flexibility, however, and if provided with the right tools, they can tap into opportunities to increase their market share, and grow and manage risk more effectively. Using ISO 31000:2009 can help organisations of all sizes increase the likelihood of achieving their objectives, improve their chances of identifying opportunities and threats, and effectively allocate and use resources for risk treatment.

ISO 31000 describes the components of an RM implementation framework as including essential steps in the implementation and ongoing support of the RM process. The main components of the ISO 31000 framework are: (1) design framework, (2) implement RM, (3) monitor and review framework and (4) improve framework.

Enterprises, be they small or large, need to identify, understand and manage the uncertainties or risks that threaten their chances of achieving success. ISO 31000:2009 provides a proven, robust and reliable approach to managing risk. With a view to helping SMEs to improve their preparedness and manage risks, the ISO, International Trade Centre (ITC) and United Nations Organization for Industrial Development (UNIDO) decided to join forces and developed the ISO 31000:2009 guide on how to implement RM consistently and effectively (Lark, 2015). This publication aims to help SMEs better understand the requirements of ISO 31000:2009, compare their RM practices with internationally recognised benchmarks and align their practices with that standard.

13.4. THE PROCESS OF RISK MANAGEMENT

The process of RM unfolds according to a list of coordinated activities. All RM plans follow the same steps that combine to make up the overall RM process (Berg, 2010; ISO, 2009b; Lark, 2015) (Table 13.1).

Table 13.1. The RM Process.

Steps	Actions
1	Establish the goals and context
2	Recognise and identify the risk
3	Analyse the risk
4	Assess and evaluate the risk
5	Treat the risk
6	Implement feedback mechanisms: (1) monitor and review performance and (2) communicate and consult

Source: Authors' elaboration, retrieved from Berg (2010), ISO (2009b) and Lark (2015).

Step 1: Establish the goals and context (the risk environment)
The purpose of this stage of planning is to understand the environment in which the respective organisations operate – that means thoroughly understanding the external environment and the internal culture of the organisation.

Step 2: Identify the risk
The next step in the process is to identify potential risks. Identify sources of risk, areas of impact, events (including changes in circumstances) and their causes and potential consequences. Risk identification establishes the exposure of the organisation to risk and uncertainty. This requires intimate knowledge of the organisation; the market in which it operates; the legal, social, political and cultural environment in which it exists; as well as an understanding of its strategic and operational objectives.

Identifying the sources of risk is the most critical stage in the risk assessment process. Sources must be managed for RM to be proactive. The better the understanding of the sources, the better the outcomes of the risk assessment process, and the more meaningful and effective the RM will be (Berg, 2010).

Step 3: Analyse the risk
Once the risk has been identified, and the context, causes, contributing factors and consequences have been described, the organisation must determine the odds of a risk occurring, as well as its potential consequences. The aim of this analysis is to further understand each specific instance of risk and how it could influence the organisation's projects and objectives.

Risk analysis can be:

> ... broadly defined to include risk assessment, risk characterization, risk communication, RM, and policy relating to risk, in the context of risks of concern to individuals, to public- and private-sector organizations, and to society at a local, regional, national, or global level. (Society for Risk Analysis, 2017)

A useful construct is to divide risk analysis into two components: (1) risk assessment (identifying, evaluating and measuring the probability and severity of risks) and (2) RM (deciding what to do about risks) (Haimes, 2015). Risk analysis can be qualitative or quantitative in nature: The former uses words or colours to identify and evaluate risks or presents a written description of the risk, while the latter calculates numerical probabilities over the possible consequences (Rausand, 2011).

Step 4: Assess and evaluate the risk
Once risks have been identified, they must be assessed for the potential severity of their impact (generally negative, such as damage or loss) and the probability of their occurrence. A decision must be made as to whether the risk is acceptable or not. Once the risks have been analysed, they can be compared to previously approved tolerable risk criteria. A risk may be considered acceptable if, for example, it is so sufficiently low that treatment is not considered cost-effective.

Whether a risk is acceptable or not relates to a willingness to tolerate that risk, that is, bearing the risk after it has been treated in order to achieve the desired objectives. The risk assessment activity contributes to identifying those risks that require management's attention. This will facilitate the ability to prioritise risk control actions in terms of their potential to benefit the organisation.

Step 5: Treat the risk (respond to significant risks)
Risk treatment is the activity of selecting and implementing appropriate strategies to modify risk. An unacceptable risk requires treatment. During this step, organisations assess their highest-ranked risks and develop a plan to alleviate them using specific strategies. The objective of this stage is to develop cost-effective options for treating risks.

Risk treatment includes as its major element risk control (or mitigation) but extends further to, for example, risk avoidance, transfer and financing. For many risks, these responses may be applied in combination. Factors to consider for a risk treatment strategy are guided by an organisation's answers to the following questions:

- Can the likelihood of the risk occurring be reduced? (through preventative maintenance, quality assurance or a change in business systems and processes), or
- Can the consequences of the event be reduced? (through contingency planning, minimising exposure to sources of risk or separating/relocating an activity and resources).

A more detailed presentation of the main RM strategies is provided in Section 13.6. The whole process of RM should lead organisations to decide on an *RM plan*. This involves selecting appropriate controls or countermeasures to measure each risk. The RM plan should propose applicable and effective security controls for managing risks. For example, an observed high risk of computer viruses could be mitigated by acquiring and implementing antivirus software. A good RM plan should contain a schedule for control implementation and identify the persons responsible for each of those actions. *Implementation* follows all of the planned methods for mitigating the effect of risks. A company could purchase insurance policies for any risks that need to be transferred to an insurer, avoid all risks (if that can be done without sacrificing the entity's goals) reduce other risks and retain/face the rest.

Review and evaluate the RM plan: initial RM plans will never be perfect. Risk analysis results and management plans should be updated periodically in order to evaluate whether previously selected security controls are still applicable and effective.

Step 6: Implement feedback mechanisms

ISO 31000 recognises the importance of feedback by way of two mechanisms: monitoring and review of performance and communication and consultation.

Monitoring and review of risk performance: this involves following up on both the risks and the overall plan to continuously monitor and track new and existing risks. It ensures that the organisation monitors risk performance and learns from experience. The overall RM process should also be reviewed and updated accordingly.

This step requires a description of how the outcomes of a treatment will be measured. A framework needs to be in place to enable responsible persons to report on the following aspects of risk and their impact: (1) What are the key risks? (2) How are they being managed? (3) Are the treatment strategies effective? If not, what else must be undertaken?

Communication and consultation: clear and effective communication is essential for the RM process, that is clear communication of the objectives, the RM process and its elements, as well as the findings and actions required as a result of the output. Communicate and consult with internal and external stakeholders during any and all stages of the RM process. Ensure that those responsible for implementing RM are kept properly informed.

Case Study 13.1: Ten Tips for Practising RM in the Tourism Industry

Tourism enterprises increasingly face incidents involving risks to both their own operations and to tourists. This includes political unrest, terrorist attacks, earthquakes, tsunamis and health-related incidents. An entrepreneur should be prepared to deal with potential crises and possible risks. It is important to learn to address RM issues and reduce the impact of crises. RM does not start with a crisis, but much earlier. The top 10 tips on how to successfully deal with risks and RM in tourism are outlined below.

1. *Identify the risks*: make an inventory of the potential risks that could threaten a specific destination. Identify the nature of the potential crisis by considering the following: cause, frequency, duration, scope of impact and destructive potential.
2. *Determine the RM strategy*: avoid the risk, reduce the likelihood of having to face the consequences, transfer or retain the risk. Learn from previous crises and disasters that have taken place in a specific area. Also look into similar crises that have occurred in other destinations.
3. *Develop an RM plan for our tourism business*: every tourism provider should have an emergency/contingency plan ready (i) to ensure the safety of tourists and employees and (ii) to secure buildings, facilities and equipment from the effects of the risk/crisis.
4. *Team up with stakeholders*: a good RM plan requires involving stakeholders in our region. Identify the structures and frameworks within which tourism businesses can develop their own capacity to prepare for, respond to and recover from, crises.
5. *Train our staff*: in a crisis, staff must step outside of their day-to-day roles and carry out tasks that are far less familiar and do so within a highly stressful environment. This means they need to be well prepared. Organise training programmes for the staff on how to handle crisis situations.
6. *Test our plan*: make sure the RM plan is ready for action. When implementing it in our business, we should test the plan. Additionally, risks may change, so it is important to maintain and update the plan.
7. *Provide clear and honest crisis communication*: communicate directly with the media and keep our website and/or social media channels up to date. Keep information neutral and factual. Most importantly: be honest!
8. *Keep informed about possible negative travel advice*: regularly check our country's safety status at the website of our target market/country's ministry of foreign affairs.
9. *Revive our business after a crisis*: use (i) post-crisis tourists who are willing to share their experiences online and in person with friends and family and (ii) social media in a smart and efficient way, e.g., online review platforms and travel blogs.
10. *Reposition the business after a crisis*: some crises have such an impact on a tourism destination that we need to think about repositioning our business. Examples: the tsunami in Thailand in 2004 and terrorist attacks in Egypt in 2015. Those countries had major image problems due to a natural disaster and political conflict, respectively. They subsequently adopted a differentiation strategy.

(For more on this, see https://www.cbi.eu/tourism/how-manage-risks-tourism/.)

13.5. ENTERPRISE RISK MANAGEMENT: ACTIVITIES

Businesses of any size have to manage risks, and this is true from their creation and remains true during their lifetime. RM is an essential business activity for all enterprises. To commence operations, business owners must manage risks related to the acquisition of a location; the identification of skills, which are valuable to the enterprise; the recruitment of employees who have these skills; and the acquisition of financing, raw materials, equipment, IT systems, etc. This list contains a few examples of the risks that are relevant to an SME. Enterprise risk management (ERM) is an integrated and inclusive approach to managing risk across an organisation and its extended networks (IRM, 2016).

This section provides an overview of the steps involved in the implementation of an ERM initiative. A very helpful approach is offered by the guide *Structured Approach to ERM* (AIRMIC, ALARM, & IRM, 2010), which advises on the implementation of an ERM initiative that is compatible with ISO 31000. The purpose of the guide is to: (1) describe the principles and processes of RM, (2) provide a brief overview of the requirements of ISO 31000, (3) give practical guidance on designing a suitable framework and (4) give practical advice on implementing ERM.

The implementation of RM that is aligned with ISO 31000:2009 is done with the primary aim of successfully achieving objectives. It is recommended that RM be implemented by (1) developing a clear plan, (2) implementing the plan as it was designed, (3) verifying that the plan is delivering the set objectives and then (4) acting to modify the plan in response to the information flowing from the monitoring and review stages (i.e. what works well, what should be adjusted to improve results). These activities are outlined below.

13.5.1. Planning and Design

A number of factors should be considered when designing and planning an ERM initiative. The range of benefits the organisation seeks to achieve will define the scope of the initiative. As for the RM framework, arrangements need to be in place to ensure continuous improvement in performance.

13.5.2. Implementation and Benchmarking

To achieve a comprehensive RM approach, an organisation needs to undertake suitable and sufficient risk assessments.

Establish risk assessment procedures: Risk assessment will be required as part of all decision-making processes, for instance, in relation to routine operations and proposed projects.

Undertake risk assessments: An organisation should develop benchmarks to determine the significance of the identified risks. The nature of these benchmark tests will depend on the type of risk. For risks that can cause disruptions to operations, the length of a disruption may be a suitable test. Having identified suitable risk assessment procedures and decided on the benchmark test of significance for different classes of risks, it will be possible to identify the attitude to that type of risk, together with the capacity of the organisation to withstand that risk.

13.5.3. Measuring and Monitoring

Risk assessments are frequently recorded in a risk register. Such a register should be viewed as a risk action plan that includes details of the current controls and any further planned actions. This will enable the internal audit function to monitor the existing controls and the implementation of any necessary additional controls.

Not only the effectiveness of existing controls and the implementation of additional controls but also the cost-effectiveness of existing controls should be monitored. Monitoring and measuring extend to an evaluation of the culture, performance and preparedness of the organisation. Evaluating the existing controls will lead to an identification of risk improvement recommendations.

13.5.4. Learning and Reporting

Completing the feedback loop on the RM process involves the important steps of learning from experience and reporting on performance. To learn from experience, an organisation needs to review risk performance indicators and measure the contribution that ERM has made to the success of the organisation.

The reasons for undertaking the RM initiative should be clearly established from the outset. If this is not done, the organisation will be unable to evaluate whether the contribution was in line with expectations. The monitoring of risk performance indicators should include an evaluation of the contribution being made by the RM.

Monitor risk performance: Learning from experience requires more than an evaluation of risk performance indicators. An annual review of the RM framework and an evaluation of the risk architecture, strategy and protocols are necessary.

Report risk performance: In addition to internal communication and reporting, there is an obligation to report externally. External risk reporting is designed to provide external stakeholders with the assurance that risks are being adequately managed. A company needs to report to its stakeholders on a regular basis, setting out its RM policies and their effectiveness in achieving set objectives.

Successful implementation of an ERM initiative is an ongoing process that entails working through the four activities and 10 steps outlined below (IRM, 2010).

The activity of 'planning and design' includes three steps, namely: (1) the identification of intended benefits of the ERM initiative, (2) the planning of the scope of the ERM initiative and develop a common language of risk and (3) the establishment of the RM strategy, framework and roles and responsibilities. The second activity, 'implementing and benchmarking', encompasses the following steps: (4) adopt suitable risk assessment procedures and an agreed risk classification system, (5) establish risk significance benchmarks and undertake risk assessments and (6) determine risk tolerance levels and evaluate existing controls.

The activity 'measuring and monitoring' includes the seventh and eighth steps, namely: (7) ensure the cost-effectiveness of existing controls and introduce improvements and (8) embed a risk-aware culture and align RM with other management tasks. The fourth and last activity, 'learning and reporting', encompasses the ninth and tenth steps, namely: (9) monitor and review risk performance indicators to measure ERM contribution and (10) report risk performance in line with legal and other obligations, and monitor improvement (IRM, 2010).

13.6. RISK MANAGEMENT STRATEGIES

After the enterprise's specific risks have been identified and the RM process has been implemented, there are several strategies which enterprises can develop in regard to different types of risk, including

- avoiding the threat;
- reducing the negative effect or probability of the threat;
- transferring all or part of the threat to another party and
- retaining/accepting some or all of the potential or actual consequences of a particular risk.

These treatment options (1) are driven by outcomes and (2) are not necessarily mutually exclusive or appropriate in all circumstances (see Table 13.2).

Ideal use of these RM strategies may not be possible. Some may involve trade-offs that are not acceptable to the entrepreneur. Let us look at these strategies in more detail.

Table 13.2. Controlling Risk: RM Strategies.

Strategy	Aim	Example
Risk avoidance	Eliminating, withdrawing from or not becoming involved, i.e. not undertaking the activity that is likely to trigger the risk	• Closing down a particular high-risk business area • Not buying a property or business so as not to take on the legal liability that comes with it
Risk reduction	Optimise – mitigate the impact, i.e. control the likelihood of the risk occurring or the impact of the consequences if the risk occurs	• Outsourcing/contracting a project of software development • Installing a fire protection system (a fire alarm)
Risk sharing	Transferring, i.e. outsourcing or insuring the risk	• Outsourcing one function (e.g. cleaning) • Transferring the risk to an external agency, such as an insurance company
Risk retention or acceptance	Accepting the risk and budgeting for it	• True self-insurance; taking over fully the risk of running the operation • A small incident

Source: Authors' elaboration, adapted from Dorfman (2007) and Hopkin (2010).

13.6.1. Risk Avoidance

A risk avoidance strategy is designed to deflect as many threats as possible, to avoid the costly and disruptive consequences of a damaging event. This includes not performing an activity that could carry risk. Avoidance may seem the answer to all risks, but avoiding risks also means missing the potential gain that accepting (retaining) the risk may have allowed. Not entering a business to avoid the risk of loss also negates the possibility of earning profits.

13.6.2. Risk Reduction

Organisations are sometimes able to reduce the extent of the effect certain risks can have on their processes. This is achieved by adjusting certain aspects of an overall project plan or organisational process or reducing its scope. Risk reduction or 'optimisation' involves reducing the severity of the loss or the likelihood of the loss occurring.

Outsourcing is an example of risk reduction, if the outsourcer can demonstrate higher capability at managing or reducing risks. Modern software development methodologies reduce risk by developing and delivering software incrementally.

13.6.3. Risk Sharing

This is briefly defined as sharing with another party the burden of loss or the benefit or gain from a risk, as well as measures to reduce a risk. Sometimes the consequences of a risk are shared or distributed among several project participants. The risk could also be shared with a third party, such as a business partner.

'Risk transfer' is often used in place of 'risk sharing', in the mistaken belief that you can transfer a risk to a third party through insurance or outsourcing. A note of caution about the purchase of an insurance contract: the risk still lies with the policy holder, i.e. the person who has been in the accident. An insurance policy simply provides that if an accident (event) occurs involving the policy holder, some compensation may be payable to him/her that is commensurate with the damage.

13.6.4. Risk Retention

This concept involves accepting the loss, benefit or gain, from a risk when it occurs. Sometimes enterprises decide that a risk is worth it from a business point of view and decide to retain the risk and deal with any potential fallout. Enterprises tend to retain a certain level of risk if a project's anticipated profit is greater than the costs of its potential risk.

Risk retention is a viable strategy for small risks, where the cost of insuring against the risk would be greater over time than the total losses sustained. All risks that are not avoided or transferred are retained by default (e.g. a war). Risk retention or acceptance is a common response to both treats and opportunities.

Case Study 13.2: A Real Business Risk: Alcohol Service and Liquor Liability

Hospitality businesses (bars, restaurants, hotels) share one common feature – a bar. Serving alcohol creates unique risks, exposing business owners to risks they must address by having specific guidelines in place. Failure to adhere to the appropriate laws and regulations for a business could result in fines, jail, licence revocation and/or bad publicity.

Failure to manage the commercial sale of alcohol in one's business could threaten its success due to increased liability exposure. What are the recommended controls? Entrepreneurs must be knowledgeable of the laws governing the service of alcohol. The success of any plan requires management's commitment to provide the necessary training, equipment and support. Training:

Barmen and waitresses should complete alcohol service training. Those involved in alcohol service need to be educated, responsible and prepared. It is the only way to make sure that they are always in control.

Staff controls: Specific actions/behaviours must be shown by management and followed by all employees. Ensure that staff have all the information required to responsibly serve alcohol at determined standards and that employees consistently observe these behaviours. Service controls: (i) drink counting −accurate drink pouring and proper drink tracking (ii) cut-off policy − a strong, consistent cut-off policy should be developed.

Security controls: a proper security programme includes procedures and training which clearly outline how employees should fulfil their duties. These training programmes provide valuable information on the best ways to de-escalate a situation, how to deny alcohol service without losing a valued customer and how to make the best of tough situations.

It is believed that the above controls can create a safer environment for customers and employees and help maintain a positive reputation/image for any enterprise.

(Source: http://www.societyinsurance.com/case_studies/).

13.7. SUMMARY

Risks constitute an integral part of tourism, sports, events and leisure activities. The concept may refer to numerous types of threats posed by the environment, technology, humans, organisations and politics. These risks could stem from a wide variety of sources, including uncertainty in financial markets, legal liabilities, management errors, project failures, credit risks, accidents, natural disasters, IT security threats and data-related risks, vandalism or events with an uncertain or unpredictable root cause. Risk involves any possible event or circumstance that can negatively influence an enterprise. Its impact can be felt or seen on the very existence, the resources (human and capital), the products and services or the customers of the enterprise, in addition to having an external impact on society, markets or the environment.

RM suggests that every probable risk must have a pre-formulated plan to deal with its possible consequences. In the field of tourism entrepreneurship, the elimination of risk by putting safety measures in place is not simply achieved by taking precautions in a haphazard manner. Rather, these tasks require an intricate, logical plan and a sensible system, which can be adhered to.

In this chapter, key issues and aspects regarding RM in tourism entrepreneurship were highlighted, such as the definitions of risk and RM, the principles of RM, the six steps of the RM process, the ISO 31000:2009 standard for RM; the main activities and actions of an ERM, and the four alternative strategies of RM. A tourism enterprise may use a single strategy – e.g. risk assumption, avoidance, retention or transfer – or a combination of these to properly manage future events. These issues were illustrated using one example and two case studies.

Review Questions

Now you may check your understanding of this chapter by answering the following questions or discussing the topics below:

- Provide a definition of risk and RM in the business field.
- Discuss the different steps in the RM process.
- Briefly discuss the standard ISO 31000:2009 for RM.
- What is the utility/value of an RM standard?
- What are the main treatments options/strategies of RM, and what is the aim of each?
- Discuss the main activities followed in implementing an RM structured approach in the business field.
- Based on your experience, provide examples of RM and discuss the ways in which the business handled this, or the strategies it used.

REFERENCES AND FURTHER READING

Association of Insurance and Risk Managers (AIRMIC), the Public Risk Management Association (ALARM) and Institute of Risk Management (IRM). (2010, 5). *A structured approach to enterprise risk management (ERM) and the requirements of ISO 31000*. AIRMIC, ALARM & IRM, London. Retrieved from: http://www.ferma.eu/app/uploads/2011/10/a-structured-approach-to-erm.pdf and www.theirm.org. Accessed on 10 April 2017.

Bentley, T. A., & Page, S. J. (2008). A decade of injury monitoring in the New Zealand adventure tourism sector: A summary risk analysis. *Tourism Management, 29*(5), 857–869.

Berg, H.-P. (2010). *Risk management: Procedures, methods and experiences*, RT&A #2(17), 1, June, 79–95.

Bhati, A., & Pearce, P. (2016). Vandalism and tourism settings: An integrative review. *Tourism Management, 57*(1), 91–105.

Business dictionary. (2016). *Risk management*. Retrieved from http://www.businessdisctionary.com/definition/risk-management.html. Accessed on 5 May 2017.

Cater, C. I. (2006). Playing with risk? Participant perceptions of risk and management implications in adventure tourism. *Tourism Management, 27*(2), 317–325.

Crockford, N. (1986). *An introduction to risk management* (2nd ed.). Cambridge: Woodhead-Faulkner.

Donohoe, H., Pennington-Gray, L., & Omodior, O. (2015). Lyme disease: Current issues, implications, and recommendations for tourism management. *Tourism Management, 46*(3), 408–418.

Dorfman, M. S. (2007). *Introduction to risk management and insurance* (9th ed.). Englewood Cliffs, NJ: Prentice Hall.

Fraser, J., Simkins, B., & Narvaez, K. (Eds.). (2014). *Implementing enterprise risk management: Case studies and best practices*. New York, NY: Wiley & Sons.

Haimes, Y. Y. (2015). *Risk modeling, assessment, and management* (4th ed.). New York, NY: Wiley & Sons.

Hopkin, P. (2010). *Fundamentals of risk management*. London: Kogan Page.

Hubbard, D. (2009). *The failure of risk management: Why it's broken and how to fix it*. New York, NY: Wiley & Sons.

Institute of Risk Management. (2010). *A structured approach to enterprise risk management (ERM) and the requirements of ISO 31000*. London: AIRMIC and IRM.

Institute of Risk Management. (2016). *Risk management*. Retrieved from https://www.theirm.org/the-risk-profession/risk-management.aspx. Accessed on 25 April 2017.

Institute of Risk Management (IRM). (2002). *A risk management standard*. IRM, London.

International Organisation for Standardisation (ISO). (2009a). *ISO/IEC Guide 73:2009: Risk management – Vocabulary*. ISO, Geneva.

International Organisation for Standardisation. (2009b). *ISO/DIS 31000. Risk management: Principles and guidelines on implementation*. ISO, Geneva.

Lark, J. (2015). *ISO 31000 Risk management: A practical guide for SMEs*. ISO, the International Trade Centre, and the United Nations Organization for Industrial Development, Geneva. Retrieved from www.iso.org. Accessed on 4 May 2017.

Piekarz, M., Jenkins, I., & Mills, P. (2015). *Risk and safety management in the leisure, events, tourism and sports industries*. Wallingford: CABI.

Rausand, M. (2011). *Risk assessment: Theory, methods, and applications*. New York, NY: Wiley & Sons.

Society for Risk Analysis. (2017). *Glossary and foundations of risk analysis*. Retrieved from http://www.sra.org/about-society-risk-analysis. Accessed on 15 May 2017.

Sönmez, S., Apostolopoulos, Y., Theocharous, A., & Massengale, K. (2013). Bar crawls, foam parties, and clubbing networks: Mapping the risk environment of a Mediterranean nightlife resort. *Tourism Management Perspectives*, 8(1), 49–59.

CHAPTER 14

TAKING THE EXIT ROUTE: REASONS, METHODS AND A PLAN

Nkoana Simon Radipere and Msindosi Sarah Radebe

ABSTRACT

Purpose — *The scope of this chapter is to present the key issues of taking the exit route from a business venture. Its aim is therefore to analyse the main strategies and suitable methods to harvest a business venture, as well as to outline the appropriate plan and the main aspects of valuation.*

Methodology/approach — *Literature review was conducted on issues and aspects that are related to harvesting of a business. These issues have been illustrated with an example and case studies.*

Findings — *This chapter highlights the fact that every mindful entrepreneur will normally have a roadmap and a plan to exit from a business venture. It provides entrepreneurs with guidance to elaborate suitable strategies and adopt appropriate methods to exit a business.*

Research limitations — *This chapter is explorative in nature, based on a literature review.*

Managerial/practical implications — *Entrepreneurs often find themselves consumed in making a business successful, while they neglect to elaborate a plan for harvesting a business venture. This chapter provides entrepreneurs with the needed guidance on how to exit a business by preparing an effective plan, in case it is not successful or for personal reasons. It also presents a set of practical advices on decision-making about related strategies and methods.*

The Emerald Handbook of Entrepreneurship in Tourism, Travel and Hospitality:
Skills for Successful Ventures, 241–257
Copyright © 2018 by Emerald Publishing Limited
All rights of reproduction in any form reserved
ISBN: 978-1-78743-530-8/doi:10.1108/978-1-78743-529-220181018

Originality/value — *The chapter analyses, in a comprehensive and practical way, the reasons, methods and strategies of harvesting, as well as the elements of an effective plan to take the exit route.*

Keywords: Exit route; harvesting; exit strategy; plan; methods; valuation and payment

---

Learning Objectives

After studying this chapter, you should be able to:

- discuss the reasons why an entrepreneur/business owner decides to 'harvest' or exit a business;
- establish which situations can cause a business owner to implement an exit strategy;
- explain the importance of having an exit or harvest plan;
- describe ways of developing an effective exit plan;
- present the different methods of harvesting;
- discuss the various valuation and payment methods used when harvesting.

14.1. INTRODUCTION

For every successful entrepreneur, the road into the business world is often more clearly laid out than the route leading away from involvement. A well-drawn roadmap for the endgame can be the difference between achieving success and missing the target on important life goals. Therefore, a well-prepared, well-crafted and effective exit plan can provide a valuable service (Butler, 2012).

Most entrepreneurs focus on growing their venture, rather fleshing out a plan for exiting that venture in years to come. It is always better for an entrepreneur to consider his/her exit sooner, rather than later. Of course, an exit strategy is also always of importance to external investors. Entrepreneurs must be aware that an exit strategy for their venture means they will exit or quit the venture which they initially started.

An exit strategy is defined as that component of the business plan in which an entrepreneur describes a method by which investors can achieve a tangible return on their investment. The entrepreneurial process is not complete until the owners and any other investors have exited the venture and captured the value created by the business. This final and important phase can be enhanced through an effective 'harvest', that is, harvesting value from the business. The goal for the businessperson is to create value during his/her entrepreneurial journey, by making a surplus and finishing well. In contemplating the harvest or exit route, the entrepreneur should be proactive by starting to plan for this at an early stage. She/he must not wait for the venture to fail or stop moving forward, because this will decrease its value, leaving him/her in a bad negotiating position and at the mercy of potential buyers. The harvesting potential of a venture which is in trouble is very low, and it may be better to think about disinvestment alternatives (Nieman & Nieuwenhuizen, 2014).

Harvesting, which is part of the venture's strategy, cannot be carried out overnight: the decision must be taken during the life cycle of the enterprise. The critical importance of elaborating or fleshing out a harvest or exit plan is based on the following considerations/reasons:

- Harvesting or exiting is the method which entrepreneurs and investors use to leave a business, while ideally still reaping the value of their investment in that business venture.
- It involves reducing business risk, capturing value and creating future options.
- The business's appeal to investors is driven by the availability of harvest options.

The main aim of harvesting is not just to sell up and leave the company; in essence, it is a long-term goal aimed at creating added value or benefit to the business and gaining from it. Harvesting could, however, be motivated by personal factors such as death, disability, divorce and many other reasons (Van Aardt et al., 2016).

The aim of this chapter is to give a brief account of harvesting as an exit strategy and to outline the process of achieving an identified end goal which can repay an entrepreneur for his/her hard work and inputs.

The focus here is on presenting and discussing key questions – why and how – in this field, with the aim of assisting businesspersons and entrepreneurs in the decision-making process, when they are considering an exit strategy as the end of the life cycle of a specific business venture.

To gain insight into the topic of exiting a business, this chapter attempts to respond to the following questions:

- Why is it important for business owners to consider reasons for exiting or harvesting an enterprise/businesses venture?
- What methods can be followed in taking an exit route?
- How can business owners develop a good exit plan?
- Which evaluation methods could be appropriate for assessing the value of a business, when implementing harvesting as an exit strategy?

14.2. REASONS FOR HARVESTING

Harvesting is essential for all entrepreneurs, as it offers a means of capturing or revealing value, reducing risk and generating exit options. In essence, it is about more than money, as it also involves personal and non-financial considerations. Therefore, despite realising an acceptable monetary value for the company, an entrepreneur who is not prepared for the lifestyle transition that accompanies the harvest may come away disappointed with the overall outcome. Thus, elaborating on, and implementing, a harvest strategy is as crucial to the entrepreneur's personal success as it is to his/her financial success (Petty, 2015).

In any business, the reasons for harvesting can vary considerably depending on the venture's size, its life cycle phase, as well as on the stage of the entrepreneur's life cycle. These reasons can be classified into four broad categories: personal reasons, financial reasons, failure and outside/external factors (Nieman & Nieuwenhuizen, 2014).

14.2.1. Personal Goals

At the early stage of a venture, the harvesting option is the last thing entrepreneurs think about − it only becomes important when they start to think of exiting the business. At that stage, entrepreneurs think about harvesting, because they want to profit from all the inputs they made over the years. When entrepreneurs start feeling dejected by an environment characterised by tedious work, are faced with long work hours and unmet expectations, then they begin to re-evaluate both the projects and their aims. Then harvesting suddenly becomes an option worthy of serious consideration.

14.2.2. Retirement

Most entrepreneurs think of retiring when they are older and have been in business for many years. Because they have put everything into the business, they think of reaping the fruits of their labours (the harvest). They might feel that it would be better to leave the business once they have made enough money and before they become too old.

14.2.3. Succession

Succession can be one of the reasons why entrepreneurs choose to harvest. For instance, when a child has to be absorbed into a business with the aim of taking leadership of the company later on, the situation can become very awkward.

Conflict can arise between the old and new generation if no proper succession plan is in place; therefore, it is important to define the roles of each party. It must also be noted that succession is not limited to an entrepreneur's own family, but might even include the in-laws.

14.2.4. Willingness to Make a Change

Entrepreneurs might prefer to pursue other business ideas or opportunities that they have identified but may lack sufficient financial resources or require capital from the existing business to start a new venture. During the harvesting process, the seeds of renewal and reinvestment are sown.

14.2.5. Other External Forces

Certain external forces are beyond the entrepreneurs' control but may force them to make a harvesting decision. These forces/factors include the death of a loved one or spouse, health-related concerns, mental or psychological breakdown, the loss of key expertise from the venture, significant changes in the institutional/legislative framework and negative developments in conditions within the external environment/market context.

14.3. THE CONTEXT: SITUATION AND FACTORS

Sometimes too much pressure can be exerted on an entrepreneur to harvest. This happens when the situation changes, the number of options diminishes, and the businessperson is required to take a step by exiting the company. It is always important to choose the right time to harvest.

An entrepreneur's decision to harvest can be influenced by internal and/or external factors. Some issues and challenges in the business/market environment may influence his/her strategy: these can be market related (customers, competitors, suppliers and intermediaries/distribution channels) or related to the macro environment (political, economic, social, technological and other factors).

Internal factors are mainly related to business performance. The impact of the harvesting strategy and the process, which is followed to arrive at that point, can be the result of the business's performance level and/or a crisis:

- *Underperformance.* This condition is not difficult to determine with proper analysis and comparison. There are many harvest options at this stage, provided the opportunity is good for the successor.

- *Good performance.* It is always advisable to harvest when the venture is performing well in terms of revenue, profitability and market share (both actual and forecast).
- *Trouble.* At the stage of trouble, the business owner's harvest options decrease, unless the buyer is ignorant about both the business and its industry. It is important for the owner to know that losing his/her strategic positioning may have an effect on his/her harvest options, more so than when the trouble emanates from a competitor who has just entered the market.
- *Crisis.* In the event of a crisis, the owner is forced to sell the business venture to a competitor or someone who is looking to make an acquisition.
- *Failure.* In the case of failure, the owner has no other harvesting options to pursue, without incurring significant losses (see Nieman & Nieuwenhuizen, 2014).

In addition to the above, several other factors may contribute to render the situation more severe. A number of these aspects are listed below.

14.3.1. Strategic Pressure

This is the case where the business loses its strategic position in the market. Sometimes this happens when market conditions are no longer conducive to the venture or its products and services, which means the entity no longer represents a good business opportunity. Here is an example: a retail business might start to lose customers because of two reasons/factors: (1) the intensification of competition in the industry and (2) a failure to adopt digital channels for sales, for instance, not investing in a website/online presence to reach the targeted market segments. The business is no longer matching or complying with changing business conditions and is therefore under strategic pressure. Its business opportunities are thus no longer good, and it is under threat from new entrants to the industry. Such a scenario can drive the business towards failure, because of lower profit margins and insufficient cash flow. Any such venture will go out of business unless it changes its operational approach and strategic positioning. The ultimate outcome will be the option (or 'forced option') to harvest.

14.3.2. Urgency and Other Factors

Urgency refers to how quickly an entrepreneur needs to harvest. It is insignificant to opt for harvesting without first looking at certain factors. Business owners need to acknowledge that time is a vital asset of the harvesting strategy and plan. Urgency is closely related to timing and patience – two variables which are the underlying principles of the harvesting process.

Another determining factor could be the venture's low performance, which might force the entrepreneur to take the exit route and harvest. Keep in mind that there are numerous issues which can complicate the choice of harvesting strategy (Nieman & Nieuwenhuizen, 2014).

14.4. TAKING THE EXIT ROUTE WITHIN A BROADER STRATEGY

An entrepreneur could take the decision to harvest as a result of (and in the context of) a broader business strategy. There are a number of broad strategies that may influence an entrepreneur's decision to harvest, including the growth, retrenchment, stability and combined/mixed strategies, as outlined below (Nieman & Nieuwenhuizen, 2014).

14.4.1. Growth Strategy

An entrepreneur who adopts a growth strategy has two options to implement this, namely (1) to grow the business internally, in size (organic growth) or (2) to grow it externally by acquiring more ventures (growth by acquisition).

- *Organic growth.* This entails the expansion of a business through increased market share, and it can be achieved by enlarging the existing business and increasing sales through market development. In other words, the business attains growth by using the available resources in the existing business more efficiently.
- *Growth by acquisition.* This strategy refers to the buying of additional related (or unrelated) ventures to enlarge business operations. Under acquisition circumstances it is difficult to expand, since the potential buyer might wonder why an entrepreneur wants to harvest at the same time. A wise way would be to do so at an advanced stage, which would prevent the entrepreneur from hampering the harvest.

14.4.2. Retrenchment Strategy

In this context, it is necessary for some operations to be downsized or fully eliminated. The impact of this strategy is that future sales and costs are limited. The elimination of fixed operational costs (e.g. labour expenses) is part of the retrenchment process. A retrenchment strategy is often related to trouble with the venture, since the potential buyer may be concerned about negative growth.

14.4.3. Stability Strategy

This strategy is followed by an entrepreneur who is satisfied with employing a small number of employees and does not want to grow the business or retrench. Under normal conditions most entrepreneurs would want their business to grow, but due to unforeseen circumstances (such as not wanting to disturb the existing order of things), they might prefer stability. Growth sometimes requires entrepreneurs to obtain more capital investment. Stability in a business may not influence the harvest decision significantly, but if it continues for a lengthy period of time, the buyer may believe that the business (or market) has stagnated.

14.4.4. Combined/Mixed Strategy

This strategy could be a combination of the growth, retrenchment and stability strategies. An entrepreneur might consider combining both strategies by growing one part of the business operations, while retrenching other business functions. This occurs when she/he wants to better position certain parts of a business unit, to render them more efficient and effective. The decision to harvest can be affected by the stage of the strategy: the current strategy in a venture can determine the intensity of, as well as the choices available for, the harvest.

14.5. THE IMPORTANCE OF HARVESTING

Business owners usually do not like to think of harvesting, though several events may occur to indicate the failure of their business venture. This may result in entrepreneurs taking the harvest decision as a result of unexpected events such as a financial crisis or a 'forced choice'. Most entrepreneurs grow their enterprises well, but fail to develop an effective harvesting plan and end up unable to capture the full value of the business they worked so hard at, for so many years. It is important for an entrepreneur to learn that harvesting encompasses many aspects, including capturing value (money), reducing risk and creating future options. Harvesting or exiting from a business signals the end of a chapter, not the end of the entrepreneur's business life or journey.

Harvesting is important to both the owner and investors (such as angels and venture capitalists), as they provide high-risk capital. Therefore, the enterprise's reputation, attractiveness and appeal to investors are driven by the harvest options available to the business. Investors will not invest in a business venture unless they are convinced that harvesting opportunities will prevail in the future (Van Aardt et al., 2016).

> **Case Study 14.1:   Issues to Consider in Decision-making about Harvesting**
>
> Twenty years ago, entrepreneur Ima R., started a restaurant with a liquor licence. At that stage, he was 23 years old − this winter he will be 43. The restaurant is a successful business which provides him with a good living. However, each day Ima feels more unfulfilled in what he is doing, because he believes that much of his business knowledge is being wasted, just doing the same thing year after year. Ima has tried some ventures on the side, and even considered selling the business, but it is too large to be bought by a local competitor and too small to attract the attention of large companies. Besides, he would not know what to do if he sold it − whatever he does next must bring in as much money as he is earning right now. Ima likes the restaurant business but does not know if he will regret letting go of the one thing he has had all his adult life.
>
> In an attempt to obtain relevant information on how to exit a business, Ima consulted one of his friends (who has an **MBA** with a major in Entrepreneurship) for advice. During their encounter, his friend identified the four categories of reasons associated with harvesting. He further indicated which broad strategies can have an impact on the decision to harvest. This greatly conflicted Ima, as he had never considered the factors which his friend highlighted. Now he was faced with the challenge of evaluating his reasons for wanting to exit, as well as the strategies he could use to his benefit when exiting.
>
> Question/issue to discuss: Are there any other options for Ima R. to consider, besides selling his business?
>
> *Source*: Authors

14.6. METHODS OF HARVESTING

Numerous small business owners do not like to think about harvesting their venture, even when the business or firm is greatly affected by turbulence. It is therefore important to remind business owners that harvesting (or exiting) is the method owners and investors use to get out of a business and, ideally, reap the value of their investment in the firm (Petty, 2015).

This section focuses on the ways in which entrepreneurs might implement the decision to take the exit route or to harvest. There are four basic ways to harvest an investment in a business, namely by: (1) selling the business, (2) offering stock to the public, (3) using private equity recapitalisation and (4) forming a partnership with another entrepreneur.

14.6.1. Selling the Business

It is always important for an entrepreneur to know the value of his/her business and how to structure payment for that business. Often an entrepreneur's motivation to sell the business relates to retirement and estate planning as well the desire to diversify his/her investment. Entrepreneurs must understand what they want to achieve from the sale if they identify possible buyers, because those buyers may come from unexpected sources (customers, suppliers, employees, friends, family or even competitors). Entrepreneurs can still make use of the services of a broker (a professional who assists in the buying and selling of a business) to find a possible buyer, as such an individual can provide valuable guidance and even facilitate negotiations.

The main types of potential buyers, when selling a business, are:

- *Strategic buyers.* this can be a firm in a similar line of business, but in a different market. Alternatively, it can be someone in an unrelated business who wants to acquire certain of the strengths which are evident in the seller's business, to help the buyer's existing business;
- *Financial buyers.* when a financial buyer acquires/takes over an existing business, she/he hopes to increase future sales growth and reduce costs. Such buyers always look to a firm's stand-alone and cash-generating potential as sources of value. Before the buyer decides to buy, the acquired firm must have the following characteristics: steady earnings over time; an attractive growth rate; an effective management team and assets that can be used as collateral on debt;
- *Employees.* some companies have 'employee stock ownership plans' which use employees' retirement contributions to buy company stock from the owner and hold it in trust. The stock is later distributed to employees' retirement plans.

14.6.2. Opting for an Initial Public Offering

If a business venture has performed well for several years, it is prudent to think about disinvestment alternatives when it becomes clear that failure is inevitable. A business can be harvested through an initial public offering (first sale of shares of a company's stock to the public). It is important for an entrepreneur to think about the costs associated with running a publicly traded business. One of the reasons for going public would be to create a ready market for publicly trading the stock of the business.

14.6.3. Choosing Private Equity Recapitalisation

As opposed to a public offering, a business venture can take a private route in exiting through a private equity recapitalisation. This is a method whereby private equity investors provide additional financing (debt and equity) to a business that allows an entrepreneur the opportunity to cash out a portion of his/her investment, while possibly continuing to run the business. The advantages of private equity investors are that an entrepreneur can sell most of his/her stock immediately, and that such investors are more flexible in structuring their investment to meet the entrepreneur's needs.

14.6.4. Forming an Alliance/Partnership with Another Business Venture

This is an interim step that leads to the complete takeover and the owner's withdrawal after a certain period of time. The entrepreneur identifies and enters into an alliance agreement with that business. The agreement can pertain to the production, purchasing or distribution of goods. It is important for an entrepreneur to realise that alliances are especially helpful when other people's resources are used to expand operations.

Business owners can employ two additional methods when planning to exit a business venture:

- *Capital cow.* This is when an entrepreneur prefers to proceed with the enterprise, but uses the cash it generates as capital to establish an alternative business. The cash can be used as an investment, rather than using it in another business. It enables the entrepreneur to exploit other windows of opportunity and serves as a source of capital;
- *Disinvestment alternative.* An entrepreneur can follow this route when other options to harvest are not possible. Alternatives include filing for bankruptcy; closing the business and selling its assets; entering a defensive merger; and splitting the business into workable units and selling those to interested parties such as employees (Spinelli & Adams, 2012).

Micro Example 14.1:   Increasing the Value of Venture

A couple owns and runs a family restaurant, the husband is the head chef and his wife is the manager. The restaurant has been in business for 30 years, has a loyal clientele, and is very profitable. If the owner and his wife leave, the recipes and cooking style go with him, and the customer service and operational efficiency go with her. There is not much left in the business except the reputation. However, if the owner and his wife begin planning for sale years before, they can make the restaurant much more valuable to a potential buyer. For instance, the chef can hire and train one or two assistant chefs, and teach them his secret recipes and cooking techniques. The wife, who manages the restaurant, can train one or two assistants. She can develop procedure manuals or at least define what the procedures should be. She can also introduce her protégées to regular clients so they know who they are. After a few years, a buyer could easily takeover the business and keep it going as long as he is able to keep the now well-trained staff on board. By following the above steps, the couple has significantly increased the value of their business.

Source: Authors' elaboration.

14.7. VALUATION AND PAYMENT METHODS

When an entrepreneur/business owner realises that the business venture is moving towards the harvest period, the main/key issues to consider and make decisions about are (1) the harvest value of the business and (2) the method of payment when the agreement to sell the business has been concluded.

14.7.1. Harvest Value

Evaluation is an important process in estimating the value of the business throughout its life cycle. For the business owner, it is important to determine this value while the business is a going concern, based on its assets (e.g. investments in the market, stocks, patents and trademarks) or liabilities (e.g. bonds). The value of the business is created when its return on investment is higher than the investor's opportunity cost of funds. The incremental value is shared between the old and the new owner, depending on the negotiation skills of each. There is no formula to determine the price of a private company, rather, the price is determined through negotiations between buyer and seller. But first, there must be a willing buyer.

14.7.2. Method of Payment

An entrepreneur or owner has three basic choices when selling the business: selling business assets; selling shares or if buyer is another company they can merge with the buyer by combining the two businesses into one. The owner may prefer to sell the business's stock, for the gain on the sale will be a capital gain. The harvesting owner can be paid in cash or in the stock. It is a disadvantage to the entrepreneur who accepts the stock in payment, since she/he is unable to affect the value of the stock once she/he has sold the business (Longenecker, Palich, Hoy, Radipere, & Phillips, 2016).

What are the issues involved in valuing a business that is being harvested and deciding on the method of payment? The key issues are strategic pressure, anticipation of the harvest, crisis or urgency and other aspects like the entrepreneur's personal situation.

Another issue that needs careful consideration is the distribution of the company's value. This strategy involves the owner withdrawing investment in the form of the company's cash flow. This can occur when the owner sells off assets and liquidates the business. During the early years of operation, cash is mostly used for growing the business. As the business grows, opportunities to continue growing start to decline, and a sizable cash flow starts to become available. Then the owner can start withdrawing cash, thus harvesting his/her investment. The advantages of harvesting by slowly withdrawing a business's cash include the following: The owner can retain control of the business while she/he harvests he/his investment and does not have to seek out a buyer or incur expenses associated with closing a sale.

14.8. DEVELOPING AN EFFECTIVE HARVEST PLAN

This section deals with the elaboration/crafting of an effective exit plan. In other words, the process explains the steps to follow to achieve a profitable harvesting.

The process encompasses five steps: forecasting or anticipating the harvest, handling emotional and cultural conflict, consulting an expert, ensuring deep understanding and planning the next move. These stages are outlined below.

14.8.1. Anticipating the Harvest

Business owners need to create a clear picture of their exit goal. This stage is associated with planning for retirement, as it requires the individual to think carefully about how his/her pension funds will be spent. Similarly, in exiting a business – this is a step that business owners do not like, because it takes a lot of time and energy (on the management side) and can be distracting. Employees are also stressed, as they are not sure about the new owner. Entrepreneurs are advised to plan their exit strategy in advance, by thinking how they are going to exit.

14.8.2. Expecting Conflict (Emotional and Cultural)

Although some entrepreneurs purchase other companies, they may not be prepared to sell their own. A buyer is unemotional and detached, while a seller is likely to be more concerned about non-financial considerations. Entrepreneurs often do not make good employees, as it may be difficult for them to work under new owners. There is also a danger of cultural conflict between the acquiring and acquired firm's management. Conflicts may occur whenever an entrepreneur remains with the company after the sale.

14.8.3. Getting Good Advice: Consult an Expert

An entrepreneur must be open-minded and must not hesitate to consult an expert or other businessperson who has had a similar experience. She/he could obtain good advice from experienced professionals and those who have gone through the harvesting process. It is important to know that the same experts who helped someone build and grow their business might not be the ideal people to turn to when the time comes to sell that business.

14.8.4. Understanding Motivations

Entrepreneurs should think carefully about their motives for exiting and what they plan to do after harvesting. They should seek advice about problems that may arise post-exit and address them effectively. People so easily forget what helped them to achieve success, for instance, their work ethic, their commitment to family or other factors that worked in their favour. Once money starts rolling in, people forget to be prudent to economise.

14.8.5. What Is the Next Stage?

After exiting, the entrepreneur needs something to bring meaning to his/her life. Many have a sense of gratitude for the benefits they received from living and doing business in a capitalist system and want to give back by giving of both their time and money (Longenecker et al., 2016).

Therefore, the challenge for the entrepreneur is to prepare and plan an exit strategy properly, to develop an effective harvest plan. The following case study provides advice on this issue.

Case Study 14.2:   Preparing for the Exit: Steps to Follow

If the entrepreneur has the luxury of time, the best approach is to postpone the harvest, the sale for a few years, and gradually put some key elements in place to maximize the company's value. Ground Floor Partners (2017) suggest, 'anything that increases transparency, efficiency, revenue or profitability, or minimizes risk or costs, should be considered'. The experts recommend the following steps and measures:

- Set up and document business processes and systems. This action supports the management and provides transparency.
- Clean up the company's books. This starts with a professional accounting audit, but ends with actually implementing the auditor's recommendations. Examples include better documentation of expenses, invoices, benefits, cash management, etc.
- Conduct a proper inventory of all physical assets, such as furniture, equipment, hardware, software, and supplies, without under- or over-estimating their value.
- Hire a competent firm to conduct (i) an inclusive audit, not just a financial audit, and (ii) a valuation for your company, as this will provide unbiased estimates.
- Review all insurance policies and make sure the company is adequately insured for all major risks.
- Review all employee, partner, and provider contracts and policies to make sure the company complies with all legislation and regulations.
- Start networking with business buyers, business brokers, and other businesspersons.
- Monitor market trends and try to not miss opportunities in the market.

Source: Adapted from Ground Floor Partners (2017).

14.9. SUMMARY

The aim of this chapter has been to assist the entrepreneur with alternative exit methods and strategies that can be used or considered as alternatives when harvesting. Harvesting is a strategic tool, but strategies are also required to achieve it. It is important for any entrepreneur to understand the harvesting process, as it offers insights that will assist him/her in anticipating, planning and executing the harvesting process successfully.

Harvesting is regarded as the means entrepreneurs and investors use to exit a business and, ideally, to unlock the value of their investment in the firm. It entails more than merely selling and leaving a business, it involves capturing value (cash flows), reducing risk and creating future options. Personal goals, retirement, succession and wanting to make a change are all possible reasons why an entrepreneur might wish to exit a business venture.

Bear in mind that the size of the harvest is very important. Business owners can make use of several strategies when planning an exit route, including strategies focusing on growth, retrenchment, stability and a combination/mix of such approaches. The importance of harvesting for business owners and investors was briefly outlined as a means of assisting in decision-making in this respect. Four harvesting methods (selling the business, distributing the business's cash flows to its owners, offering stock to the public and using private equity recapitalisation) were explored. The authors also indicated that, after the decision has been reached to exit, there are certain business valuation methods that an entrepreneur can use to reap the benefits while exiting his/her business venture.

The following suggestions or recommendations could be made to any entrepreneur who wishes to harvest his/her business venture (Petty, 2015): anticipate and plan the harvest. Remember that selling a company is not the same as buying. Cash is king. Seek sound advice from experienced professionals and from those who have personally experienced the exit process. Be careful what you wish for — you may just get it. Understand what is important before harvesting the personal and financial investments you made in your company.

The crucial issue is to flesh out a very good plan, before implementing it properly.

Review Questions

Verify your understanding of this chapter by answering the following questions or discussing the topics below:

- Explain the importance of a harvest or exit plan.
- Describe the options available to an entrepreneur when it comes to harvesting.
- Which broad strategies can have an impact on the decision to harvest?
- What are the issues involved in valuing a business that is being harvested and deciding on a method of payment?
- Advise an entrepreneur in developing an effective exit plan.

REFERENCES AND FURTHER READING

Bird, M., & Wennberg, K. (2016). Why family matters: The impact of family resources on immigrant entrepreneurs' exit from entrepreneurship. *Journal of Business Venturing, 31*(6), 687–704.

Butler, C. (2012). *Ext strategy for small business clients.* Retrieved from http://www.peoriamagazines.com/ibi/2012/jan/exit-strategies-small-business-clients. Accessed on 12 October 2017.

De Tienne, D. R., McKelvie, A., & Chandler, G. N. (2015). Making sense of entrepreneurial exit strategies: A typology and test. *Journal of Business Venturing, 30*(2), 255–272.

Ground Floor Partners. (2017). Retrieved from https://groundfloorpartners.com/exit-strategies-for-small-business-owners/. Accessed on 25 October 2017.

Hsu, D. K., Wiklund, J., Anderson, S. E., & Coffey, B. S. (2016). Entrepreneurial exit intentions and the business–family interface. *Journal of Business Venturing, 31*(6), 613–627.

Longenecker, J. G., Palich, L. E., Hoy, F., Radipere, S., & Phillips, M. (2016). *Small business management: Launching and growing entrepreneurial venture* (1st South African ed.). South-Western: Cengage Learning.

Mathias, B. D., Solomon, S. J., & Madison, K. (2017). After the harvest: A stewardship perspective on entrepreneurship and philanthropy. *Journal of Business Venturing, 32*(4), 385–404.

Nieman, G., & Nieuwenhuizen, C. (2014). *Entrepreneurship: A South African perspective* (3rd ed.). Pretoria: Van Schaik.

Petty, W. J. (2015). *Harvesting the entrepreneurial venture*. Retrieved from: http://www.blackwell-reference.com/subscriber/uid=303/tocnode?id=g9780631233176_chunk_g978140511650311_ss1-2. Accessed on 12 October 2017.

Spinelli, S., & Adams, R. (2012). *New venture creation: Entrepreneurship for the 21st century* (9th ed.). New York, NY: McGraw-Hill.

Van Aardt, I., Barros, M., Clarence, W., van Rensburg, J., Radipere, S., Venter, K., & Visser, K. (2016). *Principles of entrepreneurship and small business management*. Cape Town: Oxford University Press South Africa.

Van Aardt, I., & Bezuidenhout, S. (Eds.). (2014). *Entrepreneurship and new venture management* (5th ed.). Cape Town: Oxford University Press.

Wennberg, K., Wiklund, J., De Tienne, D. R., & Cardon, M. S. (2010). Reconceptualizing entrepreneurial exit: Divergent exit routes and their drivers. *Journal of Business Venturing, 25*(4), 361–375.

Yamakawa, Y., & Cardon, M. S. (2017). How prior investments of time, money, and employee hires influence time to exit a distressed venture, and the extent to which contingency planning helps. *Journal of Business Venturing, 32*(1), 1–17.

PART V
MARKETING THE TOURISM
BUSINESS OFFERING

CHAPTER 15

MARKETING OF TOURISM SERVICES/EXPERIENCES

Hongfei Bao

ABSTRACT

Purpose — *This chapter's aim is to present the key elements of marketing of tourism services and experiences by taking the perspective of a new tourism entrepreneur. The chapter's focus is on better understanding and efficient implementation of marketing principles.*

Methodology/approach — *This chapter was built on literature review of marketing of tourism services at business level. A practical approach has been adopted and implemented in illustrating the variables of marketing mix.*

Findings — *This chapter highlights the fact that in order to be successful in the field of marketing, tourism entrepreneurs should consider and implement all elements of marketing mix as an integral and comprehensive set; all marketing variables are interlinked and interrelated.*

Research limitations — *This chapter is explorative in nature, based on a literature review. It takes more entrepreneurial/practical than academic approach.*

Managerial/practical implications — *A marketing plan for tourism services/ experiences constitutes a chain of strong bonds that guide the tourism business forward in making the chain stronger and more efficient. When an entrepreneur/manager is considering adding a new feature or changing existing elements, he/she has to consider the whole picture of the actions and the resulting outputs.*

The Emerald Handbook of Entrepreneurship in Tourism, Travel and Hospitality:
Skills for Successful Ventures, 261–275
Copyright © 2018 by Emerald Publishing Limited
ISBN: 978-1-78743-530-8/doi:10.1108/978-1-78743-529-220181021

Originality/value — *This chapter discusses an extended marketing model; the model of 10 Ps — Product, Place, Pricing, Promotion, Partners, Presentation, People, Process, Physical evidence and Passion under two stages, before and during the experience consumption/encounter.*

Keywords: Marketing; tourism services/experiences; marketing mix; 10 Ps model; experience encounter; tools and techniques

---

Learning Objectives

After studying this chapter, you should be able to:

- present the principles of marketing tourism services;
- identify the key elements of marketing mix in tourism services;
- describe the available tools for promotional purposes for a tourism business;
- identify the objectives of promotion and present the promotional tools/techniques;
- discuss the issue of partnerships in marketing tourism services and illustrate it with an example;
- highlight the importance and the elements of the physical environment;
- discuss the adequate approach of using elements of marketing mix during the experience encounter.

15.1. INTRODUCTION

During the last two decades, economies throughout the world have undergone extensive social and economic transformation. One of the most significant of these changes is the increased share of expenditure on services. Tourism is defined as the provision of services and products to people who are travelling and staying outside their usual residence for a period shorter than one year, for leisure or business purposes. The marketing of tourism services is the managerial function of business/providers that includes all the activities that are in anyway connected to the communication with promotion and sale of their offerings in the tourism market.

The aim of marketing in tourism is the production and distribution of products that suit to tourist consumers, facilitating the exchange process in the tourism market. Marketing in tourism could be seen as a subsystem of marketing services system (Elida, 2014). As already mentioned in previous chapters, the tourism product is complex, because it consists of goods and services provided by different businesses.

Nowadays, the tourism product/experience is usually a combination of accommodation, travel, transport and entertainment/leisure services. The aim of marketing in tourism is, therefore, information gathering and analysis, based on which the tourism offering is conceived, designed and developed as an integrated offering to permanently communicate with customers.

The differences between tourism marketing and other services are: (1) tourism products are provided in terms of transportation, hospitality, recreational and leisure experiences; (2) tourists must travel to the place of production (destination) instead of a product moving to the tourist and (3) travel contributes a significant portion of the time and expenditure related to recreational and tourism experiences (Middleton, Fyall, Morgan, & Ranchhod, 2009; Srinivasan, 2009). In order to be successful in the field of marketing, tourism businesses need to fully apprehend the main differences between marketing goods and services: the behaviour, motivations and requirements of tourists, and the unique characteristics of tourism experiences. This chapter will present and discuss the key elements of marketing with the aim to provide prospective entrepreneurs with the needed knowledge and background for better understanding and efficient implementation. In this regard, the 10 Ps — namely Product, Place, Pricing, Promotion, Partners, Presentation, People, Process, Physical evidence and Passion — are introduced and discussed under two stages, namely (1) before the experience consumption (pre-encounter) and (2) during the tourism experience consumption (while providing the services).

15.2. MARKETING MIX FOR TOURISM SERVICES: THE 10 PS MODEL

Marketing in service industries, such as travel and tourism, strives towards converting the intangible product into an experience that customer will value and cherish. Tourism market is a set of relations of demand and offer focusing on the exchange of goods and services by means of money and with the extent determined by the prices of goods and services (Elida, 2014). Marketing activities play a key role in achieving the competitive position of a tourism enterprise, in the sense that they enhance to achieve the most optimal combination of marketing mix. The chosen marketing strategy varies through a specific elements' combination of the marketing mix. The goal is to meet in a more efficient way the needs of consumers in the target market segment.

Academic literature and business studies/reports encourage entrepreneurs/ managers to use marketing mix models to guide their decision-making (Kotler, Armstrong, Wong, & Saunders, 2008; Lilien, 1994). The classical marketing mix model, known as the 4 Ps (Price, Product, Place and Promotion) is the cornerstone of any marketing activity (McCarthy, 1975). This traditional marketing mix was also criticised for ignoring the impacts of the business environment on marketing decisions. The external environment factors have an important influence on the marketing strategies (Kotler, Haider, & Rein, 1993). Forces of external environment are always uncontrollable. Moreover, there might be differences between production and service that should be taken into consideration. These characteristics led to the conception and adoption of an expanded marketing mix for all services reflected in the 7 Ps (original 4 Ps, plus Physical environment/evidence, People and Process).

In this chapter, a model of 10 Ps will be introduced and discussed, as nowadays it is accepted that three additional factors to the 7 Ps, are critical, namely Partners, Passion and Presentation. Therefore, the chapter defines the 10 Ps as below.

1. *Price* is the amount the consumer must exchange to receive the offering.
2. *Place* includes the location of a business as well as the activities that make the product available to target market segments/consumers.
3. *Product* means the goods-and-service combination the enterprise offers to the target market segment/s.
4. *Promotion* includes all the activities undertaken to inform consumers about the products and to encourage potential customers to purchase these products.
5. *Physical environment* is the physical context in which the service is delivered and any tangible component that facilitates the communication of the service. It is the context in which the interaction between the provider and customer takes place.
6. *People* are all human actors who play a part in service delivery and thus influence the buyers' perceptions (the business personnel, customers and other customers in the service environment).
7. *Processes* are the actual procedures, mechanisms and flow of activities by which the service is delivered, that is, the service delivery and operating systems.
8. *Partners* and collaborations can make a successful business in the increasingly integrated tourism industry.
9. *Passion* can be an activity, an object, another person or even an abstract concept, idea, cause or goal.
10. *Presentation* includes any activity introducing products and services, contributing to increasing a company's brand awareness and sales.

The following sections are dealing with the various elements/components of marketing mix in temporal terms, before and during the consumption experience, the encounter between tourism business and consumers.

15.3. PRE-ENCOUNTER: BEFORE THE TOURISM EXPERIENCE

There are six key elements of marketing on which a tourism business should focus before the consumption experience. These are Product, Place, Price, Promotion, Partnership and Presentation. The main aim is to persuade and attract the potential consumers to experience its offering.

15.3.1. Product

From a marketing perspective, a 'product' is defined as a good or service that most closely meets the requirements of a particular market and yields enough profit to justify its continued production and offering. There are usually choices or options for product assembly, because products include both tangible and intangible elements (Benur & Bramwell, 2015; Middleton et al., 2009). In the tourism context, the tangible element could be a hotel room or the lunch and drink we have in a restaurant. The intangible element could include the service provided by the staff, their attitude and behaviour. The service provided by a tourist guide service is another example of intangible element.

The quality of tangible elements is important, namely the atmosphere/ambience in a hotel with music, lighting, interior design in rooms and display of the food. For instance, Lotte Hotel Jeju, South Korea, decorated everything from the corridor to the amenities in the theme of Hello Kitty, which succeeded in creating a space that realises every little girl's dream world. However, compared to the tangible product, the intangible element is more important in tourism industry, particularly in the online tourism context (Kotler, Burton, Deans, Brown, & Gary Armstrong, 2012). For instance, the tourism companies and other providers in a tourism destination have their own webpages to develop their unique marketing strategies in order to attract tourists. Moreover, the online intermediaries, such as Expedia and Travelocity, realise the importance of customising their offerings. They provide consumers with increased flexibility to build their package up from a 'base' model (by adding options for airlines, hotels, rental cars, and events/shows) or to exclude those features from a 'full' inclusive package (where all the features are included in the default option).

15.3.2. Place

Place is defined as the 'direct or indirect channels to market, geographical distribution, territorial coverage, retail outlet, market location, catalogues, inventory, logistics and order fulfilment' (Blythe, 2009, p. 146). The place where customers purchase the tourism product can vary greatly.

Travel agents, tour operators and tour wholesalers are a few examples of the distribution channels for tourism products. Hence, generally hotels are located at either central city or tourist zones; airlines and travel agents are around the metro city areas, malls and office complexes. Fast-food restaurants and service centres may be located in busy main streets to allow consumers walk in to experience an authentic experience value. However, certain restaurants may be located in a quiet street to maintain exclusivity and privacy. Ultimately, product or service must be available in the right place, at the right time and in the right quantity to meet tourists' requirements and needs.

With the rise and extensive use of the Internet and hybrid models of distribution, place may refer to a retail outlet, but increasingly refers to virtual stores such as a digital presence, business own website or 'a mail order catalogue, a telephone call centre or a website' (McLean, 2002). Thus, the business owners/managers should know the consumption habits and preferences of the targeted market/s, how to be there, easily accessible and guarantee the convenience to consumers. Convenience, easy information search about the product and related elements are factors of critical importance in placing and distributing business offering into the tourism markets.

15.3.3. Pricing

In simple terms, price is the amount of money that tourists pay for the product or service provided. Thus, pricing of tourism services is a very important factor compared to other elements of marketing mix. In a business environment of intense competition, higher prices could cause a decline in sales and thus influence the total income. On the other hand, the price has to cover production costs and ensure a profit (Bowie & Buttle, 2004).

Catering for the upmarket segment pricing may not fluctuate much, while businesses targeting the budget market segment may not have too much room for flexibility in pricing, and they will rely on volumes of bookings. In addition, the external environment factors, such as the government laws and regulations, weather conditions and season fluctuations in demand are very crucial for a business's pricing decisions.

The main pricing strategies are: skimming pricing, penetration pricing, premium pricing, main competition pricing, high price/quality pricing, promotional pricing, geographical pricing, price matching guarantees, cost-plus pricing, real-time pricing by competition, price discrimination and discount pricing strategy (Kotler et al., 2008)

Any pricing strategy should take into account all operational costs and commissions paid to a third party (retail travel agent, inbound tour operator or online travel agent). A more practical approach to the pricing decision-making was presented in Chapter 10 – 'Managing Financial Matters'.

15.3.4. Promotion (Communications)

In tourism industry, small- and medium-sized businesses really need to understand the importance of promotion in order to achieve the best performance. A business can utilise its human resources to the fullest and come up with strategies to promote its offering and let it flourish. There are three aims of promotional activities, namely: (1) to present the information to consumers and others, (2) to influence and increase the demand and (3) to differentiate a product (Middleton et al., 2009). The promotional plan should have specific objectives, including sales increase, new product acceptance, creation of brand equity, positioning, address a new competitor or creation of a corporate image. Promotion is the voice of an enterprise in the marketplace, sending out a loud and clear message to the audience.

A range of media and techniques can be used to convey the message and attract consumers to purchase the offering, including information kits, websites, advertising, personal selling, sales promotion, travel shows and public relations. A company's promotional tools consist of the specific blend of advertising, public relations, sales promotion and direct marketing, as briefly defined below (Philip et al., 2012):

- *Advertising.* Any paid form of non-personal presentation and promotion of ideas, goods or services by an identified sponsor.
- *Public relations.* Building good relations with the various publics of a company by obtaining favourable publicity, building up a good corporate image and handing or heading off unfavourable rumours, stories and events.
- *Sales promotion.* Short-term incentives to encourage the purchase or sale of a product or service.
- *Direct marketing.* Direct communications with carefully targeted individual consumers to both obtain an immediate response and cultivate lasting customer relationships. The adequate techniques are direct mail, telephone, e-mailing, the Internet and other tools to communicate directly with specific consumers.

The development of the Internet has changed the business environment forever. The digital presence for a tourism business, i.e. having its own website is a now a crucial ingredient to the marketing promotional strategy. Consumers can obtain instant information on products or services to enhance them in their decision-making (Middleton et al., 2009; Morrison, 2002). A more detailed analysis of marketing approach and techniques in the digital environment and online tourism market is presented in Chapter 16 — Digital Tools: Their Value and Use for Marketing Purposes.

15.3.5. Partners

Poon (1993) argues that major business actors in the tourism industry, particularly the airlines, hotels, travel agents and tour operators have increasingly integrated in an industry whose boundaries are becoming increasingly blurred. In this context, collaborations and partnerships are necessary, not a luxury (Gursoy, Saayman, & Sotiriadis, 2015). Literature (see, for instance, Hagen, 2002; Kanter, 1994) suggests 4 Cs (Compatibility, Capability, Commitment and Control) as criteria for choosing the appropriate partners. Trust has also been identified as an important factor determining whether a partnership could be sustainable or not (Medcof, 1997). The determining factors for successful partner relationships between hotels and travel agencies are trust, commitment, coordination, communication quality, information exchange, participation, usage of constructive resolution techniques and similar relative dependence (Medina & Garcia, 2000).

The main types of marketing partnerships that every small business can look to build are outlined below (Davis, 2017):

- *Revenue partners*: These could simply be the critical customers; they may justify a tailored package or their own account manager. A revenue partner may also be a valuable re-seller or maybe a key distribution channel, or a vital sponsor.
- *Product partners*: Essential suppliers are also, like vital revenue partners, difficult to replace. It could be a key product that you distribute exclusively or a vital component, such as technology or packaging.
- *Alliances*: These partnerships allow businesses to collaborate and exchange value, building and sharing plenty of smart marketing benefits.
- *Promotional and PR partnerships*: These enable the enterprise to leverage additional value by tailoring its marketing activities to fit with those from another business. The enterprise can offer value in various forms, such as cash, free products or services or access to its customer base. At best, you can get a lot from doing something very simple, such as adding reciprocal links between its website and the partner's one.

A more detailed discussion about collaborations and partnerships in the tourism field was presented in Chapter 8 – 'Collaborative Forms and Strategies for Business Venturing in Tourism Industries'.

15.3.6. Presentation

Marketing is a chain process for identifying, anticipating and satisfying consumers' requirements in a profitable manner. Marketing cannot accomplish any of its purposes without effective presentation (Cardenas, 2017). In the contemporary, highly competitive market environment cluttered with paper, audio and electronic media, the message is the foundation of the presentation that is required to attract attention, build brands and capture sales. At the same time, the Internet, social media and electronic media have exponentially expanded marketing's reach and the importance of marketing presentation. Creating relevancy, relationships and experiences is required for effective marketing presentations, and the launch should be in a variety of platforms (Kennedy, 2006). Marketing presentation has to compete for attention from people who have short attention spans, little time and overloaded schedules, making a memorable presentation key to any marketing effort (McCormick & Livett, 2012).

By using a platform in the cloud, here are four ways that presentations can be integrated and qualitative (Twila, 2017): branding and messaging consistency, brand equity/version control, time saving and cross team collaboration. Of critical importance is also the digital presence, the website design, layout and appeal (Elliot & Fowell, 2000). Consumers may reduce cognitive effort and save time through online shopping. For example, website designs that use fast presentations, uncluttered screens and easy search paths support a pleasurable and effective shopping experience by reducing shopping time and the cognitive effort of shopping.

Tourism businesses should use and implement the above-mentioned six elements/variables of marketing mix in efficient and effective way to attract potential consumers and persuade them to try, experience their offering. Once this mission has been accomplished, i.e. the consumer purchases the services/experiences on offer and becomes a customer; the business' aim is then to ensure that the offering satisfies the customers' requirements and meets the given promise.

15.4. DURING THE EXPERIENCE ENCOUNTER

Four are the key elements of marketing on which a tourism business should focus during the consumption experience, namely People, Processes, Physical environment and Passion. The main aim is to offer a high-quality offering and a memorable experience by managing the four elements/factors in an efficient way.

15.4.1. People

People are essential in the marketing of any product or service. In the service industries context in general and in the tourism industry in particular, people are not producers, but rather the products themselves (McLean, 2002). The people who provide the services are the ones who represent the company and a key to the success of the experience. People deliver services in all sorts of settings, such as travel agencies, tourist guides, hotels and restaurants and transport companies. A team of people underpins everything about the experience in an organised event (e.g. exposition, music performance and show). Behind-the-scenes, there are project managers and chefs, stewards, waiters, etc. The physical appearance, their dressing code, attitude, behaviour, knowledge/competencies and skills have a powerful impact on customers' perception of the tourism offering and experience.

Thus, many companies nowadays are interested in specially getting their staff trained in interpersonal skills and customer service with a focus on customer satisfaction/delight. All personnel need a training and skills development to ensure a high quality of personal service. Training should begin as soon as the individual starts working for an organisation during an induction. The induction will involve the person in the organisation's culture, as well as briefing him/her on operational policies and procedures. A training and development plan is designed for every staff member, which sets out personal goals linked to future performance evaluation/assessment. Customer service can add value by offering customers technical support, expertise and advice. As already mentioned in Chapter 11, 'Providing Service Quality and Customer Care in Tourism Businesses', the way staff handles a complaint could have significant impact: retaining or losing a customer, and improving or ruining a company's reputation, both affecting business performance.

15.4.2. Processes

Process refers to 'the set of activities that results in delivery of the product benefits' (Rafiq & Ahmed, 1995). A process could be a sequential order of tasks that an employee undertakes as a part of his/her job. It can represent sequential steps taken by a number of various employees while attempting to complete a task.

The various characteristics of tourism industry affect the process of tourism services. For instance, depending on the seasonality of the tourism service, the service process can be stressed, and fail, during extreme periods of demand. When the operation has too many customers, the service process can fail to cope with the demand, resulting in customer dissatisfaction. When the operation has too few customers, the atmosphere can be missing, resulting in customer disappointment. The service process management should be effective based on the actual condition and deliver a consistent service quality to the customers (Bowie & Buttle, 2004).

It is important to identify the important processes from a customer perspective and design these processes so that they contribute to customer satisfaction and customer retention. The customers who are not satisfied about the service may tell their family, friends and acquaintances (Middleton et al., 2009). These kinds of negative word-of-mouth influences can create a difficult situation for the tourism enterprise. Now, more and more professional companies are aware of the importance of handing customer complaints effectively and through the employee training programs to improve the service process. Instead of disregarding the complaints of the customer, they are encouraging customer complaints so that the company can have the chance to communicate with the customer before the negative effects emerging (Bowie & Buttle, 2004).

15.4.3. Physical Environment

Physical evidence refers to the non-human elements of the service encounter, including equipment, furniture and facilities (Bowie & Buttle, 2004). It may also refer to the more abstract components of the environment in which the service encounter occurs including interior design, colour schemes and layout. Some aspects of physical evidence provide lasting proof that the service has occurred, such as souvenirs, mementos, invoices and other livery of artefacts. Zeithaml and Arvind (2000) describe the physical environment as the space by which customers are surrounded when they experience the service. For a meal, this is the restaurant, and for a journey, it is the aircraft or other transport mode. The physical environment is made up of its ambient conditions, spatial layout and functionality, as well as signs, symbols and artefacts.

The physical environment is very important in attracting customers into the premises and in contributing to the customer experience during the service encounter. Tourism businesses have to continually investing in refurbishment in order to achieve high repeat and recommended sales and nurture customer loyalty (Bowie & Buttle, 2004; Morrison, 2002). The tourism enterprises that fail to maintain the physical environment of their premises will eventually become tired and have to compete based on lower prices to attract consumers, and this will result in lower profitability.

Case Study 15.1: Travel Aboard — Get Instant Refunds with Alipay

The business and market environment are fast changing and the tourism businesses should adapt and comply with the trends and requirements of consumers.

Alipay (or Zhifubao in Chinese Mandarin) is a third-party mobile and online payment platform, established in Hangzhou, China in February 2004 by Alibaba Group. Alipay overtook PayPal as the world's largest mobile payment platform in 2013. In the fourth quarter of 2016, Alipay had a 54 per cent share of China's US$5.5 trillion mobile payment market, by far the largest in the world, although its share fell from 71 per cent in 2015.

Alipay provides many functions and services, such as cross-border online payments, paying for daily expenses, transferring money, financing function, etc. With the growth of Chinese outbound tourism, Alipay started making face-to-face purchases in the foreign merchant's stores using the Alipay App. Alipay deducts the amount of a payment from the buyer's Alipay account in real-time in Chinese currency and settles the payment to the merchant in a foreign currency.

An increasingly number of local stores in tourism destinations realized that as the number of Chinese using Alipay increases, providing this way of payment would increase the convenience to the customers. Furthermore, Global Blue now offers an exciting new way for Alipay members to receive VAT refunds — direct to their Alipay wallet in real-time. Available in 14 major airports across Europe, this service allows Alipay members to receive refunds in their home currency within seconds, with all payments visible via the Alipay app.

Now, the participating airports are Milan Malpensa, Barcelona, Madrid, Berlin/Tegel, Amsterdam, Hamburg, Rome, Helsinki, Stockholm, Munich, Copenhagen, Zurich, Frankfurt and Oslo.

The Alipay customers travelling to these destinations can now enjoy a faster tax-free shopping journey and an improved in-airport experience. In addition, because the refund is made in your home currency, there is no further currency exchange fees, saving tourists' time and money.

Source: https://global.alipay.com; http://www.globalblue.com

15.4.4. Passion

Passion is an important aspect of entrepreneurship (Bierly, Kessler, & Christensen, 2000). Entrepreneurial passion has been defined as involving positive and intense feelings experienced from engagement in activities associated with roles that are meaningful to the self-identity of entrepreneurs (Cardon, Wincent, Singh, & Drnovsek, 2009). Vallerand (2015) points out that the object of one's passion can be an activity, an object, another person or even an abstract concept, idea, cause or goal.

This passion is an imperative in the field of marketing. Passion increases entrepreneurs' dedication and commitment to their ventures, their persistence in pursuing venture-related goals and activities, and their ability to get and stay fully engaged in their actions (Drnovsek, Cardon, & Patel, 2016). Entrepreneurial passion is also contagious to other key actors of the enterprise, such as employees. Recently, it is found that passion also affects specific domains of entrepreneurship and outcomes such as persistence (Cardon & Kirk, 2015), firm survival (Stenholm & Renko, 2016), venture growth (Drnovsek et al., 2016) and employee commitment (Breugst, Domurath, Patzelt, & Klaukien, 2017).

An entrepreneur, who does not feel passionate about what the marketing of his/her business offering, can still develop and execute an effective marketing plan. However, it is the passion for the product or service that is marketed that helps the entrepreneur keep the faith during the inevitable slow times. Passion is the driving force that inspires a 'we must win' attitude and helps the entrepreneur to design an efficient and effective marketing plan (Clow, 2013).

15.5. SUMMARY

Service industries are the source of economic leadership. Services lie at the very hub of the economic activity of any society and interlink closely with all other sectors of the economy. Tourism is no longer considered a luxury confined to economically developed countries; it has become an integral component of life-style and, thus, it has emerged as a global industry with producers and consumers being spread throughout the world. Among a host of business perspectives deal-ing with tourism-related topics, marketing is probably the most active.

The core of marketing is an exchange process where value is given and received between two or more parties. Along the continuum of such relation-ships, there are 'transactional exchanges' at one end and 'collaborative exchanges' at the other (Day, 2004). In this chapter, we have seen the eight characteristics that make marketing in tourism businesses a managerial func-tion of particular importance (Morrison, 2002). We also introduced and briefly discussed the model of the 10 Ps, the main elements of the marketing mix in communicating and promoting tourism services and experiences.

Tourism businesses should approach and implement all elements/factors of marketing mix as an integral and comprehensive set; all are interlinked and inter-related. For instance, Price and Promotional activities should be compatible with the Product and Place. As a result, a marketing mix plan constitutes a chain of strong bonds that guide the business forward in making the chain longer, stron-ger and more efficient. Whenever an entrepreneur/manager is considering adding a new feature or changing existing things, he/she has to look at the overall pic-ture and has full perception of the actions and the resulting outputs.

Review Questions

Now you may check your understanding of this chapter by answering the following questions or discussing the topics below:

- Discuss the key factors that differentiate the marketing of tourism ser-vices from the general marketing.
- Briefly present the model of the 10 Ps.
- Discuss the available tools for promotional purposes for a tourism business.
- Present some partnerships that small business can look to build.
- Outline the importance and the elements of the physical environment.
- Describe two elements/factors of marketing mix and discuss the adequate approach of using them during the experience encounter.

REFERENCES AND FURTHER READING

Alipay. (2017). Retrieved from https://global.alipay.com/. Accessed on 10 September 2017.

Benur, A. M., & Bramwell, B. (2015). Tourism product development and product diversification in destinations. *Tourism Management*, *50*(1), 213–224.

Bierly, E., Kessler, H., & Christensen, W. (2000). Organizational learning, knowledge and wisdom. *Journal of Organizational Change Management*, *13*(3), 595–618.

Blythe, J. (2009). *Key concepts in marketing*. Los Angeles, CA: Sage.

Bowie, D., & Buttle, F. (2004). *Hospitality marketing*. Oxford: Elsevier Butterworth-Heinemann.

Breugst, N., Domurath, A., Patzelt, H., & Klaukien, A. (2017). Perceptions of entrepreneurial passion and employees' commitment to entrepreneurial ventures. *Entrepreneurship Theory and Practice*, *36*(1), 171–192. Retrieved from https://doi.org/10.1111/j.1540-6520.2011.00491.x

Cardenas, H. (2017). The importance of presentation in marketing. Retrieved from http://smallbusiness.chron.com/importance-presentation-marketing-48566.html. Accessed on 23 July 2017.

Cardon, S., & Kirk, P. (2015). Entrepreneurial passion as mediator of the self-efficacy to persistence relationship. *Entrepreneurship; Theory and Practice*, *39*(5), 1027–1050.

Cardon, S., Wincent, J., Singh, J., & Drnovsek, M. (2009). The nature and experience of entrepreneurial passion. *Academy of Management Review*, *34*(3), 511–532.

Clow, B. (2013). *Everything is marketing*. Retrieved from http://allismarketing.blogspot.com/2013/01/the-many-ps-of-marketing-passion.html. Accessed on 7 September 2017.

Davis, A. (2017). *Andrew Davis: Keynote speaker & best-selling author*. Retrieved from https://www.akadrewdavis.com/. Accessed on September 15, 2017.

Day, S. (2004). Achieving advantage with a new dominant logic. Invited commentaries on 'Evolving to a new dominant logic for marketing'. *Journal of Marketing*, *68*(1), 18–19.

Drnovsek, M., Cardon, S., & Patel, C. (2016). Direct and indirect effects of passion on growing technology ventures. *Strategic Entrepreneurship Journal*, *10*(1), 194–213.

Elida, C. (2014). Marketing mix in tourism. *Academic Journal of Interdisciplinary Studies*, *3*(2), 111–115.

Elliot, S., & Fowell, S. (2000). Expectations versus reality: A snapshot of consumer experiences with Internet retailing. *International Journal of Information Management*, *20*(2), 323–336.

Global blue. (2017). Retrieved from http://www.globalblue.com. Accessed on 20 June 2017.

Gursoy, D., Saayman, M., & Sotiriadis, M. (2015). Introduction. In D. Gursoy, M. Saayman, & M. Sotiriadis (Eds.), *Collaboration in tourism businesses and destinations: A handbook* (pp. xv–xxvi). Bingley: Emerald Group Publishing Limited.

Hagen, R. (2002). Globalization, university transformation and economic regeneration. A UK case study of public/private sector partnership. *International Journal of Public Sector Management*, *15*(3), 204–317.

Kandampully, J. (2000). The impact of demand fluctuation on the quality of service: A tourism industry example. *Managing Service Quality*, *10*(1), 10–18.

Kanter, R. M. (1994). Collaborative advantage: The art of alliances. *Harvard Business Review*, *72*(4), 96–108.

Kennedy, D. (2006). *The ultimate marketing plan: Find your hook, communicate your message*. Avon, MA: Adams Media.

Kotler, P., Armstrong, G., Wong, V., & Saunders, J. (2008). *Principles of marketing* (12th ed.). London: Pearson Educational International.

Kotler, P., Burton, S., Deans, K., Brown, L., & Gary Armstrong, G. (2012). *Marketing* (9th ed.). London: Pearson Educational International.

Kotler, P., Haider, H., & Rein, I. (1993). *Attracting investment, industry, and tourism to cities, states and nations-marketing places*. New York, NY: Free Press.

Lamb, C. W., Hair, J. F., & McDaniel, C. (2012). *Essentials of marketing* (7th ed.). Boston, MA: Cengage.

Lilien, G. L. (1994). Marketing models: Past, present and future. *Research Traditions in Marketing*, *1*, 1–26.

Lotte Hotel. (2017). Retrieved from http://www.lottehotel.com/jeju/ko/accom/accommo.asp?seqNo=54&roomTypeCd=CR&roomCd=NCFK&wingDivn. Accessed on 13 September 2017.

Marketingdonut. (2017). Andrew Armour. Retrieved from http://www.marketingdonut.co.uk/marketing-strategy/cost-effective-marketing/marketing-partnerships-that-every-small-business-should-build. Accessed on 11 September 2017.

Marshall, G. W., & Johnston, M. W. (2014). *Marketing management* (2th ed.). New York, NY: McGraw Hill.

McCarthy, J. (1975). *Basic marketing: A managerial approach*. Homewood, IL: Richard D. Irwin.

McCormick, H., & Livett, C. (2012). Analysing the influence of the presentation of fashion garments on young consumers' online behaviour. *Journal of Fashion Marketing and Management*, *16*(1), 21–41.

McLean, R. (2002, October 19). *The 4 C's versus the 4 P's of marketing. Custom fit online*. Retrieved from http://www.customfitonline.com/news/2012/10/19/4-cs-versus-the-4-ps-of-marketing. Accessed on September 30, 2017.

Medcof, W. (1997). Why too many alliances end in divorce. *Long Range Planning*, *30*(5), 718–732.

Medina, D., & Garcia, M. (2000). Successful relationships between hotels and agencies. *Annals of Tourism Research*, *27*(3), 737–762.

Middleton, V. T. C., Fyall, A., & Morgan, M., with Ranchhod, A. (2009). *Marketing in travel and tourism* (4th ed.). Oxford: Elsevier.

Morrison, A. (2002). *Hospitality and travel marketing* (3rd ed.). Boston, MA: Cengage Learning.

Poon, A. (1993). *Tourism, technology, and competitive strategies*. Wallingford: CAB International.

Rafiq, M., & Ahmed, P. K. (1995). Using the 7Ps as a generic marketing mix an exploratory survey of UK and European marketing academics. *Marketing Intelligence & Planning*, *13*(9), 4–15. doi:10.1108/02634509510097793.

Rajagopal. (2007). *Marketing dynamics theory and practice*. New Delhi: New Age International.

Srinivasan, K. (2009). *Tourism marketing: A service marketing perspective*. New Delhi: AMCHSS.

Stenholm, P., & Renko, M. (2016). Passionate bricoleurs and new venture survival. *Journal of Business Venturing*, *31*(5), 595–611.

Twila, G. (2017). *The importance of presentations for marketing*. Retrieved from https://www.customshow.com/importance-presentations-marketing/. Accessed on 10 September 2017.

Vallerand, J. (2015). *The psychology of passion: A dualistic model*. New York, NY: Oxford University Press.

Zeithaml, A., & Arvind, M. (2000). E-service quality: Definition, dimensions and conceptual model. *Working Paper*. Marketing Science Institute, Cambridge, MA.

Zeithaml, C. P., & Zeithaml, V. P. (1984). Environmental management: Revising the marketing perspective. *Journal of Marketing*, *48*(2), 46–53.

CHAPTER 16

DIGITAL TOOLS: THEIR VALUE AND USE FOR MARKETING PURPOSES

Catherine Papetti, Sylvie Christofle and
Vanessa Guerrier-Buisine

ABSTRACT

Purpose — *The aim of this chapter is to present in a pedagogical way the main digital tools used by tourism-related businesses, especially by hospitality businesses. The main purpose of this chapter is to illustrate our discussion with concrete examples and to give a set of advices for efficient use of those tools.*

Methodology/approach — *Literature review was conducted on conceptual issues, as well as managerial and marketing aspects of digital tools, their value and use in the hospitality industry.*

Findings — *This chapter highlights the fact that needs in terms of digitalisation depend on the size of the hotel. The main differences can be explained by differences in terms of hotel capacity, and digital technologies should be customised to different types of structures.*

Research limitations/implications — *This chapter is exploratory in nature, based on a literature review.*

Practical implications — *It provides clear and practical guidance about the way independent hospitality businesses could use digital tools for marketing*

The Emerald Handbook of Entrepreneurship in Tourism, Travel and Hospitality:
Skills for Successful Ventures, 277–295
ISBN: 978-1-78743-530-8/doi:10.1108/978-1-78743-529-220181022

purposes. It also suggests the most efficient digital technologies to improve their performance in the field of marketing and customer relationship management.

Originality/value — *The chapter demonstrates the huge gap between best practices in the hospitality industry and the way independent enterprises really use, in practice, the digital tools for marketing purposes. It shows how digital technologies could be used in a more efficient way, to take advantage of their full potential.*

Keywords: Digital tools; online social media; marketing; hospitality industry; independent hotels; phygitalisation

---

Learning Objectives

After working through this chapter, you should be able to:

- have an overview of all the digital tools used in the tourism-related industries;
- define social media and have a better understanding of its uses and objectives;
- have a precise idea of which tools are useful for independent tourism providers/ businesses;
- discuss the opportunities for independent hotels to use some specific digital tools.

16.1. INTRODUCTION

Airlines, major hotel groups and especially online travel agencies were the first to develop digital solutions to improve the user experience and increase their online sales. The explosion over the last 15 years or so of large OTAs (Online Travel Agencies) such as Booking.com or Expedia.com has been linked to the budgets they have invested in R&D and in marketing efforts. They quickly offered tourists simple and ergonomic solutions to compose their journey. They were among the first to propose reservation systems on their websites, to develop applications, to offer packages with car rental companies. Today, airports are setting up Internet of things to improve the experience within their premises. The hotel groups create 100 per cent digitalised itineraries, allowing tourists to prepare their entire stay without leaving their smartphones and to avoid wasting their vacation time with administrative procedures. Finally, the major tourist resorts are also developing digitalised experiences, in particular, using connected objects such as beacons or bracelets allowing payment for their services without a credit card or cash.

In most small tourism businesses, human and financial resources are missing to engage in digital development. It is by taking into account multiple constraints that many start-ups deploy specialised products, offering a monthly package rather than an annual cost that is far too high for small businesses. Hotels have at their disposal a very important arsenal of technological tools to facilitate their operational and managerial management. Some of them make the most of it to streamline their staff's experience and achieve substantial savings, but existing software, tools represent a new burden on hotel budgets, and they often have to opt for one tool rather than integrating tools for each department of the hotel.

In this chapter, we will therefore take a look at all the digital technologies that tourism providers – with a special focus on hotel businesses – can deploy in the back office for all marketing and team management processes internally. In the following section, we will describe main technologies that a hotel can deploy in front office for all face-to-face operations with the customer and communication actions. In the last section, we will formulate recommendations for small independent businesses, highlighting the minimum requirements to take full advantage of these technological tools for marketing purposes, within a reasonable budget.

16.2. USE OF DIGITAL BACK-OFFICE TECHNOLOGIES

16.2.1. At the Level of the Commercialisation Process

Although most hotels today use management systems, almost all of them have basic functionalities compared to other industries. Today, there are new tools that will become real competitive advantages for hotel establishments.

The Property Management System (PMS): Tools available to facilitate procedures and optimise human or material capital are either transversal, such as the PMS (Property Management System) or specific to each department.

The PMS is the flagship and essential tool in hotel establishments. This tool concentrates all information on customers and allows hotel managers to register, bill and track their customers. All booking information is collected there. Moreover, most of technological tools are interfaced with the PMS and make it possible to condense all the useful information:

- The Central Reservation System (CRS), or the channel manager, allows real-time and two-ways connectivity with the OTAs to provide information on hotel rates and availability.

- Invoicing: Thanks to the interfaces with other services, invoicing from the PMS will group together information about consumption on restaurants, shops, spas, etc.
- The management of debtors, for a better follow-up of suppliers and customers.
- Customer relationship management (CRM), along with CARDEX that process data, allows increasingly personalised communications with customers, through emailing, push SMS texts, feedback management, loyalty programme, etc.
- The Computer-Aided Maintenance Management Tool (CAMM), which allows energy management, maintenance, teams, equipment, etc.
- Quality Management System (QMS).
- The management of links with housekeeping services for a housekeeping management.
- Monitoring of hotel statistics and key figures.

The best-known and most widely used PMSs in the hotel industry are Oracle (ex-Fidelio) and Opera, but new generations of PMS are emerging, with the aim of simplifying and making the tool more versatile, such as Hotel Optimiser. The latter concentrates all digital services found in a hotel establishment. Some tools are available to facilitate sales, such as the booking engine, which are embedded into the hotel's website, applications and social networks.

Digital revenue management tools: Hotels are increasingly investing in revenue management tools to manage their yield/income. Guests no longer expect to find fixed low/medium or high season rates but rather dynamic rates evolving, as with airlines, depending on many factors such as availability, location, average occupancy rate and competitors' rates. Large hotels, such as the Grand Hyatt Cannes Martinez, have a dedicated team working in-house yield or tools such as PMT Hotels. This is also the case of the Mas de Pierre in St-Paul-de-Vence, which uses the tool to optimise its rates and occupancy level.

CRM tools: Working on CRM is essential to attract new customers and even optimise loyalty. With tools such as Sellinity or Medallia coupled with the booking engine, hotels collect relevant data on their customers and profiles, analyse them and can communicate with them by personalising the exchanges, by e-mail or SMS. Hotels that adopt Lounge Up applications, such as the Sister Hotel in Paris, which operates the application for customer relations and upselling during the stay.

Mobile payment: The opening up to digitalised and more varied means of payment is also a competitive advantage adopted by the best hotels. In the most advanced cases, hotels such as the Moontain Hostel, located in Oz in Oissans in the French Alps, have adopted the use of connected wristbands to allow their guests to pay for all hotel services. In the Louvre Hotels group, Chinese guests can pay for their stay via the successful Alipay and WeChat applications. These new digital payment tools open up sales prospects for new markets.

16.2.2. At Organisational Level

The main uses of digital technologies for back-office purposes are presented below.

Technical and maintenance services: Other tools make everyday life easier for hotel staff, such as the 1Check application very useful in optimising all services related to accommodation.

Example 16.1: The Aubusson Hotel in Paris

If PMSs have mobile modules that can handle cleanliness issues, the scope of these applications is very limited. With my managers, we want to invent the hotel business 2.0 and move away from the traditional modes of operation where paper is omnipresent, visual checks and oral exchanges are frequent. We wanted to break this way of working and go towards 2.0 with tools made available to the staff that make them save time in their work explains the hotel's executive officer.

Hence, a hosting management tool such as 1Check, developed by the Best Artisan in France, executive housekeeper, is the solution for integrated or independent hotels to manage two functions:

1. *Inspection*. The tool registers cleanliness and maintenance issues for guest rooms and public spaces. This option updates all departments in real-time if any problem/issue is raised. This possibility increases the productivity, as all the housekeeping, technical and other team members are updated in real-time.
2. *Maintenance*. Any issue can be notified and processed through the application. Housekeeping can report the issue; the work orders are available immediately. Maintenance staff can analyse the issues and modify their preventive maintenance plan in the application.

These functionalities allow real-time efficiency and a real traceability of every hotel issue.

With tools, such as 1Check, hotels can also manage stocks of equipment and products, inventory and housekeeping planning, and have complete control and cross-functional monitoring of budgets, teams and schedule management. With such digital services, hotels gain in productivity and efficiency in the various back-office services, such as housekeeping and technical services. If 1Check gathers all the tools available for this type of services, other tools linked with the PMS can also be used to optimise the hotel durability: it is the Computer-Aided Maintenance Management Tool (CAMM).

Room services: Many room services are dematerialised: information on the hotel, menus, schedules, concierge services and laundry. This is the case of the Accor group and its service portal called My Web Valet. Customers can order meals, read the newspaper, contact the concierge service, book a taxi, a restaurant, spa treatments, to name a few. Other hotels use Facebook's Messenger and WhatsApp instant messaging applications to inform their customers and confirm reservations.

There is a range of basic customer requirements that can be automated using appropriate technology. This allows hotel staff to focus on other activities and improve the customer experience. The technologies used in back office have a direct effect on customer contact activities. There are many services dedicated to front-office activities and customer experience; this is the topic of next section.

16.3. USE OF DIGITAL FRONT-OFFICE TECHNOLOGIES: ENHANCING CUSTOMER EXPERIENCE

Numerous digital technologies are available to enhance the experience of customers during their stay.

Online check-in and check-out: Thanks to the online check-in, customers can check before their arrival from their smartphone or computer. Very practical for clients, this service reduces administrative formalities. On the day of departure, thanks to the Quick check-out, customers can simply return the key and let the staff know that the room is free. The invoice is automatically sent by e-mail.

Mobile terminal as key: Nowadays, the electronic key is widespread and is totally dematerialised in some hotels via NFC technology or the digitisation of a visual code, as many airports are doing for airline tickets.

High-tech reception areas/lobby: Customers, who are not willing to stay in their room, can use high-tech spaces/venues where there is Wi-Fi access for fun or work. The uses of technology in the hotel industry are increasingly varied, and hotels anticipate the desires of their customers by creating stylish semi-public spaces, where everyone can take advantage of new technologies. Many customers have even begun to incorporate technology into their online hotel searches. Thus, hotel establishments that do not offer these services may suffer a disadvantaged position.

High-tech meeting rooms: The modern meeting venues have evolved. It no longer boils down to well-stocked tables, chairs and service trolleys. Modern meetings need technology. The audio/video venues of yesteryear, which required dedicated staff, no longer have their place. The speakers want to make multimedia presentations and integrate remote participants by video-conference or both; for marathon meetings, they want to be able to access various services (catering, for example) with a minimum of interruptions. Most importantly, discerning hotel managers know that they must make these spaces as friendly as possible.

16.4. DIGITAL/ONLINE SOCIAL MEDIA: TOOLS THAT ARE INDISPENSABLE FOR MARKETING PURPOSES

16.4.1. Why Is It so Important to Use Online Social Media?

The widespread adoption and use of social media (SM) is undeniable. Today, digital consumers are spending more time on social networks and messaging platforms than ever before. It is therefore important for tourism provider to have a brand presence and to make a marketing effort on SM channels, especially since SM marketing has been proven more effective than traditional marketing, when implemented correctly (Inversini & Masiero, 2014). SM marketing allows a two-way communication between consumers and businesses; this interactive element helps companies build a long-term consumer relationship and loyalty. Additionally, SM marketing supports the real-time promotion of new products and services, all while yielding measurable consumer data that can be further leveraged to target, engage, and grow a customer base.[1] Among the different typologies that were proposed, we selected the one by Kaplan and Haenlein (2010) because it classifies SM according to their social presence/media richness and self-presentation/self-disclosure. We also completed this classification with Fotis, Buhalis, and Rossides (2012) work about online social networks. These different criteria lead to the following SM classification:

- Social networking sites (Facebook, LinkedIn): We add the distinction made by Zhu and Chen (2015) because these have evolved into two main types: the ones which are person-based, i.e. focused on the individual user's personal profile and network (e.g. Facebook and LinkedIn), and content-based, where the visual content is of primary importance (e.g. Pinterest, Instagram);
- Consumer reviews and rating websites (TripAdvisor, Yelp, Epinions);
- Internet fora (ThornTree, Fodor's Travel Talk);
- Blogs and microblogs (Twitter) — Content communities (YouTube, Flicker, Scribd, Slideshare, Delicious);

- Collaborative projects (Wikipedia, Wikitravel);
- Social worlds (Second Life) and
- Virtual games (World of Warcraft).

The above-mentioned SM were classified according to their use by consumers as 'Relationship', 'Self-media', 'Collaboration' and 'Creative outlets' (Zhu & Chen, 2015). We also combined this typology with the one suggested by Leung, Law, van Hoof, and Buhalis (2013) to elaborate a simplified classification of SM depending on their marketing utility. The outcome is the classification depicted in Table 16.1.

SM, characterised by their rapidity, convenience, anonymity and virtual nature, are digital tools, which are particularly effective in tourism-related industries; a field characterised by high experiential consumption and perceived risk. Thus, the tourism industry is wholly reliant on word-of-mouth, as it is the simplest distribution channel for a business. Guest loyalty does generate business, yet positive reviews provided by word-of-mouth recommendations encourages new guests and higher sales/revenues (Aluri, Slevitch, & Larzelere, 2016; Duan, Yu, Cao, & Levy, 2016). According to a recent TrustYou study, 95 per cent of all tourists use online review sites like TripAdvisor to help them make their final decision. While a hotel's overall brand reputation is still important, potential guests want to know the nuances of individual properties. A report on hotel bookings by TripAdvisor indicates that out of 12,659 responses, 77 per cent of the respondents choose to use reviews and recommendations from the website before booking a hotel room. Another recent study from Cornell University found that by boosting its overall review score by one point (based on the typical five-star rating system), a hotel can increase room rates up to 11 per cent. Hotel guests clearly want the best experience, even if it costs more. More than 75 per cent of guests are willing to pay more for a room that has positive reviews, and they are four times as likely to move to a more expensive hotel option if the ratings are outstanding. Such an information speaks loudly to the necessity for an online presence that is not only informative but also distinct and easily identifiable among the 'clutter' of hotel promotion.

The possible use of each of the main SM and their utility for a hotel are outlined in subsection 16.4.2.

16.4.2. Interesting Uses of Social Media

The main uses of SM include:

- Provision of a means of communication with customers and other potential consumers.
- Possibility of personalising the brand or product. Customers then feel that they talk to the brand and no longer to the company.

Table 16.1. A Typology of Online Social Media Depending on Their Marketing Objectives and Uses.

Type of Media	Examples	Main Consumers' Usages				Main Marketing Uses			
		Relationship Profile-based X Customised message Self-presentation, Develop relationship	Self-media Profile-based X Broadcast message Have an impact, Promote one's self	Collaboration Content-based X Customised message Help others establish reputation/fame	Creative outlets Content-based X Broadcast message Hobby sharing, Showcase of creativity	Promotion Suppliers' application for: reaching a global audience, disseminating promotional information, strengthening company's marketing forces	Distribution Suppliers' application for: facilitating online bookings, distributing products and services	Communication Suppliers' application for: facilitating communication between suppliers and customers or partners	Research Suppliers' application for: maintaining internal knowledge, improving, and customising products to suit customers' needs
Person-based social networks	Facebook, LinkedIn, Snapchat, Whatsapp	X				XXX	X	XXX	XXX
Micro-blogging and publishing media	Twitter, WordPress, Tumblr, Medium		X			XXX	X	XXX	XXX
Consumer review and rating websites	Yelp, Zomato, TripAdvisor			X		XXX	X	XXX	XXX
Discussion forums & blogs	Reddit, Quora, Digg, Fodor's Travel Talk			X		XXX	X	XXX	XXX
Content-based social communities and networks	Pinterest, Instagram, Youtube				X	XX	X	XX	XXX

Source: Authors' elaboration, retrieved from various sources.

- Opportunity for clients to inform and assist other clients in a collaborative community.
- Some websites offer the possibility to advertise for a specific group.
- Create traffic on the company's website and blog.
- Creation of a 'virtual consumer community' of the product or brand. This community will engage with reviews, evaluations and suggestions that can only be useful for the company's marketing purposes.
- Reputation management: identify influential groups and virtual consumer communities that can become ambassadors of the brand and thus contribute to the growth of its reputation.
- Cost-effective communications: most social networking sites and SM are free of charge.

16.4.3. Interesting Uses of Main Social Media in the Hospitality Industry

The main tools a hotel can use to improve its visibility on the Internet are outlined below.

TripAdvisor: Some hotels, too little in number, apart from luxury hotels, are monitoring their e-reputation for strategic purposes. A debriefing of opinions and feedback from the online review platform can lead to a questioning of certain hotel services or facilities. Opinions may therefore have a managerial and operational interest, but the sole monitoring of these reviews is not enough (Sotiriadis, 2017). The free 'owners' space on TripAdvisor allows a hotel business to activate tools such as response to reviews or Review Express to solicit TripAdvisor opinions from guests who have actually stayed at the hotel. Some hotels like Novotel ask their guests to share their experiences and make free communication with future tourists. A communication that is sometimes called 'story living' because the client will share the experience he or she has really lived in the place. Here is the message posted on the website: 'To help other travellers choose their hotel, we invite you to share your impressions on the website.'[2]

Instagram: Hotels can capitalise on this trend by motivating consumers to use branded hashtags or specific hashtags that are relevant to a current promotion or event. For example, Starwood Hotels launched a campaign in 2016 to encourage the #SPGLife branded hashtag on Instagram. Posts with this hashtag feed into the Starwood website's guest gallery of user-generated content, where guests can also book a hotel room directly via a link. A simple hashtag is effective, because it allows users to easily discover related content through a search filter. The key is to first encourage tourists to post stories, photos and videos of their visit to the SM channels (Lo, McKercher, Lo, Cheung, & Law, 2011; Stepchenkova & Zhan, 2013). Then, leverage its value by sharing across the digital network. Tourist-generated content provides independents with fresh, authentic voices that help separate them from competitors and strengthen their identity among other tourists.

Facebook: An ideal tool to interact with its customers, promote its brand and services. Ideally, it should also be a traffic provider for the company's website. Of course, the website should be regularly enriched in order to provide Facebook with sufficient material. In addition, the statistical analysis tools, through Facebook Insights, developed by the platform can be used to monitor the dynamism of the page and posts. A study published in 2017 shows that in the MICE – Meetings, Incentives, Conferences and Exhibitions – industry, visuals play a more important role on consumers' participation than texts. The relevance of tools such as Sociograph to monitor the ratio between the nature of the elements posted on the page and the rate of customer engagement was highlighted (Christofle, Papetti, & Fournier, 2017).

Snapchat: Major hotel companies have made successful forays into marketing through Snapchat, a SM messaging application that allows users to send photos and videos to friends or publish them onto 'My Story' where the users' followers can view them. The increasing popularity of Snapchat comes from the fact that photos and videos are ephemeral; they disappear after a certain amount of time once they have been viewed. Hotels cannot afford to ignore this SM, because it is the first preference – more than 70 per cent of millennial users (the 18–34 age group) – in all SM platforms. This platform, however, requires a completely different approach because re-purposing content simply will not work. It does offer an incredible level of engagement, though, and it will certainly grow significantly in 2018.[3] In 2015, Starwood Hotels experimented with Snapchat geofilters at some of its W Hotels to see how guests would use them. Geofilters allow users of Snapchat to add a sponsor-created geo-locational tag to their photo or video message that can only be used when sending a Snap within a sponsor-defined geographical area (e.g. within a 10-metre radius of the hotel). The usage rates and number of views for the geofilters were well above what Starwood had anticipated, indicating that Snapchat may be a viable option for future brand marketing initiatives. Its success is so big that Facebook has developed its own stories system on Instagram and Facebook.

Periscope: Periscope is a platform from Twitter born in 2015 that allows users to broadcast live video to their followers. Video has a high level of engagement in general, and live video is even more popular. Periscope is here to stay thanks to its interactive, instant and on-demand features. Moreover, the platform currently has 10 million accounts and people are watching 40 years' worth of videos every day, with these figures constantly growing. This platform is excellent to establish face-to-face contact with the people following the business, giving it a human face and helping build relationships much faster. Following this example, Facebook has its own live broadcast system, 'Facebook Live'.

Hyper: Hyper contains all the functions needed to create either a local playlist just for now, or an online playlist, tied to your YouTube account. It also offers geographic tags that allow users to discover new things happening in their vicinity. This feature could be a valuable asset to hotels in attracting customers because those tags are searchable.

Obviously, the objectives pursued through these various tools are numerous: to communicate, develop a brand community, inform, ensure an e-reputation monitoring, etc. The question that now arises is to know, among all the technologies, that we have just described which tools an independent hotel with limited financial and human resources must implement. The next section is dealing with this issue.

16.5. RECOMMENDATIONS REGARDING THE USES OF DIGITAL TECHNOLOGIES

In practice, hotels' owners and managers adopt different strategies and positioning depending on whether they belong to an integrated chain, a voluntary chain or they are independent business. The range of products they belong to and the target customer have an impact on the adoption of digital tools. Given the resources available to hotel groups and, in turn, to most of their franchisees, we have just seen all the technological features they use in general. The recommendations presented below are focusing on independent hotels.

16.5.1. Digital Technologies as Managerial Tools Are Not Necessary

The use of managerial tools varies mainly according to hotel capacity. A small capacity hotel will have less difficulty in monitoring the condition of its facilities and equipment and planning its maintenance because it will be easier to list and plan the work, repairs, renovations or interventions necessary. Investing in CAMM-type tools does not seem essential to small businesses, so many remain on an 'artisanal' operations management. In the housekeeping function, tools such as 1Check target hotels with an Executive Housekeeper and a large enough number of staff in rooms to set up an elaborate planning process. This tool is not fully adapted to smaller units/businesses.

16.5.2. Digital Technologies for Purposes of Customer Relations and Customer Experience: A Must

Management and marketing tools have become indispensable for all types of establishments. According to PMS Editors, hoteliers only master and exploit

20 per cent of the functionality of their tools. Rather than taking training time, they use basic functions such as check-in or invoicing, but do not expand the CRM-based customer relationship capabilities often included in large tools. Hotels, especially independent, invest in specialised tools such as CRM and consider training to be a waste of time and prefer several user-friendly tools but these duplicate services have a cost. Instead, we advise them to invest their PMS to the fullest extent possible, even if they have to go through a more extensive training phase. In addition, today's minimum necessary is to offer Wi-Fi on all floors. Wi-Fi is an equipment both awaited by tourists and the facilitator for other digital supports of the hotel, such as the application. The deployment of Wi-Fi is a real commercial argument because it has become one of the first criteria for selecting a hotel. Investing in other very modern technologies can of course improve the customer experience, but due to access costs, we will focus on the presence of hotels in the digital media.

16.5.3. Presence on Digital Social Media

We recommend that tourism providers invest in SM channels because of their low cost of entry. The important issue is to choose the most relevant ones for their clientele and above all to manage the content in a homogeneous way on all media and consistent with the business strategy. Rather than being present on Facebook, if a hotel caters for business customers, being active on Twitter can be interesting. On the other hand, we would advise a youth hostel to launch on the digital networks of generations Y or Z, because they are no longer on Facebook, and most of them are using Instagram and Snapchat (White, 2010). With a small team, running the SM accounts can be a collaborative effort. It is critically important that this endeavour be guided by a common set of shared ideas by all persons involved in managing SM accounts.

When planning and implementing a business operational SM marketing, it is important to perform the following actions:

- Keep the hotel's style at the forefront;
- Express it with a consistent voice;
- Only use an idea or piece of content if it is clearly in the top 20 per cent;
- Tailor/customise the message to each SM;
- Post videos and photos of good quality: more than 50 per cent of SM users claim that they find videos and images more engaging than posts only with text.

If independent hotels want to invest in only four networks, we recommend Facebook, Instagram, TripAdvisor and Twitter, especially if their clientele is the business segment. It is important to choose only a few SM, but to publish regularly quality and reliable content. The use of Instagram could enable an independent hotel to distinguish itself among current buyers, and imprint a lasting message and/or visual for the viewer. Obviously, visual messages are essential. Instagram has accumulated 77.6 million users in 2015 only in the United States, 50 per cent of whom are millennials.

Quality is also important on Facebook for similar reasons. That has said there is a bit more latitude for humour, self-promotion and a variety of content on Facebook. TripAdvisor allows activating free tools such as the 'Review Express' to solicit opinions from customers who have been staying at the hotel. The tool also offers hoteliers and restaurateurs the possibility of being alerted when a new notice is posted. Managers must take the time to monitor and respond to comments, either to thank them if they are positive or to try to find a solution or to dialogue with courtesy if the client's opinion is negative. Tourists say an appropriate response from hotel management is more likely to make them book (57 per cent), improves their overall impression (84 per cent) and makes them feel the hotel cares (78 per cent). Finally, with Twitter, the 140-character limit is an important factor in planning for this SM, but there are strong tools (like images with text) that can work to tell a longer story (Syed-Ahmad, Musa, Klobas, & Murphy, 2013). Twitter streams are busy places so managers can repeat messages as on another SM.

In addition, the use of free analysis tools available on these platforms makes it possible to measure the dynamism and impact of information posted. Even more interestingly, some analyses concern competitors and propose effective benchmarks and comparisons between the administrator's pages and the individuals' ones. There are some tools, available free of charge, that an independent hotel can use to improve its visibility on the Internet (Christofle et al., 2017).

Thus, very little research uses this type of quantitative tool to test hypotheses, particularly on the relationship between the nature of posts and the type of engagement of Internet users. In a very recent study, the authors attempted to verify whether the evolution of the importance of the visibility of a tourism and congresses city on Facebook and the ranking of the city in world statistics were converging. At this aim, the researchers mobilised the free benchmarking tools of the various pages for which they are not administrators, that is, Sociograph and LikeAlizer, and were able to build a cartography of congress cities whose visibility on Facebook accompanies their dynamism (Christofle et al., 2017). A series of explanations of these results are given. A research project currently under way aims at deepening the analysis by proposing to test the relationship between the precise nature of published posts (visual versus textual content) and the type of reactions aroused, in the case of the world's major tourism cities. Some of the results that negate the work on the role of photos in Internet users' level of engagement are discussed in conclusion and research proposals are set out (Papetti, 2017). In addition, independent hotels should use programming tools available directly on SM or via platforms such as Hootsuite, in order to save time.

16.5.4. Website Update

Most of the tourism providers' websites are only fed very occasionally, except for the update of prices via their booking engine. These websites benefit from the Content Management System, which allows hotel managers to modify textual and visual content without systematically referring to a specialised service provider. In addition, some hotel websites still insist on returning to an application form for a reservation, which scares away today's customers, and even when the websites benefit from a booking engine, the tool is sometimes already outdated in comparison with the behaviour of new tourists, both mobile and international. Hotels are increasingly adopting responsive design sites, but their booking tool is sometimes not convenient and customers prefer to book on OTA websites or applications on smartphones.

Finally, independent hotels should think about a synergy between SM and website in taking advantage of the growth of e-commerce services. E-commerce features are gaining ground in SM platforms, with Facebook ads already permitting users to click straight through to a business' website. In 2016, IHG (InterContinental Hotels Group) began using dynamic ads on Facebook to target 'high-potential' customers with personalised advertisements based on searches, which yielded an increase in the brand's ability to attract customers and a lower cost per booking. In the big picture, SM channels are beneficial to hotel companies because they offer an opportunity to create personalised interactions with consumers, which can be leveraged to increase direct online bookings.

In summary, the minimum SM toolkit for an independent hotel should include:

- A first or responsive mobile website encompassing: a CMS to update text and visuals; a high-performance booking engine that accepts a multitude of payment methods, including via messaging systems such as WeChat pay; a widget with certified customer reviews, so that the customer is reassured before booking and basic analytics tracking tool to react based on the behaviour of visitors to the website.
- A tool for monitoring e-reputation, with online opinions/reviews on TripAdvisor, Booking and Expedia to respond to them.
- A revenue management tool, essential to optimise hotel availability and rates.
- A SM that targets the hotel's main clientele. This requires regular feeding of the SM, using programming tools and performance monitoring tools if they exist.
- Facebook Messenger or WhatsApp channel as a communication tool.
- An easy-to-access PMS that requires minimal training, like the new generation of Thai Soft, including basic functionalities such as a good CRM.

Finally, it is believed that the employees' training for SM marketing is essential. Online training solutions are now available and less constraining for independent hotels since they do not have to send their teams for several days off their premises.

16.6. SUMMARY

Tourism-related industries are entering the era of artificial intelligence. This includes significant advances on data, voice assistants and chatbots. Big data mining and processing will soon enable hotel managers to propose a hyper-personalisation of the customer experience. A typical customer who visits the Delta Hotel website will not see the same textual and visual content as the Beta customer. The applications are already customised according to location and time of use, but these opportunities will increasingly extend to groups and independent hotels.

In this chapter, we have seen the various digital tools available to tourism businesses. Its focus has been on their value and uses for marketing purposes. CRM and website management tools will take into account the stage, the tourist's profile and behaviour in order to offer a hyper-personalised experience.

> If an establishment can [...] collect a large amount of data, it is necessary to work across the different data collection departments for a customization strategy. Agility implies exploiting millions of variables (keywords, audience, devices, location...). By crossing dynamic advertisements, remarketing and using automation systems, [hotels will gain] agility, for better customization, thus conversion. (Guerrier-Buisine, 2017a)

The learning machine allows companies to fine-tune communication in all languages with tourists. Expedia works on its Chabot to allow bookings without going through a human before the stay on site. Robots are able to have interactive and built exchanges with tourists to bring them the necessary information at any moment, without any waiting time. Guerrier-Buisine (2017b) indicate that 56 per cent of hosting providers plan work on data 'to personalize the customer experience' and 38 per cent want to automate some of the online exchanges with visitors and customers. The deployment of digital tools, such as voice assistants by the Internet giants – i.e. Amazon with Echo or Alexa and Google Home – has made this hyper-personalisation possible. Tourist consumers who are looking for inspiration, information or want to make a reservation can simply turn to this connected and intelligent object. For this purpose, a huge amount of R&D work is devoted to the learning machine, which will accompany the hotel owners of tomorrow.

Internally, projections are turning towards increasingly accessible and agile tools, as well as towards a real digitalisation of offer. From home automation, which has already invaded the luxury hotel industry, to software and applications that will allow forever more responsiveness by improving customer care, teams and equipment, hotels will have an arsenal of tools that will improve their productivity, the well-being of employees and the experience of guests. Increasingly versatile and intuitive tools will be essential for better back-office management. These tools will have to link the different hotel departments, which are fully connected to each other. Those functionalities are common to every department and transferable. Guests no longer will have a friction point during the preparation of their stay, they also want to arrive at the hotel and be recognised at each meeting point or purchase point of the hotel.

In addition, in terms of customer experience, augmented reality mobile tools can also provide substantial improvements to the hotel experience. Experiments that allow the room to immerse the client in a virtual reality are underway. The question is to know the returns of these expensive technological investments. Although mobile augmented reality should allow less passive connection such as traditional in-situ or online content delivery, beyond it the challenge of the right balance between physics and digital named 'phygitalisation' to serve the customer experience arises. Only the experiments in progress will better guide the strategic decision-making (Antonczak & Papetti, 2017).

Review Questions

Check your understanding of this chapter by answering the following questions or discussing the topics below:

- What are the different objectives of a PMS and a CRM? Is it always necessary to have both?
- What are the most relevant online SM for developing a brand community?
- How can digital tools improve your customers' experience during their journey?
- What are the key tools of the *phygitalisation* of tourism businesses?
- Discuss the opportunities for an independent hotel to implement specific *phygitalised* tools.

NOTES

1. https://www.hotel-online.com/press_releases/release/social-media-marketing-in-the-hotel-industry-trends-and-opportunities Accessed on 10 September 2017.
2. http://www.novotel.com/fr/newsletter/hotel-review.shtml Accessed on 16 September 2017.
3. https://www.hotel-online.com/press_releases/release/social-media-marketing-in-the-hotel-industry-trends-and-opportunities Accessed on 16 September 2017.

REFERENCES AND FURTHER READING

Aluri, A., Slevitch, L., & Larzelere, R. (2016). The influence of embedded social media channels on travelers' gratifications, satisfaction, and purchase intentions. *Cornell Hospitality Quarterly*, *57*(3), 250–267.

Antonczak, L., & Papetti, C. (2017). Towards a mobile enhancement of glocal heritage: Developing user experiences in relation to mobile technologies, geo-localisation and culture. *The thirteenth international conference on wireless and mobile communications*, ICWMC, 23–27 July, Nice.

Christofle, S., Papetti, C., & Fournier, C. (2017). Tourisme, trajectoires et images: les média socio numériques, outils contemporains d'adaptation communicationnelle de destinations mondiales de congrès? 7ème édition du colloque AsTRES, Université de Grenoble, 14–16 June.

Duan, W., Yu, Y., Cao, Q., & Levy, S. (2016). Exploring the impact of social media on hotel service performance. *Cornell Hospitality Quarterly*, *57*(3), 282–296.

Filieri, R., Alguezaui, S., & McLeay, F. (2015). E-WOM and accommodation: An analysis of the factors that influence travelers' adoption of information from online reviews. *Journal of Travel Research*, *53*(1), 44–57.

Fotis, J., Buhalis, D., & Rossides. (2012). Social media use and impact during the holiday travel planning process. In M. Fuchs, F. Ricci, & L. Cantoni (Eds.), *Information and Communication Technologies in Tourism* (pp. 13–24). Vienna: Springer-Verlag.

Guerrier-Buisine, V. (2017a). Adapter sa distribution aux usages numériques des voyageurs. *Journal L'Hôtellerie Restauration*, 2 juin 2017. Retrieved from http://www.lhotellerie-restauration.fr/

Guerrier-Buisine, V. (2017b). Les 5 tendances de l'e-tourisme en 2017. *Journal L'Hôtellerie Restauration*, 14 juin 2017. Retrieved from http://www.lhotellerie-restauration.fr/

Inversini, A., & Masiero, L. (2014). Selling rooms online: The use of social media and online travel agents. *International Journal of Contemporary Hospitality Management*, *26*(2), 272–292.

Kaplan, A. M., & Haenlein, M. (2010). Users of the world, unite! The challenges and opportunities of social media. *Business Horizons*, *53*(1), 59–68.

Kim, W. G., Lim, H., & Brymer, R. A. (2015). The effectiveness of managing social media on hotel performance. *International Journal of Hospitality Management*, *44*(1), 165–171.

Leung, D., Law, R., van Hoof, H., & Buhalis, D. (2013). Social media in tourism and hospitality: A literature review. *Journal of Travel & Tourism Marketing*, *30*(1–2), 3–22.

Lo, I. S., McKercher, B., Lo, A., Cheung, C., & Law, R. (2011). Tourism and online photography. *Tourism Management*, *32*(4), 725–731.

Martín-Santana, J. D., Beerli-Palacio, A., & Nazzareno, P. A. (2017). Antecedents and consequences of destination image gap. *Annals of Tourism Research*, *62*(1), 13–25.

Papetti, C. (2017). Influence du type de matériel posté sur Facebook sur les réactions des internautes: le cas des grandes villes touristiques françaises. Séminaire interne Nice, juin.

Sigala, M., Christou, E., & Gretzel, U. (Eds.). (2012). *Social media in travel, tourism and hospitality: Theory, practice and cases*. London: Ashgate.

Sotiriadis, M. (2017). Sharing tourism experiences in social media: A literature review and a set of suggested business strategies. *International Journal of Contemporary Hospitality Management*, *29*(1), 179–225.

Sotiriadis, M., & Van Zyl, C. (2013). Electronic word-of-mouth and online reviews in tourism services: The use of Twitter by tourists. *Electronic Commerce Research Journal*, *13*(1), 103–124.

Sparks, A. B., Fung So, K. K., & Bradley, L. G. (2016). Responding to negative online reviews: The effects of hotel responses on customer inferences of trust and concern. *Tourism Management*, *53*(1), 74–85.

Stepchenkova, S., & Zhan, F. (2013). Visual destination images of Peru: Comparative content analysis of DMO and user-generated photography. *Tourism Management*, *36*(3), 590–601.

Syed-Ahmad, S.-F., Musa, G., Klobas, J.-E., & Murphy, J. (2013). Audience response to travel photos and Arab destination image. *Journal of Travel & Tourism Marketing, 30*(1–2), 161–164.

White, L. (2010). Facebook, friends and photos: A snapshot into social networking for generating travel ideas. In N. Sharda (Ed.), *Tourism informatics: Visual travel recommender systems, social communities, and user interface design* (pp. 115–129). Hershey, PA: IGI Global.

Xiang, Z., Schwartz, Z., Gerdes, J. H., Jr., & Uysal, M. (2015). What can big data and text analytics tell us about hotel guest experience and satisfaction? *International Journal of Hospitality Management, 44*(1), 120–130.

Xie, L. K., & Zhang, Z. (2014). The business value of online consumer reviews and management response to hotel performance. *International Journal of Hospitality Management, 43*(1), 1–12.

Zhu, Y.-Q., & Chen, H.-G. (2015). Social media and human need satisfaction: Implications for social media marketing. *Business Horizons, 58*(3), 335–345.

CHAPTER 17

DESIGNING AND IMPLEMENTING A MARKETING PLAN

Anestis Fotiadis, Claudel Mombeuil and
Nataša Slak Valek

ABSTRACT

Purpose — *Main purpose of this chapter is to broaden current knowledge of marketing plan design and implementation. In this context, main scope is to explain why marketing planning is a crucial managerial function and procedure for tourism business ventures.*

Methodology/approach — *Literature review combined with examples and a case study is the methodological approach of this chapter.*

Findings — *This chapter presents the main components of a marketing plan and it explains in a practical way with simple steps how marketing objectives can be set up and how monitoring and evaluation can be developed.*

Research limitations/implications — *Although the study is not completely theoretical, as it has several practical examples and a case study, it still is based on literature review.*

Practical implications — *Tourism businesses have to develop marketing plans to help them cope with the market's dynamism. In this chapter, we present the main elements of a marketing plan. SMEs usually are unable on focusing on long-term goals since they have significant time constraints. This chapter explains which procedure business should follow to achieve smart objectives set by entrepreneur/manager with limited resources.*

The Emerald Handbook of Entrepreneurship in Tourism, Travel and Hospitality:
Skills for Successful Ventures, 297–311
ISBN: 978-1-78743-530-8/doi:10.1108/978-1-78743-529-220181023

Originality/value — *This chapter presents the main elements that should be taken into consideration before starting to design a marketing plan, as well as its components. Additionally, a very interesting case study is presented to illustrate a real-time example of successful implementation of a marketing plan by a tourism enterprise.*

Keywords: Marketing plan; SMART; marketing objectives; marketing mix; monitoring; evaluation

---

Learning Objectives

After studying this chapter, you should be able to:

- define a marketing plan and explain its importance;
- present the main component elements of a marketing plan;
- develop and set SMART marketing objectives;
- elaborate and discuss a marketing plan;
- present the approaches to evaluate the outcomes of a marketing plan.

17.1. INTRODUCTION

Twenty-first-century businesses are competing in a high-risk, unstable and dynamic market environment (Harackiewicz, Durik, Barron, Linnenbrink-Garcia, & Tauer, 2008; Liang, Saraf, Hu, & Xue, 2007). Many fail because they lack the capability to adapt themselves to the mutation of the business ecosystem and do not possess a deep understanding of their customers' needs, preferences and price tolerance in order to develop a compelling value proposition (Rowson, 2009). The internal and external environment should be constantly monitored and analysed in order to stay competitive in the current business era (Scheidler, Schons, & Spanjol, 2016).

Tourism is a highly complex and dynamic set of industries. To be successful in these industries, entrepreneurs must have a good understanding of their customers' needs, their consumption behaviour, patterns and preferences (Mombeuil & Fotiadis, 2017). Tourism-related industries are characterised by an increasing number of products and services with less differentiation in their offerings. This issue was presented in more detail in previous chapters, mainly Chapters 2 and 3. With the development of the Internet and information technology, human mobility, and accessibility to different means of transportation, it is increasingly challenging for businesses to identify their competitors and monitor customer behaviour (Fotiadis & Stylos, 2017).

Entrepreneurs should constantly monitor and evaluate factors that enable the attainment of their business aim and objectives. One way to keep track of how companies have reached certain objectives and how they plan to achieve future ones is a marketing plan. In this chapter, we will explain why marketing planning is a crucial managerial function and procedure for any kind of business.

In the two previous chapters of this section, two other closely related topics have been discussed. First, the marketing of tourism services and experiences by presenting the key elements/variables of the marketing model to be adopted and implemented in the context of services. Second, you have seen the appropriate approach and adequate use of media and tools in the context of digital marketing. Chapter 15 has presented the suitable approach and the utility of the digital tools available in the marketing toolkit of tourism entrepreneurs. This chapter attempts to discuss the way these issues should be planned and scheduled in a structured way by following a specific process.

The fundamental elements that should be taken into consideration before starting to design a marketing plan will be explained in this chapter. However, for a marketing plan to work, an owner/manager needs to ensure that the employees clearly understand what the business stands for, its mission, aim and objectives. Entrepreneurs and managers also need to evaluate their own competence, commitment and the available resources. That is the reason why it is important to know why a marketing plan is significant in general and in the tourism-related industries in particular. The key elements of a marketing plan will be presented and explained. Additionally, a case study will be presented to demonstrate successful implementation of a marketing plan.

It should be noted that the structure of marketing plan and its contents will vary depending on the size of the company, timescale and the market environment.

17.2. STRATEGIC MARKETING PLANNING: THE PROCESS

To start a business or launch a product/service within the tourism industry, entrepreneurs/managers are required to elaborate a strategic marketing plan. The strategic marketing plan constitutes of a sequence of steps in which one can find a number of activities that are all bound together (Middleton, Fyall, Morgan, & Ranchhod, 2013). The steps to be followed represent a process, which is similar to a receipe. It is important to mention that tourism entrepreneurs and managers need to take a holistic approach while following the process that guides the development of a strategic marketing plan.

The process of a strategic marketing plan starts with a situation audit of current situation in which the tourism business is operating or plan to operate.

At this level, the focus is both on the internal issues (internal audit) and the external issues of the business (external audit). This is often referred to as a SWOT analysis (strength, weakness, opportunism and threat) as fully explained in Chapter 4. The situation audit is where entrepreneurs often attempt to identify key success factors, such as the demand side, potential for growth and the attractiveness of the market. The step that follows the situation audit is the development of the marketing objectives that must be specific, measurable, achievable, results-focused and time-bound. We refer to this as SMART marketing objectives. The step that follows the marketing objectives in the strategic marketing planning process is a set of activities that includes deciding about specific strategies, that is, segmentation, targeting and positioning. The company will attempt to achieve its marketing objectives, by implementing the strategies decided and using the elements of marketing mix in efficient way. Finally, we have some last steps that are tactical marketing actions and plan, monitoring, control and evaluation.

17.3. MAIN ELEMENTS OF A MARKETING PLAN

Marketing efforts and activities in small- and medium-sized enterprises (SMEs) are quite different than in big corporations. It is more difficult to 'generate any real insights into how SMEs engage with their customers, find out about their competitors and other factors affecting their marketplaces, and develop their marketing mix' (Moriarty, Jones, Rowley, & Kupiec-Teahan, 2008, p. 293). SMEs tend to neglect long-term goals and objectives because they have significant time constraints. SMEs marketing plan can be defined as the procedure a SME follows, to achieve detailed goals or objectives it sets in a narrow time-frame with limited resources. There are logical steps in a systematic marketing planning process. Each element feeds into the next one with feedback loops built into the process (Middleton et al., 2013). Fundamentally, a marketing plan should begin with a clear understanding of customer needs or problems and how products or services will satisfy these needs (the value proposition).

The main component elements of a marketing plan are in logical sequence: the market analysis, development of SMART marketing objectives, development of marketing strategy and tactics, implementation of a marketing plan, as well as monitoring, control and evaluation of a marketing plan. These components are outlined in the following sections.

17.4. MARKET ANALYSIS: UNDERSTANDING THE SITUATION OF THE MARKET

Market analysis constitutes the foundation to examining and investigating market attractiveness and tailor marketing objectives, strategies and tactics accordingly given the overall situation of a business, product/service and brand (Chernev, 2015). Understanding customers' needs and meeting their expectations by developing a product/service that delivers a compelling value proposition are the most important focus of an entrepreneur. Also, an entrepreneur is concerned about competition, the competitive companies, brands and products. The elements that are likely to be investigated in a market analysis are presented below.

17.4.1. Potential Customers and the Potential of the Market

It is important to understand the needs of potential customers, their consumption behaviour and their expectations. Within the tourism industry, an entrepreneur needs to focus on offering high-quality experiences, creating memories and joyous experiences for consumers in order to attain profitability and growth (Jauhari, 2017). Also, in tourism-related industries, consumers' expectations revolve mostly around comfort, convenience and technology (Crotts, Mason, & Davis, 2009). Thus, managers should ensure that their offering satisfies at least these three expectations.

Owners and managers should investigate continuously the level of customer satisfaction by using different monitoring approaches. For example, they might ask visitors to assess the quality of their stay at a guest house by rating room décor, room cleanliness, friendliness of the staff and food and beverages purchased (Crotts et al., 2009). And also the online platforms such as TripAdvisor may unveil meaningful information on what features they like or dislike about the products/services offered by your competitors (Crotts et al., 2009).

Managers should assess the market potential in terms of revenue and number of potential consumers, as well as expected market share. In this regard, market analysis research should be based on reliable sources of data and other information.

Table 17.1 depicts the revenues and market share of guest houses (SMEs) in Rhodes Town, Greece, in 2016.

17.4.2. Understanding the Competition

Managers should have sufficient insights on products/services offered by competitors in terms of quality, characteristics or attributes, and target markets catered. It is also important to understand their branding strategy and position, their price and reputation, as well as their marketing campaign and distribution channels. Additionally, any improvement or innovation within the tourism industry needs to be monitored as well.

Table 17.1.   Example of Calculating the Market Share.

Accommodation Units	Total Sales in 2016	Market Share in 2016 (%)[a]
Elini Room	309,100	26.18
Minos Pension	182,000	15.42
Sofia Pension	168,600	14.28
Cava d'Oro	146,100	12.38
St. Artemios Boutique Hotel	134,900	11.43
Casa De La Sera	56,200	4.76
Niki's Pension	48,200	4.08
Georgia Old Town Apartments	47,200	4.00
Saint Michel	45,000	3.81
Olympos Pension	43,300	3.67
Total revenues	1,180,600	100.00

Source: Authors' creation.
[a]Market share is calculated by dividing the volume of sales of each accommodation unit by the total of revenues and multiply the result by 100.

Managers should be very mindful about existing and potential competitors and also investigate the dynamism of the segments within tourism industry. The competition analysis was discussed more analytically in Chapter 4.

17.4.3. Understanding the Importance of Technology

The development of the Internet and telecommunication technology have greatly impacted tourism-related industries and the whole tourism ecosystem (Pease, 2007; Suàrez Àlvarez, Díaz Martín, & Casielles, 2007). Most exchanges and transactions in this industry are going online. Thus, the Internet and tele-communication technology may help any business to track and get closer to their target market, provide a convenient access and deliver their product/ser-vice faster. Consequently, business success largely depends on how efficiently the Internet and all communication technologies are integrated into the busi-ness functions, operations and strategy. The previous chapter (Chapter 16) has a more detailed presentation of the marketing actions in the digital context.

17.4.4. Understanding the Social, Political and Economic Environment

Social, political and economic environment may greatly influence marketing decisions. Therefore, entrepreneurs and managers need to constantly examine how to turn these factors into their advantage or seek how to adapt their business situation to these factors. How quick strategies will be aligning with these factors may also determine a business performance and sustainable operation. Consequently, entrepreneurs and managers need to be proactive. They also have to investigate continuously the evolution and changes in the global and local markets. When examining the social and political environment, entrepreneurs and managers should consider the following:

- The evolution of the trends and attitudes of the actors (such as customers, competitors and suppliers);
- Keep updated and informed about the institutional framework, legislation, regulations and other requirements that may affect their business goals and objectives; and
- Be on your guard! For any situation that is likely to affect the results of their business venture, entrepreneurs need to elaborate a contingency plan.

17.4.5. Gathering and Analysing the Data

There are different sources from which data can be retrieved regarding the competition and customers. For example, official websites, such as chamber of commerce, local governments, consulting and marketing agencies that specialise in the hospitality and tourism industry, as well as financial reports may provide valuable information necessary for market analysis.

Having access to data is crucial for any businesses. More importantly, the data must come from reliable sources. Managers can therefore search subsequent information from primary and secondary sources in order to have a very clear picture of their target market. The data may be collected from tourism information offices, hospitality and tourism industry associations, travel agencies and business reports and market surveys produced by consulting and other agencies in the hospitality and tourism industry. Valuable data can also be gathered and retrieved on online review websites, such as TripAdvisor. Furthermore, countless insights on new trends and innovation in the hospitality and tourism industry may be retrieved from reading professional press (magazines and newspapers) and publications from tourism-related academic journals.

Here is a list of relevant data needed to prepare the marketing plan for a business of guest house/motel:

- share of leisure tourism market of each competitor in terms of revenue or percentage;
- increase or decrease in total volume of visitors for leisure tourism services;
- average length of stay among leisure visitors;
- the distribution of age groups of leisure visitors;
- average household income of leisure visitors;

- purpose of their visit (vacation, business, conferences, health and education);
- volume of leisure visitors who stay in hotels or motels;
- locations and attractions visited during their stay: theme park, shopping centres, etc.
- number of followers, visitors, likes and dislikes registered and onlines reviews on various social networks.

While collecting the data, it is important to ensure their relevance to one's business context. Therefore, the data collected need to be cleared in order to warrant their relevance and quality. Then, the data and other information have to be analysed objectively in order to be an useful input into the planning and decision-making process.

17.5. SETTING MARKETING OBJECTIVES

An entrepreneur who is launching a business venture aiming at achieving good financial performance has positive financial results. Simply put, the marketing objectives are just the WHAT questions of a business. The marketing objectives must stem from realistic assumptions and the dynamics of the market (Calkins, 2012). The marketing objectives must also be in-line/compliance with strategic objectives of the business. Additionally, objectives of any business must be SMART, that is, specific, measurable, achievable, results-focused and time-bound.

SMART objectives generally provide key performance indicators against which an entrepreneur may compare actual results achieved. That is the only way to assess and evaluate business performance in the related fields. Here are some examples of SMART objectives for a guest house:

- Increase the occupancy rate of the accommodation by 15 per cent for year 2020;
- Increase revenue by 10 per cent for year 2020;
- Reduce the total operating costs by 10 per cent for the second year of operation;
- Increase the market share by 5 per cent for by the end of 2022;
- Increase guests' awareness by 100 per cent during the next five years;
- Increase guests' length of stay by two overnights by the end of 2021; and
- Increase the own website traffic (visits) by 10 per cent on going every quarter.

17.6. MAKING THE MAIN STRATEGIC DECISIONS: MARKET SEGMENTATION, TARGETING AND POSITIONING

Many businesses failed not because they offer a low or average quality product or service but because of incorrect and inaccurate segmentation of their market.

The final outcome is generally the incorrect targeting of the potential customers. It is important to avoid targeting all things to all consumers. Therefore, entrepreneurs and managers need to take time, devote high volume of efforts to identifying the market segments, to determining who are their potential customers, which segment/s are going to be targeted and position their offering and company accordingly. By segmenting the market, entrepreneurs/managers ensure that they are not going to devote time and resources by offering a service/product to people who have no need for it, who do not really want it, or who cannot afford to pay for it.

When segmenting a market, entrepreneurs and managers should also have insights into the drivers that influence consumers' decision-making, purchase decisions and the consumption behaviour of their target segments. Social factors, individual preferences, demographic characteristics and educational background, personal interests and beliefs and experiences are among factors that may influence consumption behaviour and decisions.

The main approaches and methods of segmenting a market for a start-up SME are:

- *Geographic segmentation*. this may be the geographic location of the business or the geographic location of the target customers. For example, this may include national and international visitors, tourists, business travellers from Germany, France, Canada, USA, Greece, Norway, China, etc.;
- *Demographic segmentation*. this is based on the statistical characteristics of the target customers. The demographic characteristics include gender, age group, social class, race, marital status, level of education and income class;
- *Psychographic segmentation*. this refers to the psychological or emotional traits of consumers, belief systems or personality types, lifestyle and life stage.

Once the market segmentation has been performed, it is important to assess the potential of each market segment in terms of total sales, attractiveness, profitability and market share.

17.6.1. Defining a Marketing Strategy

The American Marketing Association defines a marketing strategy as 'a statement (implicit or explicit) of how a brand or product line will achieve its objectives'. Simply put, the strategies answer the HOW question; how the marketing variables are managed to reach the marketing objectives. The marketing variables refer to the 7 Ps (Product, Price, Place and Promotion, People, Process and Physical evidence) for a service company. The marketing strategies will target the market segment (group of consumers), as defined in the market segmentation process. That is to say, the choice and blend of 7 Ps must be the efficiency to communicate and attract potential customers. The marketing strategy must have a direct connection and must be based on the results of the market analysis. These are:

- the target customers' needs and expectations, which include the motives and factors driving their purchasing decision;
- identify the weak points in the marketing strategy of the competition and seek to address any gap/s created by competitors; and
- the market gaps can be addressed by designing and developing a unique value proposition. This is how the product/service or brand might be positioned to avoid being similar to the competition. The crucial point is that the enterprise must provide evidence that its offering is better than the competitors'.

Let us give some strategies that could be used to match the marketing objectives in the previous example of a guest house.

- *Objective 1*: Increase guest's awareness by 100 per cent during the next five years.
- *Strategy 1*: Search engines optimisation (SEO) of the guest house's website.
- *Strategy 2*: Use video as a tool/media.

17.6.2. Marketing Mix Decisions

Entrepreneurs rely on the elements of marketing mix (the 7 Ps) to communicate their offering to a particular target segments and attempt to perform better than their competitors. Thus, entrepreneurs are encouraged to grasp the nuaces of marketing mix for the tourism industry. Also, much emphasis has to be put on the assessment of every element of the marketing mix. In other words, entrepreneurs and managers have to consider the marketing mix as means to help build an effective marketing strategy and also implement tactics that result in providing customers more value for money. The issue is to manage effectively and efficiently all available resources, human and financial.

17.6.3. Marketing Tactics

Once the marketing strategy has been decided, the entrepreneur/manager should think of developing the marketing tactics and make sure that these tactics align with the marketing strategies. A marketing tactic is simply the step/s that help achieve or implement a marketing strategy.

It is important to bear in mind that business strategies, marketing strategies, objectives and tactics are closely linked; all are interconnected. Here are a few examples of tactics that may link to some of the strategies and objectives in the example of the above-mentioned guest house.

- *Objective*: Increase guests' awareness by 100 per cent during the next five years.
- *Marketing strategy*: Produce a 90-second promotional video.
- *Marketing tactic*: Post and share the marketing video on the most popular social network.

17.6.4. Budgeting

There are obviously certain expenses that emerge from the marketing plan, a business has to devote a volume of financial resources. This is because no product or service can sell itself off without proper promotion or marketing communication. So, the money the entrepreneurs pay to communicate with the market and their target market segment, to promote or increase a brand awareness, reaching more clients are closely linked to the business investment. This is important for start-up or operating small business managers to prepare a budget to support the marketing objectives and activities. The budget for the marketing has to be realistic somehow. That is, the budget for general marketing and marketing communications must match the reality of industry in which the entrepreneur is operating the business venture. Once again it is about managing efficiently available resources, that is, get most out of every euro spent.

17.7. IMPLEMENTATION: MONITORING, CONTROL AND EVALUATION

The implementation of a marketing plan constitutes the steps towards putting into action the marketing strategy and achieving the objectives of a business (Kotler, 1997; Rowson, 2009). The implementation has two basic phases: organising and executing. In the organising phase, the person who will carry out the marketing plan must clearly be identified in addition to reporting relationship among staff members. The executing phase refers to the efficiency and effectiveness of the task distribution among the staff. Thus, the implementation of a marketing plan details the tasks, the budget, the responsible person(s) for executing each task and the timeline to accomplish each of the tasks. Table 17.2 shows an example of an implementation plan of the above-mentioned guest house.

It is very unlikely that a marketing plan will go as smoothly as expected (Calkins, 2012; Chernev, 2015). This happens because there are many variables with behaviours that even the most sophisticated artificial intelligence

Table 17.2.   Example of an Implementation Plan.

Date	Tasks	Person In-charge	Budget for Year X
Oct–Dec 2019	Market research	Jackson	€10,000
Jan 2020	Prepare a list of prospects	Lynn	–
Feb 2020	Prepare the promotional materials: brochures, advertisements, etc.	Rose	€30,000
Mar 2020	Launch the marketing campaign	Chen	€15,000

Source: Authors' elaboration, retrieved and adapted from Fisher (2009).

programme may not be able to accurately predict. Therefore, entrepreneurs and managers need to develop approaches that help them measure the performance and progress of their business towards the achievement of the marketing objectives. Three are the managerial functions in assessing the outcomes of marketing plan and business performance, namely monitoring, control and evaluation.

Monitoring and control: Monitoring and control helps ensure that the activities (actions planed) are on-course, on-schedule and within budget in meeting the objectives set in the marketing plan. This provides clues on the progress of each action to date so that appropriate corrective actions might be taken on the basis of variances or unforeseen events.

Evaluation: Monitoring and control are the steps needed before the evaluation of a marketing plan. Evaluation indicates whether or not business objectives are being achieved. An entrepreneur/manager needs to assess whether the objectives were realistic-based the variables/factors of the market and whether the strategies and tactics were feasible. The evaluation is likely to focus on both quantitative and qualitative metrics that are associated with objectives, strategies and tactics. For example, the volume of sales achieved against plan is a quantitative metric, whereas customer awareness or satisfaction is qualitative in nature. The purpose of a marketing evaluation is to assess what worked or did not work properly and why. This contributes to adjust the strategies and tactics that worked and rectify or abandon what did not work.

17.8.   CASE STUDY

ECO-Z is an outdoor camping site with unique natural environment situated next to a waterfall. In 2010, the owner of ECO-Z introduced convenience tourism offerings and a rental shop for camping materials. This made ECO-Z very popular among local tourists. In 2012, the owner developed a complete range of tourism products. This reflected the growing social acceptance of these products with both male and female tourists. The owner was able to exploit her knowledge of the camping market segment by conducting market research which revealed that numerous local and international visitors are in need of suitable accommodation/hospitality facilities related to convenience tourism products. The research also indicated that both local and international visitors showed preferences to exotic characteristics in tourism products. These represented a potential growth opportunity that the manager opted to exploit.

The ECO-Z Guest House was launched in 2013. Total annual net revenue of the camping services were €100,000 at that time. Net revenue for camping product rentals was €45,000. The owner then decided to position the business as a memorable, exotic, eco-friendly environment where each € spent would bring the guests joyous memories and experiences.

Synopsis of the market:

- The province where ECO-Z is located is experiencing increases in the number of campers and tourists every year;
- Shops and convenience tourism products continue growing in the area;
- The local government expects to increase expenditure in developing and improving infrastructure;
- Increasing volume of individuals are building homes in this local area in search of a greener environment and mild climate/weather conditions and
- There are two plots/sites that could be developed because of their unique attributes.

You are required to prepare a marketing plan for the launch of ECO-Z Guest House. You are also required to show how the owner can respond to changes in tourists' expectations. Please follow the outline template of a marketing plan provided in this chapter.

17.9. SUMMARY

The global business ecosystem is becoming increasingly competitive, dynamic and unstable all at the same time. Many businesses fail because they are unable to adapt themselves to the market environment and industry in which they are operating. The development, adoption and extensive use of information and communication technologies favour business competing on a global scale and also influence customers' behaviours and preferences.

In this context, tourism businesses have to develop marketing plans to help them cope with the market's dynamism. In this chapter, we have presented the main elements of a marketing plan.

The first key element is the market analysis. The market analysis helps entrepreneurs investigate and understand the needs and preferences of their customers, the potential of the market and analyses the competition. During the market analysis, entrepreneurs also seek to understand the potential of technology in developing business strategies as well as to evaluate how the social, political and economic environment may influence the results of the business.

Market segmentation, targeting and positioning follow the market analysis. At this point, entrepreneurs/managers classify the potential customers into different groups based on their similarities and evaluate which group(s) are more likely to generate the most profit. A business is then positioned using the 7 Ps of marketing mix, which form the basis of communicating the offering and value proposition to the target segments.

Marketing objectives are determined based on the reality of the business environment. These objectives need to be SMART. In order to achieve the marketing objectives, managers elaborate and determine a set of marketing strategies and tactics. A marketing tactic is the action that helps execute a marketing strategy. The implementation of a marketing plan constitutes the steps needed to achieving both marketing strategies and objectives of a business. Monitoring, control and evaluation help measure performance and progress of strategies and tactics towards the achievement of the marketing objectives.

All these marketing activities and plans are very useful in managing the available business resources in an efficient and effective way.

Review Questions

Check your understanding of this chapter by answering the following questions or discussing the topics below:

- Discuss in simple terms the utility and value of a marketing plan.
- What is the main purpose of situation audit in the process of the strategic marketing plan?
- Explain in a few words the significance of the market analysis in a marketing plan.
- Explain the value and utility of market segmentation.
- Establish the link between SMART marketing objectives, marketing strategies and tactics.
- Explain the role of the monitoring, control and evaluation section of a marketing plan.

REFERENCES AND FURTHER READING

Bang, V. V., Joshi, S. L., & Singh, M. C. (2016). Marketing strategy in emerging markets: A conceptual framework. *Journal of Strategic Marketing*, *24*(2), 104–117. doi:10.1080/0965254X.2015.1011200

Bitner, J., & Booms, B. (1981). *Marketing strategies and organizational structures for service firms*. Chicago, IL: American Marketing Association.

Calkins, T. (2012). *Breakthrough marketing plans: How to stop wasting time and start driving growth.* Palgrave Macmillan.

Chernev, A. (2015). *The marketing plan handbook.* Cerebellum Press.

Crotts, J. C., Mason, P. R., & Davis, B. (2009). Measuring guest satisfaction and competitive position in the hospitality and tourism industry: An application of stance-shift analysis to travel blog narratives. *Journal of Travel Research, 48*(2), 139–151. doi:10.1177/0047287508328795

Fisher, S. (2009). Guide to Writing a killer marketing plan. Retrieved from http://nsbdc.org/wp-content/uploads/2010/11/Guide_to_Writing_a_Killer_Marketing_Plan.pdf. Accessed on 13 October 2017.

Fotiadis, A. K., & Stylos, N. (2017). The effects of online social networking on retail consumer dynamics in the attractions industry: The case of 'E-da' theme park, Taiwan. *Technological Forecasting and Social Change, 124*, 283–294. doi:10.1016/j.techfore.2016.06.033

Harackiewicz, J. M., Durik, A. M., Barron, K. E., Linnenbrink-Garcia, L., & Tauer, J. M. (2008). The role of achievement goals in the development of interest: Reciprocal relations between achievement goals, interest, and performance. *Journal of Educational Psychology, 100*(1), 105–122. doi:10.1037/0022-0663.100.1.105

Jauhari, V. (2017). *Hospitality marketing and consumer behavior: Creating memorable experiences.* Waretown, USA: CRC Press.

Kotler, P. (1997). *Marketing Management: Analysis, planning, implementation and control* (9th ed.). Hemel Hempstead: Prentice Hall International.

Liang, H., Saraf, N., Hu, Q., & Xue, Y. (2007). Assimilation of enterprise systems: The effect of institutional pressures and the mediating role of top management. *MIS Quarterly, 31*(1), 59–87. doi:10.2307/25148781

Middleton, V., Fyall, A., Morgan, M., & Ranchhod, A. (2013). *Marketing in travel and tourism.* New York, NY: Routledge.

Mombeuil, C., & Fotiadis, A. K. (2017). Assessing the effect of customer perceptions of corporate social responsibility on customer trust within a low cultural trust context. *Social Responsibility Journal, 13*(4), 698–713. doi:10.1108/srj-02-2017-0032

Moriarty, J., Jones, R., Rowley, J., & Kupiec-Teahan, B. (2008). Marketing in small hotels: A qualitative study. *Marketing Intelligence & Planning, 26*(3), 293–315. doi:10.1108/026345008 10871348

Pease, W. (2007). *Information and communication technologies in support of the tourism industry.* London, UK: IGI Global.

Rowson, P. (2009). *Putting it all together: Your marketing plan.* Richmond, VI: Crimson Business Ltd.

Scheidler, S., Schons, L. M., & Spanjol, J. (2016). Internal marketing of corporate social responsibility (CSR) initiatives: CSR portfolio effects on employee perceptions of corporate hypocrisy, attitudes, and turnover. In L. Petruzzellis & R. S. Winer (Eds.), *Rediscovering the essentiality of marketing: Proceedings of the 2015 academy of marketing science (AMS) world marketing congress* (pp. 553–554). Cham: Springer International Publishing.

Suàrez Àlvarez, L., Díaz Martín, A. M., & Casielles, R. V. (2007). Relationship marketing and information and communication technologies: Analysis of retail travel agencies. *Journal of Travel Research, 45*(4), 453–463.

CHAPTER 18

DESIGNING AND CREATING TOURISM EXPERIENCES: ADDING VALUE FOR TOURISTS

Yosr Ben Tahar, Coralie Haller, Charlotte Massa and Sébastien Bédé

ABSTRACT

Purpose — *In a fragmented tourism market and highly competitive industry, tourism providers aim to increase their appeal and attractiveness. Identifying opportunities and resources, which contribute to provide consumers with higher quality experiences and create added value, is challenging for entrepreneurs. This chapter aims to increase the awareness of entrepreneurs about flexible methods and tools, which are transforming the way work is performed and thus affecting management practices in the tourism industry.*

Methodology/approach — *Literature review was conducted on conceptual issues related to consumer experience and three case studies were analysed as best practices in the wine tourism industry*

Findings — *To deliver a specific consumer experience and create added value for customers, several opportunities are identified, related to authenticity and accommodation offering. Necessary resources to exploit those opportunities encompass existing (connected to the main product wine, historical buildings, family story and product characteristics) as well as newly acquired valuable resources related to the development of peripheral tourism activities.*

The Emerald Handbook of Entrepreneurship in Tourism, Travel and Hospitality:
Skills for Successful Ventures, 313–328
Copyright © 2018 by Emerald Publishing Limited
All rights of reproduction in any form reserved
ISBN: 978-1-78743-530-8/doi:10.1108/978-1-78743-529-220181024

Research limitations/implications — *This study is explorative in nature, based on a literature review. It takes more entrepreneurial than academic approach.*

Practical implications — *The balance between authenticity and attractiveness is a key factor of success for wineries as means to provide added value to customers.*

Originality/value — *This contribution helps to identify valuable and existing resources in order to exploit opportunities and deliver high-quality experiences to tourists. The uniqueness of this experience is crucial on building added value for customers.*

Keywords: Entrepreneurial opportunities; resources; consumer experience; added value; wine tourism; best practices

---

Learning Objectives

By the end of this chapter, you should be able to:

- explain and describe what customer experience in tourism industry is;
- identify the most common 'strategic experiential modules' (SEMs) and 'experience providers' (ExPros) in tourism industry to develop a successful business venture;
- evaluate and use specific tools and frameworks related to customer experiences in tourism industry;
- identify necessary resources to provide added value for tourists as an entrepreneurial opportunity;
- understand and evaluate major issues at a macro level in order to identify valuable opportunities/resources at micro level;
- illustrate the design and creation of tourism experiences by best practices in the context of wine tourism.

18.1. INTRODUCTION

Three decades ago, the concept of 'consumption experience' emerged in the seminal article of Holbrook and Hirschman (1982). It became one of the key notions for academics and managers during the last 35 years. Thanks to this framework, marketing literature moved from the investigation of the buying decision process and the cognitivist paradigm towards the understanding of an emotional and hedonic consumption of products and services. Originally, Holbrook and Hirschman (1982) defined consumption experience 'as a primarily subjective state of consciousness with a variety of symbolic meanings, hedonic responses and aesthetic criteria' (p. 132). Through literature evolution of this concept of experience, major research focuses on emotions and feelings experienced by consumers during their consumption activities and this concept can be defined as 'experience is based on both cognitive and affective sphere and results from the interaction between "people − object − situation" (i.e., POS)' (Filser, 2002, p. 15).

In tourism, the importance of consumer experience is explained by its contribution to add value for tourists and improve their satisfaction level. More specifically, in a wine tourism context, Mitchell (2004) emphasises on emotional connexions induced by consumer experience:

> … there is more to … wine tourism than the simple consumption of a beverage (albeit a hedonistic pursuit) … this experience is not limited to the senses and emotions associated with the wine alone.

This definition focus on emotional aspects of wine tourism experience for customers. The main way used to deliver this consumption experience is winery visits that have developed during the last years. This development is supported first, by the proximity with direct viticulture activities and second, by the low amount of resources required. Wineries expect a direct return on investment (ROI) on selling their wines while tourism agencies/operators are interested by a ROI in terms of brand image of the destination, increase of visitors and services consumption. In order to fulfil those objectives: wine tours, wine road ('route du vin') (Haller, Bédé, Couder, & Millo, 2016) and several cultural activities are developed to enhance attractiveness (Dodd & Beverland, 2001). This implies moving from a product-focused strategy to a more services approach to create experiences.

This chapter aims to increase the awareness of an entrepreneurial mindset; flexible methods and tools, which are transforming the way work is performed in organisations and thus impacting management practices in the tourism industry today. The first section provides theoretical frameworks about consumer experience analysed through entrepreneurial opportunities perspectives. The second section is dedicated to the analysis of three cases of wine tourism industry. This contribution helps to identify valuable and existing resources in order to exploit opportunities and deliver a unique experience. The uniqueness of this experience is crucial on building added value for customers.

18.2. CREATING A CONSUMER EXPERIENCE: AN ENTREPRENEURIAL OPPORTUNITY

There are two categories of winery visits services: one category is dedicated to large groups of tourists organised in guided tours and the other one concerns small wineries with low accommodation capacities. Both, wineries and tourism agencies/operators are concerned by the development and changes in this activity. Direct ROI of winery visits for both wineries and tourism agencies is difficult to evaluate. In fact, it seems to be under expectations and mainly unprofitable for the two actors. One reason could be that winery visits are packages, which include a visit and a wine tasting. In France, in comparison to new world wine countries (i.e. Australia, Argentina, Chile or the USA), legislation forbids the payment of wine tasting. Thus, wineries' investments and ROI are differently correlated to the objective.

In the case of wineries working with tourist, the main ROI is correlated to the number of groups, the number of guided tours and the negotiated prices with tourist operators. There is no expectation of wine selling or impact on winery brand image. Moreover, being only one step in a tour will not allow the winery to develop its brand identity and more specifically authenticity, history and shared emotions with customers. Another difficulty for the small wineries is the highly competitive context with a large number of winemakers with similar wine quality and services offering. In addition, forbidding payment for wine tasting diminishes the perspectives of ROI to direct wine purchases.

18.2.1. Entrepreneurial Opportunities

Thus, wineries have to go over structural and environmental constraints. One way to address this challenge could be the development of entrepreneurial opportunities, which are defined as 'a set of ideas, beliefs and actions that enable the creation of future goods and services in the absence of current markets for them' (Venkataraman, 1997). Three distinctive but not mutually exclusive views of entrepreneurial opportunity exist: allocative (recognition), discovery and creative (Sarasvathy, Dew, Velamuri, & Venkataraman, 2003). According to the allocative view, entrepreneurs perceive existing opportunities when there is potential to redistribute resources for the enhancement of existing product or services. Discovering opportunities refer to the emergence of opportunities from information asymmetries associated to objective evaluation of existing resources. Entrepreneurs are able to create opportunities if they seek to maximise the utility functions of multiple stakeholders and that opportunities can only truly be identified ex-post (Sarasvathy et al., 2003). It is believed that opportunities' identification, selection and evaluation are the required skills for successful entrepreneurs.

Opportunities develop through time, form an idea or perception to concrete actions and strategy. Perception, discovery and creation refer to sensing or perceiving market needs and/or underemployed resources; recognising or discovering a 'fit' between particular market needs and specific resources; creating a new 'fit' between heretofore separate needs and resources in the form of a business concept (Ardichvili, Cardozo, & Ray, 2003). This framework is coherent with the observed development of wine tourism activities. The diversification of activities about wine is aligned with developments and changes in all agricultural domains. Facing more intense competition, lower financial incomes and subsidies, farmers and mainly winemakers have to identify or discover new opportunities to exploit. These opportunities are connected to the expertise, the relationship to the land the landscape and the product. Wine tourism represents potential entrepreneurial opportunities for winemakers as it inspires different categories of consumers over the world, who are looking to enhance their awareness and knowledge through specific consumption experiences.

18.2.2. Experiential Marketing and Experience Economy

Nowadays, experiential marketing is everywhere. In a variety of industries, companies have moved away from traditional 'features-and-benefits' marketing towards creating experiences for their customers. Through its products and services, tourism is one of the greatest source of experiences. Consumers are looking for purchasing experiences, to live new experiences, re-enchanting their lives, giving meaning to their consumption acts or building their identity. What is important for consumers is no more only the product or the service but the global offering that the company can deliver to them. In the case of wine tourism, products, which are at the heart of this business, are wines, and services proposed by the wineries could be wine tasting, are not sufficient. Existing research (see, for instance, Bédé & Massa, 2017) reveals that wine tourists look for dining, shopping and cultural and recreational activities along with authentic (e.g. reflecting local elements, unique events) products and experiences.

Holbrook and Hirschman (1982) published a major paper on the consumption experience and the experiential perspective 36 years ago. This approach focuses on the 'Three Fs' or fantasies (dreams, imagination and unconscious desires), feelings (emotions such as love, hate, anger, fear, joy and sorrow) and fun (hedonic pleasure derived from playful activities or aesthetic enjoyment) as key aspects of the consumption experience (Hirschman & Holbrook, 1982; Holbrook, 2006; Holbrook & Hirschman, 1982). By purchasing and consuming, this model completes the understanding of consumer behaviour by focusing on the experiences actually lived by consumers. Since the 1980s, this concept become increasingly central for academics and managers and innovative work has taken time for researchers and consultants to integrate and apply to business.

In the 1990s, a new economic approach emerged 'the experience economy'. According to Pine and Gilmore (1999), an experience is produced when 'companies stage an experience whenever they engage customers, connecting with them in a personal, memorable way' (p. 3). Therefore, experience started to be considered as a third category of supply adapted to the needs of the consumer (products, services and experiences). For Pine and Gilmore (1999), developing and selling experiences is a way to operate and sustain in a competitive environment. Customer experience includes every point of contact at which the customer interacts with the company, product or service. In order to make the development of the customer experience strategy easier, a company has to work on a 'customer experience management' (CEM), that is, a business strategy designed to manage the customer experience. It represents a strategy that results in a win−win value exchange between the company and its customers.

18.2.3. Managing the Customer Experience: Strategic Experiential Modules and Experience Providers

Schmitt (1999) proposed a strategic framework for managing experiences based on SEMs and ExPros. The experiential modules to be managed include five types of experiences, easily manageable by small businesses, outlined below.

First, a company has to work on sensory experiences (SENSE), i.e. 'sensual and tangible aspects of a product or experience that appeal to the five senses of sight, sound, scent, taste and touch' (Schmitt, 1999, p. 61). Thanks to these sensory experiences, a company can develop a real competitive advantage and differentiate its products and services from competition and can increase perceived value by consumers. For example, in relation to wine tourism, a winery should activate this module through the wine tasting or vineyard and winery tours. Affective experiences (FEEL) represent the second type of experiential modules. This module 'is devoted to inducing affect (i.e. the creation of moods and emotions) that adhere to the company and brand' (Schmitt, 1999, p. 61). Some research has demonstrated that emotions shape the attitudes that drive decisions. Loyalty can be partly explained by the emotional attachment to a product or a service, this feeling being triggered when they consume or use this product or service. Concerning tourism activities, one of the most effective stimuli, which can trigger emotions to consumers, is all employees and salespeople who have a direct link with consumers can explain the experience and create a relationship with them (e.g. a museum guide, a winegrower, a waiter/waitress and a concierge). A better consumption experience will be delivered when an employee creates an emotional connection with a consumer.

Third, a company should design creative cognitive experiences (THINK) in order to incite consumers to engage themselves in the experience in a creative way. A good solution to do that can be to use the process of co-creation with tourists (Prahalad & Ramaswamy, 2004). Through activities and interactions, it is essential to give tourists an active role/participation in designing, producing and consuming the tourism experience.

Then, physical experiences, behaviours and lifestyles (ACT) 'enriches customers' lives by targeting their physical experiences, showing them alternative ways of doing things, alternative lifestyles and interactions' (Schmitt, 1999, p. 62). The major objective is to change long-term behaviour of consumers. The fifth and last modules are social-identity experiences that result from relating to a reference group or culture (RELATE). This module emphasises the role of relational and community marketing. Both strategies have the same objective: to deliver an experience which engage brand presence, employees and consumers in order to interact together.

To manage these SEMs, Schmitt (1999) suggests conveying them to consumers through ExPros. These providers can be active in all operational marketing elements (Schmitt, 1999), such as:

- *Communications.* advertising, external and internal company communications, public relations campaigns;
- visual and verbal identity and signage, including names, logos, colours, etc.;
- product presence, including design, packaging and display;
- co-branding, involving event marketing, sponsorships, alliances and partnerships, product placement in movies, etc.;
- *Physical environments.* which include the external and internal design of corporate offices and sales outlets;
- *Digital presence.* websites and social media networks; and
- *People.* including salespersons, company representatives, customer service providers and call centre operators.

18.2.4. Evaluating the Performance: Customer Feedback

Delivering experiences to consumers is a long-term and evolving strategy, which needs to capture customer feedback. Several solutions exist to collect consumer feedback. First, a company can ask in real-time (by employees) or post-visit (by automated tools as email) what people think and feel about their experience. Another solution is directly linked to the digital revolution and the tendency to 'give your opinion' online. Companies have access to a huge free amount of information by these review websites. Tourism-related industries are particularly concerned by this information sharing through websites such as TripAdvisor or Oyster.

In this long-term perspective, finally, it is essential to measure the effects on performance of the company in the field of managing consumption experience. Through its ROI specifically due to this strategy, a company can measure if all investment to deliver the experience (people, processes and setting/environment) are working and are efficient. Consumer experience can also be measured by using brand image and its perception by consumers or by using a specific metric, the 'net promoter score' (NPS). Many companies use NPS because this metric is a single question ('Would you recommend this company to a friend or relative?'), which can be easily implemented, monitored and analysed.

18.3. ADDED VALUE FOR TOURISTS: THREE CASES/ BEST PRACTICES OF ENTREPRENEURIAL WINE BUSINESSES

During a family lunch, on a nice spring day in June 2017, as most tourists were enjoying the sunshine, and the different 'terroirs' of Alsace, a winemaker was discussing with his parents about the ways to enhance the tourist appeal of their vineyards:

> I think we should develop a wine tourism offering based more on customer experience. The atmosphere of the cellar and the exchanges/interactions we have with potential customers should be at stake. It is crucial that client feel like home in our winery as each one of them is a potential ambassador for our winery.

This statement highlights the fact that wine tourism is a topic at stake for both the wine and tourism industries as it can support business success for different stakeholders.

In fact, winemakers consider wine tourism as an opportunity to sell their wines and build proximity/connexions with their customers. Visitors are looking for experiencing through tasting, visiting and discussing with winemakers grape wine region attributes (Hall et al., 2000). There are different wine tourism activities that winemakers can implement: vineyards and wineries visits, wine tasting, wine festivals and wine shows and also focus on the promotion of wines attributes produced in a specific spatial area/zone. Moreover, wine tourism contributes to the attractiveness of one destination, motivating local and foreign visitors to come for a visit (Quadri-Felitti & Fiore, 2013). According to Getz, Dowling, Carlsen, and Anderson (1999), three main aspects define wine tourism activities: marketing strategy and wine companies, destination planning and marketing strategy as well as consumer behaviour. Therefore, wine tourism activities need to be analysed on a global strategic level (Beverland, 1999) integrating customer, winemakers and tourism agencies expectations and perspectives (Getz, 2000).

Regarding the French wine tourism, there are 10,000 wineries which offer wine tourism activities to 10 million visitors per year, 39 per cent of them are coming from overseas. The Alsace region is the fourth most visited region in France with the oldest wine road created in 1953, which attracts 2.2 million tourists every year. Gastronomy and wineries visits are the second reason why tourist come to Alsace, with 41 per cent of them stating that they have visited or bought wine during their stay. Figures highlight the importance of wine tourism in this region and provide a rationale to identify the key factors of success of different wineries in Alsace.

18.3.1. First Case/Best Practice: Zeyssolff's House

The history of 'Zeyssolff's house' as winemakers started in 1778, a dozen generations ago. The vineyard is well exposed and spread over an interesting geological variety of territories, which allows producing well-typed wines. Honours and awards obtained at different competitions testify their value. The 'Zeyssolff's house' is located at Gertwiller, halfway between Strasbourg and Colmar, geographically at the centre of the Alsace region. Changes in the wine processes, wine tourism offering and other services occurred with the last generation. The son started working with his parents in the vineyard in 1997 and took over the winery in 2005. He and his wife consider the wine tourism services as a pool of available entrepreneurial opportunities.

The starting point of the wine tourism business was the need for financial resources in order to maintain the family property. The historical buildings are valued as assets that help to develop the business. The induced authenticity of the historical characteristic of the buildings is considered as a keystone of wine tourism offering. Wine tourism as entrepreneurial opportunities encompass complementary services developed for better customer targeting. Current developments at 'Zeyssolff's house' have been identified through interactions with customers and proactive behaviour regarding opportunities targeting. In this regard, 'Zeyssolff's house' created and developed accommodation services and a wine and terroir boutique.

First, the existing cottages (bed and breakfast) have been renovated and accommodation capacity was increased through the expansion and creation of two additional cottages. Currently, fine cottages and 28 beds are available to accommodate visitors in a four-star hostel. Moving towards services that are more expensive is a conscious strategy. Simultaneously, a delicatessen was developed enhancing the attractiveness of 'Zeyssolff's house'. The attractiveness for domestic customers evolved rapidly to reach international tourists. The main objective is to attract visitors who are interested in high-quality wines and make them stay longer in the cottage.

The main objective of selling their wine is still guiding the exploited opportunities. Discussing with customers is the main source to discover opportunities such as asking for a place where they can take a glass of wine or a coffee. Customers help the owners to see that there is no place like that in the village. This place would be very helpful for tourists in the winter. The identification of this potential opportunity is associated with a positive evaluation of existing resources such as the available place within the renovated building. It leads the creation of some kind of artistic gallery tapas place. This place is the combination of owners' interests, customers' expectations and available resources. It reveals the importance of resources identification to go further in the opportunity elaboration and implementation.

In this context, Zeyssolff's house owner indicates:

> We thought about creating a dedicated space, within the boutique, where we could offer entertainment to customers and allow them to have a light meal at the same time (...). Having an independent place, apart from the wine boutique, like a museum, will not ensure that people will pay to see "old-fashioned things". We have many things to show and share with visitors, and we decided to integrate all of them directly in the wine boutique. It is a mean of learning and understanding both for children and adults as they can have experience by themselves.

Several activities are offered from time to time, with artistic/creative aspects, such as workshops about fragrance and flavour. Nevertheless, wine is still the core of the business model, the peripheral/auxiliary elements contribute to build a distinctive customer experience. On the one hand, winery visits with historical background about the family, buildings, wine processes and regional grape attributes contribute to enhance the authenticity of the experience. Wine tasting is a constituent element of the tour with five white wines tasted, presented and described by the winemaker and an inlaid wine glass as a souvenir. Storytelling is reinforced through presentation's film and anecdotes. On the other hand, the delicatessen is the place where customers may discover other local wines and regional gastronomy. They can enjoy these products on-site in the ambience of a historical cellar.

'Zeyssolff's house' success is explained by the awareness of owners to identify opportunities and value existing resources and assets. The key point of this success is related to the ability to deliver authentic and unique customer experience. Emotional connexion with the historical aspects of the place, family story and wine's discovery are induced by the storytelling.

18.3.2. Second Case/Best Practice: Hauller Family Winery — La Cave du Tonnelier

Established in Dambach-la-ville since 1776, and run by several generations, the Hauller family winery was first a winegrower only, bringing the grape to the local cooperative cellar. The winemaking activities began in 1960 with the grandfather of the current owners. These changes were induced by climatic incidents affecting crops. The opportunity to develop winemaking activities was identified and well exploited because of technical knowledge and available plot of land well located. The grandfather focused on production and enhancing wine quality while the father developed partnerships with distributors.

Currently, the Hauller family winery has 40 hectares in production with 400 thousand bottles. Hauller's wine is mainly distributed in supermarkets

(80 per cent of production) with recent export activities representing 10 per cent over the USA, Austria, Poland and Denmark markets. A small part — 10 per cent — of the production is sold through cafés, hotels and restaurants and direct channel through cellar-doors activities, which was the main distribution channel 20 years ago. The historical cellar is located in the downtown-fortified village of Dambach-la-ville with a dedicated employee for selling activities.

Changes in consumer behaviour with the development of supermarket wine distribution led to stop this activity for several winemakers including Hauller family winery as they stated

> The low volume of production, together with the fragmented offer and the decrease of market shares, have reduced the visibility for Alsace wines in France. It is crucial to find new innovative prospects, find new opportunities, new ways of doing, to prevent the wine industry to fail.

Awareness about economic and social risks induced by this situation, local tourist agency is engaged in a dynamic strategy. The main aim is to become more attractive for international wine tourists in order to support winemakers and revitalise the tourist activities. Being more attractive involves wine's culture sharing and developing high-quality services including accessibility, accommodation, events and dining services.

Inspired from other regions and countries, Hauller's managers offer summer programme of events in the cellar through which new products are promoted. They chose to build a new cellar out of the fortified downtown of Dambach-la-ville, as it was not possible to extend the historical cellar. New buildings have been designed in coherence with the expected developments of the activities including wine production and tourist accommodation. Located near the highway with bus parking, the new cellar induced several opportunities to collaborate with wine tour operators and event organisers. The tasting-reception bar is in the centre of a large outdoors space opening onto modern vats. The customer experience is conceived as authentic by the story of the family and the different developments occurred in its activities. Most important for management is to share feelings and emotions about wine, grapes and senses.

The development of winery visits and tasting remains limited because of structural and economic problems related to the seasonality of the activity, free charges and the lack of human resources dedicated to it. In fact, the owner argued

> ... in order to better develop the quality of services offered, it would be necessary to allow winemakers to charge for wine tastings. We could then imagine hiring a sommelier, who would be able to make the customer live a real experience. Those are possible answers to the recurrent question of what is missing to develop and render professional the wine tourism activities.

To cope with this challenge, several winemakers hire trainees over the summer period. Because of low direct ROI, winery visits and wine tastings are not highly valued by winemakers. Thus, low investments are done to develop this activity. In the Hauller's case, managers are thinking about how to exploit this opportunity. They are convinced that engaging time and money helps to provide a unique customer experience. They have been inspired by wineries offering shows, festivals or events organised around wine tasting. Professionalisation of wine tourism activities is necessary to enhance consumer perception of experience, brand image and more importantly direct selling.

18.3.3. Third Case/Best Practice: Vidivino

Vidivino is a wine tourism specialist whose main activities are the offering of regular and private wine tours, incentives and workshops for French and international customers. The Vidivino team is quite diverse, with a variety of professional profile/expertise, such as sommelier, winemakers and people passionate about wine. This team composition allows the creation and offering of complementary service experience.

Historically, business activities where located and focused on the 'Provence' region (Southeast of France), but recent developments have been conducted in the Alsace region, due to the founder's family attachment to the region. Moreover, additional reasons to expand in Alsace are related to the existing connexions of this owner with Alsatian winemakers, the international attractiveness of the region, and the limited wine tourism offering. The business model is based on medium and large groups of wine tours with a mission statement to make wine universe affordable to anyone in a friendly atmosphere. The aim is to give customers some basic elements to understand, appreciate and evaluate wines. This is carried out in collaboration with cellars and winemakers meet during wine tours.

Vidivino's founder see himself as a mediator between winemakers and customers as he stated, 'I think intermediaries are relevant, we are facilitators, but winemakers need to grasp this opportunity.' Low ROI in wine activities are the main reason for the low level of development of wine tourism activities. Aligned with this idea, Vidivino's founder supports the reluctance of winemakers to enrol in wine tourism activities.

> We take the clients in the vineyards and show them the cellar. The winemaker only takes part to the wine tasting. This will save him around 40 minutes over the winery visit. It is quite appreciable!! (...). But I can understand, that it can be complicated, for a winemaker, who recognizes himself as a farmer, to make efforts to welcome people who are not always concentrated though demanding when they come for a winery visit.

More precisely, the main issue is to find out relevant resources to develop wine tourism activities. Two are the main resources, time and staff, to explain their reluctance to invest in the development of wine tourism activities. The need to hire at least one person dedicated to wine tours is the recurrent argument against the development of wine tourism activities. Agriculture domains are characterised by low level of workforce, and the wine domains suffer of this constraint. Moreover, for winemakers, wine tourism ROI is difficult to evaluate because of free charges induced by French legal constraints and low levels of direct selling.

Thus, by outsourcing such an activity, wineries will have an opportunity to develop their brand image and turnover. Winemakers will spend less time on the project and would not need to dedicate human resources. The customer experience delivered by this wine tour operator is focused on enthusiastic attitude towards wine. It encompasses grapes specificities, regional traditions, winemaking process, the notion of 'terroir' and enlist senses. The tours are organised with wineries having a high tourist and aesthetic qualities. What is of value is 'to find the right balance between authenticity and an appropriate approach of welcoming tourists on site. And this can be sometimes quite complicated!'

Another challenge could be related to the necessary investments in facilities' renovation, which is costly and constrained by the historical location of the wineries. For some small wineries, creating a reception area and parking spaces for buses is impossible. For several Alsatian wineries located in centre of the village, fortifications and exclusive pedestrian access reduce the ability to develop amenities for this activity.

That is the reason why the design and development of wine tourism activities has to be co-created and supported by tourism agencies/operators. According to Vidivino's founder, customer experience in wine tourism is to build up in collaboration with winemakers. Customers have to be considered as ambassadors of the destinations they come to visit. Tourists continue sharing the experience they lived further after their visit through word-to-mouth and social networks by posting pictures and online reviews. Their experience helps to provide other prospective tourists with an immersion in wine world, through shared knowledge about 'terroir', winemaking processes and wine tasting. These aspects are focused on product, but peripheral elements and services related to facilities and accommodation are also important.

18.4. SUMMARY

The development of wine tourism activities is challenging for wine and tourism stakeholders. Their shared objectives are to be attractive for wine and non-wine consumers, domestic and international visitors, enhance the ROI by relying on a pool of resources and collaborations. Three are the main lessons to be taken from the discussion of this chapter, which are presented below.

The first lesson is a focus on customer experience as a distinctive factor based on authenticity, peripheral services and easy accommodation. Wine tourists may be organised in two categories: experts and novices. Experts are interested on wines, grapes, tastes, production process and regional characteristics. Novices are occasional wine consumers while experts are generally regular ones. Challenge for wine tourism industry is to be attractive for both categories through unique consumer experiences. Considering that delivering customer experience is an entrepreneurial opportunity for winemakers lead to develop a global perspective as a level of analysis. The different cases analysed provide a comprehensive overview about the development of wine tourism activities and entrepreneurial opportunities in this segment.

There are three success factors in delivering a memorable consumer experience, namely, authenticity, peripheral services and easy accommodation. Authenticity is the key characteristic of the added value expected by the customer. It is correlated to historical aspects of the region, buildings and family storytelling about wine activity. It contributes to create an emotional connexion to destination and tasted wines. Emotional connexion enhances positive perception of the experience and stronger relationship with the brands (destination, region's wines). This connexion is supported by the winemaker's storytelling. The winemaker, as a host, becomes the central actor of wine tourism experience. Winemaker's availability for winery visits and wine tasting is not sufficient for attractiveness. The development of cultural peripheral activities in wineries and/or tourist destinations contributes to increase in visitation. Artistic, creative, gastronomic and other kinds of events contribute to attract a large number of people during short periods. It represents a relevant balance between the necessary winemaker availability and the lack of available time he/she can dedicate to wine tourism activities.

The second lesson is the imperative for appropriate investments in wine tourism activities as a balance among existing and valuable resources. The development of wine tourism activities main obstacle is the difficulty to measure and evaluate the ROI for winemakers. This issue restricts and delimits entrepreneurs to fully exploiting potential opportunities.

The exploitation of opportunities is considerably dependent on positive evaluation of investment, profitability and available/necessary resources. The main concerns and challenges are the pooling of adequate resources in terms of time, staff and infrastructure in the projects, along with achieving the rights balance between the allocation of these resources.

The third lesson is the need for partnership and collaboration among stakeholders as a key factor for success for the destination. The design, creation and development of wine tourism activities are determined by regional strategies of tourism and the commitment of winemakers. More specifically, collaborations with wine tourism businesses/tours can be considered as a mean to improve ROI for both winemakers and regional tourism agencies/operators.

In fact, it represents an interesting opportunity as it helps to reduce necessary investments in organisation, communication and time to spend on wine tourism activities for winemakers. Successful stories are built up on a positive evaluation of existing resources, collaboration, alliances and long-term strategies; these factors are contributing to create and offer a distinctive customer experience.

Review Questions

Check your understanding of this chapter by answering the following questions or discussing the topics below:

- What are the major elements of the consumption experience?
- Identify different issues and challenges related to customer experience in the tourism industry from entrepreneurship perspective.
- Discuss critical factors of success of customer experience in tourism industry in order to provide added value for tourists.
- Explain why the development of tourism activities as a service-focused strategy is a valuable approach.
- How would you enhance the tourist experience in order to generate more revenues for SMEs?

REFERENCES AND FURTHER READING

Ardichvili, A., Cardozo, R., & Ray, S. (2003). A theory of entrepreneurial opportunity identification and development. *Journal of Business Venturing, 18*(1), 105–123.

Bédé, S., & Massa, C. (2017, May). Wine tourism and consumption: A netnography to determine the key elements of winery experience. Communication presented at the 33th French Association of Marketing Congress, Tours, France.

Beverland, M. (1999). Wine tourism: A missed opportunity or a misplaced priority. *Pacific Tourism Review, 3*(1), 119–131.

Dodd, T., & Beverland, M. (2001). Winery tourism life-cycle development: A proposed model. *Tourism & Recreation Research, 26*(2), 11–21.

Filser, M. (2002). Le marketing de la production d'expérience: Statut théorique et implications managériales. *Décisions Marketing, 28*(4), 13–22.

Getz, D. (2000). *Explore wine tourism: Management, development, destinations.* New York, NY: Cognizant.

Getz, D., Dowling, R., Carlsen, J., & Anderson, D. (1999). Critical success factors for wine tourism. *International Journal of Wine Marketing, 11*(3), 20–43.

Hall, C. M., Johnson, G., Cambourne, B., Macionis, N., Mitchell, R. D., & Sharples, L. (2000). Wine tourism: An introduction. In C. M. Hall, L. Sharples, B. Cambourne, & N. Macionis (Eds.), *Wine tourism around the world: Development, management and markets* (pp. 1–23). Oxford: Butterworth-Heinemann.

Haller, C., Bédé, S., Couder, M., & Millo, F. (2016). Pink wine and movie star: How the Provence Wine trail was established. In L. Thach & S. Charters (Eds.), *Best practices in wine tourism: Case studies from around the world* (pp. 95–114). Putnam Valley, NY: Miranda Press.

Hirschman, E. C., & Holbrook, M. B. (1982). Hedonic consumption: Emerging concepts, methods and propositions. *Journal of Marketing, 46*(3), 92–101.

Holbrook, M. B. (2006). Consumption experience, customer value, and subjective personal introspection: An illustrative photographic essay. *Journal of Business Research*, *59*(6), 714−725.

Holbrook, M. B., & Hirschman, E. C. (1982). The experiential aspects of consumption: Consumer fantasies, feelings and fun. *Journal of Consumer Research*, *9*(2), 132−140.

Mitchell, R. (2004). *Scenery and chardonnay: A visitor perspective of the New Zealand winery experience*. Unpublished Phd thesis, University of Otago, Otago, New Zealand.

Pine, J. B., & Gilmore, J. H. (1999). *The experience economy*. Boston, MA: Harvard Business Press.

Prahalad, C. K., & Ramaswamy, V. (2004). Co-creation experiences: The next practice in value creation. *Journal of Interactive Marketing*, *18*(3) 5−14.

Quadri-Felitti, D., & Fiore, A. M. (2013). Destination loyalty: Effects of wine tourists' experiences, memories, and satisfaction on intentions. *Tourism and Hospitality Research*, *13*(1), 47−62.

Sarasvathy, D., Dew, N., Velamuri, S. R., & Venkataraman, S. (2003). Three views of entrepreneurial opportunity. In Z. J. Acs & D. B. Audretsch (Eds.). *Handbook of entrepreneurship research: An interdisciplinary survey and introduction* (pp. 141−160). Dordrecht: Kluwer Academic Publishers Springer.

Schmitt, B. (1999). Experiential marketing. *Journal of Marketing Management*, *15*(1−3), 53−67.

Venkataraman, S. (1997). The distinctive domain of entrepreneurship research. *Advances in Entrepreneurship, Firm Emergence and Growth*, *3*(1), 119−139.

PART VI
SPECIFIC TOPICS OF
ENTREPRENEURSHIP IN TOURISM

CHAPTER 19

CROWDSOURCING FOR TOURISM VENTURES

Vincent Grèzes, Roland Schegg and
Antoine Perruchoud

ABSTRACT

Purpose — *The aim of this chapter is to present techniques to involve the crowd in the ideation and funding process of tourism ventures. The typologies of those techniques are presented before analysing their key success factors and advantages. Finally, a design model is presented in order to help managers and project holders to implement a crowd ideation and funding process.*

Methodology/approach — *Literature review, quantitative and qualitative methods such as data analysis and interviews were employed to encompass several aspects of crowdsourcing related to tourism ventures.*

Findings — *This chapter highlights the key success factors and advantages of crowdsourcing and crowdfunding for tourism ventures, formulates recommendations and proposes a concrete tool for every project holder or manager who would like to engage in those activities.*

Research limitations/implications — *Although several types of crowdsourcing are operative, we only focused on two particular types that are interesting for tourism entrepreneurs.*

Practical implications — *The key success factors and key advantages presented in this chapter constitute tracks for reflection and for action for the*

The Emerald Handbook of Entrepreneurship in Tourism, Travel and Hospitality:
Skills for Successful Ventures, 331–349
Copyright © 2018 by Emerald Publishing Limited
ISBN: 978-1-78743-530-8/doi:10.1108/978-1-78743-529-220181025

managers and project holders. The crowdsourcing design model is a tool to help entrepreneurs to elaborate campaigns of crowdsourcing/crowdfunding.

Originality/value — *This chapter summarises the evolution of involving the crowd in the innovation and funding process of a project. The reasons and success factors are exposed and illustrated with numerous examples from the tourism industry. Finally, a practical model is presented in order to allow the creation of a crowdsourcing/crowdfunding campaign.*

Keywords: Tourism venture; crowdsourcing/crowdfunding; crowdsourcing/crowdfunding typology; open innovation; key success factors; crowdsourcing/crowdfunding canvas

---

Learning Objectives

After studying this chapter, you should be able to:

- explain the typology of crowdsourcing practices;
- describe the main steps of a general crowdsourcing campaign and its possible adaptation;
- identify the best type of crowdsourcing campaign according to specific business objectives;
- build a successful crowdsourcing campaign based on key success factors;
- present and discuss examples of best practice illustrating the use of crowdsourcing campaigns in tourism;
- design a crowdsourcing campaign.

19.1. INTRODUCTION

This chapter will help to clarify the role of crowdsourcing in supporting entrepreneurship in tourism and highlight the key issues that people who want to use crowdsourcing need to know. The chapter is based on the following sources and resources:

- analysis of a detailed literature research on the experiences of crowdsourcing in tourism;
- analysis of crowdsourcing and crowdfunding projects conducted in Switzerland and in the canton Valais as one of the major tourism destinations in Switzerland, during the period 2010−2016;
- interviews with project leaders (regional actors as well as private actors) and crowdsourcing platform owners;
- case studies of crowdsourcing and crowdfunding projects.

19.2. THE EMERGENCE OF CROWDSOURCING

This section presents the value and benefits of crowdsourcing skills in tourism entrepreneurship.

19.2.1. Engaging the Users in the Innovation Process

Consideration of the economic environment is of fundamental importance, particularly in the case of tourism, both with regard to resource management and to adapting value propositions to the market, to finally realise relevant innovation for customers.

A paradigm shift has emerged in the end of the 1980s, with the work of E. von Hippel (1988). According to E. von Hippel, the sources of innovation varied greatly, in a functional way, from the manufacturer and the supplier to the user of the innovation. In 2005, the author deepened his findings about the innovation power of users and explained: 'User-centered innovation processes offer great advantages over the manufacturer-centric innovation development systems that have been the mainstay of commerce for hundreds of years. Users that innovate can develop exactly what they want, rather than relying on manufacturers to act as their (often very imperfect) agents' (von Hippel, 2005, p. 1). With his studies, von Hippel popularised the concept of *lead users*, which represents 10 to almost 40 per cent of users that engage in modifying and developing products (von Hippel, 2005).

Later, Steve Blank confirmed these considerations in the field of entrepreneurship by describing the product development model as the path to disaster and the customer development model as the path to epiphany (Blank, 2013). His concept of customer development consists of the following four steps:

1. *Customer discovery.* This first step consists of converting the vision of the founders of a start-up venture into assumptions for the business model. As a result, a plan is developed to test how potential customers respond to these assumptions and subsequently transform it into concrete facts. This step involves discovering what the entrepreneur's vision is, how the product or service addresses a need and how the response to that need is important to potential clients. Thus, this phase consists of testing the proposed hypotheses and going 'outside the building' to verify their conformity with expectations and market needs.

2. *Customer validation.* The aim of this second step is to draw up a plan for the application and distribution of the product or service and to check whether this plan can be used more than once and flexibly. If not, the entrepreneur must go back to the first step. These first two steps are used to validate the target market, to locate the customer, to validate the perceived value of the

product or service, to identify buyers and to establish pricing and distribution strategies.

3. *Customer creation.* This step must be based on the first two steps and in particular on the initial validation of the suitability of the product for customer needs. This strengthens the demand of end consumers and leads them to the company's distribution channels.

4. *Company building.* This stage corresponds to a phase of formalisation and organisational strengthening of the company, by assigning more firmly the operational divisions of the company, built on the successes of the previous stages.

In the area of entrepreneurship, this approach can also be usefully supplemented by an approach to identifying customer needs, which helps managers to develop a performance promise tailored to the needs, tasks to be completed or the problems to be solved by their customers (Osterwalder, Pigneur, Barnada, Smith, & Papadakos, 2014). Indeed, the authors base the value creation process on the observation of the customers and the test on the market.

These approaches, which are used to meet the expectations and needs of the local population and hosts, are based on a continuous dialogue with the end users of tourist products and services to produce innovations for businesses. Therefore, customer needs discovery and customer development is close to the concept of crowdsourcing, because it places the user at the centre of the innovation process.

The next subsection deals with the distinction between two postures of companies involving the customer into its innovation process: the open innovation and the crowdsourcing.

19.2.2. From Open Innovation to Crowdsourcing

Open innovation and crowdsourcing are two innovation processes in which the innovation process opens up to the outside world. Chesbrough was the first to employ the term 'Open innovation' back in 2003 and defined it as follows:

> Open innovation is a paradigm that assumes that firms can and should use external ideas and internal and external paths to market, as the companies look to advance their technology. (Chesbrough, 2003, p. 43)

The term 'Open innovation' does not only cover cooperation between individual competitors or complementary companies but also includes, and above all, consideration of all types of knowledge sources such as research institutes or customers.

This outward-looking attitude responds to the need for specific information from tourism and non-tourism companies to generate innovation. Thomke (2003) defined two types of information needed in the innovation process:

(1) initially, information on the needs of the market, the preferences and the desires of the customers and (2) secondly, information on solutions to meet these needs, in particular technological expertise, with which information on needs can be transformed into concrete offerings.

However, according to Gassmann, Frankenberger, and Csik (2013), managers consider solutions and approaches that help them to innovate their business model to be more important than product or service innovations in order to achieve competitive advantages.

This implies that, in a problem-solving process, information on needs and solutions needs to be collected by firms (von Hippel, 2005). The contribution of this 'market participation' to the innovation process of the company is described by Köpcke (2008) as evident, because external collaboration allows better acceptance of the innovations by the public (in a context where the failure rate of innovations is between 30 per cent and 70 per cent). Open innovation is therefore a means to better capture the needs of consumers. According to this logic, customer discovery (Blank, 2013) and value proposition design (Osterwalder et al., 2014) are primarily related to open innovation.

For its part, the term 'crowdsourcing' appeared in the *Wired Magazine* in June 2006 (Howe, 2006). In contrast to outsourcing, crowdsourcing refers to the crowd and the sourcing outside the boundaries of the firm. However, the author distinguishes between the two processes in terms of the identification of the agent. In outsourcing, as in crowdsourcing, the outsourced object is a job that is normally performed by an employee; in a crowdsourcing process, however, the agents to whom the task has been outsourced are not identified beforehand.

Crowdsourcing is a practice resulting from the development of digital tools and the Internet. The new ICT infrastructure provides an easy and quick way to reach out to a large community to collect ideas about a problem (Mendonca & Sutton, 2008). The authors believe that the benefits for the company are limited to the savings from outsourcing a task and reducing responsibility for employees. In addition, it becomes easier for firms to attract 'brains', which increase the likelihood to find innovative ideas and improve resulting benefits. However, the quality of the ideas might not be sufficient, e.g. due to an unfavourable composition of the respondents. It is therefore essential that the company looks out for a promising target group. Wikipedia is probably the best known example of crowdsourcing, to this day. We will discuss the crowdsourcing's advantages and key success factors in Section 19.4.

Gassman (2013, p. 6) describes the crowdsourcing process as follows: 'Crowdsourcing is an interactive strategy for transferring new knowledge and problem solving to external actors through public and semi-public call to a large group. Creative themes are typically at the centre of attention, but repetitive tasks are also possible. In general, this call is made through a website.' In summary, the author defines crowdsourcing as 'an interactive, community-based innovation strategy' (translations by the author).

The crowdsourcing method consists in opening up the process of innovation to the outside world by making it accessible to customers and to the population, which is so important in tourism-related industries. These can be interactively linked in the value creation process: tourism providers can thus benefit from valuable impetus coming directly from important actors in tourism. On the basis of the ideas created and received by customers and the population, new models of activities can be achieved.

In the next two sections, we will describe different types of crowdsourcing activities and discuss principal forms of crowdsourcing for entrepreneurship in the tourism industry.

19.3. THE TYPOLOGY OF CROWDSOURCING

Crowdsourcing activities have grown rapidly and the tasks entrusted to the crowds can be grouped into six main types of activities: idea generation or 'collective creativity', opinion gathering on policy choices or 'civic engagement', online-distributed work or 'cloud labour', community building, the call for common knowledge or 'collective knowledge' and the participatory funding or 'crowdfunding'.

Table 19.1 summarises the six main types of crowdsourcing and gives some international examples.

In the next sections, we will discuss the two most relevant types of crowdsourcing − i.e., idea generation and crowdfunding − in the context of entrepreneurship in tourism-related industries, with a focus on their respective advantages, key success factors and some examples.

19.4. BENEFITS AND OPPORTUNITIES OF CROWDSOURCING IN TOURISM VENTURES

This section presents successively the advantages of the crowdsourcing for idea generation and of the crowdfunding, their processes and key success factors. The following illustrations deal with the concepts and give some recommendations.

19.4.1. Crowdsourcing for Idea Generation in the Context of Tourism Entrepreneurship

The main advantages of this type of crowdsourcing for entrepreneurship in tourism, travel and hospitality are primarily to collect a large amount of ideas relative to a problem, to promote innovation or to test and improve existing ideas.

Table 19.1. The Typology of Crowdsourcing and Corresponding Examples.

Type	Activity	Description/Aim	Examples of Platforms
Collective creativity (Crowd-creation; broadcast search; open innovation)	Idea generation	An organisation mobilises a crowd to find a solution to a problem or to test a hypothesis. Ideal for solving (scientific) problems. When an organisation uses external sources to generate, develop or implement ideas, it is called 'open innovation'	Graphic design Writing Illustration 99Design CrowdSpring Atizo[a] Innocentive[a] I-Brain
Civic engagement (Crowd-voting; peer-vetted creative production)	Opinion on future choices	An organisation mobilises a crowd to come up with a solution to a problem that has a response that is subjective or dependent on public assistance. Ideal for design, aesthetics or policy issues	E-democracy.org Change.org
Cloud labour (Distributed human intelligence tasking)	Online-distributed work	An organisation has a set of information and mobilises a crowd for processing or analysing information. Ideal for processing large datasets that a single computer can't do easily	Amazon MechanicalTurk PeoplePerHour ClickWorker **Find my itin** **AFAR**[b]
Community building	Creation of communities	Development of communities of interest, sharing of passions, beliefs, etc.	Facebook CrowdTogether Kindling **Trippy** **Under30Experiences** **Geeks on a plane**.
Collective knowledge (Crowd-wisdom; knowledge discovery and management)	Call to popular wisdom	An organisation mobilises a crowd to find and gather information. Ideal for creating collective resources	iStockPhoto Wikipedia Quora **TripTease**
Crowdfunding	Participatory funding	An organisation or project sponsor call on the crowd to receive funding from online investors, sponsors or donors to finance a project or a business	KickStarter MyMajorCompany Croix-Rouge (CAN) WeMakeIt

Source: Authors' creation, synthesis from Howe (2008), Crowdsourcing Inc. (2011) and Daren (2013).
[a]Specialized actors of open innovation.
[b]Some tourist crowdsourcing platforms are highlighted in bold.

The crowdsourcing process: The general process is based on five general phases: preparation, initiation, execution, evaluation and valorisation, as outlined below.

1. During the preparation phase, the company or project owner has to identify a problem to solve or a hypothesis to test, and a main target audience in order to focus the communication of the campaign. At this stage, too, the aim is to establish the reward rules, criteria and framework conditions for the expected contributions and to create balanced and motivating incentives to attract contributors. Finally, the problem or hypothesis has to be converted into relevant questions that will be addressed to the crowd.
2. The initiation phase consists of broadcasting the challenge online and asking the crowd to participate and give solutions.
3. The execution or implementation phase is fulfilled with the idea collection while crowd submits solutions.
4. The evaluation phase consists of several types of evaluation: an evaluation by the crowd itself, and/or an evaluation by the initiators and/or an evaluation by a pool of experts. Regardless of the type of assessment, the aim of this phase is to discriminate the given ideas and to bring out the best items according to the goal of the company or the project owner, and according to the rules of the challenge.
5. During the valorisation phase, the company or project owner rewards the winning idea generators. In the open innovation processes, and according to the rules of the challenge, the company owns the solution and can use it to generate profits.

Success factors within the context of the tourism industry: Based on case studies conducted in an Alpine region of Switzerland, Doctor, Schnyder, and Bürcher (2016) defined six key success factors for the tourism industry.

During the preparation phase, the authors recommend to:

1. Define precisely the problem question addressed to the crowd in order to improve the quality of the ideas;
2. Ask support from the platform operator (without paying an additional contribution);
3. Be careful of the representativeness of the sample of participants (the crowd) according to the population concerned by the question.

For the execution phase, the authors advise to:

4. Encourage the participants to read carefully the question before putting ideas;
5. Be assisted by a system that classifies the ideas according to certain criteria to simplify the phase of evaluation;

6. Involve experts in the field of the problem addressed in order to stimulate reactions between participants and to exclude bad ideas and reduce evaluation time.

Examples in the tourism industry: In Switzerland, crowdsourcing is activated for the generation of ideas on both public and private initiative. Public crowdsourcing initiatives are developed at different levels: (1) at the national level, supported by the Swiss Confederation, such as the Innovations Generator; (2) at the regional level, supported by regional tourism organisations, such as Innovation Grisons and (3) at the local level, supported by local development agencies, such as Davos Klosters Innovation. As for the private crowdsourcing initiatives in the Swiss tourism industry, these are known from a cable car company. Several other examples of crowdsourcing in the hotel industry emerged outside Switzerland, for example, in France with the Club Med Val Thorens experiment[1] or the 17John project in New York.

19.4.1.1. Three Examples of Public Initiatives

1. At the national level, the Innovations Generator (www.innovationsgenerator. ch) aims to select the most promising proposals among a multitude of ideas for sustainable tourism. The aim is to support three to five concrete projects with initial aid. The Innovations Generator started activity in 2017, which was declared the International Year of Sustainable Tourism by the UNWTO. This project, supported by the State Secretariat for Economic Affairs (SECO), is organised as follows: experts and researchers participated during the preparation phase. An online platform as well as workshops with *lead users* support the crowdsourcing execution phase. Then, field/industry experts perform the evaluation of the ideas. Finally, seed funding and entrepreneurship coaching support the valorisation phase.
2. At the regional level, the Economic Development and Tourism Agency of the canton of the Grisons (AWT Amt für Wirtschaft und Tourismus) aims to optimise the framework conditions in the tourism industry in the region, to secure jobs and to strengthen the economic development of the region. It drives a crowdsourcing platform (www.innovationgr.ch/programm) for the promotion of tourism projects in the context of the tourism program Graubünden 2014–2021. Within the framework of this crowdsourcing project, a self-assessment tool to check the correspondence of the idea with the criteria and the goals is provided in order to facilitate the evaluation process. The platform also provides a detailed description of the program and the complete program objectives with a lot of basic information in order to improve the quality of the submitted projects.
3. At the local level, the Davos Klosters Innovation Initiative (www.innovation-davosklosters.ch) provides the crowd (essentially residents and tourists of Davos Klosters) with a platform in order to collect news ideas and solutions to problems related to what is missing in the destination, and what could be

improved or done differently. Criteria are non-limitative according to the field of the ideas, and the evaluation is proceeded by Davos Klosters visitors. Finally, the destination may eventually develop the most promising idea in the valorisation phase. At the time of writing this chapter, about 10.5 per cent of the 877 submitted ideas were implemented, such as a disco-on-ice event.

19.4.1.2. Three Examples of Private Initiatives

1. The cable car company of the Crans-Montana mountain resort in the Valais region conducted a crowdsourcing campaign, with the tool: www.i-brain.ch, in order to collect ideas regarding new activities for the summer and winter season, which are linked to its transport modes. The criterion was that the activities are based at the top of the cable car. Everybody could participate.
2. Club Med launched a page on Facebook related to the selection of elements of the resort by the public and co-create the future Club Med Val Thorens. The 'fans/ambassadors' chose the name during the first week and then selected the activities. To involve the users, Club Med offered every week a stay for two persons in the future resort. As a marketing means, the application offered to discover the future resort through several pictures and videos.
3. The Prodigy Network used crowdsourcing design and marketing in order to develop its extended-stay hotel in Manhattan's Financial District, calling on to architects, interior designers and creative minds (http://prodigydesignlab.com). The crowdsourcing approach was driven through a competition and a call for inputs from its potential customer base.[2]

In the next section, we will present and discuss crowdfunding activities used for validation and support of entrepreneurship and tourism projects.

19.4.2. Crowdfunding for Validating an Idea and Supporting Projects in the Tourism Industry

Crowdfunding follows the same logic as crowdsourcing, but with the aim of collecting financial resources from the crowd. It allows testing engagement and collecting opinion of potential customers or users, about the validation of an idea, of a product or service concept/idea, by subscribing to a funding campaign, with or without direct counterparts.

A study of 680 projects funded on Swiss crowdfunding platforms (Grèzes et al., 2015) characterised 156 of them as 'potentially linked to the tourism sector', i.e. less than 23 per cent of the projects analysed, of which only eight were classified as 'strictly tourism', i.e. less than 1.2 per cent of the total. Another group of 148 projects was classified as containing 'tourist characteristics'. This study showed the difficulty to separate tourism activities from other economic activities, as well as the nascent character of this practice in the tourism sector.

The eight 'strictly tourism' projects represented a total fund raising of more than CHF 553,000, reaching a financing rate of 104.5 per cent. Five of them concerned culture, and three were related to accommodation and recreation activities. The 148 other projects containing tourist characteristics collected almost CHF 1.35 million with a financing rate of 108.3 per cent. Most of these projects concerned activities or events.

Table 19.2 presents the main types of crowdfunding platforms.

The respective advantages of crowdfunding: The advantages of crowdfunding are manifold. They can be categorised according to the beneficiary and financial character of the advantage. The results stem from a survey (sample of tourism professionals: 44 persons) that was conducted during a tourism professional meeting in Switzerland[3] in 2015.

Table 19.2.   The Typology of Crowdfunding.

Type	Activity	Description/Aim	Examples of Platforms
Crowd-investing	Participatory funding in exchange for a capital increase	New form of investment and democratisation of investor activity. Project between CHF 400,000 and 500,000	Bee invested C-crowd Companisto Investiere Raizers Swiss-Crowd Swiss Starter
Crowd-donating	Participatory financing in the form of a gift (without counterpart)	Validate an idea Preorder Make Buzz	100-days Miteinander-erfolgreich.ch Conda
Crowd-supporting	Participatory financing in exchange for a reward (pre-order, in kind benefit, etc.)	Charity	Donobot Fairfundr Feinfunding Fengarion GivenGain GoHeidi I believe in you Indiegogo International Create Challenge Kickstarter LémaNéo Moboo Progettiamo

Table 19.2.   (*Continued*)

Type	Activity	Description/Aim	Examples of Platforms
			ProjektStarter
			Sosense
			Startnext
			WeMakeIt
Crowd-lending	Participatory financing in the form of loans	Simple and transparent borrowing	Cashare (also active in crowdsupporting)
		Diversification of funding sources	CreditGate24
			Direct-lending
			Veolis
			Wecan.Fund

Source: Authors' creation, synthesis based on Swiss Crowdfunding Association (2015) and Institute of Financial Services Zug (2015).

The financial advantages of crowdfunding for the project owners: These are the first motivation of the project owners (crowdlending, crowdinvesting). A crowdfunding campaign can also constitute a first round of funding (reward-based donating). The main financial advantages identified by tourism professionals for project owners are 'access to funds' and 'diversification of funds', which were raised 26 times out of 95 during the workshops. Then there are the advantages in terms of the absence of risk (8/95), the marketing and promotion (7/95) and the less rigorous funding conditions than with banks (6/95).

The financial advantages of crowdfunding for the investors: The purpose of crowd investment and crowdlending is almost exclusively financial: investors expect a risk-adequate return. Crowdinvesting supposes return on investment, appreciation and dividends. Crowdlending offers interests payment and loan repayment (BHP Hanser und Partner AG, 2015). The main financial benefits identified by tourism professionals for investors or donors are counterparties (14/51), return on investment (9/51) and tax reductions (6/51).

The non-financial advantages of crowdfunding for the project owners: According to the successful experiment of a Swiss hotel owner (Grèzes, 2015), who was able to finance his SPA through crowdfunding, the main non-financial advantages of crowdfunding are:

- the visibility at the regional, national and international levels by becoming a best practice case study;
- the engagement of customers in direct dialogue with the project owner;
- increasing the reputation and image of the company;
- the spirit of community with the people who supported the project.

The success of the counterparts, which mainly consist of vouchers or hotel packages, confirmed the relevance of the concept and ensured that the offer found its customers, according to the project manager. This case is detailed in a subsection below.

These findings complete the work of Beier, Früh, and Wagner (2014), who propose the following non-financial advantages of crowdfunding for SMEs:

- *Range.* Crowdfunding helps companies in the establishment and expansion of an online community through targeted online communication.
- *Marketing.* As part of a crowdfunding project, a SME has the opportunity to launch communication and promotional activities for a specific product.
- *Branding.* By focusing on the individual project during the crowdfunding campaign, it is possible for SMEs to re-establish their own brand or to sharpen the contours of an existing brand or to revisit their positioning.
- *Pre-market check.* As part of a crowdfunding project, it is possible for SMEs to test new concepts/ideas for products and services for public interest, to explore potential target groups and to assess market potentials.
- *Open innovation.* It is also possible to identify customer needs and impulses for product enhancements from the crowd.
- *Distribution channel.* Products and services can be sold in advance before extensive production and preparation costs are incurred.
- *Customer relationship management.* Crowdfunding projects help SMEs to reach new target groups and develop initial customer relationships.

The main non-financial benefit identified by the tourism professionals for project owners is the marketing impact, which was cited 13 times out of 95 during the workshops, followed by advantages in terms of market test (12/95), visibility (10/95) and networking and creation of community of interest (9/95).

The non-financial advantages of crowdfunding for the investors: Especially regarding crowdsupporting and crowddonating, incentives range from purely philanthropic initiatives, with the possibility of obtaining a special product at a preferential price, to the simple pleasure of participating, entering a club, or obtaining a distinction (BHP Hanser und Partner AG, 2015). The main non-financial benefits identified by the tourism professionals for investors or donors are the participation in a project and in a community (15/60), counterparts and in-kind payment (11/60), philanthropy, support and consciousness (9/60).

Key success factors for crowdfunding campaigns: According to an extensive review of thousands of projects in the USA and in Switzerland, the key success factors can be divided into four aspects: the project owner, the project, the communication and the target audience (Beier et al., 2014; Grèzes et al., 2015; Institute of Financial Services Zug, 2015; Mollick, 2014).

The quality of the project owner and his motives are fundamental success factors related to:

- the choice of the appropriate type of crowdfunding;
- the experiences and skills especially for crowdinvesting and crowdlending campaigns;
- the social network size;
- the transparency and security of investments (role of the platform);
- the definition of the rules of intellectual property (role of the platform).

The quality of the project as success factor is characterised by:

- simple and easy to understand objectives as well as clear funding impact and support effectiveness;
- reasonable financial objective (sufficient and realistic);
- spelling and presentation elements (video presenting motivations and product/service, etc.);
- equitable and interesting counterparties, not distracting from the essential;
- financial forecasts for crowdinvesting and crowdlending.

The quality of the follow-up and the communication are fundamental success factors related to:

- the support of the campaign before, during and after funding;
- the presentation on the homepage of the platform;
- the ongoing information on progress, word-of-mouth online;
- strengthening investor confidence to support the project;
- gaining the maximum number of investors from the first days in order to increase the confidence of the followers by a signal of popularity.

Finally, the quality of the target audience and its motivation are fundamental aspects concerning the quality of the project. In the tourism field, it is particularly important to take into account the local aspect of the public and the origin of visitors.

The above results have been complemented by the application of a statistical analysis on 30 variables related to 3,740 Swiss projects proposed on the platform WeMakeIt (www.wemakeit.com) conducted between 2012 and 2017. We used a logistic regression to elicit the weight of variables in the observed result (funded or not funded). The Nagelkerke coefficient of determination (r^2) is 0.7, confirming the strength of the model. Indeed, the model was able to predict the correct result of a crowdfunding campaign at 86 per cent rate for the 3,740 projects. According to our model, the most influential variables (with positive impact) are related to:

- the quality of the project owner (high experience in completed and supported projects);
- the quality of the project, of the spelling and the definition of the objectives;
- the quality of the follow-up and the communication.

19.4.2.1. A Case Study: The First Crowdfunding Campaign in the Tourism Industry in Switzerland, Financing a Hotel SPA

This case is a study based on a qualitative research method such as in-depth interviews (Grèzes et al., 2015). Among 31 Swiss crowdfunding platforms, 100-days was the first crowdfunding platform to introduce a specific 'tourism' category launched with the project 'Straw Bale Hotel: Sauna and photovoltaic wellness system in nature', which was submitted by the Maya Boutique Hotel, located in Nax in the Valais region, Switzerland (www.maya-boutique-hotel.ch).

This project was the first in the accommodation industry to develop a Scandinavian sauna and a photovoltaic wellness system in nature. The initiators of the project wanted to raise CHF 9,500. A hundred days later, 64 people supported the project, which rose more than CHF 23,000, thereof 65 per cent came from private persons (individuals, inhabitants of the region and tourists).

According to the project owner, the success factors are mainly related to a strong and regular communication campaign, fair and attractive counterparts and the local nature of the project. The project owner stressed that through this campaign, the Maya Boutique Hotel has withdrawn much more than just funding for its new spa. Indeed, the crowdfunding campaign made it possible to enhance the visibility of the hotel at the regional level, at the national level as well as at the international level, becoming a case study for foreign academics, while creating a spirit of community with those who supported the project.

Taking into account the success of counterparts mainly composed of vouchers or hotel packages (see Fig. 19.2), this campaign also enabled the project owner to validate the relevance of its concept and to test the concept and to ensure that the offer would be able to find its customers.

Finally, the financial contribution reached around 242 per cent of the initially expected amount. This was possible due to stretched goals, i.e. once the first financial goal was reached (the sauna structure), the project owner reactivated the community to ask for a second and higher financial round related to the solar system.

In the next section, we will present a pattern encompassing the success factors relative to the key aspects of crowdsourcing. The illustration is based on the above presented case study.

19.5. CROWDSOURCING DESIGN AND EXAMPLES

In this section, we present a model that helps entrepreneurs to design crowdsourcing and crowdfunding campaigns. The model regroups the five fundamental elements of a crowdsourcing campaign: the activity or the problem to solve, the crowd, the motive, the filter and the motivation. The prototyping can be

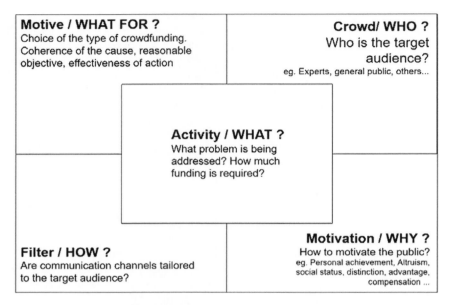

Fig. 19.1. The Crowdsourcing Canvas. *Source*: Adapted from Rosselet (2015).

facilitated by asking questions about success factors for each of these elements (see Fig. 19.1).

Fig. 19.2 presents the application of the crowdsourcing design canvas to the successful crowdfunding campaign driven by the Maya Boutique Hotel in Switzerland, presented in the case study.

19.6. SUMMARY

Crowdsourcing is an evolution of outsourcing with the help of the web. Nowadays every kind of organisation, public or private, is able to launch this sort of interactive campaign to gather ideas, collect financing or to call for action among a specific group of individuals, that is the 'crowd'.

Several types of crowdsourcing are operative but we focused on two particular types that are interesting for tourism entrepreneurs, namely, crowdsourcing for idea generation and crowdfunding. The main steps of a crowdsourcing process are the preparation, the initiation, the implementation, the evaluation and the valorisation. The key success factors for this kind of challenge are based on the precise definition of the problem question, the representativeness of the

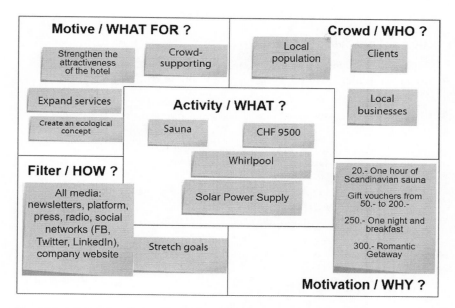

Fig. 19.2. Example of the Crowdsourcing Canvas of a Successful Crowdfunding Campaign. *Source*: Data from Grèzes (2015), model adapted from Rosselet (2015).

target audience, the degree of involvement of the participants, and the expertise of the evaluation and communication team.

In this chapter, the above aspects have been illustrated by several examples stemming from both private and public initiatives at the national, the regional and the local level, as well as the accommodation industry in Europe. Then several types of crowdfunding were presented according to the kind of proposed relationship and counterparts (gift without counterpart, interests, participation and loans). This sort of funding method has several advantages for the project owner as well as for the investors. The advantages can be classified into financial and non-financial. Apparently, the non-financial advantages, such as visibility, community building, pre-market check, etc., have great importance for crowdfunding projects.

There are three key success factors of crowdfunding campaigns, namely, the quality of the project owner, such as his/her previous experiences and expertise; the quality of the project, such as its aim and financial objectives and the quality of monitoring and communication.

Finally, this chapter proposed a crowdsourcing design model that helps entrepreneurs to facilitate the design of such a campaign. This method was illustrated by a case study outlining the first crowdsourcing campaign in the accommodation industry in Switzerland.

Review Questions

Now you may check your understanding of this chapter by answering the following questions or by discussing the topics below:

- Provide a definition of crowdsourcing. What are the most relevant types of crowdsourcing for tourism ventures?
- Present the main phases of a crowdsourcing campaign.
- Discuss the difference between some types of crowdfunding.
- Present the key factors that positively influence the success of a crowdfunding campaign.
- Discuss the main opportunities related to a crowdsourcing and to a crowdfunding campaign and compare them.
- Draw a systematic model that can facilitate the design of a crowdsourcing campaign.

NOTES

1. Retrieved online and accessed on 28 September 2017.
2. More details can be found online at: http://lodgingmagazine.com/crowdsourcing-is-changing-hotel-design-and-marketing. Accessed on 28 September 2017.
3. More information about the Tourism Professional Meeting can be found online at: http://etourism-monitor.ch/tpm/. Accessed on 28 September 2017.

REFERENCES AND FURTHER READING

Beier, M., Früh, S., & Wagner, K. (2014). *Crowdfunding für Unternehmen − Plattformen, Projekte und Erfolgsfaktoren in der Schweiz*. Forschungsbericht [Crowdfunding for companies − Platforms, Projects and Success Factors in Switzerland. Research Report]. HTW Chur.

BHP Hanser und Partner AG. (2015). *Crowdfunding − Nouvelles possibilités pour les financements du public*. Document de travail à l'intention de Forum Suisse Tourisme 2015 [Crowdfunding − New possibilities for public funding. Working Document for the Forum Suisse Tourisme 2015]. State Secretariat for Economy (SECO), Bern.

Blank, S. G. (2013). *The four steps to the epiphany: Successful strategies for products that win*. Pescadero, CA: K & S Ranch.

Chesbrough, H. W. (2003). *Open innovation: The new imperative for creating and profiting from technology*. Boston, MA: Harvard Business School Press.

Crowdsourcing Inc. (2011). *Infographic: Crowdsourcing industry landscape*. Retrieved from www.crowdsourcing.org. Accessed on 3 December 2015.

Daren, C. (2013). *Crowdsourcing*. Cambridge, MA: MIT Press.

Doctor, M., Schnyder, M., & Bürcher, S. (2016). Potential of open innovation models in the tourism sector: Three case studies. In R. Egger, I. Gula, & D. Walcher (Eds.), *Open innovation, crowdsourcing and co-creation challenging the tourism industry* (pp. 333−341). Berlin: Springer.

Gassman, O. (2013). *Crowdsourcing − Innovationsmanagement mit Schwarmintelligenz* [Innovation Management with Wisdom of Crowds]. München: Hanser Verlag.

Gassmann, O., Frankenberger, K., & Csik, M. (2013). The St. Gallen business model navigator. *Working Paper*. ITEM-HSG, St. Gall.

Grèzes, V. (2015). Best practice: Maya Boutique Hôtel. Leçons du premier cas de crowdfunding dans le tourisme en Suisse. In: hotelleriesuisse, Bern & Schweizerische Gesellschaft für Hotelkredit, Zürich (Eds.), *Jahrbuch der Schweizer Hotellerie*. Retrieved from https://www. hotelleriesuisse.ch/files/pdf9/Jahrbuch_der_Schweizer_Hotellerie_2015.pdf. Accessed on 3 October 2017.

Grèzes, V., Emery, L., Schegg, R., & Perruchoud, A. (2015). Crowdfunded tourism activities: Study on the direct impact of Swiss crowdfunding platforms on the Tourism Industry. *Travel & Tourism Research Association 2015 European Chapter Conference*, Innsbruck, Austria, TTRA European Chapter.

Howe, J. (2006). The rise of crowdsourcing. *Wired Magazine, 14*(6), 1–4.

Howe, J. (2008). *Crowdsourcing: Why the power of the crowd is driving the future of business*. New York, NY: Crown Publishing Group.

Institute of Financial Services Zug. (2015). *Crowdfunding monitoring Switzerland 2015*. Lucerne School of Business, Lucerne.

Köpcke, F. L. (2008). *Phänomen Open Innovation; Mythen und Paradoxien neuer Innovationswege* [Phenomenon Open innovation; Myths and paradoxes of new ways of innovation]. Retrieved from http://roennefahrt.de/mediapool/12/122269/data/D_/OpenI_creaktivmythen.pdf

Mendonca, L. T., & Sutton, R. (2008). Succeeding at open-source innovation: An interview with Mozilla's Mitchell Baker. *McKinsey Quarterly*, January 2008, 1–8.

Mollick, E. (2014). The dynamics of crowdfunding: An exploratory study. *Journal of Business Venturing, 29*(1), 1–16.

Osterwalder, A., Pigneur, Y., Barnada, G., Smith, A., & Papadakos, T. (2014). *Value proposition design: How to create products and services customers want*. New York, NY: John Wiley & Sons.

Rosselet, U. (2015). *Impacts des technologies de l'information sur les modes de coordination à travers quatre études en systèmes d'information* [Impacts of information technology on the coordination modes through four information systems studies]. Ph.D. thesis, Department of Information Systems, Faculty of Business and Economics, HEC Lausanne.

Swiss Crowdfunding Association. (2015). *Livre blanc: Le crowdfunding en Suisse 2015 [White paper: Crowdfunding in Switzerland 2015]*. Geneva: HEG Haute Ecole de Gestion de Genève.

Thomke, S. H. (2003). *Experimentation matters: Unlocking the potential of new technologies for innovation*. Boston, MA: Harvard Business School Press.

von Hippel, E. (1988). *The sources of innovation*. Oxford: Oxford University Press.

von Hippel, E. (2005). *Democratizing innovation*. Cambridge, MA: MIT Press.

CHAPTER 20

SOCIAL ENTREPRENEURSHIP IN TOURISM: BUSINESS OPPORTUNITIES IN THE CONTEXT OF DEVELOPING COUNTRY

Evelyn G. Chiloane-Tsoka

ABSTRACT

Purpose — *The aim of this chapter is to present social entrepreneurship as the main driver of poverty alleviation in emerging economies. The concept is aimed at providing innovative solutions to unresolved social problems; a transformative and sustainable, innovative market solutions towards addressing societal problems.*

Methodology/approach — *Literature review was conducted on conceptual issues relating to boost entrepreneurship and economic development within the context of emerging economies and its connection to tourism.*

Findings — *This chapter identifies opportunities to resolve social unjust equilibrium by developing a value chain proposition and bringing creativity to forge a stable equilibrium in the market place. The rationale behind lies in a solution to alleviate poverty by creating an environment that encourages job creation. Social entrepreneurship is not a science as such but a multidisciplinary that intends to equip people with business competencies and skills.*

The Emerald Handbook of Entrepreneurship in Tourism, Travel and Hospitality:
Skills for Successful Ventures, 351–368
Copyright © 2018 by Emerald Publishing Limited
All rights of reproduction in any form reserved
ISBN: 978-1-78743-530-8/doi:10.1108/978-1-78743-529-220181026

Research limitations/implications — *This chapter is explorative in nature, based on a literature review.*

Practical implications — *Social entrepreneurship is a practical response to unmet societal needs with a globalised business environment. It values corporations and introduces the concept of social entrepreneurship. The chapter also suggests a linkage between various research fields, such as entrepreneurship, corporate entrepreneurship and intrapreneurship.*

Originality/value — *The chapter analyses frameworks and models, as well as the disruptions driven by the fourth industrial revolution, evolving challenges and opportunities in the fields of business and employment.*

Keywords: Social entrepreneurship; tourism; opportunities; challenges; fourth industrial revolution; South Africa

---

Learning Objectives

After you have studied this chapter, you should be able to:

- define social entrepreneurship and its context;
- discuss the importance of social entrepreneurship in the tourism field;
- outline the benefits of social entrepreneurship in tourism;
- establish the role played by entrepreneurship and tourism in South Africa;
- identify the challenges facing social entrepreneurship in South African context;
- present the influence of the fourth industrial revolution on social entrepreneurship.

20.1. INTRODUCTION

In most emerging economies, social entrepreneurship is part of the solution, as it explicitly aims to provide innovative solutions to unsolved social problems, putting social value creation at the heart of its overall strategy in order to meet individuals' and communities' needs and improve their well-being. This goes far beyond our current conceptions of entrepreneurship and small business development in South Africa. The concept also exemplifies 'organic growth' or 'bottom-up growth' and deals with the overall social development of a community rather than an individual. It is, in a sense, inclusive development.

In essence, social entrepreneurship is the work of a social entrepreneur. Traditional education has always been focused on teaching knowledge and rules in order to respond to a rapidly changing world, what is needed is empathy and teamwork that will unlock the ability to turn new ideas into reality (Shimbun, 2015). The change in mind-set that will shift and challenge old pathways of thinking and inculcate the new order of critical thinkers. The entrepreneurs possess the skills, confidence and self-efficacy to integrate the digital technology that connects the global market. Further, it promotes positive social change and invests in social entrepreneurs whose innovative solutions are sustainable and replicable both nationally and globally (Shimbun, 2015). Social entrepreneurship lies in epistemology that provokes thoughts to identify problems relating to market failures with transformative and financial sustainable innovations aimed at solving such social problems.

This chapter seeks to establish what is social entrepreneurship and its role in providing solutions as a way towards economic development in emerging economies. It also provides the context in which this type of entrepreneurship is stimulated and developed. The chapter also discusses this issue and related aspects with connection to tourism activities.

20.2. THE CONCEPT AND CONTEXT OF SOCIAL ENTREPRENEURSHIP

Literature suggests various definitions that all have one main underlying idea/principle, creating an impact on the society. According to Roger and Osberg (2007, p. 30), social entrepreneurship consists of three components, namely:

1. identifying a stable but inherently unjust equilibrium that causes the exclusion, marginalisation or suffering of a segment of people that lacks the financial means or political clout to achieve any transformative benefit on its own;
2. identifying an opportunity in this unjust equilibrium, developing a social value proposition and bringing to bear inspiration, creativity, direct action, courage and fortitude, thereby challenging the stable state's hegemony and
3. forging a new, stable equilibrium that attempts to alleviate the suffering of the targeted group (vulnerable groups), through the creation of a stable ecosystem around the new equilibrium, ensuring a better future for the targeted group and society in general.

Peredo and McLean (2006, p. 56) define social entrepreneurship as 'the development of innovative, mission-supporting, earned income, job creation, ventures undertaken by social entrepreneurs, non-profit organisations'.

Social entrepreneurship is a term that captures a unique approach to economic and social problems, which cuts across sectors, industries and disciplines that stem in certain values and processes common to each social entrepreneur irrespective of focus area (Rankhumise, 2016). This chapter argues that social should be considered as a creation of a benefit/value to a society in three areas, namely (1) economic benefit to the society; (2) ecological benefit to the environment and (3) social benefit to people and quality of their life.

The social entrepreneurship is fast becoming an ideal trajectory for entrepreneur to solve social problems while offering practical solutions. Social entrepreneurs serve as the change agents in society by means of finding new and innovative ways to solve some of the social issues. While, the main motivation and aim of entrepreneurship is generally profit oriented and economic development, the social entrepreneurship focuses on addressing social problems within the communities. The concept of entrepreneurship directly affects the lives and well-being of individuals. This means that through entrepreneurship, a society can draw confidence in their innovative ways to change its status quo for the better (Davie, 2011, p. 17). The principles of value creation, innovation, creativity and more can be seen as some of the key ingredients of entrepreneurship's economic and social impacts that leads to economic growth and sustainability.

The main aspects of social entrepreneurship are outlined in the following subsections.

20.2.1. Benefits for the Society and Tourism

The tourism-related industries continue to grow and serve as a base to bring on board previously neglected people becoming hosts and tourists themselves. It is believed that the two components of tourism – domestic and international – are equally important. Domestic tourism is a significant player and has important role in a developing economy, such as South Africa (SA). International tourism, on the other hand, is a vital element of any tourism industry. The potential of tourism to spawn entrepreneurship and create new services such as local entertainment, handicrafts as well as other industries and productive branches of the economy are to strengthen rural communities, generate income and create jobs.

It is generally accepted that the social entrepreneurs can contribute to provide solutions to problems and to address some challenges in the following areas/fields:

- Education;
- Medical and health care;
- Social deprivation and isolation;
- Sanitation;
- Infrastructure development;
- Sustainable environmental development; and
- Poverty reduction.

The societies are constantly changing old models for providing services, and support may no longer be possible or they have never even existed in some societies. That is the reason why it is nowadays important to have a more innovative approach and thinking ways in supporting different groups of people. The above areas offer potential to everyone who can make great, big or small contributions.

20.2.2. Benefits for the Entrepreneur

The implementation of social ventures results in a series of benefits for the entrepreneur, such as

- Possibility/opportunity to provide an alternative to become their own bosses and work for something they have a passion for and believe in.
- Essential contribution to the fulfilment of their personal and professional goals.
- Opportunity to pursue a dream/passion and believe in the business initiative with interest, having higher probability to succeed.
- Offer of equal opportunities to both genders to develop and put into practice their ideas, by addressing the gap of talent and skills of women.
- Potential to apply a business model to solve a social problem, a local or regional problem, that government cannot address.

20.3. SOCIAL ENTREPRENEURSHIP AND TOURISM IN THE CONTEXT OF A DEVELOPING COUNTRY

Tourism offers the potential and many business opportunities, jobs creation and income generation for local populations, while social enterprises could play a significant role in this field. Social entrepreneurship is a niche for contributing to an ecosystem of support for social entrepreneurs in different ways. Knowledge sharing is spurred as a major driver for entrepreneurship while many organisations began independently replicating support to social entrepreneurs. As change agents, such knowledge has the potential to empower SMEs, and thus efficiently conducted, it is possible that peace in communities create another vehicle for tourism.

20.3.1. The Importance of Social Entrepreneurship in the Tourism Field

It is believed that social entrepreneurship in tourism is by nature beneficial to local community and population. It constitutes one kind of social innovation and is likely going to bring benefits to a number of interest groups in the following ways.

- The first major economic value that social entrepreneurship creates is the most obvious one because it is shared with entrepreneurs and businesses alike: job and employment creation in tourism enterprises and attractions.
- Social enterprises provide employment opportunities and job training to disadvantaged social groups, such as long-term unemployed, disabled, homeless, at-risk youth and gender-discriminated women.
- Development and promotion of ecotourism, activities providing services that are environmental friendly as they build environmental and cultural awareness and respect.
- Offer positive experiences for both visitors and hosts creating financial benefits and empowerment for local populations.
- Raise sensitivity to host countries, political, environment and social climate for local business to increase its turnover and profits, visitation, loyalty and satisfaction and to enhance positive reputation that leads to increased visitation.
- Target social groups might benefit in terms of reduction of high unemployment rates and alleviation of poverty within local populations.

Therefore, social enterprises should be seen as a positive force, as change agents providing leading-edge innovation to unmet social needs, closely related to local infrastructure and tourism.

20.3.2. Low Barriers of Entry

The tourism industry accommodates a thriving and dynamic informal sector that involves the previously disadvantaged groups in the tourism-related businesses, such as entertainment, laundry and transport services. The tourism industry has low barriers of entry, which can promote easy entry into entrepreneurship. Tourism employs a multiplicity of skills because of its cross-cutting nature, which means it promotes entrepreneurship directly and indirectly. McKay (2013) acknowledged that lifestyle entrepreneurs are able to function as business catalyst. Lifestyle entrepreneurship has the potential to become a non-binding introduction into the world of entrepreneurship, as the lifestyle entrepreneur is involved in business to substitute their income while business growth is not a major objective. According to Christie, Fernandes, Messerli, and Twining-Ward (2014), tourism performs well as other industries regarding the opportunities for small and medium enterprises. The disruption created by technology operators, such as Uber and Airbnb, has meant that there would be a category of tourism entrepreneurs, who provide services such as taxi services (Uber) and Air BNB (accommodation), creating lifestyle entrepreneurs.

Table 20.1. Business Opportunities and Challenges in Tourism Social Entrepreneurship.

Opportunities	Challenges
Potential to design and implement enterprises in the field of: • Local infrastructure development (water, sanitation) • Informal education/training (skills development) • Medical and health care • Improvement of accessibility to knowledge, human/social capital and networking • Career path: the growing prevalence of entrepreneurship as a career is more attractive among young people and women who are venturing to contribute and take entrepreneurship as a career rather than panacea of hope	• Limited resources for marketing is a challenge for most SMEs • Efficient and effective use of resources • Access to funding and capital • Skilful and trained human resources • Collaboration: partnerships and strategic alliances • Creation of entrepreneurial ecosystem in education • Curricula not aligned to industry demands and inadequate internship. Programmes that foster skill development to youth to reduce unemployment • Entrepreneurship education that foster confidence, self-efficacy and mind-set for employability rather than job-seeking mentality

Source: Author's creation.

20.3.3. Improving Life Conditions in Rural Areas

Rural areas are usually suffering from high rate of unemployment. Rural populations have less expertise due to the domestic migration (out-migration of skills), and less economic opportunities to provide employment and a decent standard of living (Briedenhhamn & Wickens, 2004, p. 71). The tourism-related industries have been identified as an opportunity to bring in highly sought after investments and money from tourists. This could address the rural-urban migration of poverty by providing jobs in tourism for locals. Diversification of the economic base of the rural areas is important, as tourism activities provide temporary migration to the rural areas.

Table 20.1 outlines the opportunities and challenges in the field of tourism social entrepreneurship.

20.4. SOCIAL ENTREPRENEURSHIP IN A DEVELOPING COUNTRY: THE CASE OF SOUTH AFRICA

In recent years, government, donors and public are increasingly recognising social entrepreneurship as a vehicle to address social issues in SA (Karanda & Toledano, 2012). These issues include major problems, such as insecurity, unemployment, food shortages and environmental degradation.

Urban (2008) believes that private sector, corporate governance and social responsibility have essentially gained prominence in the modern business world. The importance of social entrepreneurs contributes to an economy by way of providing alternative business model for firms to trade commercially in a socially sustainable way (Urban, 2008). It is worth pointing out that social entrepreneurs provide solutions to issues such as health, education, housing and community support of some kind − All these aspects that are pandemic and threatens community and, therefore, there is a dire need to come up with social solutions to ensure that the communities are supported in the ills that they encounter in their daily lives.

In SA, social innovations emerging as new ideas should address pressing unmet needs. That resulted through poverty, homelessness and violence. There is a strong need to apply new strategies to solve social problems. Innovation should have measurable impact on the larger social, political and economic context that created the problem. Social entrepreneurship is regarded as a solution since traditional government initiatives are not able to fulfil the social deficit, where a quest to reduce dependency on social welfare handouts/subsidies, such as grants, is being implemented. This type of dependency emanated from social context characterised by inequalities of the past such as education, housing, high rate of unemployment and poverty in the communities.

20.4.1. Importance of SMMEs in South Africa and Its Challenges for Policy Makers

According to Zulu (2014), it is critical that SME development be prioritised to create a supportive environment to establish new and to grow existing small businesses, to unlock the potential of small- micro- and medium-sized enterprises (SMMEs) that will be sustainable to assist poverty alleviation especially to youth, women and disabled. Supporting small businesses will defeat the scourges of poverty, unemployment and inequality. The Global Entrepreneurship Monitor (GEM) (2016) highlights the low levels of entrepreneurial activity in SA. The focus globally is around sustainability of entrepreneurs rather than the number of start-ups introduced into the ecosystem. While Fatoki (2014) points out a concern that business failure rate in SA has escalated to 70−80 per cent for starts-up in the five years of operation.

Albeit, the SMMEs have currently observed an increase in tourism by the previously neglected population groups that are now seen entering the market at an alarming pace. The volume of SMMEs is expected to contribute to growth rate and promote tourism. SA is regarded as a key performance among the countries in the sub-Saharan promoting inbound trips for international markets. SA Tourism budget increase from R1.14bn (€79.5mn) to R1.23bn (€85.8mn), an 8% increase well ahead of inflation. This growth rate is attributed to increasing interaction between various factors and industries, such as transport, digital integration mapping the tourism landscape, social media, online travel, short-term rental markets, luxury travel all connecting customer and service providers in a very easy and convenient way.

According to South Africa Web (2015), small businesses contribute 30 per cent to SA's GDP which is less than small businesses in developed countries that contribute around 50 per cent to the GDP and those in Asia that contribute around 40 per cent. With regard to employment, SMMEs in SA absorb up to 80 per cent of the employed population and contribute less than 4 per cent to export earnings, leaving a large margin for growth.

Nieman (2006) points out that SMMEs are the main drivers and are expected to function as vehicles in SA's social and economic stability due to the following factors:

- The labour-absorptive capacity of the small business sector is higher than that of other bigger businesses.
- The average capital cost of a job created in the SMME sector is lower than the big business sector.
- They are more competitive markets that push tourism-related industries in many ways.
- They can adapt more rapidly than larger organisations to changing market conditions and trends.
- They often use local resources.
- They provide opportunities for aspiring entrepreneurs, especially those who are unemployed, under-employed or retrenched.
- Employees at the lower level often require limited or no skills.
- Subcontracting by large enterprises to SMMEs lends fertility to production processes.
- They play a vital role in technical and other innovations.

20.4.2. A Basic Needs Approach

The main aim of the basic need approach is to develop sustainable projects based on the community to continue to assist and meet the basic needs. It is mainly offering a bottom-up approach to social entrepreneurship and social innovation can be a long-term contributor to sustainable growth within communities.

There is a need to meet the basic needs of people, especially the poor as they are regarded as important role players in every effort of development in the emerging economies. This model/approach focuses on the development that is directed to alleviate poverty challenges in assisting human requirements of the needy, being the poor of the society.

20.4.3. An Alternative Model of Entrepreneurship

The development of new micro and small businesses and entrepreneurship are paradigms that are to be crafted to respond to social, economic and environmental challenges. Government funding and donors from private sector should benefit public interest that will foster and nourish the entrepreneurial model. Economic systems are designed to stimulate growth through market mechanism that channels investment capital based only on financial results though government seeks to address market failures through spending and aid.

Moving beyond the social enterprise as the unit of analysis, Urban (2008) quantitatively examines the intentions of SA students to engage in social entrepreneurship activity and the skills and competencies required for success. In further justification, the same author comments that social entrepreneurship is not only under-researched in a SA context, but given the sustainable development challenges the country faces, social entrepreneurship is also critical as 'a phenomenon in social life' (p. 347). In a more recent study, Karanda and Toledano (2012) consider narratives and discourses of social entrepreneurship, reflecting on the meaning of 'social' changes in SA and other developing world contexts.

Social entrepreneurship is seen as a way of doing business that makes positive social and/or environmental changes. ASEN (2014) defines social enterprises as:

> ... the organizations social entrepreneurs have established to put their innovations into practice encompassing small community enterprises, co-operatives, NGOs using income generating strategies to become more sustainable, social businesses or companies that are driven by their desire to bring social or environmental change.

Finally, UnLtd South Africa (2015) identifies social entrepreneurs as 'passionate people who are committed to deliver sustainable solutions to social challenges in South Africa'. These local definitions illustrate the growing embeddedness of social entrepreneurship in SA. Yet interestingly, they also suggest a significant international influence on the definition of social entrepreneurship, enterprise and entrepreneur in SA and in how these terms are implemented by local stakeholders.

20.4.4. Social Entrepreneurship in Tourism Field

Social entrepreneurship has quite a long history in SA in promoting existing ecotourism sites and its impact has been with the US Ashoka Foundation first establishing offices in the country in 1991. There are now more than 300 Ashoka change makers in Southern Africa, mainly in SA. However, as early as 1892, SA's first cooperative was formed in Pietermaritzburg, during the apartheid period, SA also developed a strong civil society and tradition of social activism. Yet it is in the last 10−15 years in particular that social entrepreneurship as a phenomenon has blossomed. For instance, in 2001, PhytoTrade Africa, the trade association of the Southern African natural products industry, was established with the aim of alleviating poverty and protecting biodiversity. Three years later in 2004, Cooperation for Fair Trade in Africa (COFTA) was formed, including members from SA. More recently in 2009, ASEN was created (though it suspended activities late 2014), and in 2012, the SEAA began, both based in SA. As previously discussed, growing practitioner activity has also been accompanied by increasing academic engagement; in 2010, the Centre for Social Entrepreneurship and the Social Economy (CSESE) was founded at the University of Johannesburg. The burgeoning of social entrepreneurship in SA is perhaps best typified by Johannesburg and CSESE hosting the 2011 Social Enterprise World Forum.

The tourism industry faces two main concerns and challenges that are briefly presented below.

Safety and security: Personal safety and security is one of the key challenges for the growth of the tourism industry in SA. Potential tourists increasingly consider their personal safety and security as a determining factor of the choice of destination. According to Hughes (1996, p. 172), SA has the highest per capita rate of murder with a firearm in the world, the second highest for manslaughter, the second highest for rape rate, the fourth highest murder rate, the second highest assault rate, the fourth highest burglary rate and the fourth highest robbery rate. Overall, SA is the fifth most crime-ridden country in the world. Township tourism suffers from a negative image from a product-offering perspective and about personal safety and security. Much needs to be done to change this image, and any failure to do so will limit the developmental ability of tourism in townships, the place where the developmental impacts of tourism are mostly required (Henama & Sifolo, 2015).

'Undocumented', 'illegal' or 'unauthorized' migration: Another challenge that SA's tourism industry has to face is the issue of illegal or undocumented immigrants. According to Hoogendoorn and Marais (2008), the high rates of crime in South African cities have created 'fear-based' spatial distribution. This in turn has an important negative effect on the tourism industry. Hindson, Meyer-Stamer, Schoen, and Wegmann (2009, p. 1) assert that addressing red tape is an important building block of a local economic development initiative. It is crucial to highlight what Shaw and Williams (1994, p. 183) pointed out, that is, how in-migration happens − when the labour demands of the tourism industry exceeds those of the local supply. SA's economic success compared to other African countries has led to a steady migration, both documented and undocumented, for job-seeking within SA.

The tourism industry is a supplier of jobs for the poorly skilled illegal migrant in SA, a country having high unemployment rate. Social entrepreneurship should focus on areas and industries that can help people who have restricted access to resources, skills and help to improve the livelihood of the society. SMEs operating as social entrepreneurs in the tourism industry need to diversify their product offering and adapt their strategies in order to attract local and international clientele and ultimately continue to grow and sustain their business and employee numbers. Social entrepreneurs should explore the environment and conditions that essentially provide opportunities to address social problems by implementing appropriate initiatives and plans.

20.4.5. Strengthening Linkages between Entrepreneurship and Tourism

A study by Taskov (2011) indicates the following:

- One of the strengths of entrepreneurs is that they have the ability to innovate;
- The growth of tourism industry will bring benefit that will facilitate job creation;
- Small tourism enterprises should form sustainable relationship with stake-holders in order to have a vision that drives the entire entrepreneurial and tourism ecosystem;
- Small business networks contribute to sustainable destination development;
- An understanding of business network is critical to the success of making decisions by entrepreneurs as well as giving business support and make tourism destination policies;
- The social network relates to family, friends and the wide cultural dimensions in which the business are immersed. Using a networking and a destination development framework fosters a cultural understanding and
- Social structures enable the operators of small enterprises to build the level of trust in the development of the local tourism offering and enhance the network to mobilise the relationship and learn from each other.

Research into small tourism enterprises identifies limited marketing and management skills, which serves as the core capacity to work with other actors in an efficient and competent way (Van Laer & Heene, 2003). Entrepreneurs have recognised that many skills and resources leading to small businesses success are outside of the firm and start working in cooperatives. It is important to consider tourism business networks collectively; such activities of small business entrepreneurship are sustainable to economic and community development of scale and destination as well as opportunities influenced by the business environment.

The owner/manager is an important factor in an industry such as tourism, because it aims to maintain a competitive advantage in as far as customer, markets and technology intelligence that has a bearing in introducing innovations.

It is, therefore, a necessity to prioritise the proliferation of small businesses in the tourism-related industries to take advantage of its full potential in the field of social entrepreneurship.

20.5. THE FOURTH INDUSTRIAL REVOLUTION AND SOCIAL ENTREPRENEURSHIP IN GLOBAL ECONOMY

According to Schwab (2016) and Mawasha (2017), the fourth industrial revolution (FIR) brings forth hope to entrepreneurs and is seen as creating environment for critical and innovators a platform for employment creation. It has features that will affect all countries and populations biologically, physically and digitally. The main features, the benefits, the new organisational models, as well as the challenges of the FIT are outlined below.

20.5.1. Main Features

The first industrial revolution used water and steam power to mechanise production. The second used electric power to create mass production. The third used electronics and information technology to automate production. Now a FIR is building on the third, the digital revolution that has been occurring since the middle of the last century. It is characterised by a fusion of technologies that is blurring the lines between the physical, digital and biological spheres (Schwab, 2016).

Computers can retreat and store massive amounts of data and are unbiased in their decision-making. While humans can be more stubborn, they can also read their opponent's weaknesses, evaluate complex patterns and make creative and strategic decisions to win. The world will always need human brilliance, human ingenuity and human skills. Software and technology have the potential to empower people to a far greater degree than in the past unlocking the latent creativity, perception and imagination of human beings at every level of every organisation.

This shift will enable employees on the front line and in the field to make smarter decisions, solve tougher problems and do their jobs better. This combination will allow the power of data and the power of people across global industries. The advantage is that when the mechanic and the technology work together, the work is done faster, with fewer errors and better results. The knowledge, the talent and the tools to solve some of the world's biggest problems such as hunger, climate change and disease. Machines will supply us with the insight and the perspective that are needed to reach those solutions. Nevertheless, they will not supply the judgement or the ingenuity. People will always serve as important catalysts.

20.5.2. Benefit of the FIR to Entrepreneurs and Tourism

The main benefits resulting are presented below.

- Accelerate existing programmes that support innovation and entrepreneurship and create new platforms in making it easier for many more people to start and grow businesses.
- Promote mass engagement and the energies around entrepreneurship and innovation can contribute to social as well as economic value, and tap the creativity and intelligence of all parts of the population.
- Offer new metrics that can help us measure what's working as well as measure the values that guide and shape entrepreneurship.
- Provide education that prepares young people to be makers and shapers of their careers.
- Mainstream curriculum to a more project-based learning, entrepreneurship and problem solving and enhance radical alternatives that use education as a lever for entrepreneurship.
- Universities which are looking to complement mastery of disciplines by encouraging students to work on real-life problems often in partnership with businesses and NGOs.
- Students engagement on live problems around implementation of new generation technologies, by setting groups of students to work on practical projects to radically cut traffic congestion, emissions or elderly isolation.
- Speed up the new opportunities to bring wealth and prosperity. Focus on reconfiguring parts of cities to help drive up social interaction and health levels, combining technologies with new models of 'people-powered' health so that people could take better control of their own health, with tools to monitor, diagnose and nudge.

The above-mentioned benefits could be achieved by adopting suitable organisational models.

20.5.3. New Organisational Models for Tourism

The FIR is shaking up old business models and presenting strategic options that enhance efficiency.

- Accelerate existing programmes that are to support entrepreneurship developed on the network platform. Digital applications will create new platforms in making it easier for many more people to start and grow businesses.
- Smart cities/destinations: The benefit for tourism lies in smart platforms on urban transport (and other infrastructure) organised in anonymised forms as a commons rather than as proprietary.

- In real-time, reliable and accessible information for small and microbusinesses.
- Combination of local business initiatives with global corporations/digital brands, such as Uber and Airbnb, to ensure that local populations benefit more from globalisation and digitation of services, to make sure that more value distribute within local economies.

20.5.4. Challenges and Opportunities of the FIR

The FIR creates a new business environment. On the supply side, developments in energy storage, grid technologies and real-time processing of customer and asset performance are transforming operating models. On the demand side, customers value and expect personalised interaction at all points of their consumer experience (Schwab, 2016).

In this context of an exponential speed of change in technology, the main challenges and opportunities are:

- Availability and accessibility to new products and services that increase the efficiency and pleasure of our personal lives. Ordering a cab, booking a flight, buying a product, making a payment, listening to music, watching a film or playing a game.
- Transportation and communication costs will drop, logistics and global supply chains will become more effective, and the cost of trade will diminish, all of which will open new markets and drive economic growth.
- As automation substitutes for labour across the entire economy, the net displacement of workers by machines might exacerbate the gap between returns to capital and returns to labour. On the other hand, it is also possible that the displacement of workers by technology will, in aggregate, result in a net increase in safe and rewarding jobs.
- More than 30 per cent of the global population now uses social media platforms to connect, learn and share information. In an ideal world, these interactions would provide an opportunity for cross-cultural understanding and cohesion.

20.6. SUMMARY

Societies are constantly changing and old models for providing services and support may no longer be possible or may have never even existed in some societies. That is the reason why it is important to become more innovative and think of new ways to support different groups of people nowadays. Furthermore, tourism aims to attract visitors from other regions and countries that need services at the destination. Tourism is one of the leading industries in the global economy and is mostly promoted for its economic benefits across the world. Tourism economy is not an autonomous/distinct entity but is intricately woven with the social and political fabric of society and should be seen as serving a linkage with entrepreneurship, business opportunities and job creation to improve the well-being of local populations.

In this chapter, we presented and discussed the main issues and aspects of social entrepreneurship with connection to tourism. First, a definition and the context of social entrepreneurship were provided. This was followed by presenting the issue of social entrepreneurship and tourism in the context of a developing country. Then the chapter discussed the social entrepreneurship in a developing country focusing on the case of SA. The chapter was completed by presenting the main characteristics, as well as the challenges and opportunities of the fourth industrial revolution.

The social entrepreneurship will greatly open up to promote mass engagement that will finally provide a platform for entrepreneurs to be makers and shapers through innovative landscape as well as energies around entrepreneurship and innovation. The ultimate result should be to benefit the creativity and social knowledge and capital of all parts of population in order (1) to make a significant contribution to social economic and (2) to address the local and regional problems and challenges.

Review Questions

Now you may check your understanding of this chapter by answering the following questions or discussing the topics below:

- Define social entrepreneurship in your own terms.
- Contrast the basic needs model approach to alternative entrepreneurship model.
- Present the benefits of social entrepreneurship to the society.
- Discuss the importance of social entrepreneurship in tourism.
- Present the challenges for tourism social entrepreneurship in the context of a developing country.
- Discuss the main features of the fourth industrial revolution.
- Outline the challenges and opportunities of the fourth industrial revolution.

REFERENCES AND FURTHER READING

Alegre, I., & Berbegal-Mirabent, J. (2016). Social innovation success factors: Hospitality and tourism social enterprises. *International Journal of Contemporary Hospitality Management*, *28*(6), 1155–1176.

ASEN. (2014). *African social entrepreneurs network*. Retrieved from https://asenetwork.org/

Bornstein, D. (2007). *How to change the world: Social entrepreneurs and the power of new ideas.* New York, NY: Oxford University Press.

Briedenhhamn, J., & Wickens, E. (2004). Tourism routes as a tool for economic development of rural areas-vibrant hope or impossible dream? *Tourism Management, 25*(1), 71–79.

Brock, D. D., & Steiner, S. (2010). *Social entrepreneurship. Be the change.* Anderson University: Entrepreneurship Program.

Bruwer, J. (2003). South African wine routes: Some perspectives on the wine tourism industry's structural dimensions and wine tourism product. *Tourism Management, 24*(4), 423–435.

Christie, I., Fernandes, E., Messerli, H., & Twining-Ward, L. (2014*). Tourism in Africa: Harnessing tourism for growth and improved livelihoods.* Washington, DC: International Bank for Reconstruction and Development.

Crush, J., William, V., & Peberdy, S. (2005). *Migration in Southern Africa.* Pretoria, SA: Global Commission on International Migration.

Davie, G. (2011). Social entrepreneurship: A call for collective action. *Organisational Design Practices, 43*(1), 17–34.

Elkington, J., & Hartigan, P. (2008). *The power of unreasonable people: How social entrepreneurs create markets that change the world.* Boston, MA: Harvard Business School Publishing.

Fatoki, O. (2014). The causes of the failure of new small and medium enterprises in South Africa. *Mediterranean Journal of Social Sciences, 5*(20), 922–927.

Henama, U. S., & Sifolo, P. P. S. (2015). A tourism theoretical gap: The case of the Northern Cape Province in South Africa. *African Journal of Hospitality, Tourism and Leisure, 4*(1), 1–14.

Herrington, M., Kew, J., & Kew, P. (2016). *Global entrepreneurship monitor 2016: The state of entrepreneurship in South Africa.* Cape Town: University of Cape Town.

Hindson, D., Meyer-Stamer, J., Schoen, C., & Wegmann, M. (2009). *Addressing red tape at the local level: Options and tools.* Working Paper No. 13. MesoPartner, Duisburg.

Hoogendoorn, G., & Marais, L. (2008). Perceptions of crime and the built environment: The case of Bloemfontein Central Business District (CBD). *Acta Structilia, 15*(2), 75–96.

Hughes, T. (1996). Africa: The contrarian big African state. In C. Clapham, J. Herbst, & G. Mills (Eds.), *Big African states: Angola, Sudan, DRC.* Ethiopia: Wits University Press.

Karanda, G., & Toledano, N. (2012). Social entrepreneurship in South Africa: A different narrative for a different context. *Social Enterprise Journal, 8*(3), 201–215.

Laeis, G. C. M., & Lemke, S. (2016). Social entrepreneurship in tourism: Applying livelihoods approaches. *International Journal of Contemporary Hospitality Management, 28*(6), 1076–1093.

Mawasha, M. (2017). *The 4th industrial revolution: The new era of Africa.* Fin24.google search: Retrieved from https://www.fin24.com/the-fourth-industrial-revolution-an-africa-perspective-2017. Accessed on 25 September 2017.

McKay, T. J. M. (2013). Adventure tourism: Opportunities and management challenges for SADC destinations. *Acta Academia, 45*(3), 30–62.

Nieman, G. (2006). *Small business manager: A South African approach.* Pretoria, SA: Van Schaiks.

Oguzhan, I., & Arikboga, S. (2015). The effect of personality traits on social entrepreneurship intentions: A field research. *Procedia – Social and Behavioural Sciences, 27*(4), 1191–1195.

Peredo, A. M., & McLean, M. (2006). Social entrepreneurship: A critical review of the concept. *Journal of World Business, 41*(1), 56–65.

Rankhumise, E. (2016). *Social entrepreneurship a tool for poverty alleviation.* Pretoria, SA: Van Schaiks.

Rey-Marti, A., Ribeiro-Soriano, D., & Sanchez-Carcia, J. L. (2016). Giving back to society: Job creation through social entrepreneurship. *Journal of Business Research, 69*(6), 2067–2072.

Roger, L. M., & Osberg, S. (2007). Social entrepreneurship: The case for definition. *Stanford Social Innovation Review, Spring,* 29–39. Retrieved from www.ssirview.org. Accessed on 20 September 2017.

Schwab, K. (2016). *The fourth industrial revolution.* Geneva: World Economic Forum.

Sekliuckiene, J., & Kisielius, E. (2015). Development of social entrepreneurship initiatives: A theoretical framework. *20th International Scientific Conference Economics and Management*, 213(1), 1016–1019.

Shaw, G., & Williams, A. M. (1994). *Critical issues in tourism: A geographical perspective*. Oxford: Basil Blackwell.

Sheldon, P. J., & Daniele, R. (Eds.) (2017). *Social entrepreneurship and tourism: Philosophy and practice*. Cham (ZG): Springer International Publishing.

Shimbun, A. (2015). Ashoka's vision plan for social entrepreneurship. Japan's Second-Largest Newspaper. Japan.

Sigala, M. (2016). Learning with the market: A market approach and framework for developing social entrepreneurship in tourism and hospitality. *International Journal of Contemporary Hospitality Management*, 28(6), 1245–1286.

Smith, R., Bell, R., & Watts, H. (2014). Personality trait differences between traditional and social entrepreneurs. *Social Enterprise Journal*, 10(3), 200–221.

Taskov, N. (2011). The influence of tourism on economic development: Entrepreneurship in tourism industry lead to business benefits. *2nd Biennial International Scientific Congress*: April-27–29, Macedonia.

Urban, B. (2008). Social entrepreneurship in South Africa: Delineating the construct with associated skills. *International Journal of Entrepreneurial Behaviour and Research*, 14(5), 346–364.

Van Laer, K., & Heene, A. (2003). Social networks as a source of competitive advantage for the firm. *Journal of Workplace Learning*, 15(6), 248–268.

Wang, C., Duan, Z., & Yu, L. (2016). From non-profit organization to social enterprise: The paths and future of a Chinese social enterprise in the tourism field. *International Journal of Contemporary Hospitality Management*, 28(6), 1287–1306.

Williams, A. M., & Shaw, G. (1995). *Tourism and economic development: Western European experiences* (2nd ed.). New York, NY: John Wiley & Sons.

Yunus, M. (2010). *Building social business: The new kind of capitalism that serves humanity's most pressing needs*. New York, NY: BBS Public Affairs.

Zulu, L. (2014). *Small business development: National Assembly Speech*. Cape Town: National Parliament.

CHAPTER 21

GREEN ENTREPRENEURSHIP
IN TOURISM

María del Mar Alonso-Almeida and
María José Álvarez-Gil

ABSTRACT

Purpose — *This chapter aims to discuss the key issues of green entrepreneurship in tourism (GEiT), paying special attention to the environmental performance of green entrepreneurs and its relationship with strategy, brand reputation and long-term business growth.*

Methodology/approach — *Literature review is conducted on conceptual issues and several hotels first-hand experiences that were categorised to provide readers with business-world examples.*

Findings — *This chapter highlights how small- and medium-sized entrepreneurs are the agents who started green innovation initiatives and how larger corporations tested and validated them. A myriad of small green interventions awaits to be undercovered and implemented. Most of them can bring financial improvements to the entrepreneurs as the required initial investments are not necessarily high.*

Research limitations/implications — *This chapter is explorative in nature, based on a literature review and interviews-based analysis of consolidated green initiatives, most of them being successful ones.*

Practical implications — *The forces driving green initiatives are identified and classified. Most important categories of green entrepreneurs are*

The Emerald Handbook of Entrepreneurship in Tourism, Travel and Hospitality:
Skills for Successful Ventures, 369–386
Copyright © 2018 by Emerald Publishing Limited
ISBN: 978-1-78743-530-8/doi:10.1108/978-1-78743-529-220181027

described and emphasis was placed on the managerial and marketing benefits linked to green initiatives and action plans.

Originality/value — *This chapter presents models and concepts in an integrated way, facilitating a useful knowledge for prospective entrepreneurs wishing to acquire a better understanding of the opportunities and challenges related to eco-friendly business.*

Keywords: Green entrepreneurship; tourism; green initiatives/action plans; eco-labels; case studies; environmental performance

---

Learning Objectives

After studying this chapter, you should be able to:

- define the concept of green entrepreneurship in tourism;
- identify the main drivers of green entrepreneurship in tourism;
- analyse strategies of green entrepreneurship in tourism;
- discuss the areas in which tourism entrepreneurs can implement sustainable/green initiatives and plans;
- present examples of best practices of green initiatives and projects in the field tourism entrepreneurship.

21.1. INTRODUCTION

This chapter attempts to define the main concepts regarding green entrepreneurship in tourism (GEiT). As a matter of fact, a growing number of tourism companies are treating environmental performance as an important objective in their strategy and operations, as they try to increase growth and competitive position. GEiT is giving way to substantial financial and environmental benefits, enhanced brand reputation and long-term business growth from environmentally sound operations. Green practices have been widely studied in tourism over the last decade; this is a fact, but, nevertheless, GEiT is not well defined yet, making the GEiT system still confusing and little known.

The first remark to be made in this introduction is that while researchers and practitioners look for the causes of green problems when they want to come to effective and efficient green solutions, entrepreneurs are more prone to develop creative initiatives. The second remark is that industry practitioners, as well as established companies/brands, use to offer better chances for testing the related initiatives and to produce green innovations in tourism. We have to take into account that very frequently what we characterize as green innovations in the tourism industry were originally created and developed by green entrepreneurs.

Tourism companies have been accused of being high consumers of energy and water, high producers of waste and damages in the environment, leading to a serious dissatisfaction of residents. Alonso-Almeida (2012) stated that tourism-related activities engender at least two types of environmental impact. On the one hand, some environmental impacts are linked to the movement of tourists around the destinations. On the other hand, residents could be also damaged by the environmental effects induced by the many diverse activities that local businesses perform to meet the visitors' needs. So, green tourism entrepreneurs are currently dealing with tourism products that seek to avoid or minimise environmentally negative impacts. These offerings attempt to preserve cultural heritage at the same time and provide learning opportunities and contribute to the preservation or improvement of local community structures, including positive benefits for the local economy. This chapter discusses, among other issues, the main drivers of GEiT, with a specific focus on hospitality industry.

The hospitality industry still struggles with the most effective ways to promote their green status, and this is partly due to the fragmentation that characterises this industry. World Tourism Organisation (UNWTO, 2017) points out that tourism is unique in that it comprises many small and micro enterprises (SMEs) worldwide. Indeed, given the organisational structure and size of tourism companies, the link between entrepreneurship and environmental management has become a high priority among tourism providers. Hall, Daneke, and Lenox (2010) indicate that 'entrepreneurship has been recognised as a major conduit for sustainable products and processes, and new ventures are being held up as a panacea for many social and environmental concerns'. Given that sustainable degradation is considered a market failure by environmental economics, GEiT could contribute to boost sustainable development and set an example for other industries.

This chapter is dealing with the theoretical and practical issues and aspects of green/ecologically friendly projects and initiatives in the field of tourism entrepreneurship.

21.2. THEORETICAL AND KNOWLEDGE BACKGROUND

In this section, we will present the general knowledge background on the topic. In addition, we attempt to give a global definition of green entrepreneurship. The same approach is used for drivers, practices and strategies. This knowledge will be very useful for prospective entrepreneurs in order to acquire a better understanding about this topic. Furthermore, they will improve their

M. M. ALONSO-ALMEIDA AND M. J. ÁLVAREZ-GIL

capabilities in adopting and managing green operations. Finally, an open mind-set could be developed to give an opportunity for new strategies and innovative practices.

21.2.1. The Concept of Green Entrepreneurship and the Forces Driving Green Initiatives

There is neither a consensus about what is green entrepreneurship, in general, nor more in tourism, in particular. According to the OECD (2012), 'green or eco-innovation is a somewhat elusive concept, but can be identified by its favourable impact on the environment' and it can be defined as an innovation that results in a reduction of environmental impact and/or optimises the use of resources throughout the lifecycle of related activities. Hall et al. (2010) asserted that 'it remains an open question as to what extent entrepreneurs have the potential to create sustainable economies, how they are motivated and incentiv-ized, if there are structural barriers to the capture of economic rents for sustain-able ventures and if sustainability-oriented entrepreneurs differ from traditional entrepreneurs'.

Nowadays, these questions remain without answers although previous stud-ies have shown that the main drivers for tourism companies to adopt green practices are external (see Table 21.1).

Besides these external drivers, entrepreneurs need some influencing factors to start implementing GT, such as motivations and some specific conditions. The most important factor is an enabling environment that provides boost and support to the entrepreneur, that is a supportive institutional framework with policies offering easy access and support to the entrepreneur. It is believed that the other influencing factors include:

Table 21.1. External Drivers to Adopt Green Practices in Tourism.

Regulation
Customer pressure
Searching of new markets
Supplier influence
Need to keep up with competitors
Social pressure of local communities
Interest of certain stakeholders such as suppliers, investors and banks
Image

Source: Compilation from Alonso Almeida, Robin, Pedroche, and Astorga (2017).

- Internal motivations: such as the need for achievement, the desire for independence, job satisfaction at − and from − work and the willingness to play the entrepreneurial role.
- Skills and expertise, meaning current know-how plus confidence to be able to keep updated to address the future challenges.
- Expectation of personal economic gain and/or psychological benefits and
- Adoption of new technologies, smart digital, as well as information and communication technologies (ICTs).

21.2.2. Categories of Green Entrepreneurs

Entrepreneurs used to be keener to adopt green practices or been identified as green companies in order to be successful in the market (Alonso-Almeida, Bagur-Femenias, Llach, & Perramon, 2015). Various studies (for instance, Alonso-Almeida, 2012; Jang, Kimb, & Bonn, 2011; Perramon, Alonso-Almeida, Llach, & Bagur-Femenias, 2014) show that green practices not only serve to lure certain types of clients, who seek an explicit commitment to the natural environment, but also provide hotels with a source of competitive advantage (reduction of operational costs and improvement of image). Big corporations have more resources and possibilities to access the latest technologies. However, recent research shows that smaller tourism companies do not differ from bigger ones in terms of implementation of green practices. In most cases, small companies have more creative and innovative strategies and initiatives than bigger ones, which have to cope with structural rigidities and are slow in decision-making (Alonso Almeida et al., 2017).

Literature suggests that the conjoint analysis of the degree of green adoption practices and of the adoption of innovations contribute to identify four green entrepreneurs' categories, as outlined below (see Fig. 21.1).

1. *Green laggards.* This category shows low levels of activity in both green practices and innovations adoption. In this group, traditional long-established tourism companies could be included. Hockerts and Wüstenhagen (2010) pointed out that 'green laggards' have the advantage of their long experience in the market, which allows them to enjoy a better understanding of their customers. So far, they adopt new practices in a reactive way, only when their customers ask for green practices. They neither pretend to play a model role nor pioneers in the field. Their behaviour is reactive and they only respond under pressure by their clientele demand.
2. *Green followers.* These entrepreneurs show low level of innovations, but they are investing in best green practices. In other words, these entrepreneurs monitor very closely their competitors in order to identify market success and best practices and adopt them. For that reason, they have adopted a big number of green practices.

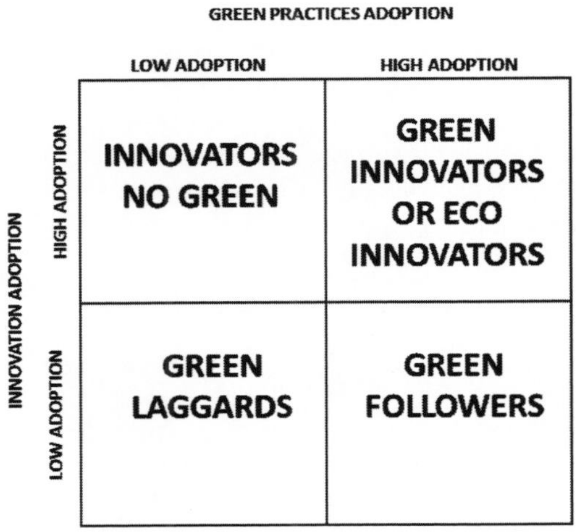

GREEN PRACTICES ADOPTION

	LOW ADOPTION	HIGH ADOPTION
HIGH ADOPTION	INNOVATORS NO GREEN	GREEN INNOVATORS OR ECO INNOVATORS
LOW ADOPTION	GREEN LAGGARDS	GREEN FOLLOWERS

INNOVATION ADOPTION

Fig. 21.1.   Types of Green Entrepreneurs. *Source*: Authors' own elaboration.

3. *Grey innovators.* These innovators identify market opportunities and have the ability to generate ideas and create disruptions by means of developing new products and innovations within the organisation. However, environmental issues are not their main concern and, therefore, they do not look for innovating; they would adopt some green practices if these practices can help their business. It is important to mention that for tourism and other predominantly service-oriented industries, non-technological innovation will play an increasingly important role in the transition to a green economy. Examples include the adoption of environmental management systems and new business models.

4. *Green innovators or eco-innovators.* Advanced innovators and strong green adopters compose this type of entrepreneurs. They are always looking for new ways to improve sustainability in their business in a wider sense, i.e. organisational, technological and products or processes. As a result, they are in a position to achieve great benefits. Notwithstanding with it, the challenge for GEiT is to develop the ability to create a clear profile and differentiate from competition, while they master business model innovations.

21.3. GREEN ENTREPRENEURSHIP IN THE TOURISM CONTEXT

Although tourism areas/destinations can be a good breeding ground for innovations, the predominance of SMEs in tourism-related industries leads to a situation wherein businesses often lack the capacity to make innovations. Tourism industry suffers from low productivity, often resulting in difficulties to attract the necessary level of capital investment and highly qualified staff. As tourism is a labour-intensive industry, process innovations can help to improve the productivity levels, enabling tourism providers to decrease operational costs, leading to quality improvements, lower prices and increased profitability.

Entrepreneurs in tourism react to external factors/pressure by implementing some basic green operational practices, such as saving water and energy and recycling hazardous product waste (Perramon et al., 2014). Some authors (Perramon et al., 2014; Withiam, 2011) have identified and classified the most common green practices in restaurants; these are: (1) recycling and composting of products such as glass, plastic, metal, cardboard and soil, (2) efficient use of energy and (3) water-efficient equipment. They also adopted the use of eco-friendly cleaning supplies and packaging and eco-friendly dish, table and floor cleaners.

Restaurants are considered high consumers in terms of resource usage and waste generation. Thus, restaurants have opportunities to adopt a green strategy, not only to be more appealing but also to save financial resources and achieve efficient operation. By adopting green strategies, restaurants may introduce innovations in their product portfolio, for instance, 'green menus' offering green and healthy food items, greener waters, organic wines and certified meats and other items. Consumers' demand for this type of nutrition has increased over the past decade due to customers' healthier lifestyles and environmental concerns (Jang et al., 2011). Pursuing this strategy, restaurants can attract new market segments and achieve a sustainable competitive advantage. There are, of course, other types of green practices they could adopt, such as regulating cooking temperatures, checking freezing options, updating the air conditioning and heating systems, and of course, improving their inventory management for fresh and non-fresh food items. There is still ample room for restaurants willing to reduce their energy and water consumption (Chen, Sloan, & Legrand, 2009).

In the same way, hotels and other accommodation units could implement some basic green practices; the main focus of their strategies is on attracting more environmentally conscious customers or on positioning as a green brand or eco-friendly company. They could benefit in the long term, helping local population to preserve their environment and showing other providers the pathway to follow (Alonso Almeida et al., 2017).

The American Green Hotel Association has defined 'green hotels' as those environmentally friendly properties whose managers are eager to introduce and implement programmes that save water, save energy and reduce solid waste, while saving money. Alonso-Almeida (2012) and Chen et al. (2009) suggested various practices for independent operations, such as the use of water-saving sanitary equipment (mist spray installations), low water consumption dishwashers, the installation of LED light or replacing incandescent lamps, optimising the amount of food prepared, minimising the waste generated in the kitchen and installing grease traps in the kitchen drainage system. The adoption and

Table 21.2. Benefits by Implementing Green Practices in Tourism.

Field/Area	Specific Benefits
Human resources	Environmental knowledge and experience
	Improvement of employee commitment
	Improvement of employee satisfaction
Internal	Improvement of environmental performance
	Reduction of operational costs
	Improvement of operational performance
	Increase of internal efficiency
	Better financial performances
External	Enhancement of business image
	Attainment of stakeholders/owners' satisfaction
	Improvement of competitive position.
	Appeal and attraction to new market segments
	Access to institutional support for green issues

Source: Llach, Perramon, Alonso-Almeida, and Bagur-Femenias (2013) and Alonso Almeida et al. (2017).

implementation of green practices could result in a series of benefits for tourism businesses, as presented in Table 21.2.

Enz and Canina (2011) argue that green entrepreneurs may generate some innovation as innovation may flourish in the absence of established operating procedures. More particularly, independent entrepreneurs could gain competitive advantage because they are in a more flexible position from external relationships with various partners and suppliers. Independent hotel entrepreneurs are in a position to actively examine new technologies or participate in external knowledge communities (e.g. social networks). Innovative independent entrepreneurs may wish to keep their options open by making smaller investments in external knowledge rather than a long-term commitment to a franchise to ensure as much flexibility as possible. The new limited-service hotels, for instance, might lend themselves to successful operations by independent green entrepreneurs. As a matter of fact, entrepreneurs are tagging on to a hot global trend in the hospitality industry, which is represented by 'boutique hotels', i.e. typically small, upscale, aspirational hotels (10−100 rooms) that have unique settings and provide personalised services, such as Edition Hotels that offer a unique and customised experience.

Chong and Ricaurte (2016) indicate that full service properties, meaning well-established hotels, are not always 'greener' than limited service hotels (closer to the concept of SME entrepreneurs). Although full service hotels generally have more resources and can do more about sustainable operations, limited service hotels are continually improving in the field of sustainability, going toe-to-toe with full service properties and in some cases even beating them in adoption rate. The same authors point out that limited service properties are consistently showing higher intention to implement green initiatives and improve their service quality.

Based on the above-mentioned statement by Chong and Ricaurte (2016), this chapter identifies common green practices and most trending eco-friendly initiatives implemented by well-established businesses over the last five years, under the assumption that GEiT are resulting in better performance and benefits.

Case Study 21.1:   The Sustainability Performance Operation Tool

The Sustainability Performance Operation Tool (SPOT) developed by the International Tourism Partnership is a sustainability check instrument for business operations. SPOT graphically demonstrates the sustainability of an operation pertaining to the three pillars: (i) environmental, (ii) social and (iii) economic, which can be used either as a management information tool or as part of a training process. SPOT structures key principles and indicators of sustainability into a robust framework, from which an appraisal of performance can be undertaken and reported against. By setting objectives for the coming years and monitoring and reviewing the performance, the SPOT tool contributes to a property's balanced scorecard system. It also sets standards for a company award-based system using third-party validation. Lastly, SPOT compiles a Corporate Social Responsibility (CSR) Impact assessment.

The methodology is easy to use and fully adaptable to all types of operations. The process encompasses four steps, namely: (i) assessment by online questionnaire; (ii) results presented dynamically (incorporated into the SPOT chart showing performance at a glance); (iii) customisable reporting (used as a powerful and effective tool that compares options that help strategic operation decision making); (iv) data export (the charts can be added to documents and presentations).

Source: International Tourism Partnership (www.tourismpartnership.org) in Chen et al. (2009).

21.4. AREAS/FIELDS TO IMPLEMENT GREEN ACTIONS AND SUSTAINABLE INITIATIVES

In recent years, sustainability and the measurement of environmental performance have become standard within most major hotel companies around the world. The sustainability orientation has been driven by interest in improving operational efficiency, reducing costs and mitigating business' environmental negative impact. It should be stressed that the tourism-related industries keep forward by setting new, ambitious goals, for energy, water and waste reduction, while it is still a challenge to acquire a better knowledge about GEiT practices.

In this context, what are the chances left for green entrepreneurs to bring environmental and competitive initiatives into the fore? It is believed that there are strong connections between creativity and entrepreneurship. Creativity can provide the basis for innovation and business growth, as well as have a positive influence on society in general. Creativity is the crafting of creative solutions into new products, processes or services. Innovation relates to the successful implementation of creative ideas and acceptance by various stakeholders in organisations. It is a process of divergent and convergent thinking: divergent thinking has an indirect effect on venture growth through generating original business ideas. A more detailed discussion about creativity and innovation was presented in Chapter 5 of this book.

Entrepreneurs are more likely to be embarked onto green creativity, while well-established companies are more akin to innovate thinking. This does not mean that entrepreneurs do not innovate; on the contrary, in SMEs, entrepreneur's creativity can facilitate bricolage, which in turn influences innovation performance.

We have processed data from customer surveys and existing business records, along with available literature and official and business reports performed over the last five years (2012–2017) to generate a list of the various green/sustainable initiatives implemented at business level.[1] This analysis identified two main types of green tools: (1) internal management tools and (2) external management tools, as outlined below.

Internal management tools aim at minimising the consumed resources and the waste generation. These actions influence the sustainability improvement/ green performance without significantly affecting the enterprise's budget. *External management* tools are used for three purposes, namely: (1) reuse and recycle consumed resources and generated waste, (2) incorporate new alternative resources for energy and water and (3) give special attention to alternatives taking advantage of local resources and knowledge/social capital.

A summary of our research's findings is presented in Tables 21.3 and 21.4. Obviously, these initiatives are related to a wide range of green practices, from simple practical measures to extensive renewable energy projects. Tables 21.3 and 21.4 summarise previous GEiT that have become innovations, which are widely used by the tourism industry nowadays. Today's utilities' suppliers are venturing into digital transaction, with smart moves to improve efficiency and expand their customer base. The smart metres and smart grid merely are an example. These innovations constitute the foundation of the digital utility, supplying the massive volumes of data that are its lifeblood; they enable data-based analyses, planning and diagnostics. With these tools, utilities can optimise staffing levels at power

Table 21.3. Most Common Internal Management-related GEiT Innovations.

Innovations that can significantly decrease energy consumption and a property's overall carbon footprint

Low VOC or VOC-free paints, i.e. non-toxic substances in paints used to paint guestrooms and public spaces

Non-smoking guestrooms

Choosing menu items that contain less meat

Stop delivering newspapers to guest's rooms

Growing food on-site

Guestrooms have occupancy sensors for reducing heating/cooling when they are empty

Digital thermostats

Windows have some type of reflective film to reduce heating and cooling loads

Humidity sensors in bathroom fans to turn them off when not needed

Recovering waste heat for reuse (in the kitchen and in the laundry)

Generating some of their own power on-site

Changing the hotel layout

Use of notices in bathrooms that encourage customers to mitigate consumption

Composting organic waste to produce fertiliser

Giving old furniture to charities or selling used equipment

Switching to refillable dispensers for bathroom amenities

Repurposing the tiny amenity containers by donating them to shelters and charities

Small-scale waste reuse practices

Operate as much as possible during daylight hours

Adopting linen reuse programmes

Intensive maintenance programmes to repair leaks and drips in guestrooms

Donate leftover food to the needy

Use of glass kitchenware instead of disposable packages

Place recycling bins thorough the premises

Source: Authors' own elaboration.

Table 21.4. Most Common External Management-related GEiT Innovations: Investments and Acquisitions.

Acquisition of eco-friendly amenities

Adopt a local procurement policy

Acquisition of renewable energy technology

Investment in solar thermal for water or space heating

Handling of laundry wash

Installing solar photovoltaic systems

Reducing solar gain with solar control film to coat windows

Table 21.4.   (*Continued*)

Updating the heating system used in hotel swimming pools

Switching to an air-to-water heat pump from a conventional heating system

Replace electricity with gas as a source of energy for the laundry and catering services

Replacing current appliances with water-efficient ones in all facilities

Installing low-flow showerheads and aerated faucets

Installing grey water recycling systems

Install new ceramic tiles and toilets

Localised irrigation systems in gardens

Acquisition of new linen with greener tissues, easier to iron

---

Source: Authors' own elaboration.

plants and manage the intricate energy terrain of renewable and conventional sources, trading options and patterns in demand. Thus, we can expect relevant savings in energy and waste consumption as well as a considerable diminishing in waste generation. Digitalisation also leads to a more efficient management of the back-office processes.

21.5.   EXAMPLES AND BEST PRACTICES FROM THE BUSINESS WORLD

In this section, we are going to present some examples to illustrate key concepts and best practices of green entrepreneurship in the field of tourism-related industries.

21.5.1. Social Responsibility and Certifications

Some consolidated companies have gone a long distance in getting environmental and sustainability certifications, as highlighted by CSR reports. There are some hotels that are truly green all around – those that have been certified by the Leadership in Energy and Environmental Design (LEED) rating system. Submitting a hotel for LEED consideration is prohibitively expensive for some smaller properties, only a couple dozen in the USA have been certified so far. Sustainability certification is important in gaining favourable image and reputation, particularly ISO 14001 and LEED. A study of over 2,000 independent hotels in Spain by Segarra-Oña, Peiró-Signes, and Verma (2011) found that hotels that implemented the ISO 14001 environmental standards displayed better financial performance than those that were not certified. The new version four scorecard of LEED certification system is specifically designed for the hospitality industry and is intended to create incentives for new hotel construction that meets sustainability criteria. A study of 93 LEED-certified hotels found that these hotels had better financial performance than a larger sample of non-certified ones (Chan et al., 2008). Besides, certification labels such as Green Key (FEE), Green Key (Global) and Travelife all have criteria that the hotels must adhere to in order to obtain their certification (Nicholls & Kang, 2012).

We have included these examples because small- and medium-sized hotels may always imitate the protocols and actions undertook by the larger accommodation firms. By benchmarking their green initiatives against the protocols of larger certified hotels, they can save big money and realise outstanding environmentally friendly improvements.

Example 21.1: Tourism-related Eco-labels and Certifications

Other approach to signal out the concern for green initiatives related to various entrepreneurship programmes can be found in the adoption of international and national tourism-related eco-labels, such as the examples summarised in Table 21.5.

Table 21.5. Eco-labels and Certifications: Some Examples.

Region or Country	Examples of Eco-labels and Certifications
North America (USA and Canada)	Green Seal (http://www.greenseal.org/) US, facilities
	Ecologo (http://www.ecologo.org/en/), Canada products, including hospitality products and hotel facilities.
Europe	The Eco-label (http://www.ecolabeltourism.eu/), products and service, including tourism accommodation services
	Green Tourism Business Scheme (http://www.greenbusiness.co.uk/); UK sustainable tourism certification scheme
	Nordic Swan (http://www.svanen.nu/) Norway, Sweden, Finland, Iceland and Denmark, products and services, including hotel and restaurant operations.
	Viabono (http://www.viabono.de/), Germany, accommodation facilities.
Australia	Good Environmental Choice (http://www.aela.org.au/) products or service.
India	Ecomark (http://envfor.nic.in/cpcb/ecomark/ecomark.html), products, useful in planning the sourcing and purchasing activities of a hotel or restaurant.
Japan	EcoMark (http://www.ecomark.jp/english/index.html) sourcing and purchasing activities in hotels and restaurants.
International	The Green Key (http://www.greenkey.org/) is the first international environmental label for accommodation facilities.

Source: Authors' elaboration, retrieved from Chen et al. (2009) and related websites.

In addition to the labels that are designed specifically for the tourism-related industries, the International Organization for Standardization has developed certifications that do not apply to one industry in particular. ISO 14001 certification is a process-led approach that guides companies through the process of setting up an Environmental Management System, the ISO/EMAS 14001. It assesses the attempts of an organisation to minimise harmful effects on the environment caused by its activities; it strives to support the company in the continual improvement of its environmental performance.

Should entrepreneurs wish to go for a more closely related accreditation, they could study the challenges posed by 'The Green Globe 21' scheme.

Case Study 21.2:   The Green Globe 21

The Green Globe 21 (GG21) scheme is a global benchmarking, certification and improvement system for sustainable tourism. It is one of the first self-regulation systems and currently the most widely recognised initiative within the tourism-related industries. The World Tourism and Travel Council (WTTC) and the International Hotel and Restaurant Association (IH&RA) as a result of the 1992 Earth Summit in Rio launched it in 1994. It is based on the principles of Agenda 21 and ISO-type standards. The Green Globe 21 initiative is dedicated to improving the environmental performance of all tourism companies, regardless of size, segment, location or level of environmental activity.

It uses quantitative indicators to benchmark the key aspects of environmental and social performance of an enterprise in all segments of the tourism industry. The results of indicators for a particular type, activity, market and location of a tourism operation are compared with the relevant baseline and best-practice levels. This scheme works in two phases. *Phase one* is devoted to benchmarking activities and it takes about three months; it lasts about eight indicators that are used: the installation of a sustainable development policy, water consumption, energy consumption, waste management, paper consumption, pesticide usage, maintenance and cleaning products usage, and engagement with local communities.

Phase two is certification, and it takes approximately seven months. The hotel management team is required to install an action plan based on good practices. And all hotel employees must be implicated in the process, and training procedures are requested by an external and independent auditor who reviews the progress. Auditing takes place yearly, with visits on property every two years. The hotel is certified if it is in conformity with the requirements of the standard Green Globe.

Source: http://www.ec3global.com/, 2017.

One more time, this programme looks rather interesting and useful but is very time consuming and expensive for SMEs as well. Thus, we provide our readers with another example closer to the real situations experienced by green entrepreneurs in tourism.

21.5.2. A Best Practice

The following case illustrates in a practical way the strategies a small accommodation business can adopt and implement in the field of GEiT.

Case Study 21.3:   Green Boutique Hotel

Chen et al. (2009) highlighted the case of AHB, a boutique hotel located in Melbourne, Australia, as an example of green entrepreneurship. AHB is a purpose built and designed green hotel. The hotel is participating in the programme Savings in the City — Green Hotels, a municipal programme that helps hotels make environmental improvements. AHB management reported that the primary reason for introducing wide-ranging green measures was a deep sense of responsibility towards protecting the environment. This was undertaken in three areas — waste, water and energy — as outlined below.

Waste: They do not supply throwaway plastic toiletries containers. The hotel has developed some great ways in minimising their waste output (see Tables 21.3 and 21.4). They also recycle all their organic waste. Tracking the savings, the hotel's waste audit and results speak for themselves. They produce only 4.7 litres of waste per guest night, almost half the best practice targets for waste efficiency in hotels!!

Water: They have reduced the cistern capacity of toilets and it has had an enormous impact. AHB incorporates a range of water-saving techniques (e.g. rain water tanks on the hotel's roof that provide water for gardening and cleaning). These investments are saving vast amounts of the city's precious drinking water. AHB's water use for its first year of the city programme was a mere 119 litres per guest per night, lower the best practice target of 194 litres.

Energy: Management has introduced a vast array of measures to minimise the hotel's energy consumption, and the hotel has reported that they resulted in huge long-term savings in maintenance and replacement and reduced energy bills. Its energy consumption of 37 megajoules per guest per night is far below the best practice target of 140 megajoules.

(*Source*: City of Melbourne, www.melbourne.vic.gov.au/greenhotels in Chen et al., 2009)

21.6. SUMMARY

An increasing volume of research and industry reports shows that sustainability has become an established part of corporate agendas. There are numerous examples of environmental management systems and practices have been successfully implemented by tourism companies worldwide: an extensive adoption and implementation of GEiT.

With regard to managerial practices, it is possible to draw several interesting conclusions that may be of direct interest to the tourism industry practitioners. First, green operations may be one form of efficiency improvement and competitive way of differentiation that entrepreneurs can develop to survive economic downturns and achieve better positioning in the market. Second, practitioners must consider green practices as a way to improve competitiveness internally by means of improving employee commitment to achieve reduction in resources consumption. Third, green practices can be used to build and reinforce company image/reputation by means of attaching the brand to an 'eco-friendly concept'.

Fourth, companies' involvement in green practices leads to the acquisition of new capabilities and skills. Fifth, there is not one unique green strategy; every entrepreneur should pursue a green strategy suitable to his/her business. Sixth, economic viability and sustainability improvement are important criteria in the selection processes, as the final decision should be evaluated in terms of economic, ecological and ethical suitability for the relevant context before being implemented.

There is an imperative to create a wider set of indicators that do reflect the greater sustainability impacts of the industry (positive and negative). This set of sustainability indicators will place the tourism industry ahead of many other industries and take a great leap forward in demonstrating the importance it places on sustainability. One significant methodological challenge for sustainability research in tourism is the identification of sources of impacts and the allocation of responsibility for mitigating them. By nature, tourism products are complex combinations of economic activities (transport, entertainment, accommodation, etc.); each using multiple materials flows (water, energy, land, eco-systems, bio-diversity, etc.). Logically, evaluating the performance, outputs and effects of tourism activities requires comparable measures along multiple materials and energy streams (Budeanu, 2007).

It is believed that GEiT initiatives and plans should contribute to developing a management model that takes into consideration all dimensions of sustainability, as well as stakeholders' interests and increased involvement of communities, ensuring economic development. An inclusive development that is ethical and politically oriented, as well as environmentally socially and culturally conscious.

<hr>

Review Questions

Now you may check your understanding of this chapter by answering the following questions or discussing the topics below:

- Discuss the ways to identify potential niches for starting to implement sustainability entrepreneurship.
- How do you understand the concept of green entrepreneur in tourism?
- Identify green practices based on your experience.
- How does an effective environmental management system affect the service operations?
- Present the main differences between internal and external innovations in GEiT.
- Discuss why eco-labels and environmental management certifications are useful.

<hr>

NOTE

1. The useful publications/sources included: Cornell Hospitality Report, 2014; Hotel Sustainability Benchmarking Study, Energy, Water, and Carbon; the Hotel Sustainability Benchmarking Index 2016; Global Hotel Study 2016; Second Annual Green Lodging Trends Report 2017, STR Global; UNWTO, World Travel and Tourism Council (WTTC), Pacific Asia Tourism Association.

ACKNOWLEDGEMENT

The authors wish to thank the financial support provided by The Spanish Government: Research Projects RETOS 2016, ECO2016-75961-R and ECO2016-79659-R.

REFERENCES AND FURTHER READING

Alexander, S. (2002). *Green hotels: Opportunities and resources for success*. Portland, OR: Zero Waste Alliance.

Alonso-Almeida, M. M., (2012). Water and waste management in the Moroccan tourism industry: The case of three women entrepreneurs. *Women Stud. Int. Forum*, *35*(5), 343−353. doi:10.1016/j.wsif.2012.06.002

Alonso-Almeida, M. M., Bagur-Femenias, L., Llach, J., & Perramon, J. (2015). Sustainability in small tourist businesses: The link between initiatives and performance. *Current Issues in Tourism*, 1−20. doi:10.1080/13683500.2015.1066764

Alonso Almeida, M. M., Robin, C. F., Pedroche, M. S. C., & Astorga, P. S. (2017). Revisiting green practices in the hotel industry: A comparison between mature and emerging destinations. *Journal of Cleaner Production*, *140*(7), 1415−1428. doi:10.1016/j.jclepro.2016.10.010

Bruns-Smith, A., Choy, V., Chong, H., & Verma, R. (2015). Environmental sustainability in the hospitality industry: Best practices, guest participation, and customer satisfaction. *Cornell Hospitality Report*, *15*(3), 6−16.

Budeanu, A. (2007). Sustainable tourist behaviour? A discussion of opportunities for change. *International Journal of Consumer Studies*, *31*(5), 499−508. doi:10.1111/j.1470-6431.2007. 00606.x

Chan, W. W., Mak, L. M., Chen, Y. M., Wang, Y. H., Xie, H. R., & Hou, G. Q. (2008). Energy saving and tourism sustainability: Solar control window film in hotel rooms. *Journal of Sustainable Tourism*, *16*(5), 563−574.

Chen, J., Sloan, P., & Legrand, W. (2009). *Sustainability in the hospitality industry*. Oxford: Butterworth-Heinemann.

Chong, H. G., & Ricaurte, E. E. (2016). Hotel sustainability benchmarking tool 2016: Energy, water, and carbon. *Cornell Hospitality Reports*, *15*(9), 6−11.

Dupeyras, A., & MacCallum, N. (2013). Indicators for measuring competitiveness in tourism: A guidance document. *OECD Tourism Papers, 2013/02*, OECD Publishing. doi:10.1787/ 5k47t9q2t923-en

Enz, C. A., & Canina, L. (2011). A comparison of the performance of independent and franchise hotels: The first two years of operation. *Cornell Hospitality Report*, *11*(21), 6−13.

Hall, J. K., Daneke, G. A., & Lenox, M. J. (2010). Sustainable development and entrepreneurship: Past contributions and future directions. *Journal of Business Venturing*, *25*(5), 439−448.

Hockerts, K., & Wüstenhagen, R. (2010). Greening Goliaths versus emerging Davids: Theorizing about the role of incumbents and new entrants in sustainable entrepreneurship. *Journal of Business Venturing*, *25*(5), 481−492. doi:10.1016/j.jbusvent.2009.07.005

Jang, Y. J., Kimb, W. G., & Bonn, M. A. (2011). Generation Y consumers' selection attributes and behavioral intentions concerning green restaurants. *International Journal of Hospitality Management*, *30*(4), 803−811. doi:10.1016/j.ijhm.2010.12.012

Llach, J., Perramon, J., Alonso-Almeida, M. M., & Bagur-Femenias, L. (2013). Joint impact of quality and environmental practices on firm performance in small service businesses: An empirical study of restaurants. *Journal of Cleaner Production*, *44*(1), 96−104. doi:10.1016/j.jclepro. 2012.10.046

Nicholls, S., & Kang, S. (2012). Going green: The adoption of environmental initiatives in Michigan's lodging sector. *Journal of Sustainable Tourism*, *20*(7), 953−974. doi:10.1080/ 09669582.2011.645577

OECD. (2012). Green innovation in tourism services. Tourism papers. Paris: *OECD Publications*.

Perramon, J., Alonso-Almeida, M. M., Llach, J., & Bagur-Femenias, L. (2014). Green practices in restaurants: Impact on firm performance. *Operations Management Research*, *7*(1−2), 2−12. doi:10.1007/s12063-014-0084-y

Ricaurte, E. (2012). Developing a sustainability measurement framework for hotels: Toward an industry-wide reporting structure. *Cornell Hospitality Report*, 11(13), Cornell Center for Hospitality Research.

Ricaurte, E. (2016). *Hotel sustainability benchmarking index 2016: Energy, water, and carbon*. The Center for Hospitality Research (CHR), 7−8-2016.

Segarra-Oña, M. A., Peiró-Signes, A., & Verma, R. (2011). Environmental management certification and performance in the hospitality industry: A comparative analysis of ISO14001 hotels in Spain. *Cornell Hospitality Report*, *11*(22).

UNWTO. (2017). *Tourism Highlights* (2017 ed.). Madrid: UNWTO.

Withiam, G. (2011). The challenge of hotel and restaurant sustainability: Finding profit in being green. *Cornell Hospitality Roundtable and Conference Proceedings*, *3*(2). Cornell Center for Hospitality Research.

CHAPTER 22

CONTRIBUTION OF CREATIVE TOURISM TO ENTREPRENEURSHIP

Agusdin Agusdin

ABSTRACT

Purpose — *The main purpose of this chapter is to discuss the design and development of creative ventures and activities in tourism-related industries. This chapter also aims to provide prospective entrepreneurs with practical guidance to pursue business opportunities and manage creative tourism business.*

Methodology/approach — *Literature review was conducted on main conceptual issues and practical aspects of entrepreneurship and creative tourism business. These issues have been illustrated by case studies from the business world.*

Findings — *This chapter outlines and highlights the main components/segments of the creative tourism, the profile of entrepreneurs in this industry, the main elements of creative tourism experiences, as well as the requirements and expectations of creative tourists.*

Research limitations/implications — *This chapter is explorative in nature based on a literature review and case studies. It takes an entrepreneurial perspective and approach.*

Practical implications — *An in-depth understanding the concept of creative tourism and its implementation is really useful in designing, managing and marketing the appropriate offering of experience opportunities in the creative tourism business. Therefore, to provide high-quality offering and memorable*

The Emerald Handbook of Entrepreneurship in Tourism, Travel and Hospitality:
Skills for Successful Ventures, 387–401
Copyright © 2018 by Emerald Publishing Limited
All rights of reproduction in any form reserved
ISBN: 978-1-78743-530-8/doi:10.1108/978-1-78743-529-220181028

experiences in this field, prospective entrepreneurs should fully understand and apprehend the characteristics, the requirements and expectations of creative tourists.

Originality/value — *This chapter analyses conceptual frameworks and presents practical examples of business ventures through case study development. In doing so, it provides a better understanding of the entrepreneurship in the field of creative tourism.*

Keywords: Creative industries; creative tourism; business ventures; consumer behaviour; creative tourism experiences; best practices

---

Learning Objectives

After studying this chapter, you should be able to:

- explain the concepts of creative industry, entrepreneurship and business creation;
- describe the characteristics and profile of entrepreneur in tourism industry;
- explain the concepts of tourism entrepreneurship and creative tourism;
- discuss the contribution of creative tourism to entrepreneurship;
- present and discuss examples of best practices illustrating the application of creative business in tourism-related industries.

22.1. INTRODUCTION

The creative economy is currently considered as one of the most rapidly growing industries of the world economy. The creative economy is a new economy that intensifies technology, information and creativity by relying on the ideas and knowledge capital of human resources as the main factor for its economic activities. Therefore, the creative economy relies on creativity and knowledge possessed by human resources as the determining factor. Human creativity and innovation, at both individual and group level, are the key drivers of this industry, and these qualities have become the true wealth of nations in the twenty-first century (UNESCO and UNDP, 2013, p. 15).

Many scholars studied creative economy and suggested definitions for the concepts of 'creative industries' (Hesmondhalgh, 2002, p. 12; Howkins, 2001, pp. 88−117; UNCTAD and UNDP, 2008, pp. 11−12), 'cultural industries' and 'creative economics' (Hesmondhalgh, 2002, pp. 11−14; UNCTAD and UNDP, 2008, p. 12). The UK Government Department for Culture, Media, and Sport (DCMS) defines the creative industries as 'those industries which have their origin in individual creativity, skill, and talent and which have a potential for wealth and job creation through the generation and exploitation of intellectual property' (DCMS, 2001, p. 4).

The above definition by DCMS suggests that there are nine creative industries, namely (1) advertising and marketing, (2) architecture, (3) crafts, (4) designs (product, graphic and fashion), (5) film, television, video, radio and photography, (6) information technology (IT), software and computer services, (7) publishing, (8) museums, galleries and libraries and (9) music, performing and visual arts.

This chapter discusses the concept of creative industries with connection to tourism entrepreneurship, the design and development of creative ventures and activities in tourism-related industries. The chapter begins by outlining the concepts of creative industry, entrepreneurship and business creation (Section 22.2). The second section focuses on the topic of tourism entrepreneurship by outlining the characteristics and profile of entrepreneur in tourism-related industries and presenting a case study on an example/best practice of entrepreneurship in these industries (Section 22.3). The following section then presents the concept of creative tourism and analyses a case study on Lombok pottery making lessons in the tourism village of Banyumulek, Lombok Island, Indonesia. This case study illustrates an example of how creative tourism can contribute in developing business opportunities and entrepreneurial ventures to boost community wealth and well-being (Section 22.4). The last section discusses the issue of collaboration and partnership between businesses and other stakeholders to offer high-quality creative tourism experiences. This issue is illustrated by a case study on accessible tourism in Spain. This case study presents the accessibility of tourism destinations for all people in Spain through developing an inclusive tourism programme for collaborative work in awareness-raising, training, consultancy and research on accessibility and attention to the public. The main aim is to involve all interested stakeholders in order to achieve the best possible outcomes (Section 22.5).

22.2. CREATIVE INDUSTRY, ENTREPRENEURSHIP AND BUSINESS CREATION

This section briefly discusses the concepts of creative industry, entrepreneurship and creation of business.

22.2.1. Creative Industry

The British writer and media manager John Howkins (2001) popularised the term 'creative economy'. This author suggested that the term could be applied into 15 industries: advertising, architecture, art, crafts, design, fashion, film, music, performing arts, publishing, research and development (R&D), software, toys and games, TV and radio and video games. On the other hand, Santiago (2015) stresses the economic and social contributions of cultural and creative industries (CCI) by including under this term, television, visual arts, newspapers and magazines, advertising, architecture, books, performing arts, gaming, movies, music and radio. According to Santiago (2015), the CCI in Europe, North America, Latin America, Africa, the Middle East and the South Pacific region reached US$2,250 billion, representing 3 per cent of global GDP. Creative industries also generated 29.5 million jobs, which account about for 1 per cent of the world's active population.

It should be pointed out that the term 'cultural industries', which referred to the forms of cultural production and consumption, was popularised worldwide by UNESCO in the 1980s and has come to encompass a wide range of fields, such as music, art, writing, fashion and design and media industries (such as radio, publishing, film and television production). Its scope is not limited to technology-intensive production since a great deal of cultural production in developing countries is labour-intensive. Investment in the traditional rural craft production, for example, can benefit female artisans by empowering them to take ownership of their lives and generate income for their families, particularly in areas where other income opportunities are limited or inexistent.

The term 'creative industry' is applied to a much wider productive set, including goods and services produced by the cultural industries and those depending on innovation, including many types of research and software development. At the same time, the term 'creative industries' began to become integral part into policy decision-making and plans, such as in the national cultural policy of Australia in the early 1990s. This development was followed by the transition made by the DCMS in the UK from cultural to creative industries at the end of the last decade. The use of the term 'creative industry' also stemmed from the linking of creativity to the urban economic development and city planning (UNDP and UNESCO, 2013).

All of these productive branches and activities have significant economic values as well as social and cultural meanings. Hence, they offer entrepreneurship opportunities.

22.2.2. Entrepreneurship and Business Creation

Bygrave (1994) suggests that the term 'entrepreneur' refers to someone who perceives an opportunity and creates an organisation (venture) to pursue this opportunity. This means that entrepreneurship refers to new venture creation. While, the term 'venture creation process' refers to the process that begins with the idea for a business and culminates when the products or services are offered to customers in the market (Bhave, 1994). In other words, the entrepreneurial process involves two phases: (1) an invention phase, during which new ideas are generated and (2) an innovation phase, during which new ideas are developed into marketable goods and services. A more detailed discussion about the term 'entrepreneurship' was presented in Chapter 1, and about the concepts of creativity and innovation was already presented in Chapter 5.

22.3. ENTREPRENEURSHIP IN TOURISM INDUSTRY

Russel and Faulkner (1999) identify the significant roles of entrepreneurship in the evolution of tourism destination. They also established the significant connection between innovative individuals known as entrepreneurs and the development of the Gold Coast as a famous tourism area in Australia. It is generally accepted that entrepreneurs have significant contribution to and role in the development of a tourism destination. In the following subsections, we are going to present the features and profile of entrepreneurs in tourism-related industries and their relation with and valuable contribution to the development and implementation of local business initiatives.

22.3.1. Characteristics and Profile of Entrepreneur in Tourism-related Industries

Various studies analysed the characteristics of entrepreneurs in a series of industries. The findings of these studies indicated that there are six key characteristics of entrepreneurs:

1. The need for achievement (David, Dent, & Tyshkovsky, 1996);
2. Risk-taking (Brockhaus, 1980);
3. Desire for independence (Chen, Zhu, & Anquan, 2005);
4. Innovation (Schumpeter, 1934);
5. Self-confidence (Timmons, 1978) and
6. Ability to learn from failure (Shepherd, Covin, & Kuratko, 2008).

Furthermore, a number of researchers were interested in identifying the key features of and determining the profile of entrepreneurs in tourism industry. Specifically, a study conducted by Litzinger (1965) found that entrepreneurs are innovative and willing to take risks. The studies on entrepreneurs' background of small and medium enterprises (SMEs) in tourism industry portrayed their profile. Their dominant age groups are between 25–50 (Avcikurt, 2003) and 45 and older (Getz & Carlsen, 2000; Szivas, 2001), and the majority are married males (Avcikurt, 2003; Getz & Carlsen, 2000). In Australia, entrepreneurs with tertiary education and degree represent 34 per cent (Getz & Carlsen, 2000), while in the UK and Turkey have 70 per cent (Szivas, 2001).

22.3.2. Tourism Entrepreneurship

Entrepreneurship is necessary to form a new enterprise and to set-up new business ventures. Therefore, individual entrepreneurial characteristics and actions that create jobs in tourism-related businesses significantly contribute to the growth of a local, regional and national economy. New small tourism businesses contribute to the flourishing of entrepreneurship as important catalysts or actors in technological innovations, as agents of change in market structure and competitive business environment and as critical drivers in industrial restructuring and improvement of a country's comparative advantage and competitiveness (Hart, Doherty, & Ellis-Chadwick, 2000; Porter, 1990). Saayman and Saayman (1998, p. 55) define tourism entrepreneurship as 'the activities related to creating and operating a legal tourism enterprise'. Legal enterprises refer to those businesses that operate for-a-profit, lucrative basis and seek to satisfy the tourists' needs. In addition, Ramukumba, Mmbengwa, Mwamanyi, and Groenewald (2014) indicate that tourism contributes to reducing poverty, by creating job opportunities. The result is the improvement of well-being and living standards of local populations.

In this regard, Morrison (1996) pointed out that there are several reasons justifying the high number of small-sized hotels in the tourism industry. The main reasons are: (1) the low capital and lack of specific qualifications and professional requirements needed to start a business, (2) the demand for services is very localised and segmented, enabling small accommodation providers to offer a wide range of products, facilities and special services to a niche market, (3) the nature of a small enterprise allows an owner/manager to respond quickly to customer needs and expectations and (4) small accommodation units are normally owned and managed by families, making them profitable and financially sustainable.

Russell and Faulkner (2004) found that the characteristics of entrepreneur, the business environment and market conditions, as well as the particular stage of the development of tourism destinations determine the involvement of entrepreneur in the tourism industry. Barr (1990), for instance, describes the small-scale local entrepreneur as being more prevalent at the involvement phase, while migrant tourism entrepreneurs contribute a significant impact during the later phases of tourism development. Therefore, entrepreneurial personality or characteristics are considered as a very important/determining factor in setting an attractive and sustainable business landscape in any destination.

Case Study 22.1: 'Merapi Lava Tour': An Entrepreneurial Initiative in Tourism-related Industries

The eruption of Mount Merapi, Yogyakarta, Indonesia, on 26 October 2010 caused 347 casualties, and 410,388 persons were forced to abandon their homes. The eruption has damaged houses, agricultural land and community-owned businesses in the surrounding area. Inspired to restore the living and economic conditions of the surrounding communities, one of the residents (Triyono) took the initiative to design a tour for tourists called 'Merapi Lava Tour' using off-road vehicles accompanied by drivers and tour guides. This tour itinerary was conceived and designed to provide an experience for tourists to see the impact of the eruption while visiting a museum called 'Hartaku', built by the local community to commemorate the event and the victims of the volcano's eruption. Triyono started his efforts by buying one vehicle (Jeep mark) and established a 'Jeep community' by inviting surrounding villages to join as community members.

The offering of the 'Merapi Lava Tour' experience attracts many tourists visiting Yogyakarta and its surroundings. In 2016, the increasing interest of tourists has led to the extension of the jeep community and the purchase of more off-road vehicles. The tourism visitation resulted in an increase of jeep communities to 28 with more than 600 vehicles. The ownership of vehicles is arranged and agreed by the local community; the vehicles being registered by members of the community are the only vehicles owned by local residents with a clause stipulating the rule of one vehicle per family.

The tourism product 'Merapi Lava Tour' is fully managed by the local community under the coordination of the 'Kampong Head'. The income earned is proportionally and fairly distributed to vehicle owners, drivers and communities. The entrance fee is collected and managed by the 'Kampong Head' and is provided to help elderly locals who cannot make a living after the eruption. Thus, the management of the 'Merapi Lava Tour' is community-oriented by giving priority to the economic empowerment of the population affected by the eruption, based on the principle of community cooperation and not-for-profit orientation (Mulyowati & Indarwati, 2016).

The above case is an example of applying the concept of tourism entrepreneurship by a creative member of community. The entrepreneurial mind-set and creativity of a person like Triyono has contributed to: (1) address a challenge of survival for the local communities, (2) create job opportunities for local population, (3) support elderly persons and ultimately (4) improve the well-being of the local population (Ramukumba et al., 2014).

22.4. BUSINESS VENTURES IN CREATIVE TOURISM INDUSTRY

UNESCO (2006) argues that creative tourism is considered as the third genera-tion of tourism industry, the first being the 'beach tourism' in which people visit a place for relaxation and leisure purposes, and the second generation 'cultural tourism', which is oriented towards cultural activities, such as visit of museums and cultural tours. The creative tourism involves more interaction, in which the visitor has an educational, emotional, social and participative interaction with the place, its living culture and the people who live there. Creative tourism offers visitors the opportunity to develop their creative potential through active participation in courses and learning experiences, which are characteristics of the visiting tourism destination (Raymond & Richards, 2000). Therefore, the focus of creative tourism businesses is on providing products and services involving tourism experiences with participation and interaction, as well as edu-cating them in the field of arts, heritage, culture or special character of an area/ destination. In addition, it should provide a connection with the community and its culture and everyday life (Creative Tourism Network, 2017).

In order to be in a position to offer memorable, adequate and high-quality experiences, the prospective entrepreneurs should have a very good understand-ing of the tourists interested in creative experiences. Who are creative tourists and what are their expectations? Compared to conventional tourists, creative tourists are more skilled in information technology, languages and humanities; they belong to a wide array of social groups; they produce valuable contents and experiences themselves, and they seek for more interactivity (Couret, 2015).

The main characteristics of creative tourists are: (1) they can be a single, couple, family or bigger party of tourists; (2) they can plan their trip themselves or contract professional/experts and (3) the nature of their activities can be edu-cational (courses, workshops), creative (art residency, co-creation with local artists) or performing arts, such as events, concerts, theatre and exhibitions.

The below are some examples of creative tourists (Couret, 2015; Creative Tourism Network, 2017):

- a single tourist who participates in a cooking class/workshop, in order to meet local residents or to share his/her experiences/know-how with others;
- a choir or orchestra of amateurs who travel with the purpose of offering con-certs in each place they visit;
- a group of dance, theatre or photograph lovers, whose travelling purpose is to practice their hobby and
- families participating in a mosaic class/workshop during their stay, in order to feel themselves 'less tourists'.

In terms of expectations, creative tourists are usually having the following behaviour: they (1) are keen to experience the local culture by participating in artistic and creative activities, (2) eager to live experiences where they can feel themselves as a local, (3) are reluctant to look for the 'monumentality' or the 'spectacularity', (4) are willing to share their experiences on social medias (blogging and online reviews), (5) are exclusive regarding the way they travel: once experienced the creative tourism, they no longer want to come back to a conventional circuit, (6) spend a substantial part of their budget to these activities/experiences and (7) usually combine many types of tourism activities during the same trip, such as creative, culinary, eco-tourism and slow tourism (Creative Tourism Network, 2017).

Therefore, creative tourism is considered as a new generation of tourism by involving the tourists and the locals in the creation of the tourist products and services. Raymond and Richards (2000, p. 1) define creative tourism as 'tourism which offers visitors the opportunity to develop their creative potential through active participation in courses and learning experiences, which are characteristic of the holiday destination where they are taken'. The following case study is illustrating an example of such a learning experience.

Case Study 22.2:   The Lombok Pottery Making Lessons

The Lombok pottery making lessons at Banyumulek Tourism Village, Lombok Island, Indonesia, is an example of the implementation of business venture in the field of creative tourism. Banyumulek is a village that has been popular since the 1990s as a pottery producer with more than 3,000 pottery artisans, most of them being housewives. The pottery products include pots and vases of flowers, ashtrays, cups, mugs and plates. Banyumulek pottery has been widely used for household, hotel and office needs, and the products are even exported to other regions of Indonesia and abroad. Banyumulek pottery has attracted many domestic and international tourists to visit this village for business and leisure purposes. However, since 2010 there has been a decline in the tourists' demand to purchase Banyumulek pottery resulting in a shutting down of many businesses, and consequently a considerable loss of the main source of income.

In 2014, one of the local residents (Hasan), who previously worked as tourist guide and pottery owner in the village of Banyumulek, designed and developed a creative tourism experience named 'Lombok pottery making lessons'. The main purpose of providing such an experience is to optimise the knowledge and skills of artisans and to develop a sustainable income from tourism. The creative tourism offering of 'Lombok pottery making lessons' is outlined below.

Starting from the 'Anan pottery gallery' as a meeting point located in Banyumulek village, tourists are transported to pottery making lessons using traditional Lombok horse-carriage called 'cidomo' accompanied by the English-speaking guide for international tourists, and Indonesian-speaking guide for domestic ones. After arriving at the location, the guide explains the history of pottery making and then proceeds with a demonstration by instructors (local artisans) on how to make pottery. Furthermore, tourists are offered the opportunity to practice the pottery making under the guidance of a trained and skilful local artisan. Tourists also have the opportunity to practice in finishing and polishing the pottery that they had made while enjoying lunch with traditional Lombok menu. Tourists can take the pottery products they made with them at home or return them to Anan pottery gallery, the meeting point at the beginning of this learning experience.

The duration of each session of Lombok pottery making lesson is between one and two hours. This creative tourism experience/offering has attracted a substantial volume of domestic and international tourists who visited Lombok, developing the source of income for the artisans at Banyumulek village. The above case study is an example of the implementation of creative tourism to meet the expectations of tourists and, simultaneously, of jobs creation for local population.

22.5. THE COLLABORATION AND PARTNERSHIP BETWEEN BUSINESSES AND OTHER STAKEHOLDERS TO OFFER HIGH-QUALITY CREATIVE TOURISM EXPERIENCES

The Creative Tourism Network® considers the creativity as the ability to create meaningful new ideas and elements, from the traditional and existing ones. That is the reason why each destination develops its own creative context from their historical and social background, as well as all the events that have shaped the character of their people (Couret, 2015, p. 195). Richards and Marques (2012) suggest that creative tourism is a form of networked tourism, which depends on the ability of providers and tourists to relate each other and to generate value from their encounters. In this regard, Couret (2015) indicates that there are three levels of collaboration and partnerships to establish and promote creative tourism:

1. The co-creation of tourism experiences between local communities/residents and tourists (Binkhorst & Den Dekker, 2009);
2. The collaboration and alliances between local stakeholders at a destination level, between citizen, artists, artisans, NGOs, private companies and public organisations and
3. The networking at a global level, between creative tourism destinations that, in spite of their diversity, share a common objective which is to reach the creative tourists.

The same author also pointed out that it is a very delicate point wherein the locals, artists, artisans and other actors of the creative experience have to find a balanced partnership with the tourism companies and tourism travel trade and intermediary agencies in order to 'package' the activity, while maintaining its 'freshness' and 'singularity' (Couret, 2015, p. 197). Therefore, it is believed that the collaboration and partnership between businesses and other stakeholders are key factors in carrying out the adequate design and successful development of creative tourism.

The following case study on accessible tourism in Spain illustrates an example of partnership between businesses and other stakeholders to offer high-quality creative tourism experiences aiming at meeting the tourists' needs and requirements.

Case Study 22.3:   Accessible Tourism in Spain

The importance of tourism for people with disabilities or movement limitations has become a prime business opportunity in Spain. According to the 2008 AGE (Survey of Disabilities, Personal Autonomy and Situations of Dependency) of the National Statistics Institute, there are 3.85 million Spaniards with disabilities and/or mobility problems, representing 9 per cent of the total population. The inclusion and non-discrimination of people with disabilities is an obligation enshrined in Spanish law, and tourism must consider that these people have the right to leisure and to enjoy their vacation time with a suitable transportation and accommodation, as well as to use and enjoy the infrastructure, environment and tourism products and services in a standard, autonomous and secure way. Therefore, accessible tourism is the solution to this right to be implemented.

In 2014, the social enterprises of ONCE and its foundation were reorganised to group the human capital and professional experience of the Ilunion Hotels under one name, E Ilunion Hotels, with 100 per cent accessible and all hotels (25 units in 12 destinations throughout Spain) are certified in universal accessibility and also the only hotel chain with 100 per cent socially committed and promote inclusion through the employment of people with disabilities.

These hotels adopt an inclusive design that favours all the population, including the elderly or those with temporary disability – a design to break the physical barriers that prevent the use and enjoyment of all facilities. Hotel facilities include rooms with adequate turning spaces; bathrooms with support bars to the elements, with accessible design and height; continuous floor shower enclosures; telephones with several adaptations; information in braille in the door locks and in the articles of welcome; elevators with voice and display system; portable vibration alarm; alarm clock; light timbre; rod holders and a chair-crane in swimming pools (Pacha, 2016).

Some new travel agencies specialised in accessible tourism have also emerged, as they have identified a niche market; for example, Tour Adapt, Travel for All, Accesit Travel or Viajes 2000. Until July 2015, Viajes 2000 develops two clear lines of business: firstly, travel and MICE (meetings, incentives, conferences and exhibitions) business within the umbrella of BCD Travel; secondly, a business model focused on the development and programming of accessible tourism, or tourism for all.

The last boost to accessible tourism has come from the hand of technology and its many options, accessible websites to consult the tourism offering, make reservations or provide opinions/online reviews and recommendations, as well as the digital applications taking advantage of features such as GPS positioning to customise accessibility information (such as routes, reserved parking spaces). Finally, there is a technology linked to the mobile terminals, the beacons, that allows offering services of guidance and guidance indoors, which is very useful for making transport facilities or museums accessible, for example. For its part, Predif (State representative platform for people with physical disability), with the support of Vodafone Spain Foundation, has developed the TUR4all application, which contains all the resources published in the guides of the platform and is continuously updated. E Ilunion Hotels has implemented Nou-u technology, aimed at offering providers the accessibility measures of the different spaces of the hotels, and allowing their management and marketing in a more agile and integral way as these measures are visible in 14 languages. This means that all organisers have access by making sure that they meet the needs of their MICE customers.

Source: Pacha (2016).

22.6. SUMMARY

The development of the creative industry, in general, and of the creative tourism businesses, in particular, has been rapidly increasing over the last decade. This chapter outlined the related issues and aspects and presented practical examples of the creative tourism regarding the entrepreneurship and the creation of business ventures. The main aim of the chapter was to provide prospective entrepreneurs with practical guidance to pursue business opportunities and manage creative tourism business.

In this chapter, we have seen the main components/segments of the creative industry. The characteristics and the profile of entrepreneurs in the tourism industry were also highlighted.

The chapter also indicated the main elements and treats of creative tourism experiences. Creative tourism involves more interactions, in which the visitor has an educational, emotional, social and participative interaction with the place, its living culture and the local population/community. Thus, an in-depth understanding the concept of creative tourism and its implementation is really useful in designing, managing and marketing the appropriate offering of experience opportunities in this field. In order to be in position to provide high-quality offering and memorable experiences in the creative tourism business, prospective entrepreneurs should fully understand and apprehend the characteristics, the needs and requirements/expectations of creative tourists.

Review Questions

The following questions are intended to evaluate your understanding of this chapter. Answer the following questions or discuss the relevant topics:

- Why is creative industry considered as one of the most rapidly growing industries of the global economy?
- Discuss the concepts of creative industry and business creation.
- Discuss the concepts of creative tourism and tourism entrepreneurship.
- Present the characteristics and profile of entrepreneur in tourism industry.
- Explain the application of creative tourism entrepreneurship in the business world.
- Explain the contribution of creative tourism to entrepreneurship.
- Discuss the potential challenges and opportunities for prospective entrepreneurs in the field of creative tourism.

REFERENCES AND FURTHER READING

Avcikurt, C. (2003). Auditing managerial training needs of Turkish small and medium-sized hotel enterprises. *Managerial Auditing Journal, 18*(5), 399–404.

Barr, T. (1990). From quirky islanders to entrepreneurial magnates: The transition of the Whitsundays. *Journal of Tourism Studies, 1*(2), 26–32.

Bhave, M. (1994). A process model of entrepreneurial venture creation. *Journal of Business Venturing, 9*(3), 223–242.

Binkhorst, E., & Dekker, T. D. (2009). Agenda for co-creation tourism experience research. *Journal of Hospitality Marketing and Management, 18*(2–3), 311–327.

Brockhaus, R. (1980). Risk taking propensity of entrepreneurs. *Academy of Management Journal, 23*(2), 509–520.

Bygrave, W. (1994). *The portable MBA in entrepreneurship.* New York, NY: John Wiley & Sons, Inc.

Chen, J., Zhu, Z., & Anquan, W. (2005). A system model of corporate entrepreneurship. *International Journal of Manpower, 26*(6), 529–565.

Couret, C. (2015). Collaboration and partnership in practice: The creative tourism network. In D. Gursoy, M. Saayman, & M. Sotiriadis (Eds.), *Collaboration in tourism businesses and destinations: A handbook* (pp. 191–204). Bingley: Emerald Group Publishing Limited.

Creative Tourism Network. (2017). *What do we mean by creative tourism?* Retrieved from http://www.creativetourismnetwork.org/about/. Accessed on 20 July 2017.

David, R., Dent, M., & Tyshkovsky, A. (1996). The Russian entrepreneur: A study of psychological characteristics. *International Journal of Entrepreneurial Behavior and Research, 2*(1), 49−58.

Department for Culture, Media and Sport (DCMS). (2001). *Creative industries mapping document 2001* (2nd ed.). Retrieved from https://static.a-n.co.uk/wp-content/uploads/2016/12/DCMS-Creative-Industries-Mapping-Document-2001.pdf. Accessed on 10 September 2017.

Getz, D., & Carlsen, J. (2000). Characteristics and goals of family and owner-operated business in the rural tourism and hospitality sectors. *Tourism Management, 21*(3), 547−560.

Hart, C., Doherty, N., & Ellis-Chadwick, F. (2000). Retailer adoption of the internet-implications for retail marketing. *European Journal of Marketing, 34*(8), 954−974.

Hesmondhalgh, D. (2002). *The cultural industries.* London: Sage Publications.

Howkins, J. (2001). *The creative economy: How people make money from ideas.* London: Penguin.

Litzinger, W. (1965). The motel entrepreneur and the motel manager. *Academy of Management Journal, 8*(2), 268−281.

Morrison, A. (1996). Guest houses and small hotels. In P. Jones (Ed.), *Introduction to hospitality operations* (pp. 73−85). London: Cassell.

Mulyowati, A., & Indarwati, A. (2016). *The empowerment of local people and ecotourism for the development of creative economy in Indonesia* (Case study: Mount Merapi). National Seminar on Economics and Business.Faculty of Economics and Business, University of Muhammadiyah, Sidoardjo, East Java, Indonesia.

Pacha, F. (2016). *SAVIA Amadeus Magazine*: Accessible tourism. Retrieved from http://www.revistasavia.com/economia/adasd/. Accessed on 20 October 2017.

Paredo, A., & Christman, J. (2006). Toward a theory of community-based enterprise. *Academy of Management Review, 31*(2), 309−328.

Porter, M. E. (1990). *The competitive advantage of nations.* New York, NY: The Free Press.

Ramukumba, T., Mmbengwa, V., Mwamanyi, K., & Groenewald, J. (2014). Analysis of the socio-economic impacts of tourism for emerging tourism entrepreneurs: The case of George Municipality in the Western Cape Province, South Africa. *Journal of Hospitality Management and Tourism, 3*(1), 39−45.

Raymond, C., & Richards, G. (2000). *What do we mean by creative tourism?* Retrieved from http://www.creativetourismnetwork.org/about/. Accessed on 5 August 2007.

Richards, G., & Marques, L. (2012). Exploring creative tourism: Editors introduction. *Journal of Tourism Consumption and Practice, 4*(2), 1−8.

Russel, R., & Faulkner, B. (1999). Movers and shakers: Chaos makers in tourism development. *Tourism Management, 20*(2), 411−423.

Russell, R., & Faulkner, B. (2004). Entrepreneurship, chaos and the tourism area lifecycle. *Annals of Tourism Research, 31*(3), 559−579.

Saayman, M., & Saayman, A. (1998). Tourism and the South African economy: Growing opportunities for entrepreneurs. *African Journal of Health, Physical Education, Recreation, and Dance, 5*(1), 55−68.

Santiago, J. (2015). *What is creativity worth to the world economy?* Retrieved from http://www.weforum.org/agenda/2015/12/creative-industries-worth-world-economy/. Accessed on 5 August 2017.

Schumpeter, J. (1934). *The theory of economic development.* Cambridge, MA: Harvard University Press.

Shepherd, D., Covin, J., & Kuratko, D. (2008). Project failure from corporate entrepreneurship: Managing the grief process. *Journal of Business Venturing, 24*(6), 588−600.

Szivas, E. (2001). Entrance into tourism entrepreneurship: A UK case study. *Tourism and Hospitality Research, 3*(2), 163−172.

Timmons, J. (1978). Characteristics and role demands of entrepreneurship. *American Journal of Small Business, 3*(1), 5−17.

UNCTAD and UNDP. (2008). *Creative economy report 2008, the challenge of assessing the creative economy: Towards informed policy making.* Retrieved from http://unctad.org/es/Docs/ditc20082cer_en.pdf. Accessed on 5. August 2017.

UNESCO. (2006). *Towards sustainable strategies for creative tourism: Discussion report of the planning meeting for 2008 International Conference on Creative Tourism,* 25–27 October. Retrieved from http://unesdoc.unesco.org/images/0015/001598/159811e.pdf. Accessed on 5 August 2017.

UNESCO and UNDP. (2013). *Creative economy report 2013 (special edition): Widening local development pathways.* Retrieved from http://www.unesco.org/culture/pdf/creative-economy-report-2013.pdf and http://academy.ssc.undp.org/creative-economy-report-2013. Accessed on 5 August 2017.

CHAPTER 23

SHARING ECONOMY AND ENTREPRENEURSHIP IN TOURISM

Vasiliki Avgeli

ABSTRACT

Purpose — *This chapter aims to present and analyse the phenomenon of 'sharing economy' or 'collaborative consumption' in relation to tourism entrepreneurship. It presents and highlights the factors contributing to the growth of sharing economy and its business models, as well as strategically analyse related opportunities, challenges, concerns and threats in the field of tourism entrepreneurship.*

Methodology/approach — *Literature review was conducted on conceptual issues and main aspects of sharing economy, combined with examples and case studies within the tourism business environment.*

Findings — *This chapter highlights the fact that tourism businesses face new developments, trends and changes in tourist consumer behaviour and travel technology. It shows that sharing economy is on the rise, already affecting all segments of tourism industry, offering significant opportunities, as well as challenges and threats.*

Research limitations/implications — *This chapter is explorative in nature because the discussed is based on a literature review.*

Practical implications — *The sharing economy/collaborative consumption is transforming the way people access goods and services changing all elements of trip planning. This is of great significance to the tourism industry, considering the business opportunities in all segments of related businesses. It is*

The Emerald Handbook of Entrepreneurship in Tourism, Travel and Hospitality:
Skills for Successful Ventures, 403–421
Copyright © 2018 by Emerald Publishing Limited
All rights of reproduction in any form reserved
ISBN: 978-1-78743-530-8/doi:10.1108/978-1-78743-529-220181029

suggested that tourism entrepreneurs – existing, new and prospective – should elaborate the suitable strategies to address the new challenges.

Originality/value – *It analyses main issues and aspects of the sharing economy within the tourism context. This analysis contributes to an improved knowledge and understanding that are very useful to all existing and prospective tourism providers.*

Keywords: Sharing economy; key drivers; tourism business environment; entrepreneurship; business models; opportunities and challenges

---

Learning Objectives

After working through this chapter, you should be able to:

- define the concept 'sharing economy';
- describe the tourism business environment;
- identify the factors driving the sharing economy;
- discuss the various business models in the sharing economy;
- present the conflicting opinions about the sharing economy;
- discuss the business opportunities for entrepreneurship and venturing;
- identify the challenges and threats in the arena of the sharing economy.

23.1. INTRODUCTION

Three of the megatrends that are likely to affect tourism over the next 20 years are: (1) that individuals are increasing their networks of trusted peers who inform their tourism choices, (2) that consumers have access to increasing amounts of information in real time and (3) that consumers take more control and seek personal interactions. Nowadays, technology is enabling alternatives – like the sharing economy (SE) – that aim to disrupt and change the tourism industry.

SE or collaborative economy is broadly defined as 'an economic model based on sharing, swapping, trading, or renting products and services in a way that enables access over ownership. This can include business-to-consumer, business-to-business, and/or peer-to-peer transactions' (BSR, 2016, p. 3). This definition builds on leading collaborative thinker Rachel Botsman's definition of collaborative consumption (Botsman, 2015).

The SE puts pressures on traditional tourism businesses that stand to lose a significant market share and struggle to survive. The SE is mainly revolutionising three segments of tourism-related industries: accommodation, transportation and in-destination activities (entertainment and organised excursions and tours).

This chapter presents the main aspects of this economic and social phenomenon with regard to entrepreneurship in tourism-related industries. Its specific objectives are: (1) to define the concept SE and describe the tourism business environment, (2) to present the factors contributing to the growth of the SE, (3) to provide a useful summary of the business models of SE and (4) to analyse the related opportunities, issues and challenges of tourism entrepreneurship.

23.2. WHAT IS SHARING ECONOMY?

Sharing is a phenomenon as old as time itself, whereas the SE and collaborative consumption are phenomena born of the Internet age (Botsman, 2014). Internet services based on user-generated content such as social networks sites (SNSs) encourage individuals to share in various ways. SE is also known as 'collaborative consumption', 'peer-to-peer' (P2P) and 'access economy' (Hbscny, 2011).

The term 'sharing economy' (SE) was added to the Oxford Dictionaries in 2015 and is defined as 'an economic system in which assets or services are shared between private individuals, either for free or for a fee, typically by means of the Internet' (cited in Heo, 2016). In what is called the SE, collaborative consumption or the peer economy, individuals participate in sharing activities by renting, lending, trading, bartering or swapping goods, services, transportation solutions, space or money.

Other definitions proposed are: (1) 'An economy created by tech companies, enabling people to make money out of their spare assets, by providing the interface between them and consumers' and (2) 'An economic model based on sharing underutilized assets from spaces to skills to stuff for monetary or non-monetary benefits' (Botsman & Roos, 2011). Eckhardt and Bardhi (2015) argue that the correct term for this activity is 'access economy' and point out that 'When "sharing" is market-mediated — when a company is an intermediary between consumers who don't know each other — it is no longer sharing at all. Rather, consumers are paying to access someone else's goods or services.'

In 2011, collaborative consumption was named one of *Time Magazine*'s 10 ideas that would change the world (*Time*, 2011). The SE concept has indeed emerged in the tourism marketplace, and businesses based on this concept continue to grow at a phenomenal rate. The benefits of SE include the following (Brady, 2014; BSR, 2016; Cohen & Muñoz, 2015):

- It provides people with access to goods and services that they cannot afford, or do not require for long-term usage.
- It creates stronger communities.

- It saves costs as items can be borrowed and recycled.
- It enables increased independence, flexibility and self-reliance.
- It reduces negative environmental impacts, such as the consumption of resources.
- It accelerates sustainable consumption and production patterns in cities around the globe.

A very optimistic opinion is that 'this transition of sharing economy will have a positive impact on economic growth and welfare, by stimulating new consumption, by raising productivity, and by catalysing individual innovation and entrepreneurship' (Sundararajan, 2013).

There are approximately 10,000 website listings of organisations claiming to be part of the SE (Collaborative Consumption, 2017). Some examples of P2P sharing platforms per segment of tourism-related industries are presented in Table 23.1.

According to a study undertaken by Hawksworth, Vaughan, and Vaughan (2014), the global SE revenues amounted to approximately $15 billion in 2014 and could increase to US$335 billion by 2025. This study identified five key industries of the SE: P2P finance, online staffing, P2P accommodation and travel, car sharing and music/video streaming. All five are growing at a rapid rate, and the SE is showing no signs of slowing down.

> Over the next decade, our analysis highlights the potential for significant value to be created by five of its most prominent industries, playing an ever more pronounced role in the commercial landscape. Global revenues could rise to well over $300 billion by 2025. But achieving this potential will require important regulatory and competitive challenges to be overcome. (Hawksworth et al., 2014)

Table 23.1. Examples of SE Online Platforms per Industry.

Accommodation	Transport
• *Airbnb*	• *Uber*
• *Co-housing*	• *Bike sharing system*
• *Couchsurfing*	• *Carpooling.com*
• *Home exchange*	• *Carsharing*
• *Peer-to-peer property rental*	• *Transfer cars*
• *HomeAway*	• *Lyft*
• *OnefineStay*	• *Zipcar*
• *Roomoram*	• *BlaBlacar*
Travel	**Dining/Catering**
• *EatWith*	• *Cookening*
• *Local hosts*	• *SuperKing*
• *Local tour guides*	• *Housebites*
• *ToursByLocals*	• *Surfingdinner*

Source: Retrieved from various Internet resources (2017).

Although Airbnb is the most recognised SE company in the accommodation industry, it is not alone. Toursbylocals and Tripforeal offer a platform that allows tourists to search for experiences at their destinations while enabling local residents to earn money as tour guides in their hometowns. EatWithalocal, Meal Sharing and Cookening help individuals to organise culinary experiences that enable them to pay to dine in private homes.

Example 23.1: Cookening: A Digital Platform for Collaborative Gastronomy

Cookening, an online platform that was launched in July 2012 by Sébastien Guignot, Cedric Giorgi and Julien Pelletier and is based in Paris, enables its users to host or attend authentic home-cooked meals and meet people from all over the world (www.cookening.com). Cookening provides a method to establish an online profile and a table page showing pictures of its users' favourite dishes and sets a contribution price for guests. It is believed that Cookening is 'Come dine with me' on an industrial scale.

This digital platform combines elements of both Airbnb and Housebites (enabling people to sell home-cooked meals as an alternative to take-out meals). Starting with France, a country known for its gastronomy, it enables locals to be matched with foreigners – tourists in particular – so they can invite them into their homes to experience an authentic French home dining experience. Cookening targets that segment of tourists who, when travelling, do not always find it easy to meet local people and experience authentic food. It is not easy to invite new and suitable people to share a home-cooked meal, and it is in this regard that Cookening aims to assist. Every host who creates a profile on Cookening includes a table page showing photos of their favourite home-cooked dishes, a pre-set menu/meal structure and the price. Cookening manually vets the profile. Non-locals then simply choose a host/table booking and make contact. Like similar P2P marketplaces, Cookening handles payments in order to help establish and maintain trust between hosts and guests, and the host only receives payment on the day after a successful meal. The start-up makes money by charging 20 per cent commission.

This concept, known as 'table d'hôte', is well known in France, where people host home-cooked meals. According to the CEO, the practice is highly regulated: 'We want to globalize and ease this concept so that everyone can experience the wonderful moment of sharing a meal with people you don't know and that have different origins'. Another important element of the Cookening concept is that hosts dine with their guests. This adds further trust as both parties are eating the same food and the meal; it is as much a social as a gastronomic experience and cultural exchange. Israel's EatWith is probably a competitor, but does not currently target France. Although there are also some local rivals in the 'table d'hôte' tradition, the CEO pointed out that they lack Cookening's P2P model. In 2013, Cookening was looking to raise external funding; however, in February 2015 it was acquired by VizEat after a promise by 'Airbnb for Meals' had fallen short.

Source: TechCrunch (2013).

23.3. THE CONTEXT: THE TOURISM BUSINESS ENVIRONMENT

Tourism businesses have to face different kinds of challenges. According to a survey by ReportLinker Insight (2016), the top three challenges in tourism are:

1. *Political situation and security*. Political instability and the fear of terrorism have a severe effect on the global tourism industry since they prevent people from travelling and decrease demand in all tourism-related industries.
2. *Diversification*. Customer satisfaction is also challenging as businesses need to provide unique experiences for every taste. Since tourists demand a wider variety of experiences, the development and provision of unique services, such as cultural heritage, sport and wellness tourism, are becoming strategic for the industry.
3. *Competition*. New online companies and services are also a threat for traditional tourism businesses. Increasing competition with new SE online companies, such as Airbnb, HomeAway and VizEat, means that differentiation is a key issue. In order to face this new kind of competition, the development of the required technology and communication presents a tremendous challenge.

Business reports confirm that changes in tourist consumer behaviour and travel technology are global trends that have a considerable effect on the tourism business environment (see, for instance, WTM, 2016). Travel technology and digitisation are about to transform the tourism experience by making it richer and more enjoyable, based on tourists' personal preferences. These changes in tourist consumer behaviour, and mainly the advent of savvy, experienced tourists with specific aspirations and requirements, are of crucial importance (WTM, 2016).

These two trends are very influential to the development of SE. The emergence of profit-based online platforms for the P2P sharing of goods and services provides new ways for consumers to generate income from their possessions. However, Geron (2013) states that P2P sharing is moving from a way to bolster personal income in a stagnant wage market to becoming a disruptive economic force. The rise of P2P online platforms is of great significance to the traditional tourism industry, which has embraced the SE with the opportunities that it offers in all segments of related business. These companies have become real stakeholders and are changing all elements of trip planning: accommodation, travel experiences, travel advice and meals (Euromonitor International, 2014).

A common premise is that when information about goods is shared (via an online marketplace), the value of those goods may increase for the business, for individuals, for the community and for society in general (Botsman & Ross, 2011; BSR, 2016). Improved knowledge and understanding of the main factors that have caused this phenomenon are very useful to all prospective and current tourism providers.

23.4. THE KEY DRIVERS FOR THE GROWTH OF THE SHARING ECONOMY

The formation of the business models of the SE and the popularity that the respective markets enjoy among many consumers have been driven by a series of distinct yet interrelated factors. The driving forces behind the rise of the SE include (Botsman, 2014; Ertz, Durif, & Arcand, 2016a, 2016b; Hamari, Sjöklint, & Ukkonen, 2015; Puschmann & Alt, 2016):

- *Global economic crisis.* Unemployment, frozen or decreased household incomes and the rising cost of consumer goods have been common themes throughout the developed world. These factors have led providers to start sharing their goods, and consumers to search for more cost-effective goods and services. The global economic crisis has provoked a greater awareness of the need for self-sufficiency among individuals. In short, this crisis has given rise to consumers' desire to utilise existing resources more effectively and increased interest among consumers to develop new sources of income.
- *Changes in consumer behaviour.* Changes in this regard are: (1) a cultural shift towards sharing, i.e. a preference for sharing many goods and services, rather than owning them, (2) the eternal quest to save money and (3) internationalisation and cultural transformation — consumers have steadily become more comfortable with the efficiency and safety of purchasing goods and services online from countries they have never visited and from people they have never met.
- *Technological advancements (Information technology, Web2.0 and SNSs).* Advances in technology are the strongest drivers of the sharing and trading of private assets, since SNSs and electronic markets more easily link consumers. The many enabling technologies, such as open data, low-cost of mobile phones and SNSs that have reached the mainstream make it easy for networks of individuals and organisations to transact directly. These technologies dramatically reduce the friction of share-based business and organisational models.

- *Increasing volatility in cost of natural resources.* Rising prosperity across the developing world, coupled with population growth, is putting greater strain on natural resources and has caused a spike in costs and market volatility. This has led to increased pressure on traditional manufactures to seek design, production and distribution alternatives that will stabilise costs and smooth projected expenditures.
- *Mobile technology.* Mobile devices and electronic services make the use of shared goods and services more convenient, and devices such as tablets and smartphones are rapidly becoming the principal devices used by people to manage their lives online. They offer the following features: cheap and efficient Wi-Fi, cloud computing, ultraprecise geolocation, crowdsourcing and Internet access to everything. In the context of the SE, mobile devices equipped with GPS and near-field technology have made it possible for residents and visitors alike to search for and access the nearest available guest room, car, parking space or home-cooked meal.
- *A younger demographic, millennials* lead the way. Millennials are commonly identified as individuals born between 1980 and 1999, and those who entered their teenage years from the year 2000, which currently puts them in the age group 18−35 years. Younger generations, who started making their independent consumer decisions in the era of 'Internet everywhere', have created strong demand for providers (whether they are shops, airlines or banks) to conduct their business online. This age group is the fastest-growing market segment in the tourism industry and is expected to represent 50 per cent of all tourists by 2025.

A closely related issue is the business models of SE outlined below.

23.5. THE BUSINESS MODELS

As already mentioned, the market technology and the Internet offer the key to making the old idea of sharing new again in the digital age.

23.5.1. How Does SE Work?

The main rationale is that: (1) technology companies are at the top of vast supply systems (where the costs are) and interface with the consumers (where the profits are) and (2) the interface is where the big profit is. SE companies do not assume any normal operating costs, such as the cost of running an accommodation unit, owning a fleet of cars, or running a catering business. Therefore, its heart is crowdsourcing, and crowdsourcing's heart is trust.

It is important to understand that SE is an economic/business activity built on trust. The SE relies on the willingness of users to share, but in order to make an exchange users have to be trustworthy. SE companies say that they are committed to building and validating relationships of trust between the members of their community, including producers, suppliers, customers and participants (Matzler & Kathan, 2015). The use of SNSs has enabled individuals to grow and maintain a network of trusted contacts, which has led to the creation of a powerful and influential force on consumer behaviour and therefore also a powerful tool for marketers. SE platforms have connected users and providers and have built trust among strangers.

Although convenience and cost savings are beacons, it is trust that ultimately keeps this economy spinning and growing. Trust is the elixir that enables individuals to feel reassured about staying in a stranger's home or hitching a ride from someone they have never met (PWC, 2015). The SE creates benefits for consumers, providers and intermediaries (Hamari et al., 2015). Both providers and intermediaries can benefit from new business models and new services and can either position themselves as platforms where consumers share goods and services, or provide additional value-added services.

23.5.2. Business Models in the SE

As a model, the SE differs from the 'traditional economy' in respect of the four core pillars as depicted in Table 23.2 (PWC, 2015).

Arend (2013) points out that there is lack of consensus regarding the definition of a business model. Cohen and Kietzmann (2014, p. 282) approve of the definition proposed by Teece, who explains that a business model is:

> ... the design or architecture of the value creation, delivery and capture mechanisms. The essence of a business model is that crystallizes customer needs and ability to pay, defines the manner by which the business enterprise responds to and delivers value to customers, entices customers to pay for value, and converts those payments to profit through the proper design and operation of the various elements of the value chain. (Teece, 2010, p. 179)

Literature suggests that there are literally dozens of unique business models in the SE (Table 23.3). If, *from the business perspective*, we consider the issue regarding the providers, the transactions and the interaction types, we may identify three broad models (Puschmann & Alt, 2016):

1. Business-to-Consumer (B2C);
2. Business-to-Business (B2B) and
3. Consumer-to-Consumer (C2C) or Peer-to-Peer (P2P).

B2C: Although the SE focuses on the exchange of goods and services among consumers, the access to these resources is disintermediated by companies providing value-added services for consumers (Eckhardt & Bardhi, 2015).

Table 23.2.   Differing Core Pillars of SE.

Pillars	Operationalisation/Meaning
Digital platforms that connect spare capacity and demand	SE business models are hosted through digital platforms that enable a more precise, real-time measurement of spare capacity and the ability to dynamically connect that capacity with those who need it (e.g. Airbnb matches spare rooms with tourists in need of accommodation).
Transactions that offer access over ownership	Access can come in a number of forms, all of which are rooted in the ability to realise more choice while mitigating the costs associated with ownership: renting, lending, subscribing, reselling, swapping and donating.
More collaborative forms of consumption	Consumers who use SE business models are often more comfortable with transactions that involve social interactions that are deeper than traditional methods of exchange.
Branded experiences that drive emotional connection	Nowadays the value of a brand is often linked to the social connections it fosters. In the case of sharing, experience design is critical to engendering emotional connections. By providing consumers with ease of use and confidence in decision-making, a company moves beyond a purely transaction-based relationship to become a platform for an experience — one that feels more like friendship.

Source: Author's elaboration, retrieved from PWC (2015).

Table 23.3.   Business Models and Examples in the SE.

Business Model	Industries and Examples		
	Transport/Mobility	Travel	Work
B2C	Uber	Onefinestay	Wework
	car2go (Daimler)	Tripping.com	Workspace on Demand (Marriott)
C2C or P2P	Getaround Parkatmyhouse (BMW)	Airbnb	Freelancer.com TaskRabbit (Walgreen)

Source: Adapted from Puschmann and Alt (2016, p. 94).

A primary reason for this is the lack of trust among individuals, such as an owner's concern about damage to a shared item, which is solved by an intermediary providing services such as insurance services.

C2C or P2P: This model considers the simultaneous role of service producers and consumers. Single individuals and single organisations often participate in both roles and also move between them. This is precisely what 'collaborative consumption' entails, as it focuses on the P2P consumption of services without involving any intermediary.

On the other hand, we may consider the issue *from the standpoint of building blocks of a business model*. Based on the aforementioned definition (Teece, 2010), literature suggests four business model building blocks: a value proposition, supply chain, customer interface and financial model (Boons & Ludeke-Freund, 2013).

1. *Value proposition* provides measurable social value in concert with economic value.
2. *Supply chain* involves suppliers who take responsibility for both their own and the focal company's stakeholders.
3. *Customer interface* motivates customers to take responsibility for their own consumption as well as that of the focal company's stakeholders.
4. *Financial model* reflects on the appropriate distribution of economic costs and benefits among actors involved in the business model and accounts for the company's ecological and social impacts.

Cohen and Kietzmann (2014) develop a summary of each major business model within the ridesharing segment by applying these elements to emerging business models for sustainability in the shared mobility arena (Table 23.4).

The management literature identified different strategies for companies to succeed in the SE, regardless of the maturity and size of a company (start-ups or incumbents). These strategies include: (1) sharing and swapping (selling the

Table 23.4. Ridesharing Business Models.

Segment	Value Proposition	Supply Chain	Customer Interface	Financial Model	Examples
Carpooling (C2C)	Reduces congestion and subsidises driver costs	Personal vehicles	Colleagues or neighbours	Small fees charged for users Many non-profit intermediaries charge no fees to riders	Carpooling.com Liftshare
Vanpooling (B2C)	Reduces congestion	Vans offered by private vanpooling operator, companies for use by employees	Business-to-consumer interaction, corporation to employee or public service to citizens	Fees charged to riders	WSDOT
Ridesharing (P2P)	Able to support larger numbers of riders/cheaper and faster than taxis	Private vehicles and drivers Smartphone applications with location-based service	Smartphone applications and social network	Drivers earn extra money while intermediaries earn up to 20 per cent of each transaction	Uber

Source: Adapted from Cohen and Kietzmann (2014, p. 285).

use not the ownership), (2) trading (supporting re-ownership of products by selling goods and services), (3) renting products and services (exploiting unused resources and capacities), (4) providing services (personal, repair and maintenance services) and (5) extending markets: targeting new segments of customers (Matzler & Kathan, 2015, p. 72; Puschmann & Alt, 2016, p. 96).

The SE has taken various forms. Through e-commerce websites and applications, businesses are seeking to harness the power of the Internet.

Example 23.2:   Some SE Platforms

Couchsurfing (www.couchsurfing.com): Its interface works like a social network. Users have profiles and can connect via existing Facebook friendships. Its motto states: 'Stay with locals instead of at hotels'. It is a P2P that simply connects users around the world, for the sole purpose of providing a couch to crash on.

Brewster (www.brewster.ca): An example of a digital platform where a tourist can book every part of his/her vacation: accommodation, activities and transportation – as long as they stay within the Brewster sphere. Brewster claims to employ Canadian locals who can give tourists the local experience. The Brewster model is similar to building one's own pizza (DIY) and ordering online.

Marriott/LiquidSpace: The ideas and practices of the SE have already driven major hotel chains to introduce the provision of innovative services in their units. Currently 432 Marriott hotels have meeting spaces listed with LiquidSpace. Marriott offers both guests and locals the opportunity to use lobbies and other vacant areas of its hotels as meeting and work spaces. Since many of those who reserve space are not guests, the arrangement helps Marriott to reach new consumer segment.

Source: Retrieved from http://socialhospitality.com/contact/, March 2017.

23.6. A CASE STUDY: HOMEAWAY, A P2P ACCOMMODATION PLATFORM

At the forefront of the SEs have been the platforms that allow users to stay in private accommodation. Over the past decade, we have seen an explosion in the types of accommodation available, which is in line with the growth and increasing diversity of users and providers. This vacation rental marketplace is booming around the world. Let us take a look at HomeAway (www.homeaway.com).

HomeAway, Inc. is a digital vacation rental marketplace with more than 2,000,000 vacation rentals in 190 countries, operated through 50 websites in 23 languages. The company offers a comprehensive selection of rentals for families and groups to find types of accommodation such as cabins, condominiums, castles, villas, barns or farmhouses.

HomeAway, Inc. which has its headquarters in Austin, Texas, USA, was founded as CEH Holdings in February 2005 and became a publicly traded company in 2011. The company acquired several sites and consolidated them into a single digital vacation marketplace, launching HomeAway.com in June 2006. It raised a total of $405 million in venture capital, which was funded by US venture capital firms. The acquisitions made by HomeAway between 2005 and 2015 include:

- *USA*. A1Vacations.com; BedandBreakfast.com; CyberRentals.com; Dwellable; Escapia; Glad to Have You (GLAD) GreatRentals.com; Instant Software; TripHomes.com; VacationRentals.com.
- *Europe*. Abritel.fr; FeWo-direkt.de; Homelidays.com; OwnersDirect.co.uk; Toprural.com; VRBO.com.
- *Oceania*. Bookabach.co.nz; RealHolidays.com.au; Stayz Australia.
- *Other regions (Brazil, Canada, Turkey and Singapore)*. AlugueTemporada.com.br; CanadaStays; Flat4Day (locally known as Hemenkiralik); Travelmob.

In 2015, its total turnover was approximately $520 million in 2015, which corresponds to an increase of 126 per cent over a period of four years. In December 2015, Expedia Inc. acquired HomeAway.

Before HomeAway introduced its new optional performance-based model in 2013, subscription fees paid by homeowners to list their own property or display their vacation rentals on the company's platforms averaged $442 annually. To promote the vacation rentals, property owners and managers could purchase paid listings on one or more of the company's platforms as a form of advertising to potential tourists. Paid listings appear in search results when tourists search for vacation rentals based on their search criteria. The new performance-based model represented a second option for those wishing to list a home on HomeAway, even though they could still opt for the original annual subscription model.

In 2016, HomeAway introduced a controversial service fee payable by the tourist when booking through the HomeAway platforms. The fee varies from 4 to 10 per cent of the rental cost, with a maximum amount of $499. The company claims that the fee covers the cost of providing 24/7 customer support, enhanced website and mobile features for both owner and tourists, plus expanded marketing efforts to generate more exposure to global audiences.

HomeAway simultaneously instituted a Confidence Guarantee Book for tourists who opt to book and pay through HomeAway. Also in 2016, the company cancelled its tiered subscription model, which enabled owners and property managers to pay for placement in search results, and instituted an annual subscription option to complement a pay-per-booking option that adds 8 per cent of the quoted total rental fee to the cost of each booking.

HomeAway also introduced a Professional Referral Network of 40 partner companies. The network's members assist vacation rental owners in managing their listings, guest inquiries and reservations, and include Evolve Vacation Rental Network and No Worries Vacation Rentals.

It is worth mentioning here that SE brands are attempting to break the business travel market; therefore, it is likely that private rental brands will eventually enter the GDS channel (e.g. Amadeus) and will also partner with an increased number of online travel agents (e.g. Booking and Expedia).

Source: Information retrieved from the websites of the company Home-Away, TechCrunch, TheNextWeb, June 2017.

23.7. BUSINESS OPPORTUNITIES AND THREATS

For millions of people, the SE is making it easier and more affordable for users to access goods and services than those that can be done by using traditional models (BSR, 2016). According to Sundararajan (2014), there is very little doubt that the P2P digital platforms will lead to an expansion in entrepreneurship and innovation. For many individuals, the relatively low-risk micro-entrepreneurship allowed by P2P business may be the first step to broader entrepreneurship, perhaps an 'on-ramp' of sorts to freelancing, or starting an independent business, by generating supplemental income, extending expertise and creating a broader professional network. This section attempts to outline the main opportunities, issues and challenges in this field.

23.7.1. Opportunities

The SE is too big an opportunity to miss — or too big a risk not to mitigate (PWC, 2015). It has grown exponentially over the past decade and is expected to multiply at an even faster rate in the decade to come. Hence, the SE:

- can create profitable business opportunities that expand access to markets, goods and services;
- unleashes new business opportunities that expand access to goods and services for low-income and underserved communities. Companies can access significant untapped revenue through user acquisition, build stronger relations with stakeholders and establish more resilient businesses;
- creates marketplaces that provide consumers with the suitable value proposition;
- can contribute significantly to local economic growth because SE suppliers and users are spending within the local economy. Such spending can have

multiplier effects on job creation, entrepreneurship and general economic health;

- enhances partnerships with other companies: Many SE companies are starting to see the value in partnering with their peers;
- provides alternative finance and money systems, such as cooperative finance or digital currencies, that could help more users participate in the SE; and
- creates opportunities to promote more sustainable use of resources. By promoting the sharing of assets with businesses, companies are able to reduce or eliminate waste or unused assets.

The above opportunities are not without challenges, concerns and threats.

23.7.2. Challenges and Issues

The growing expansion of the SE has brought a number of reactions inside and outside the boundaries of the tourism industry. Is the SE disrupting or enabling? Opinions are divergent (Toposophy, 2015). Some claim that SE may change the face of the tourism industry forever. Other experts, however, suggest that the marketplace is expanding and that the number of key players is growing. The main issues in the business are:

- New entrants need to be aware of the limitations due to existing legislation and regulations.
- *Legal status.* SE providers should be subject to the same regulations governing traditional businesses.
- *Licensing and certification.* SE providers should comply with the licensing and certification requirements that apply for traditional businesses.
- *Public safety and quality control.* Setting appropriate rules to ensure safety and public benefit; gaps in safety standards.
- *Issues of friction and trust.* Mitigating the potential unreliability of stranger is still a challenge. The SE is appealing because it offers better pricing, more unique experiences and more choices, but security, hygiene and uncertain quality still loom as big concerns.
- *Legal liability.* Concerns exist about consumer protection (security of transactions), including price transparency and privacy of customer data.
- Taxation regime.

The main challenges are:

- *Consumer focus.* Effectively competing in the SE requires clear insight into the consumer mind-set and competitive marketplace. Providers should bear in mind the main benefits as perceived by consumers: trust between providers and users, more affordable, more convenient and efficient, better for the environment, and more fun than engaging with traditional companies.

- *Efficiency*. Whether the model is C2C, B2C or B2B, companies should create and utilise the exchanges efficiently and creatively.
- *Cooperation/partnering*. In many cases, SE platforms can increase competition and put pressure on traditional businesses that face common challenges. Many traditional businesses that previously saw the SE as a threat are now seeking to partner as a way to innovate, retain and expand their market reach. These partnerships include traditional and even competing businesses – for instance, in car rental or hospitality industries – as well as partnerships with payment and technology companies that serve as facilitators or enablers.
- Small business ownership can contribute meaningfully to the economic security of low-income individuals. However, they often face a number of hurdles that can prevent them from successfully starting and growing their businesses, including lack of access to capital, limited access to business-development services and cost constraints for office space, equipment and transportation. To help address this challenge, there are 'materials marketplaces' that facilitate B2B reuse of materials (e.g. renting space).
- *Establish regulatory and policy frameworks*. When regulation is solidified, the SE businesses will be fully legitimised – not just by law, but also in the minds and hearts of consumers. The regulatory, legal and tax framework needs to be fit for the new digital age.
- By design, the SE disrupts the balance of the marketing mix for nearly every industry it touches. Price points are upended. The product has a new set of metrics – of which quality gets a new premium. Place is reconsidered as new points of access emerge. The very nature of promotion has shifted, with 'sharing' engendering new means of trial and exposure. Brand remains very relevant.
- *Never settle for stable*. If the SE has proven anything, it is that business models cannot be taken for granted in a highly connected, fast-changing marketplace. The ridesharing model could be obsolete when self-driving cars materialise – or these companies could adapt by purchasing their own fleet of self-driving cars, removing the cost centre of today's drivers. Companies need to capitalise on opportunities for expansion, assessing ways in which new models can be leveraged to reach untapped consumers.

Last, but not least, maximising the potential of the SE will depend on not only innovation by individual businesses, but also on collaboration among companies, policymakers and public authorities, in other words, the whole entrepreneurial ecosystem.

23.8. SUMMARY

The SE is transforming the way people access goods and services by matching people who need these items with those willing to provide them, drawing on a diverse range of providers. The SE is on the rise and is already affecting all segments of tourism-related industries. This new entrepreneurial ecosystem is creating business opportunities and challenges for new and prospective business persons. This chapter attempted to present and highlight the main aspects of the SE regarding the tourism entrepreneurship. It is believed that the SE (1) is here to stay because there is a demand for this segment, (2) is equally a consequence of the rapid and creative use of the most contemporary technologies and applications, and of the global economic crisis and (3) comes with both business opportunities and challenges for the tourism entrepreneurship.

We have explained the concept and definition of the SE and its position within the tourism business environment, the main factors influencing and driving the SE, how it functions, various business models, as well as a strategic analysis sketching the main opportunities, concerns and challenges of entrepreneurship in the field of tourism. These issues were illustrated by way of two case studies and one example.

Review Questions

Check your understanding of this chapter by answering the following questions or discussing the topics below:

- Provide a definition for the SE: Is this concept the most appropriate for expressing the social and economic phenomenon?
- Discuss the features of the tourism business environment that contribute to boost the SE.
- Present the key factors that positively influence the growth of the SE.
- Discuss the main building blocks of a business model.
- Name and give examples of the main types of business models of SE platforms.
- Discuss the main business opportunities of the SE.
- Discuss the main issues and challenges raised in the entrepreneurial ecosystem for venturing in the tourism SE.

REFERENCES AND FURTHER READING

Arend, R. (2013). The business model: Present and future — Beyond a skeumorph. *Strategic Organization, 11*(2), 390—402.

Boons, F., & Ludeke-Freund, F. (2013). Business models for sustainable innovation: State-of-the-art and steps towards a research agenda. *Journal of Cleaner Production, 45*(1), 9—19.

Botsman, R. (2014). Sharing is not just for start-ups. *Harvard Business Review, 92*(9), 23—26.

Botsman, R. (2015). *Defining the sharing economy: What is collaborative consumption and what is not?* Retrieved from https://www.fastcoexist.com/3046119/. Accessed on 10 April 2017.

Botsman, R., & Roos, R. (2011). *What's mine is yours: How collaborative consumption is changing the way we live.* New York, NY: HarperCollins Business.

Brady, D. (24 September 2014). *The environmental case for the sharing economy.* Bloomberg.

BSR. (2016). *An inclusive sharing economy; Unlocking business opportunities to support low-income and underserved communities.* Working Paper. Business Leadership for Inclusive Economy and the Rockefeller Foundation. Retrieved from www.bsr.org. Accessed on 10 July 2017.

Carter, G. (2015). *Secrets of the sharing economy: Unofficial guide to using Airbnb, Uber, & more to earn $1000's.* New York, NY: The Casual Capitalist Series.

Cohen, B., & Kietzmann, J. (2014). Ride on! Mobility business models for the sharing economy. *Organization & Environment, 27*(3), 279–296.

Cohen, B., & Muñoz, P. (2015). Sharing cities and sustainable consumption and production: Towards an integrated framework. *Journal of Cleaner Production, 134*(1), 87–97.

Collaborative consumption. (2017). Directory. Retrieved from http://www.collaborativeconsumption.com/directory/. Accessed on 9 May 2017.

Eckhardt, G., & Bardhi, F. (2015). The sharing economy isn't about sharing at all. *Harvard Business Review.* Retrieved from http://hbr.org/2015/01/the-sharing-economy-isnt-about-sharing-at-all. Accessed on 26 March 2017.

Ertz, M., Durif, F., & Arcand, M. (2016a). Collaborative consumption or the rise of the two-sided consumer. *International Journal of Business and Management, 4*(6), 195–209.

Ertz, M., Durif, F., & Arcand, M. (2016b). Collaborative consumption: Conceptual snapshot at a buzzword. *Journal of Entrepreneurship Education, 19*(2), 1–23.

Euromonitor International. (2014). *Passport report on travel and sharing economy.* London: Euromonitor International.

Fraiberger, S. P., & Sundararajan, A. (2015). *Peer-to-peer rental markets in the sharing economy.* NYU Stern School of Business Research Paper. Retrieved from http://ssrn.com/abstract=2574337. Accessed on 2 May 2017.

Geron, T. (2013). *Airbnb and the unstoppable rise of the share economy.* Retrieved from https://www.forbes.com/sites/tomiogeron/2013/01/23/. Accessed on 10 March 2017.

Hamari, J., Sjöklint, M., & Ukkonen, A. (2015). The sharing economy: Why people participate in collaborative consumption. *Journal of the Association for Information Science and Technology, 67*(9), 2047–2059.

Harvard Business School Club of New York. (2011). *What's mine is yours: The rise of collaborative consumption.* Retrieved from www.hbscny.org. Accessed on 15 January 2017.

Hawksworth, J., Vaughan, R., & Vaughan, R. (2014). *The sharing economy – Sizing the revenue opportunity, 2025.* London: PricewaterhouseCoopers. Retrieved from: www.pwc.co.uk. Accessed on 16 February 2017.

Heo, C. Y. (2016). Sharing economy and prospects in tourism research. *Annals of Tourism Research, 58*(C), 166–170.

Kostakis, V., & Bauwens, M. (2014). *Network society and future scenarios for a collaborative economy.* Basingstoke: Palgrave Macmillan.

Matzler, K., & Kathan, W. (2015). Adapting to the sharing economy. *MIT Sloan Management Review, 56*(2), 71–77.

Möhlmann, M. (2015). Collaborative consumption: Determinants of satisfaction and the likelihood of using a sharing economy option again. *Journal of Consumer Behaviour, 14*(3), 193–207.

PricewaterhouseCoopers. (2015). *The sharing economy.* Consumer Intelligence Series. London: PWC LLP. Retrieved from http://www.pwc.com/cis on 30 April 2017.

Puschmann, T., & Alt, R. (2016). Sharing economy. *Business Information Systems Engineering, 58*(1), 93–99.

Reportlinker. (2016). Official site. Retrieved from https://insight.reportlinker.com/top-3-challenges-in-the-tourism-industry. Accessed on 29 February 2016.

Scaraboto, D. (2015). Selling, sharing, and everything in between: the hybrid economies of collaborative networks. *Journal of Consumer Research, 42*(1), 52–76.

Smith, A. (2016). *Shared, collaborative, and on demand: The new digital economy*. Pew Research Center. Retrieved from http://www.pewinternet.org/2016/05/19/the-new-digital-economy/. Accessed on 20 April 2017.

Social Hospitality. (2016). Corporate website. Retrieved from http://socialhospitality.com/contact/. Accessed on 20 February 2017.

Sundararajan, A. (2013). From Zipcar to the sharing economy. *Harvard Business Review*. Retrieved from https://hbr.org/2013/01/from-zipar-to-hte-sharing-eco/. Accessed on 15 January 2016.

Sundararajan, A. (2014). *Peer-to-Peer businesses and the sharing (collaborative) economy: Overview, economic effects and regulatory issues*. NYU Stern School of Business, NYU Center for Urban Science and Progress, US House of Representatives, 15 January 2014.

Swedish Entrepreneurship Forum. (2015). *The sharing economy: Embracing change with caution*. Retrieved from http://eng.entreprenorskapsforum.se/. Accessed on 25 November 2016.

TechCrunch. (2013). *Cookening*. Retrieved from https://techcrunch.com/2013/05/22/cookening/. Accessed on 1 June 2017.

Teece, D. (2010). Business models, business strategy and innovation. *Long Range Planning*, *43*(2), 172–194.

Time. (2011). 10 ideas that will change the world. *Time*, 17 March 2011.

Toposophy. (2015). *The sharing economy in the tourism and hospitality industry in Greece. Report commissioned by the Hellenic Chamber of Hotels*. Athens: Destination Marketing Agency.

World Travel Market. (2016). *The WTM global trends report 2016*. London: WTM & Euromonitor International.

ABOUT THE AUTHORS

Agusdin Agusdin is Senior Lecturer in the fields of Entrepreneurship and Human Resources Management at the undergraduate and postgraduate programmes of the University of Mataram, Indonesia. He is currently Chairman of the Center for Entrepreneurship and Innovation and a Researcher at the Tourism Study Center, Faculty of Economics and Business, University of Mataram. He holds a DBA in Entrepreneurship (Southern Cross University, Australia), MBA in Human Resource Management and Financial Management (Central Queensland University, Australia) and SE in Management Science (University of Mataram, Indonesia). His main research interest is in the area of entrepreneurship and innovation in which he has developed a model of new venture creation and development, the role of cooperatives in cluster development, tourism cluster development and tourism competitive strategy. Agusdin is the author and co-author of national accredited journal articles and a number of accredited national and international conference proceeding papers.

María del Mar Alonso-Almeida is Lecturer of Business Administration at Autonomous University of Madrid, Madrid, Spain. Her research interests focus on the corporate governance and sustainability in organisations. She has written several articles and has participated as co-author in two books about sustainability from the strategic, operational and practical perspective. In addition, she is interested in the study of the operations that affect these companies, as well as in the analysis of their organizational structures and the role of women in sustainability development.

Martha Alicia Alonso-Castañón is Coordinator of the Bachelor in Business Management at the Polytechnic University of San Luis Potosi, Mexico. She holds a Master's degree in Management with a specialty in International Finance from Instituto Tecnológico y de Estudios Superiores de Monterrey, Mexico, and a Bachelor's degree in Business Management from the Autonomous University of San Luis Potosi, Mexico. She is part of a research team dedicated to studying local development and business competitiveness as well as management of human and social capital. She has participated in inter-institutional research projects, applying the socio-economic management model. She has industry experience in the areas of human resources, customer service and finance.

Marisol Alonso-Vazquez is Academic Associate in the Tourism and Event Management clusters in the University of Queensland and Griffith University. She is also a Research Contractor for entertainment-related ventures. Marisol holds a PhD from the University of Queensland, Business School, Australia; a Master's degree in Marketing from the Autonomous University of Madrid, Spain; and a Bachelor in Foreign Trade from the Autonomous University of San Luis Potosi, Mexico. She has previous experience in assisting micro-, small- and medium-sized ventures to improve their competitiveness via business consultancy and adoption of new technologies. One of her research streams focuses on entrepreneurs' behaviours in disruptive economies.

María José Álvarez-Gil is Full Professor of Operations and Supply Chain Management in Universidad Carlos III de Madrid, Madrid, Spain. Her research interests focus on the following paths: (1) Total Environmental Quality Management, (2) Advanced Manufacturing Technologies, (3) Supply Chain Environmental Management, (4) Performance Measurement Systems and (5) Innovation and New Technologies in the services sector, with special consideration in the health and hospitality industries. These five branches start from a common trunk that is the investigation of the Corporate Strategy of Operations and the new challenges posed today by the Circular Economy movement. She has published in leading international journals and has co-authored two well-known operations management textbooks (in Spanish) and three research-oriented books in the areas of Reverse Logistics, Advanced Manufacturing Technologies and Supply Chain Management 4.0. She is the co-supervisor of a dozen PhD proposals and acts as reviewer in many academic journals in the service and operations management areas.

Stavros Arvanitis is Associate Professor in Applied Economics, Department of Accounting and Finance, School of Management and Economics, TEI of Crete. He graduated from the Macedonia University of Business and Economics (BA in Economics, 1985), from the University of Aix-Marseille III (DEA Economie Mathematique et Econométrie, 1987) and from the University of Piraeus (PhD in Labor Economics, 2006). Since 1990 he has worked for the TEI of Crete. He has professional experience as a scientific staff in the Region of Crete and has collaborated in national and EU operational programmes and frameworks. His research and writing interests include labour economics, businesses economics and econometric models. His articles have been published by international journals and have been presented at conferences.

Vasiliki Avgeli graduated from the University of Abertay Dundee, UK, with a BA (Hons) Tourism degree and a Master's in International Marketing with Languages. She has a doctorate from Brunel University, UK, in the area of development and promotion of alternative forms of tourism in rural/mountainous areas. She was Lecturer in Buckinghamshire New University, UK, and currently teaches at the Technological Educational Institute of Crete, in the

Department of Business Administration, School of Management & Economics, and the Master Program in School of Agriculture & Food Nutrition. She also teaches at MBA College of Crete (in partnership with Staffordshire University, UK) and is Program Leader of the MBA Program. Her research interests focus in the area of marketing and tourism. She has organised various international academic conferences.

Hongfei Bao is Lecturer in Tourism Management at Jeju National University of South Korea, and serves for Jeju tourism organisation as a Researcher. Hongfei has authored and co-authored accredited journal articles related to incentive tours, tourism information service and young Chinese tourists. She has been engaged with the project from Industry–Academic Cooperation Foundation, Jeju Free International City Development Center, Jeju Tourism Organization, Korea Tourism Organization and Jeju Special Self-Governing Province. Her study areas include cruise, casino and business tourism.

Sébastien Bédé is Associate Professor in Strategy at the EM Strasbourg Business School in France, and a Researcher at the Humans and Management in Society (Humanis) Research Centre. His primary research interests focus on governance of tourism destination. His research fields concern remembrance tourism and wine tourism. He completed his PhD at Nice Sophia Antipolis University, France, in 2013. Dr Bédé's teaching deals with wine tourism, organisational theory, strategy of internationalisation and strategic management. His professional experience in hospitality industry spans over five years as a business manager and marketing manager in France and in Asia. Sébastien Bédé is member of Association Francophone de MAnagement du Tourisme (AFMAT).

Yosr Ben Tahar completed her PhD on entrepreneurial burnout at University of Montpellier, France, in 2014. Her primary interests focus on entrepreneurship and organisational behaviour. Her research fields expanded to include marketing and wine business as she is a permanent member of the Chair 'Wine and Tourism'. Her teaching deals with strategy, organisational behaviour, occupational stress and research methods.

Elricke Botha is currently the Acting Coordinator for Postgraduate Studies in the College of Economic and Management Science, University of South Africa (Unisa). She is also Senior Lecturer in the Department of Entrepreneurship, Supply Chain, Transport, Tourism and Logistics Management. Her research focus areas include ecotourism, tourism management and related subfields on the topics. Her passion for these research fields is also evident in the consultations with the tourism industry. Elricke completed her PhD at North West University, Potchefstroom, and since then has published on the topic in both international and local academic journals. Elricke is External Examiner and moderator for many universities offering tourism qualifications and is a local and international peer reviewer for academic journals. Elricke has six years of teaching experience at Unisa and has since then served on college committees. Her dedication to the institution was awarded in 2016 where she received the College Award for Academic Administration.

Evelyn G. Chiloane-Tsoka is currently Professor of Entrepreneurship in the School of Public and Operations Management Sciences at the University of South Africa. She obtained her Doctoral degree in 2009. She has valuable years of experience and her research focus is on small business and entrepreneurship. She is currently researching on youth unemployment, climate change and social entrepreneurship. She has published extensively in accredited journals and has presented at both national and international conferences. She is co-author of multi-disciplinary research with other scholars from universities in South Africa. She is Editor of entrepreneurship and emerging economies. She holds a fellowship award from Academy of Business Retail and Marketing (ABRM) based in London. She also holds a prestigious award for Southern SADEC best female entrepreneurship of 2013. Her landscape in entrepreneurship ecosystem is informed by seeking ways to resolve youth unemployment and women by creating awareness that entrepreneurship is a career.

Sylvie Christofle is Associate Professor at the University of Nice Sophia Antipolis and is Specialist in geography, event and tourism studies. After graduating from the University of Montpellier in Geography and in History, she received her PhD in Geography, at the University of Montpellier and a Certificate in Tourism and Leisure Planning at the School of Architecture of Languedoc-Roussillon. Her research interests include territorial urban strategies, their influence on city planning and development, particularly in the tourism and event fields. She is the author of several articles edited in journals, presented at conferences and published a book about Convention tourism. Sylvie is also Director of the Master in International Hospitality, at the IAE, Business School of the University of Nice Sophia Antipolis.

Leticia Estevez has over 10 years of experience in the tourism sector and has worked in both public and private organisations as a Consultant, specialised in project development and management of tourism. She has a Tourism and Hospitality degree and a Master's degree in Tourism Development and Management. She is Former Fellow of the Indian ITEC Programme Course 'Capacity Building Programme on Learning South-South Cooperation'. She currently works as a Consultant at the Ministry of Tourism in Argentina and as Professor at the National University of Avellaneda and Univerisdad Autonoma de Chiapas, Mexico. Previously, she has worked in Brazil, Spain, Turkey and the Netherlands, representing Argentina's national tourist board at events promoting international tourism. She worked as Consultant on an Argentinian International cooperation project at Dominica Island. She has also contributed as a writer for the book *Collaboration in Tourism Businesses and*

Destinations: A Handbook (2015; Emerald Publishing), and in many other tourism publications.

Anestis Fotiadis, PhD is a member of the academic teaching and research staff of the College of Communication and Media Science at Zayed University, Abu Dhabi, United Arab Emirates. He researches and lectures in the fields of tourism principles, research methods, project management, events and venue management. He has published more than 40 research papers in international academic journals such as *Tourism Management, Journal of Business Research* and *Journal of Technological Forecasting and Social Change.*

Vincent Grèzes, PhD is Associate Professor at the High School of Management and Tourism of the University of Applied Sciences and Arts of Western Switzerland in Valais, and Researcher at the Entrepreneurship & Management Institute (IEM). His main research activities focus on regional development, innovation and new business models, including the creation of shared values, service design, open innovation and crowdfunding. His teaching activities are focused on corporate strategy, international management and strategic intelligence.

Vanessa Guerrier-Buisine is Lecturer at the University of Nice Sophia Antipolis and Specialist in web marketing, social media and digital communication in hospitality. After graduating from the University of Nice, she works now for several years as a Journalist. Her articles focus on social media, digital marketing and tech trends affecting the tourism industry. She helps hospitality stakeholders to enhance their guests' experiences and to optimise their digital efforts. She is also considered as an expert in digital communication, running that 'blog des experts' column in *L'Hôtellerie Restauration* magazine. Vanessa is also Professional Lecturer at the Master 2 'Hôtellerie Internationale', at the IAE Nice, Graduate School of Management, University of Nice Sophia Antipolis.

Coralie Haller obtained a PhD in Management Sciences from Aix-Marseille University, France, after seven years of professional experience within various companies and educational environments in France and Australia. Her research interests and teaching expertise concern information systems and knowledge management, and entrepreneurship in the wine and tourism industry. She is currently in charge of the International Wine Management and Tourism program and the Master of Tourism Management and has created a corporate Chair in 'Wine and Tourism' at EM Strasbourg Business School in France.

Marta Magadán has a doctor cum laude in Economics and Business Administration, postgraduate in Business Administration and Applied Economics (University of Oviedo) and degree in Economics (Oviedo University). She is Professor at the Department of Business Administration (International University of La Rioja) and Director of the university press SEPTEM EDICIONES, the first university publishing group of Asturias (Spain). Dr Magadán has been a Visiting and Guest Professor at the Autonomous University of Guadalajara (Mexico) and at the Autonomous University of Colima (Mexico), among other universities. She has published over one hundred academic works related to industrial economics, public finances, experimental economics, applied economics, environmental economics and tourism.

Charlotte Massa is Associate Professor in the field of Marketing at the EM Strasbourg Business School, University of Strasbourg, France, and a Researcher at the Humans and Management in Society (Humanis) Research Centre. Since her PhD in Consumption Behaviour at Toulouse 1 Capitole University in 2014, her research interests have focused on consumption experience, sensorial marketing and wine tourism. Her teachings deal with consumption behaviour, data analysis and direct marketing in wine business. Dr Massa is permanent member of the Chaire 'Wine and Tourism' and she is member of Association Francophone du MAnagement du Tourisme (AFMAT) and of Association Française du Marketing (AFM).

Claudel Mombeuil, MSc, is Assistant Professor at Université Quisqueya, Port-au-Prince, Haiti, and Business Consultant at Centre d'Entrepreneuriat et Innovation, a Unit of Université Quisqueya, that provides entrepreneurial training and consulting services to small and medium enterprises. He is also the co-founder and Executive Director of an NGO named Rezo Inovasyon Edikatif Ayisyen (RINOVEDA), which has mission to support and promote innovation in education in Haiti. His research interest encompasses an interdisciplinary approach which includes corporate social responsibility, (sustainable) entrepreneurship, local governance, grass-roots innovation and development of SME. He is also Certified Project Management Analyst and has accumulated many years of work experience in NGOs and private institution in addition to some years of work experience in Taiwan.

Eugenia Papaioannou received her PhD degree from the Department of Applied Informatics, University of Macedonia, Greece. She received her Master's degree in Computing from the same university. Moreover, she has received Diploma in Marketing from Newcastle University of UK. Her Bachelor's degree in Business Administration is from TEI of Serres, Greece. Dr Papaioannou's current research interests include e-commerce services, service quality issues and management and entrepreneurship. She is member of the Scientific Committee of the International Conference on Contemporary Marketing Issues (ICCMI's) and she took part in several European and National projects as a researcher. She works as Assistant Professor (Adjunct) at the Business Administration Department of the Technological Educational Institute of Thessaloniki, Greece. Furthermore, she is Director of a lifelong learning centre Iason.

Catherine Papetti is Associate Professor at the University of Nice Sophia Antipolis and is a specialist in marketing, online social media, digital data-driven marketing and tourism. After graduating from the Ecole Supérieure de Commerce de Paris (ESCP), she received her PhD in Marketing from the University of Nice. Her research interests include online social networks and media, and their influence on consumer decisions and experiences, particularly in the tourism industry. She is the author of several articles edited in journals and presented at conferences and published business cases on aspects of tourism and hotel sector. Catherine is also Director of the Digital Master in Marketing, at the IAE Business School of the University of Nice Sophia Antipolis.

Antoine Perruchoud is Full Professor at the University of Applied Sciences and Arts Western Switzerland in Valais with years of interest and experience in developing and teaching about innovation, business model and entrepreneurship. He initially studied at the Swiss University of Fribourg (BA in Business Administration) and afterwards at the US Western Washington University (Master in Political and Environmental Sciences). He first became involved in sustainable development, and then moved on to become a scientific collaborator at the Swiss Federal Office for the Environment. Following this, Antoine became Professor at the University of Applied Sciences where he initiated and founded a new entrepreneurship programme: Business Experience. Most recently, he has launched the Team Academy programme in the Bachelor of Business Administration.

María del Pilar Pastor-Pérez is Professor in Economics at the Faculty of Accounting and Business Management, in the Autonomous University of San Luis Potosi, Mexico. She holds a PhD in Economics with specialty in Management granted by the Institute of Organization and Management in Industry ORGMASZ, Poland; a Master's degree in European Studies from the European University Centre Nancy 2 University, France; and a Bachelor's degree in Economics from the University of Zaragoza, Spain. She has previously worked for the aviation industry in Europe as Full-time Professor. She participates in research and consulting industry-related projects in collaboration with public and private organisations. Her research interest is in the field of innovation.

Msindosi Sarah Radebe has been Lecturer at the University of South Africa (UNISA) since January 2006. For the past eight years she has been lecturing General Management courses. At present, she is in the entrepreneurship section offering entrepreneurship and family business management courses. She studied a junior degree at Vista University and measured in Education and Business Management. She also did her postgraduate studies at Vista University (Bcom Hons in Business management) and Master's in Business Management at the University of Johannesburg (UJ). Being published in one of the international journals about social issues has kept her spirits high. Mrs Radebe is looking forward to contributing to the economy of SA through community engagement projects in empowering the aspiring business people as well as through publishing in accredited journals on topics such as technology, strategy and open distance learning.

Nkoana Simon Radipere was Associate Professor and Chair of the Department of Entrepreneurship, Supply Chain, Transport, Tourism and Logistics Management at University of South Africa (UNISA) before his passing in October 2017. He holds a BCom (Hons), an MCom and a DCom degrees in Business Management. With over 15 years of academic experience, Professor Radipere served as Head of the Entrepreneurship Section, and had previously worked as Lecturer at the former Vista University. He was Chair of Centre for Sustainable Small Business Development. He was involved in various community engagement projects in the entrepreneurship field. Before his departure on earth, he was one of the facilitators and leaders for the business and entrepreneurship track at the Young African Leadership (YALI – President Barack Obama's initiative).

Jesús Rivas holds a doctor cum laude in Economics and is Professor at the Department of Business Administration (International University of La Rioja), Postgraduate in Applied Economics (University of Oviedo), Degree in Economics (University of Oviedo) and Diploma in Law (UNED). He is also Director of Marketing and Strategy at SEPTEM EDICIONES, first university press group of Asturias. He has been a visiting and guest professor at the Autonomous University of Guadalajara (Mexico) and at the Autonomous University of Colima (Mexico) among other universities. Professor Rivas has published over one hundred of academic works related with public finances, experimental economics, applied economics, environmental economics and tourism.

Roland Schegg is Full Professor at the University of Applied Sciences and Arts Western Switzerland in Valais, Switzerland, and researcher at the Institute of Tourism (ITO). Between 2000 and 2004, he was with the Ecole Hôtelière de Lausanne (EHL). He earned his BS from the Swiss Federal Institute for Technology in Zurich (ETHZ) and his PhD from the University of Geneva. His research interests include various topics in the field of eTourism (distribution, website benchmarking, eService metrics, technology adoption and diffusion of innovation).

Shiwei Shen is Associate Professor in Tourism Management and Vice-Dean of the Ningbo University, and University of Angers joint Institute/Sino-European Institute of Tourism and Culture, Ningbo University, P.R. China. He received his PhD in geography from the University of Angers, France. His research and writing interests include tourism economy, heritage tourism, rural tourism, evolution of tourist places and cruise, etc. His articles have been published by national and international journals and presented at international conferences.

Nataša Slak Valek, has a PhD in Business, specialising in Tourism. She teaches tourism-related courses at undergraduate and graduate level at Zayed University in Abu Dhabi, UAE. Dr Slak Valek earned her doctorate in Business from the Faculty of Economics, University of Ljubljana. Her research focuses on tourism, sport tourism and tourism marketing. Prior joining to ZU UAE, she taught at University of Maribor in Slovenia and I-Shou University in Taiwan. She also has 10 years' industry experience working at Slovenian Tourism Board, first as Professional Researcher of tourism and was later promoted to Marketing Manager position. She is registered as Professional Researcher at a Slovenian Research Agency, and is member of Travel and Tourism Research Association and a reviewer for several tourism academic journals.

Magdalena Petronella (Nellie) Swart is an Associate Professor in Tourism at the University of South Africa, and Certified Meeting Professional. She developed a service quality scorecard to predict business tourist retention for a DCom in Leadership Performance and Change (University of Johannesburg). Nellie has authored and co-authored accredited journal articles, book chapters and a number of accredited conference proceedings articles. Her community engage-ment project includes the offering of various guest lectures as part of the National Department of Tourism (NDT) capacity building programme. Nellie is Executive Committee member of the Tourism Educators South Africa (TESA) and the Southern African Association for the Conference Industry (SAACI) Tshwane branch. She is Programme Leader for the Executive Development Programme for Women in Tourism (EDP for WiT), commis-sioned by NDT. Since 2011 she has been the primary researcher for HuntEx, Africa's biggest hunter and sport shooter expo.

Anne Taylor is an academic, having held Senior Lecturer position at the University of Johannesburg at the School of Tourism and Hospitality for many years, before taking up an opportunity in Romania. She holds a Master's degree in Education from the University of the Witwatersrand, where her thesis focused on the differing knowledge forms in academic and vocational knowl-edge at institutions of higher education, and the challenges and explanations they hold for higher education planning. Anne is Head of MSc programme at the American Hotel Academy in Brasov, a private tourism and hospitality academy in Romania. Her role includes the management of the programme which is done in partnership with Manchester Metropolitan University in the UK; and programme development and writing of future programmes within the Hospitality and Tourism Education spectrum for the Academy. Her years of experience within the higher education teaching and learning spectrum for hospitality allows for a deep understanding of the challenges that meet both educators and students to ensure qualified and experienced students enter the labour market successfully in a dynamic, demanding and skill-conscious environment.

Cina van Zyl is Professor in Tourism Management and currently acting Head of the Office of Graduate Studies and Research in the College for Economic and Management Sciences, at the University of South Africa (UNISA), where she has been employed since 1988. She obtained HonsBEcon in Transport Economics at the University of Stellenbosch, MPhil (cum laude) in Tourism Management at the University of Pretoria, and DCom in Tourism Management at UNISA. Her special research interests are in the fields of transport, tourism and logistics. She is author or co-author of specialist publications in national and international professional journals and has also read papers at national and international conferences.

Stelios Varvaressos is Professor at Department of Business Management (Degree/Course: Tourism Business Management), at the Technological Educational Institute (TEI) of Athens and Tutor of the Hellenic Open University, Greece, on the post-graduate programme (MSc) Tourism Business Management. He received his PhD in Tourism Economy from the University of Paris VIII, Paris, France. He is the author of eight books, on aspects of tourism economy, tourism development and tourism policy. He has undertaken a variety of research and consultancy projects of the tourism industry (public and private sectors). His articles have been published by international journals and presented at international conferences. He is a member of the editorial board of four scientific journals in tourism. His research and writing interest includes tourism economy, tourism development and tourism policy.

INDEX